Upper   Harmonics

Piccolo

	E₄	F₄	G₄	A₄	B₄	C₅	D₅	E₅	F₅	G₅	A₅	B₅	C₆	D₆	E₆	F₆	G₆	A₆	B₆	C₇	D₇	E₇	F₇	G₇	A₇	B₇	C₈	5000.0	6000.0	7000.0	10000.0

A-440

| 311.13 | | 369.99 | 415.30 | 466.16 | | 554.37 | 622.23 | | 739.99 | 830.61 | 932.33 | | 1108.7 | 1244.5 | | 1480.0 | 1661.2 | 1864.7 | | 2217.5 | 2489.0 | | 2960.0 | 3322.4 | 3729.3 | |

| 329.63 | 349.23 | 392.00 | 440.00 | 493.88 | 523.25 | 587.33 | 659.26 | 698.46 | 783.99 | 880.00 | 987.77 | 1046.5 | 1174.7 | 1318.5 | 1396.9 | 1568.0 | 1760.0 | 1975.5 | 2093.0 | 2349.3 | 2637.0 | 2793.0 | 3136.0 | 3520.0 | 3951.1 | 4186.0 |

| 44 | 45 | 47 | 49 | 51 | 52 | 54 | 56 | 57 | 59 | 61 | 63 | 64 | 66 | 68 | 69 | 71 | 73 | 75 | 76 | 78 | 80 | 81 | 83 | 85 | 87 | 88 |

Audio in Media

Audio in Media

Stanley R. Alten
Syracuse University

Wadsworth Publishing Company
Belmont, California
A Division of Wadsworth, Inc.

Senior Editor: Becky Hayden
Production Editor: Helen Sweetland
Managing Designer: Detta Penna
Designer: Rick Chafian
Art Editor: Nancy Benedict
Copy Editor: Carol Reitz
Illustrator: Don Felich
Cover Designer: Michael Rogondino

Photographs by William Storm: 2-1; 2-7a; 2-15; 2-16; 2-37; 3-12; 4-3; 4-4; 4-8; 4-9; 4-10; 5-7; 5-8; 5-19 (top); 5-23 (far left); 5-24a; 5-28; 5-30a, b; 5-46; 5-47; 5-48; 6-5; 6-9; 6-10; 6-11; 7-10; 7-17; 7-18; 7-19; 7-20; 7-21; 7-22; 7-23; 7-24; 7-25; 7-26; 7-27; 7-28; 7-29; 7-30; 7-31; 7-32; 7-33; 8-1; 8-7; 9-2; 9-6; 9-9; 9-10; 9-11; 10-3; 10-4; 10-5 (right); 10-8; 10-11; 10-16; 10-17; 10-23a; 10-24b; 11-8; 13-1; 13-2; 13-3; 13-5; 13-6; 13-7; 13-8; 13-12; 13-13; 13-15; 13-16; 13-17; 13-18; 13-19; 13-20; 13-21; 13-22; 13-23; 13-35; 13-37; 13-38; 13-39; 13-40; 13-41; 13-42; 13-47; 14-6; 14-7; 14-12; 14-13; 14-15; 14-16; 14-17; 14-18; 14-19.

Printed in the United States of America

1 2 3 4 5 6 7 8 9 10—85 84 83 82 81

Library of Congress Cataloging in Publication Data

Alten, Stanley R.
  Audio in media.

  Includes index.
  1. Sound—Apparatus. 2. Telecommunication—Apparatus and supplies. I. Hayden, Becky. II. Title.
TK7881.4.A46   621.38   81-1109
ISBN 0-534-00946-8   AACR2

Acknowledgments

AKG Acoustics: 5-20b; 5-30c; 5-32; 5-35; 5-42; 5-43; 5-49 (right); microphone models: 414 (p. 112), 451 system (pp. 112–114), C-24 (p. 119), 424 (p. 120), 224E (p. 120), 110 (p. 123), 900E (p. 124); 11-15.

Allen and Heath Brenell Ltd., England: 3-20; 3-21.

Allison Research, Inc.: 11-25.

Ampex Corporation: 9-13 (top right, bottom left); 10-5 (left); 10-6; 10-19; 10-28a; 10-32; 12-3; 12-5a, c; 13-28; 13-33a.

Ampro Broadcasting, Inc.: 4-1a.

Aphex Systems, Ltd.: 11-31.

Atlas Sound: 6-6; 6-7; 6-8 (top).

Audio Designs and Manufacturing, Inc.: 2-10; 3-2.

Broadcast Communications Magazine: 2-6a.

Broadcast Electronics, Inc.: 3-14; 3-18; 4-2 (QRK 12c turntable with Rek-O-Kut S-320 tone arm); 10-23b, c; 10-25.

Burns Audiotronics, Inc.: 5-5; Beyer M160 (p. 125).

CADAC Audio: 15-2c.

Calrec Audio, Ltd.: 5-44.

Cetec Sparta: 3-2a.

Cine 60, Inc.: 12-5b.

Cinema Products Corporation: 12-10.

Countryman Associates: 5-40a.

Crown International, Inc.: 5-41; 6-21b, c.

Datatron, Inc.: 13-29.

dbx, Inc., Newton, MA: 11-21; 11-29.

Dolby Laboratories: 11-27; 11-28.

Dual/United Audio Products: 4-11.

EECO: 13-31; 13-33b.

Electro-Voice, Inc.: 5-21; 5-22; 5-23 (left); 5-27; 5-31; 5-33; 5-50 (top left, top right); microphone models: CS15 (p. 114), CO85 (p. 118), DS35 (p. 121), RE15 (p. 121), RE16 (p. 121), RE20 (p.121), 635A (p. 122), RE50 (p. 122), RE55 (p. 122), 649B (p. 124), DL42 (p. 125); 6-21a.

Eventide Clockworks: 11-19; 11-20; 11-32.

Everything Audio: 2-4 (p. 15, bottom); 2-8d.

Farinon Electric: 12-7.

Fuji Photo Film USA, Inc.; Magnetic Tape Division: 9-12.

The Gerstenslager Company: 12-8; 12-9a.

Samuel Goldwyn Studios: 2-5a, b; 2-8a, b, c; 14-2.

Gotham Audio Corporation, N.Y.C.: 4-1c; 5-19 (bottom); 5-50 (top middle, bottom); Neumann microphone models: KM86 (p. 115), KM88 (p. 115), U-47fet (p. 116), U-87 (p. 116), U-89 (p. 116), KMR82 (p. 118), SM69 (p. 119); 6-32; 11-14.

Harris Corporation: 3-17.

Harrison Systems, Inc., P.O. Box 22964, Nashville, TN: 3-19 (bottom right).

Helpinstill Designs, Inc., Houston, TX: 5-40c.

HM Electronics, Inc.: 5-38b.

International Tapetronics Corporation: 10-1.

JBL: 8-3a.

McIntosh Laboratory: 8-3b; 8-9 and 8-10 concept from McIntosh.

Magnasync/Moviola: 12-16 (far left).

Magna-Tech Electronic Company, Inc.: 12-16 (left).

Marshall Electronic: 11-30.

MCI: 3-19 (top right); 10-7.

Mole-Richardson Co., Hollywood, CA: 5-49 (left); 6-12.

MXR Innovations, Inc.: 11-5; 11-18; 11-33.

Nagra/Kudelski: 10-27.

Rupert Neve, Inc.: 2-2; 3-19 (bottom left); 15-2a, b.

Orban Associates, Inc.: 11-24.

Otari Corporation: 10-12a (bottom right); 10-18.

Panasonic: 13-30.

Penny & Giles: 3-2b.

Posthorn Rec'gs, N.Y.C.: Schoeps Collette System microphone (p. 117).

Quad-Eight Electronics: 2-7c.

RCA: 5-4; microphone model 77DX (p. 126).

R.D. Systems of Canada Ltd., Toronto, Ontario: 5-37.

Saki Magnetics: 10-12b.

Scully/Ampro: 10-12a (top, bottom left).

Selco Products Company: 3-7; 3-10.

Sennheiser Electronic Corporation: 5-9; 5-11 (top, middle); 5-20a; 5-26; microphone models: 416 (p. 118), 816 (p. 119), MKE 2002 (p. 119), 421 (p. 122), 441 (p. 122); 12-1b (left).

Shure Brothers, Inc.: 4-5; 4-6; 5-1; 6-8 (bottom); microphone models: SM81 (p. 117), SM53 (p. 123), SM54 (p. 123), SM58 (p. 123), SM11 (p. 124), SM5 (p. 125), 300 (p. 126), SM33 (p. 126); 6-13; 12-1a.

Sony Corporation of America: 5-25; microphone models: C-37P (p. 117), C-47 (p. 117), ECM-50 (p. 118).

Sony Video Products Company: 12-2; 12-4.

Steenbeck, Inc.: 13-36.

Studer Revox America, Inc.: 12-1b (center, right).

Swintek Enterprises: 5-38a; 5-39c; 6-14.

Switchcraft, Inc.: 2-11; 2-12.

Taber Manufacturing & Engineering Company: 10-9.

Tangent Systems, Inc., Phoenix, AZ: 3-9.

TEAC Professional Products Group (TASCAM): 3-19 (top left).

Technics: 4-1b; 10-2.

Telex Communications, Inc.: 5-39a, b.

3M: 9-13 (top left, bottom right); 10-10; 10-22; 13-34.

Tweed Audio: 11-3.

United Recording Electronics Industries (UREI): 11-4; 11-10.

U.S. Gypsum: 2-35.

Westlake Audio: 2-4 (p. 14); 2-4 (p. 15, top); 2-6b; 2-29b (right).

for   *Claudette*

          Ariane   *Renee*

                    and

                Mom

Contents

Preface

The importance of audio in media seems obvious. Without it, radio and records would not exist, and television and film would have considerably less impact. Even "silent" film had accompanying music and sound effects. Nevertheless, the obvious is often overlooked or taken for granted. How else does one explain the dearth of literature about this vital and powerful part of communications?

One intent of this book, then, is to help close the gap between the importance of audio in media and its lack of recognition. A second purpose is to treat the subject of audio generically by providing a broad theoretical and practical foundation in the techniques and aesthetics of sound and by applying them to the particular demands of radio, television, film, and music production. A third intent is to introduce audio using a nontechnical approach and to avoid, whenever possible, references to makes and models of equipment, prescribed techniques, and rules.

Audio in Media is designed to be read as a whole or selectively with no disruption in continuity. Some chapters, or parts of chapters, are basic to sound in general and other sections apply to sound in a particular medium, such as radio, television, film, or records.

Chapter 1, "Sound and Hearing: An Introduction," and Chapter 2, "Sound Studios," introduce the physical behavior and psychological effects of sound, the types and characteristics of the rooms in which audio is produced, and, for those in broadcasting, signal transmission. Chapter 3, "Consoles," is divided into two sections: one section deals with the one- and two-output channel consoles used mainly in broadcasting, and the other section describes the more complex multichannel consoles used in television, film, and music production. This chapter, as well as Chapter 4, "Turntables," and Chapter 5, "Microphones," are basic to the four mechanical-electronic media since most audio production requires their use. The first part of Chapter 6, "Miking Speech," is basic to microphone technique. The rest of the chapter is divided into two parts: one about miking speech in radio and the other about miking speech in television. Chapter 7, "Miking Music," applies microphone techniques to music production for records, television, and film.

Chapter 8, "Monitor Loudspeakers," is fundamental to audio since all recorded and broadcast sound is heard and evaluated through a loudspeaker. As the title suggests, Chapter 9, "Tape and Film," is divided into two sections: one on audio and video tape and the other on motion picture film. Chapter 10, "Tape Recorders," is also in two parts: audio tape recorders and video tape recorders. Since signal processing has become such an important part of audio production, Chapter 11 covers the most commonly used signal-processing devices and their effects on sound. This chapter can be read in whole or in part based on need.

Another widespread application of audio production is in on-location production, which is discussed in Chapter 12. This chapter covers techniques and aesthetics in general and their application to radio, television, and film in particular. A section about miking on location is included here rather than in Chapter 6 or 7. Chapter 13, "Editing," describes techniques of editing audio tape, video tape, and sound film, and the aesthetics that apply to editing sound. Chapter 14, "Additional Production Techniques and Procedures," discusses important aspects of audio production that do not fit neatly into any of the other chapters. Chapter 15, "Mixing Sound," is basic to the four media since it covers combining, or layering, sounds.

Acknowledgments

Although a single name appears as the author of this book, *Audio in Media* is the product of the efforts of many people.

To Bill Storm, Assistant Director of Syracuse University's Audio Archives, go special thanks for his encouragement, attention to detail, and investment in time as both manuscript reader and photographer of many of the pictures in this book.

Sincere appreciation goes to Lesa Ouellette and Henry Scot Brent, who created and drew sketches for most of the graphics. They were a delight to work with.

Thanks to Peter Dart, University of Kansas, for his detailed editing and extremely helpful criticisms, and to John Craft, Arizona State University, for his knowledgeable and perceptive comments. Thanks also to the following for their encouragement and suggestions in reviewing the manuscript: Vincent Ialenti, Mount Wachusett Community College; David Martin, City College of San Francisco; Howard Pactor, University of Florida; Steve Runyon, University of San Francisco; and Barbara Tirre, Southern Illinois University at Edwardsville.

Several people from media and industry made important contributions to this book. Among them are Bob Costas, NBC-TV Sports, Donald Rogers, technical director of Samuel Goldwyn Studios (now Warner Hollywood Studios), Larry Schneider, CBS-TV, and Richard Stumpf, director of sound at Universal Pictures. Thanks also to the many representatives from the companies credited on p. v.

Gratitude is expressed to Bill Cooper, Bill Denne, and John Soergel of the audio and video technical support services at Syracuse University.

To Wadsworth Publishing Company and its first-rate professionals go heartfelt thanks. In particular, I thank Becky Hayden, who understood, advised, pushed, and supported at all the right times, and Helen Sweetland for her gentle guidance. I cannot imagine any author having a publisher more helpful and responsive.

Finally, thanks to my wife, Claudette, for her inestimable contribution of love, understanding, and strength. To her this book is dedicated.

Stanley R. Alten

1

Sound and Hearing: An Introduction

What is sound? The answer depends on who you ask. A physicist will tell you that sound is both a disturbance of molecules caused by vibrations transmitted through an elastic medium (such as air) and the interaction of these vibrations with an environment. That definition does not mean much to the psychologist, who thinks of sound as a human response.

To put the question another way: If a tree falls in a forest and there is no one to hear it, does the falling tree make a sound? The physicist would say yes because a falling tree causes vibrations, and sound is vibration. The psychologist would probably say no because without a perceived sensation there can be no human response; hence, there is no sound. In practical terms, both the physicist and the psychologist are right. Sound is a cause-and-effect phenomenon, and the psychological cannot really be untangled from the physical. Thus, in audio production you need to understand both the objective and the subjective characteristics of sound. Not to do so is somewhat like arguing about the falling tree in the forest—it is an interesting, but unproductive exercise.

The Sound Wave

Imagine yourself listening to a guitarist performing at a live concert. The guitarist plucks a string and it vibrates, setting into motion the air molecules closest to the string. These molecules begin moving to and fro, like a pendulum, bumping into nearby molecules and starting a chain reaction. The chain reaction carries the original vibrations from the guitar string through the air to you. What makes the chain reaction possible is air, or more precisely, a medium with the property of **elasticity.**

1

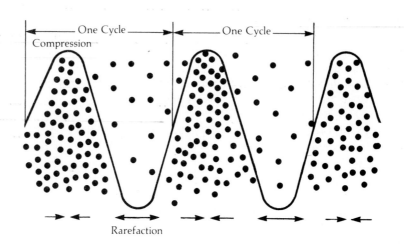

1-1 *Sound pressure waves are formed when a vibration causes molecules to bump into nearby molecules, thus compressing them, increasing the sound pressure, and triggering a chain reaction. The original molecules then return to their original position and thereby create a reduction in sound pressure, or rarefaction.*

One Cycle — One Cycle
Compression
Rarefaction

✓-missed on test
expansion
and
contraction

Compression
Rarefaction
frequency
cycles/sec.
hertz.

B. Four characteristics of sound

✓ Elasticity is the characteristic that tends to pull a displaced molecule back to its original position after its initial momentum has caused it to displace the nearby molecules. **Compression** occurs when the disturbed molecules have enough momentum to bump against other molecules. As the molecules return to their original position, a partial vacuum, called a **rarefaction,** is created. When a vibration has passed through one to-and-fro motion, from compression to rarefaction, it has completed one cycle (see **1-1**).

The number of cycles that a vibration completes in 1 second determines its **frequency**. If a vibration completes 50 **cycles per second** (cps), its frequency is 50 **hertz** (Hz); if it completes 10,000 cps, its frequency is 10,000 Hz.*

Frequency and Pitch

Every vibration has a frequency, and generally humans are capable of hearing frequencies from 20 Hz to 16,000 Hz. Frequencies just above or below this range are felt more than heard, if perceived at all. Psychologically, we perceive frequency as **pitch—the relative highness or lowness of a sound.** The more times per second a sound wave vibrates, the higher its pitch. A whistle vibrates more times per second than a fog horn; therefore, its pitch is higher. The G string of a guitar vibrates 196 times per second, so its frequency is 196 Hz. Relative to the A string, which has a frequency of 110 Hz, the pitch of the G string is higher.

---

*The term "cycles per second" was used to designate frequency until a few years ago, when the term "hertz" was adopted in honor of the nineteenth-century German physicist Heinrich Hertz. We shall use "hertz" throughout this book.

Pitch also relates to our perception of a sound's tonal characteristic—that is, whether we hear it as tinny, bright, raspy, warm, hissy, and so on. The range of audible frequencies, or **frequency spectrum,** can be divided into sections, each of which has a unique and vital quality. The usual divisions in Western music are called **octaves.** An octave is the interval between any two frequencies that have a ratio of 2 to 1. The range of human hearing covers ten octaves. Starting with 20 Hz, the first octave is 20 to 40 Hz, the second 40 to 80 Hz, the third 80 to 160 Hz, and so on (see the diagram inside the back cover).

Octaves one and two: lower bass, power, boom, fullness.

The first two octaves are the very low bass. These are the frequencies that give sound power, boom, and fullness. The lowest notes of the piano, organ, and bass are in this range, as are the lower frequencies of traffic, thunder, and explosions. The third and fourth octaves are the upper bass frequencies—the foundation of musical structure. Most tones generated by rhythm instruments such as drums and the bass are in this range. In fact, pitches in the first four octaves are very satisfying to the ear because we perceive them as giving sound an anchor or "bottom." One reason for the bass control on most home receivers and stereo systems is so that we can enhance these foundation frequencies.

Octaves three and four: Upper bass—foundations of musical structure

If the **low end** of the frequency spectrum gives sound power and fullness, the **midrange**—the fifth, sixth, and seventh octaves—gives it energy. The midrange contains most of the **fundamental** frequencies in sound and music. A fundamental is the lowest or basic pitch of a sound. Due to the sound energy generated, the ear is quite sensitive to the midrange, and long listening sessions during which midrange frequencies predominate can be annoying and fatiguing.

Octaves five, six, and seven: energy

We are also very sensitive to frequencies in the eighth octave, a rather curious range. Pitches in the lower half are extremely unpleasant to our ears; they sound harsh, lispy, and abrasive. The upper half of the eighth octave, however, contains rich and satisfying pitches that give sound definition, clarity, and realism. We perceive the frequencies in the upper eighth octave as being close to the listener, and for this reason it is also known as the **presence range.**

Eighth octave: definition, clarity, realism

Although the ninth octave and the audible part of the tenth generate only 2 percent of the total power output of the frequency spectrum, they give sound the vital, lifelike qualities of brilliance and sparkle. If there is too much emphasis on this range, however, sound will be hissy. The treble control on most home receivers and stereo systems is used to control ninth- and tenth-octave frequencies.

Octaves nine and audible part of tenth: brilliance and sparkle

(A) Pure
(B) Harmonics
(C) Overtones

Amplitude and Loudness

We have noted that vibrations stimulate molecules to move in pressure waves at certain rates, and that rate determines frequency. Vibrations not only affect the molecules' rate of movement, however; they also determine the number

Size of the sound wave = amplitude (loudness)

*(1) Pitch
(2) Volume
(3) Duration
(4) Quality
(5) Distance*

of molecules that are set in motion. This number depends on the intensity of a vibration; the more intense it is, the more molecules are displaced. The greater the number of molecules displaced, the bigger is the sound wave. The number of molecules in motion, and therefore the size of a sound wave, is called **amplitude** (see **1-2**). Our subjective impression of amplitude is **loudness**.

The ear's ability to hear wide variations in loudness is extraordinary. We measure loudness using the **decibel** (dB)—a unit that measures the relative intensity of acoustic pressure or voltage. Acoustic pressure is measured in **sound pressure level** (dB-SPL). Humans have the potential to hear a range from 0 dB-SPL, the threshold of hearing, to 120 dB-SPL, the threshold of pain, and beyond (see **1-3**). This range of quietness to loudness is called **dynamic range**.

Since this range is logarithmic, it means that humans have the capability to hear loudness at a ratio of 1 to 10,000,000 and greater. If the loudness of a sound of 100 dB-SPL were doubled, it would be 103 dB-SPL. Nevertheless, it takes an increase of at least 6 dB for most people to perceive a sound level as doubled.

The Ear and Hearing Loss

Although the human ear can hear sounds over a wide dynamic range, hearing loss results if it is exposed to excessively loud levels for too long. Unfortunately, hearing loss from exposure to loud sounds is not regenerative, or self-corrective. The ear is a durable, but delicately integrated mechanism. It is divided into three parts: (1) the **outer ear,** (2) the **middle ear,** and (3) the **inner ear** (see **1-4**).

Sound waves first reach the outer ear, where they are collected and directed to the **auditory canal.** The auditory canal channels the sound waves to the eardrum, which then starts to vibrate. These vibrations are transmitted by three small bones in the middle ear to the inner ear. The inner ear is a spiral

1-2 *The number of molecules displaced by a vibration creates the amplitude or loudness of a sound. Since the number of molecules in the sound wave in part b is greater than the number in the sound wave in part a, the amplitude of the sound wave in b is greater.*

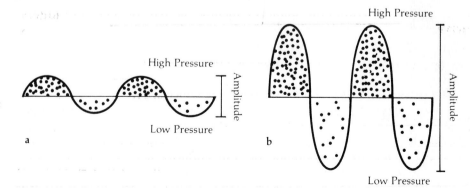

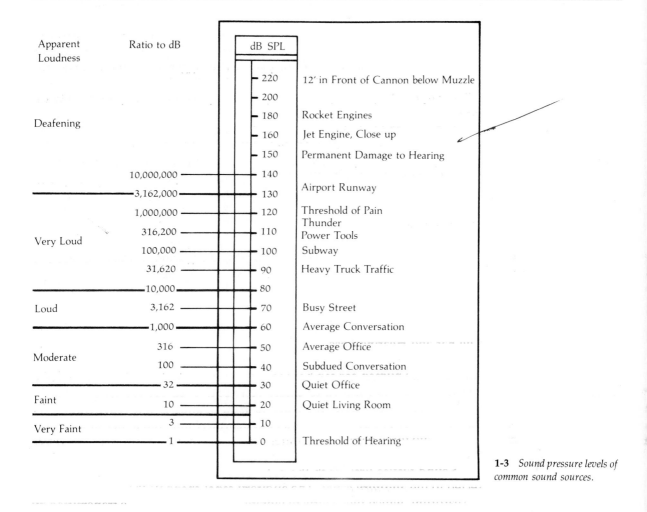

Apparent Loudness	Ratio to dB	dB SPL	
		220	12′ in Front of Cannon below Muzzle
		200	
Deafening		180	Rocket Engines
		160	Jet Engine, Close up
		150	Permanent Damage to Hearing
	10,000,000	140	
	3,162,000	130	Airport Runway
	1,000,000	120	Threshold of Pain
			Thunder
Very Loud	316,200	110	Power Tools
	100,000	100	Subway
	31,620	90	Heavy Truck Traffic
	10,000	80	
Loud	3,162	70	Busy Street
	1,000	60	Average Conversation
	316	50	Average Office
Moderate	100	40	Subdued Conversation
	32	30	Quiet Office
Faint	10	20	Quiet Living Room
	3	10	
Very Faint	1	0	Threshold of Hearing

1-3 *Sound pressure levels of common sound sources.*

filled with fluid. Within the spiral is a membrane that contains the **auditory nerve** endings. Vibrations in the fluid excite these nerve endings, which transmit impulses along the auditory nerve to the brain.

Deterioration of the auditory nerve endings occurs through the natural aging process and usually results in a gradual loss of hearing first in the higher frequencies and then in the lower frequencies. Prolonged listening to loud sounds adversely affects the auditory nerve endings and hastens their deterioration. It is not uncommon for young people who are constantly exposed to loud sound levels to have the hearing acuity of a 70-year-old person. To avoid premature deterioration of your auditory nerves, do not expose them to excessively loud sound levels for extended times (see **1-5**).

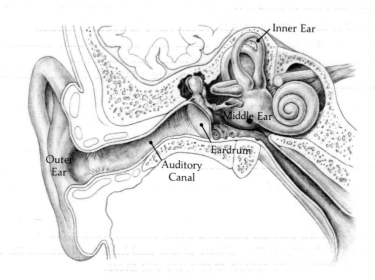

1-4 *Cross section of the human ear.*

1-5 *Hours of exposure to high sound levels permitted by the U.S. Government and the British Occupational Hygiene Society.*

U.S. Government—Occupational Safety and Health Act		British Occupational Hygiene Society	
Sound Level (dB)	Daily Permissible Hours of Exposure	Sound Level (dB)	Daily Permissible Hours of Exposure
90	8	90	8
92	6	91	6
95	4	93	4
97	3	94	3
100	2	96	2
105	1	99	1
110	½	102	½
115	¼	105	¼

Frequency and Loudness

It is natural to assume that the greater the amplitude, the louder is the sound. This is not always so, however. If a guitarist plucks all six strings equally hard, you do not hear each string at the same loudness level. The high E string (328 Hz) sounds louder than the low E string (82 Hz). To make the low string sound as loud, the guitarist would have to pluck it harder.

This suggests that the high E string may sound louder because of its higher frequency. If you sound three tones—50 Hz, 1,000 Hz, and 15,000 Hz—at a fixed loudness level, however, the 1,000-Hz tone sounds louder than either the 50-Hz or the 15,000-Hz tone.

These observations show that the human ear is not equally sensitive to all audible frequencies; we do not hear low and high frequencies as well as we hear middle frequencies. This, oddly enough, is the principle of *equal*, rather than unequal, loudness (see **1-6**), and it has important implications for recording and listening. For example, if you have the loudness of a sound at a high level during recording and at a low level during playback, both low and high frequencies disappear. The converse is also true: If loudness is low when recording and high when playing back, the low and high frequencies predominate. We have noted that the bass and treble controls on a home receiver and stereo allow you to adjust the volume of low and high frequencies; the equal loudness principle is one reason they were put there.

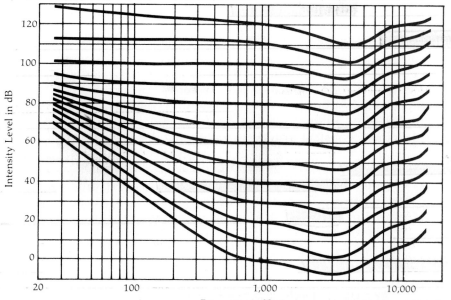

1-6 Equal loudness curves illustrate our relative lack of sensitivity to low and high frequencies compared with middle frequencies. A 50-Hz sound would have to be at 50 dB to seem as loud as a 1,000-Hz sound at 0 dB. If music is recorded at 100 dB and played back at 50 dB, the bass frequencies and the frequencies between 3,000 and 4,000 Hz sound weaker. (Based on Fletcher-Munson.)

Speed of a sound wave 1130 ft/sec @ sea level, 70°F 1°

F_0 Velocity

Although frequency and amplitude are the most important physical components of a sound wave, a third component—**velocity,** or the speed of a sound wave—should be mentioned. Velocity usually has little impact on pitch or loudness and is relatively constant in a controlled environment; sound travels 1,130 feet per second at sea level and 70 degrees Fahrenheit. Velocity changes significantly in very high or low temperatures, however, increasing as air warms and decreasing as air cools. For every change of 1 degree Fahrenheit, the speed of sound changes 1.1 feet per second. If velocity increases or decreases greatly, the pitch of a sound rises or falls proportionately. *to pitch change*

A. External Interference = outside the medium
B. Internal Interference = something broadcast in the medium

Interference

So far we have discussed the propagation and perception of sound under ideal conditions. However, in any form of communication generated by humans—spoken, written, played, painted, projected, or broadcast—some interference is not only possible but also probable. Interference may be external or internal. External interference is caused by something outside the transmitting medium—such as people munching popcorn during a movie, coughing during a concert, or shouting during a speech—or it may be due to a scratchy record, a smeared painting, or a torn page.
Internal interference is directly related to the transmitting medium—such as an out-of-tune instrument, a hoarse announcer, a "snowy" TV screen, or a noisy sound system. In audio, two of the most common types of internal interference are **distortion** and **noise**.

Distortion = undesired changes in the quality of sounds.

DISTORTION Distortion is any undesirable change in the **timbre**—the quality or color—of a sound. It can make a violin sound screechy, a trumpet raspy, or a voice scratchy. Usually, however, distortion is not so obvious but quite subtle; after you listen for a period of time it becomes apparent through a feeling of annoyance, uneasiness, or fatigue. Distortion exists in several forms: **harmonic distortion, intermodulation distortion, frequency distortion, loudness distortion, transient distortion,** and **spatial distortion**.

System-added sounds

Harmonic Distortion Harmonic distortion is actually quite unharmonious. It occurs when the audio system introduces sounds into a recording that were not present originally. This usually happens when the input and output of a sound system are *nonlinear*—that is, do not change in direct proportion to each other.

interacting frequencies overtones

Intermodulation Distortion Intermodulation distortion occurs when two or more different frequencies pass through an amplifier at the same time and interact to create combination tones and dissonances that are unrelated to the original sounds. <u>Audio systems are most vulnerable to intermodulation distortion when frequencies are far apart</u>, as when a piccolo and a baritone saxophone are playing at the same time. Intermodulation distortion usually occurs in the <u>high frequencies</u> because <u>they are weaker</u> and more delicate than the low frequencies.

Frequency Distortion Frequency distortion is caused when <u>frequencies that</u> are present in the input source are <u>not present, or not equally reproduced,</u> in the output. This usually occurs with <u>inexpensive audio systems</u> that cannot reproduce all audible frequencies at the same loudness, or that are incapable of reproducing the bass and treble frequencies.

lost or unequally produced frequencies

Loudness Distortion Loudness distortion arises when a signal is recorded or played back at a level of <u>loudness that is greater than the sound system can handle</u>.

Overloading the amplifier

Transient Distortion Transient distortion relates to the <u>inability</u> of an audio component to record or reproduce **transients—sounds with sudden, explosive attacks and quick decays,** such as drumming, crashing, and popping. Sometimes transient distortion produces a <u>ringing sound</u>.

Lack of proper response to fast attacks and quick decays (sloppy response)

Spatial Distortion Spatial distortion is a factor in stereophonic, quadriphonic, and binaural recording and reproduction, <u>where the position of sounds between two or four loudspeakers coming from front, rear, left, center, and right is important to aural balance</u> (see Chapters 6 and 7). In stereo, for example, the sound of a vocalist usually comes from between the two loudspeakers and the accompaniment comes from the left, from behind, and from the right of the vocalist. If it sounds like the vocalist is coming from the left or right of center or like the accompaniment is in front of the vocalist, the problem is spatial distortion.

Performers seem to sound out of place

NOISE Noise is <u>any unwanted electric or electromagnetic disturbance</u>, <u>other than distortion, that is heard at the output of an audio system.</u> Three types of noise are: (1) **equipment noise** generated by components in the system or by fluorescent lights, power cables, or air conditioners; (2) **tape noise** generated by the recording tape (see Chapter 11); and (3) **system noise**, <u>a combination of equipment and tape noise.</u>

three types: 1 Equipment noise 2 Tape noise 3 System noise (both)

For a sound system to be professionally acceptable, <u>the difference between the loudest sound it can record or reproduce and the inherent system noise generated by the sound must be as great as possible.</u> This difference is known as **signal-to-noise (S/N) ratio** and is measured in decibels. Most professional audio systems have S/N ratios of at least <u>55 to 1.</u> This means that it is possible to produce 55 dB of sound before the system generates 1 dB of noise. S/N ratios actually are expressed in <u>negative numbers</u>; hence, a S/N ratio of −55 to 1 is better than a S/N ratio of −50 to 1.

Broadcast quality −55:1

Summary

1. Sound is caused when a body vibrates and sets into motion the molecules nearest to it, which starts a chain reaction. This chain reaction creates pressure waves through the air, which are perceived as sound when they reach the ear and brain.

2. Sound acts according to physical principles, but it also has a psychological effect on humans.

3. The number of times a sound wave vibrates determines its frequency or pitch. Humans can hear frequencies between, roughly, 20 Hz and 16,000 Hz—a range of ten octaves. Each octave has a unique sound in the frequency spectrum.

4. The size of a sound wave determines its amplitude or loudness. Loudness is measured in decibels.

5. Humans can hear from 0 dB-SPL, the threshold of hearing, to 120 dB-SPL, the threshold of pain, and beyond. The scale is logarithmic, which means that doubling the level of a 100-dB sound would bring it to 103 dB.

6. If the ear is exposed to loud sounds for extended periods of time, the auditory nerve endings in the inner ear could deteriorate.

7. The ear does not perceive all frequencies at the same loudness even if their amplitudes are the same. This is the principle of equal loudness. Humans do not hear lower- and higher-pitched sounds as well as they hear midrange sounds.

8. Velocity, the speed of a sound wave, is 1,130 feet per second at sea level and 70 degrees Fahrenheit. Sound increases or decreases in velocity by 1.1 feet per second for each change of 1 degree Fahrenheit.

9. Distortion is any undesirable change in the timbre of a sound. Distortion exists in several forms: harmonic, intermodulation, frequency, loudness, transient, and spatial.

10. Noise is any unwanted electric or electromagnetic disturbance, other than distortion, that is heard at the output of an audio system. Three types of noise are equipment, tape, and system.

11. The signal-to-noise ratio is the ratio between the loudest sound level a sound system can reproduce or record and the inherent system noise.

2

Sound Studios

Most audio in media is produced, processed, and routed in sound studios—rooms designed to accommodate the personnel and equipment necessary to produce acoustically controlled program materials. Generally, a sound studio is used as a **control room,** a performance studio, or both.

Control Room

The audio control room houses the equipment that combines, processes, and routes sound from its source to its destination. That equipment usually includes at least the following items (see **2-1**):

Microphone—a familiar, almost ubiquitous piece of sound equipment that changes sound energy into electric energy. It is used in control rooms designed for broadcast and off-air production.

Turntable—a sturdy record player especially designed for use in professional audio facilities.

Tape Recorder—a device that records or plays information in the form of magnetic energy. Most control rooms have two types of recorders: the familiar reel-to-reel machine and the cartridge tape recorder that uses a continuous tape loop enclosed in a plastic cartridge.

Console—a device that takes all incoming audio signals from microphones, turntables, audio and video tape recorders, film projectors, magnetic film reproducers, and other sound sources and amplifies, balances, mixes, and routes them to record or broadcast.

Signal Processors—devices that change the shape, time, or quantity of a signal and, hence, its original sound. A few of the more common signal processors are the equalizer, limiter-compressor, and reverberation unit.

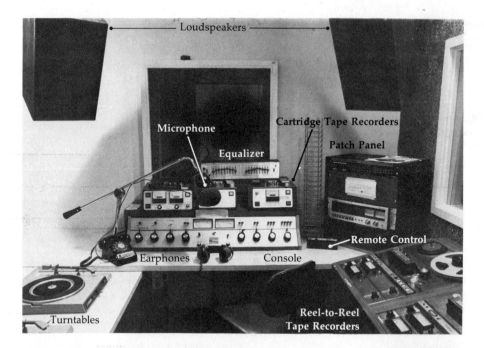

2-1 *Basic types of equipment found in most audio control rooms.*

2-2 *A radio production control room.*

Loudspeaker—a device that makes electric signals audible and intelligible by converting them into sound.

The design of a control room and the type of equipment in it depend on its function.

RADIO Radio control rooms are usually designed so that the equipment is within arm's reach of the operator. Equipment that is not in arm's reach is remote controlled. Since some control rooms are used for on-air broadcasting, the operator is often the performer as well.

Radio stations also have off-air control rooms for recording and editing commercials, jingles, announcements, news stories, and other program materials. These facilities, called *production studios* or *production control rooms,* house basically the same type of equipment as an on-air control room (see **2-2**).

TELEVISION Two types of television control rooms are: production control, used for broadcasting and recording, and postproduction control, used for editing after a production has been recorded.

Production control is divided in two sections, one for video equipment and the other for audio equipment (see **2-3**). The two areas are usually in separate rooms next to or near each other, however, so that the audio operator can monitor the program sound without disturbing the director and other control room personnel. The audio operator and director communicate through headsets that contain a mouthpiece and an earpiece.

2-3 *An audio control room used in television.*

The audio section contains a console that is usually more elaborate than those used in radio because TV deals with more sound sources, including video tape recorders, film projectors, and sometimes several additional microphones for recording music. TV audio control also has reel-to-reel and cartridge tape recorders, turntables (sometimes), and signal-processing equipment.

Postproduction control houses the tape recorders and editing equipment used to edit a production that has already been videotaped. Audio may also be enhanced or "sweetened" during postproduction.

MUSIC RECORDING Control rooms used for music recording usually contain very large consoles, with several inputs and outputs, capable of handling many sound sources at once (see 2-4). Reel-to-reel tape recorders are in one-track, two-track, and various multitrack formats; several different types of signal processors are available; and two, three, or four sets of loudspeakers are used to compare how a tape sounds on different monitoring systems.

Special lighting is often part of the design of a recording control room and studio. Its function is not only to illuminate but also to establish a mood that complements the setting and its purpose.

FILM In film, the closest thing to a control room is the **rerecording room** (see 2-5). In a rerecording room, the various elements of a film sound track are combined, or **mixed**.

2-4 *Control rooms used for music recording.*

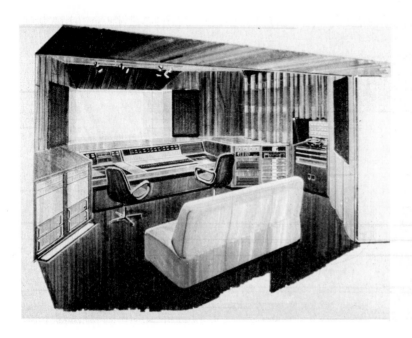

2-5a *Rerecording console and theater in acoustically controlled environment.*

2-5b *Rerecording machine room with film recorders/reproducers.*

Rerecording rooms are large and contain an elaborate console similar to those used in music recording, a screen, a film projector, several magnetic film sound reproducers, and a multitrack audio tape recorder.

Performance Studios

As the term suggests, a performance **studio** is where the talent performs. Studios vary in size from a small announce booth used by a single announcer to a large sound stage where productions are photographed and recorded. Performance studios also contain microphones, lights, cameras, loudspeakers, furniture, scenery, or an audience, depending on the studio's function (see **2-6a,b**).

In radio and music recording, performance studios are usually next to control rooms. They are divided by a glass so that the operator and the performer can see each other (see **2-7a,b,c**). In television, the studio and the control room may be separated, sometimes on different floors or even in different buildings. Visual communication is maintained through studio cameras and control room TV monitors. Aural communication is facilitated by headsets worn by appropriate control room and studio personnel, or by direct **talkback** through a control room microphone–studio loudspeaker system.

The control area may be separated from the studio for logistical reasons, such as having one control room to serve two or more studios, or to locate a control area central to other video sources, such as video tape recorders and film and slide projectors.

2-6a *Combination control console and performance studio used for telephone talk, interview, and panel programs.*

2-6b *Performance studio for music recording.*

2-7a *Television control room with visual access into the studio.*

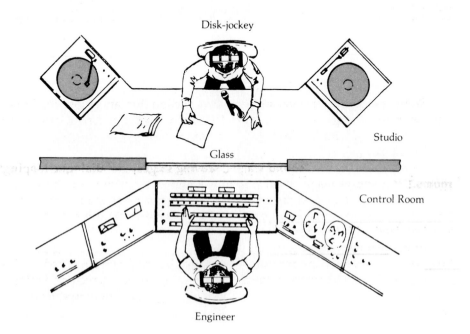

2-7b *Sometimes a disc jockey performs from the studio and an engineer operates the console from the control room.*

2-7c *Film sound rerecording facility with visual access between control room and performance studio, and between control room and recording/reproducing room.*

Some television studios also have a section for an audience. These studios must be large, and they have TV screens so the audience can follow on-stage action that is blocked by TV cameras, microphone booms, and production personnel.

Film studios include **sound stages, scoring stages,** and **dialogue looping rooms.** In a sound stage, productions are filmed (or taped) and recorded.

The scoring stage is similar to a large music recording studio, but it also has film projectors and a large screen. Music sound tracks are recorded and synchronized with the picture.

In the dialogue looping room, dialogue that is not taped during production, or that needs to be rerecorded, is recorded and synchronized to the picture (see **2-8**). The room contains both a studio with a screen and microphones and a control area with a console and magnetic film reproducers and recorders.

2-8a *(Right) Dialogue looping studio designed with variable acoustics provides a range from the "deadest" exterior sound to the "livest" interior sound.*

2-8b *(Far right) Control panel in studio, with footage counter, operates the recording/reproducing machines, which interlock sound and picture in synchronization.*

2-8c *(Right) Recording/ reproducing machines.*

2-8d *(Far right) Another example of a dialogue looping studio.*

Master Control

Broadcast stations have another control area—**master control**. This is where signals from the control room(s) are fed for final boosting and processing before they are sent on to broadcast or, sometimes, recording. Master control is usually a separate room with highly technical equipment operated by specially trained engineers and technicians. In some smaller stations, part of the main on-air control room may be used to house the master control equipment.

Signal Flow: The Sound Chain

Signal flow refers to the paths a signal can take on its way through the equipment in the **sound chain**, from its source to its destination. Signal flow is the product of two functions: **input**—signals that are fed into a component or circuit, and **output**—signals that are emitted by a component or circuit. The more routes a signal can travel, the more flexible is the operation. Such flexibility depends on how the equipment is connected or wired. This can be done in two ways: by **hard wiring,** or through **patching.**

HARD WIRING   When one or more components are wired directly to each other (for example, a microphone to a tape recorder, or the output of a microphone, turntable, and tape recorder to the input of another tape recorder), they are considered hard wired. The signal can travel only one route (see **2-9**). In a small production control room with little equipment, hard wiring usually presents no problem (see **2-10**).

   Most sound facilities, however, contain not only more pieces of the basic equipment with more complex designs, but also additional components such as equalizers, limiter-compressors, noise reducers, and special setups for talk programs and broadcasts done away from the studio. In these circumstances, the multiple routes a signal may have to take make hard wiring impractical.

PATCHING   In most sound studios, the pieces of equipment are not wired directly to each other but to a central routing terminal called the **patch panel**

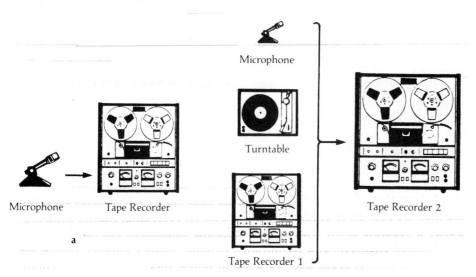

Microphone

Turntable

Tape Recorder 2

Microphone   Tape Recorder

a

Tape Recorder 1

b

2-9 *Hard wiring can limit signal flow. In part **a**, signal flow can go only one way, so hard wiring makes no difference. In part **b**, however, the microphone could feed to tape recorder 1, tape recorder 2 could feed to tape recorder 1, and so on. If these sound sources are hard wired as shown, such flexibility is not possible.*

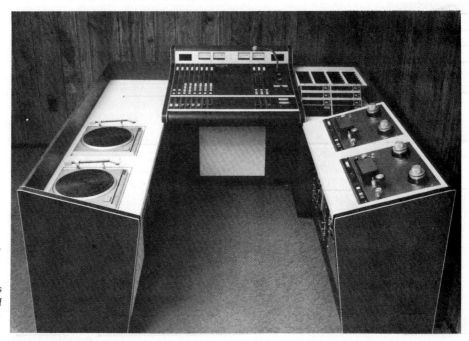

2-10 *In this small radio production studio with so few sound sources, hard wiring does not reduce flexibility in the signal flow. The console is adequate to combine and feed most of the sound sources at once.*

(see **2-11**). Each hole in the panel, called a **jack**, becomes the connecting point to the input or output of each electronic component in the sound studio. Patching is the interconnecting of these inputs and outputs using a **patch cord** (see **2-12** and **2-13**). In this context, the patch panel is like an electronic extension cord.

But such flexibility is not without its problems. In a well-equipped and active facility, the patch panel could become a confusing jungle of patch cords. In all studios, regardless of size and activity, however, a signal travels some paths more often than others. For example, it is more likely that a signal will travel from microphone to console to tape recorder than directly from one tape recorder to another.

As a way of both reducing the clutter of patch cords at the patch panel and simplifying production, terminals wired to certain equipment can also be wired or *normaled* to each other. A *normal* connection is one that permits a signal to flow freely between components without any patching. To route a signal through components that have terminals not wired to each other, patch cords are put in the appropriate jacks to *break normal*—that is, interrupt the normal signal flow—thus rerouting the signal (see **2-14**).

The ability to reroute a signal is also advantageous when equipment fails. Suppose a turntable is normaled to one of the loudness controls—input

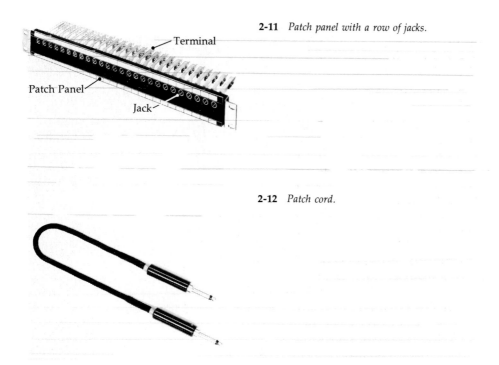

2-11 *Patch panel with a row of jacks.*

Terminal

Patch Panel

Jack

2-12 *Patch cord.*

Output

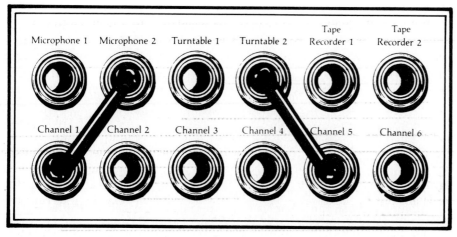

Microphone 1 Microphone 2 Turntable 1 Turntable 2 Tape Recorder 1 Tape Recorder 2

Channel 1 Channel 2 Channel 3 Channel 4 Channel 5 Channel 6

Input

2-13 *Any sound source wired to the patch panel can be connected to any other one with a patch cord plugged into the appropriate jacks.*

2-14 *The terminals connecting the output of microphone 1 to the input of channel 1 on the console, the output of microphone 2 to the input of channel 2 on the console, and so on, have been wired. The signal will flow from one to the other with no patching necessary. These sound sources are normaled. By patching, the normal signal flow is broken and the output of microphone 1 is routed to the input of channel 2, and the output of tape recorder 1 is routed to the input of channel 3. (This diagram is designed to introduce a concept; it is not drawn to scale or precisely accurate.)*

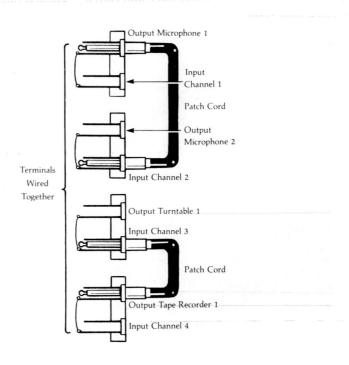

A—on the console, and the control becomes defective. If all inputs and outputs are connected to the patch panel, the defective control can be bypassed by patching the turntable's output to the input of another of the console's loudness controls—input B.

Some other features of patch panels are listed below:

Input/Output—most patch panels are wired so that a row of input jacks is directly below a row of output jacks (see **2-15**).

Full-Normal and Half-Normal—Input jacks are wired so that a patch cord always interrupts the normal connection. These connections are called *full-normal*. Output jacks may be wired as either full-normal or *half-normal*—connections that continue rather than interrupt signal flow. Half-normal connections are useful when a signal must be fed to its normal destination and, via patching, elsewhere as well. Half-normal outputs also permit patching from output to output.

Multiple—most patch panels have special jacks called **multiples**, which are wired to each other instead of to any electronic component. Multiples provide the flexibility to feed the same signal to several different sources at once (see **2-16**).

Broadcast Signal Flow

In broadcasting, once a signal leaves the control room, it begins its journey to your home receiver. Whether it is AM or FM radio, VHF or UHF television, the principle of signal transmission is the same.

After the program signal leaves the *control room*, it goes to *master control*, where it gets the power boost needed to send it to the *transmitter*. At the transmitter, the program signal is superimposed or **modulated** onto a carrier

Output
Input
Output
Input

2-15 *Patch panels are wired so input is directly below output. Here the output of "M8 Rec Out 9" is wired to the input of "MM-1000 In 9"; the output of "BRDG Out 1" is wired to the input of "361-1 Rec In."*

Output
Inputs

2-16 *The output of one sound source is patched into a multiple. Three patch cords feed that sound from the multiple to three separate inputs.*

wave and sent to the antenna, which beams the modulated carrier wave to the *home receiver*. The home receiver contains a demodulator that separates the carrier wave from the program signal and changes the program signal back into the original sound (see **2-17**).

Cable Signal Flow

Cable broadcasting has a somewhat different signal flow from direct broadcasting. Instead of a transmitted signal being picked up by the home receiver, it is picked up from relay antennas or from a satellite and transmitted by direct cable to paying subscribers (see **2-18**). This method of transmission makes it possible for subscribers to receive distant signals that are otherwise impossible to pick up.

Acoustics and Psychoacoustics

When vibrations occur in an enclosed space, they create sound waves that bounce around from surface to surface (see **2-19**). Unless these waves are absorbed or dissipated in some way, several things can happen to degrade their quality. They may continue to bounce around the room, thus creating too many reflections and making the sound seem hollow; or the waves may reflect at such a rate that they have difficulty dying out. This creates **standing waves** —waves that continue vibrating between two opposing surfaces and thereby reinforce each other for an abnormally long time before they decay.

Although too much reflected sound causes problems, too much sound absorption is not good either. Waves that are almost completely absorbed have a lifeless, close, oppressive quality.

The challenge is to create an environment in which the proportion of reflected to absorbed waves generates realistic, natural sound. The science of creating such an environment is known as **acoustics**—the objective study of the physical behavior of received sound. Acousticians, however, must also be sensitive to the subjective or **psychoacoustic** effect of received sound on people. Although both subjects are complex, some basic principles will help you understand their critical influences on studio design.

When you hear a sound, it is actually the product of three separate stages in the sound's "life cycle": its **direct sound**, its **early reflections** or **echo**, and its **later reflections** or **reverberation** (see **2-20**). Together they give information about the pitch, loudness, timbre, and direction of a sound source within an environment, and also about the size of the environment.

DIRECT SOUND   Direct sound comes straight from the source to the listener; it is the first sound heard (see **2-21**). It consists of the strongest, purest sounds a source emits, and it is essential to the perception of a sound's location and dimension.

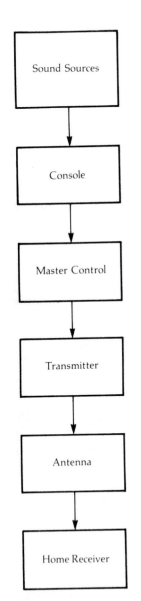

2-17 *Broadcast signal flow.*

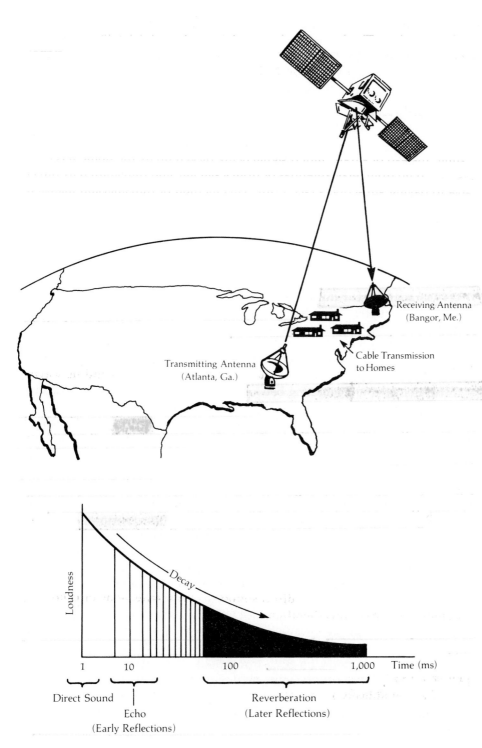

2-18 *Cable signal flow. The broadcasting station's signal is picked up by a relay antenna and sent either to other relay antennas or to a satellite. At the cable system's "head-end," the receiving antenna picks up the signal from the relay antennas or the satellite and feeds it through a cable directly to a subscriber's home.*

Receiving Antenna
(Bangor, Me.)

Transmitting Antenna
(Atlanta, Ga.)

Cable Transmission
to Homes

Loudness

Decay

Time (ms)

Direct Sound

Echo
(Early Reflections)

Reverberation
(Later Reflections)

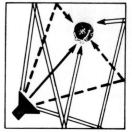

2-19 *Behavior of sound waves in an enclosed space.*

2-20 *"Life cycle" of a sound wave in an enclosed space.*

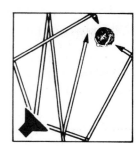

2-21 *Direct sound.*

2-22 *Early reflections (echo).*

2-23 *Later reflections (reverberation).*

"INDIRECT SOUNDS"

EARLY REFLECTIONS (ECHO) Next to reach the listener are the early reflections, better known as *echo*—which are distinctly spaced sound waves that hit one surface before they reach the listener (see **2-22**). Since there are many of them and they reach the listener at different time intervals, early reflections in a controlled acoustic environment give body to the total sound.

LATER REFLECTIONS (REVERBERATION) Later reflections, more commonly called *reverberation*, or *reverb* for short, bounce off two or more surfaces before reaching the listener and continue to reflect until they **decay**, or die out (see **2-23**). They are so closely spaced that the time intervals between them are imperceptible.

Reverberation serves the following purposes: (1) gives sound its overall timbre, (2) fills out the loudness of the sound, (3) contains most of a sound's total energy, and (4) contains most of the information about room size. Together, the early and later reflections constitute the **indirect sound**.

The ratio of direct and indirect sound is one indication of the size of a room. If there are more direct than indirect sound waves, you perceive the room as being small and feel closer to the sound source. If there are more indirect than direct sound waves, you perceive the room as being larger and feel farther from the sound source.

TIME AND RATE OF DECAY Another indication of a room's size is the **decay time**—how long it takes a sound to drop from average loudness to silence (or more precisely, to drop 60 dB-SPL, from about 85 dB-SPL to 25 dB-SPL). In a controlled acoustic environment, the longer it takes sound to decay, the larger is the room.

Studios vary in their decay times depending on the purpose for which they are designed. Announcers and disc jockeys use studios with short decay times (0.3 to 0.5 second) so the sound is close and intimate. Studios used for drama and music have longer decay times (0.7 to 3.0 seconds) because we tend to experience these events in theaters and concert halls and, therefore, expect the feel of the larger, more open space.

Also important to a sound's decay time is its **rate of decay**—the rate at which a sound fades to silence. A smooth rate of decay ensures good sound **diffusion**—the proportion of reflected to absorbed sound that prevents erratic fluctuations in loudness and softness (see **2-24**).

Studio Design

Now that you have some idea of how sound waves behave in an acoustic environment, and how that behavior affects what you hear, it is logical to consider the factors that influence this behavior. There are three: (1) the size of a room, (2) the shape of a room, and (3) the construction materials in the room.

[SIZE] One basic principle of good acoustics is that the three dimensions of a room—height, width, and length—should not be the same or multiples of each other. If the height is 10 feet, the width and length should not be 10, 20, 30, 40 feet, etc. If the height is 15 feet, the width and length should not be 30, 45, 60 feet, etc. Room dimensions that are the same or multiples of each other create acoustics that reinforce rather than diffuse sound waves.

Each sound that is generated (except pure tones—sound with no harmonics and overtones) consists of a combination of pitches: the **fundamental** —the lowest pitch of a sound; the **harmonics**—pitches that are exact multi-

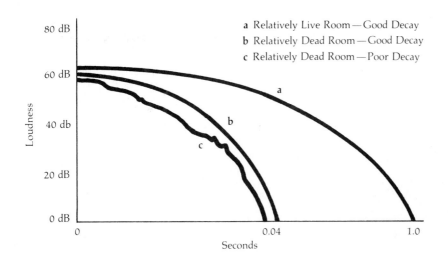

2-24 *A smooth rate of decay is important to good sound diffusion.*

a Relatively Live Room — Good Decay
b Relatively Dead Room — Good Decay
c Relatively Dead Room — Poor Decay

ples of the fundamental; and the **overtones**—pitches that are not exact multiples of the fundamental.

✳ Suppose a studio's height is 10 feet and a sound source generates a fundamental of 150 Hz. The harmonics of the sound traveling the height of the studio would be 300 Hz, 450 Hz, 600 Hz, 750 Hz, 900 Hz, etc. If the studio is 20 feet wide, the pitch of the fundamental traveling across the width would be halved to 75 Hz with harmonics of 150 Hz, 225 Hz, 300 Hz, 375 Hz, 450 Hz, etc. If the studio is 30 feet long, the pitch of the fundamental is lowered by one third to 50 Hz with harmonics of 100 Hz, 150 Hz, 200 Hz, 250 Hz, 300 Hz, etc.

Notice that the frequencies 150 Hz and 300 Hz recur in all three dimensions. If you continued the calculation of the harmonics, several other frequencies would also recur in each dimension (see **2-25**). These reinforced frequencies, which are disproportionately louder than the other frequencies, inhibit good sound diffusion and thus color sound by changing its timbre.

To avoid the sound coloration generated by improperly proportioned studios, acousticians have computed "preferred dimensions" for studios of various sizes. By avoiding dimensions that are the same or multiples of each other, no frequency (ideally) or few frequencies (realistically) are generated more than once (see **2-26a, b, c**).

SHAPE Acoustics is a science of interacting relationships. Although a studio may have preferred dimensions, its shape is also important to good sound diffusion.

Sound behaves like light; its *angle of incidence is equal to its angle of reflectance* (see **2-27**). If a studio has parallel walls, sound waves reflect into each other, creating standing waves. If there are concave surfaces, they serve as collecting points, generating unwanted concentrations of sound (see **2-28**). A studio should be designed to break up the paths of sound waves to prevent their building momentum.

Typical studio designs have adjacent walls at angles other than 90 degrees, different-shaped wall surfaces, and glass between the control room

2-25 *Reinforced frequencies in a room 10 by 20 by 30 feet. If this table were continued, each frequency that occurs in the height dimension would recur in the other two dimensions.*

	Height—10 Ft.	Width—20 Ft.	Length—30 Ft.
Fundamental	150 Hz	75 Hz	50 Hz
1st Harmonic	300 Hz	150 Hz	100 Hz
2nd Harmonic	450 Hz	225 Hz	150 Hz
3rd Harmonic	600 Hz	300 Hz	200 Hz
4th Harmonic	750 Hz	375 Hz	250 Hz
5th Harmonic	900 Hz	450 Hz	300 Hz
6th Harmonic	1,050 Hz	525 Hz	350 Hz
7th Harmonic	1,200 Hz	600 Hz	400 Hz
8th Harmonic	1,350 Hz	675 Hz	450 Hz

	Height	Width	Length
a	1.0	1.14	1.39
b	1.0	1.28	1.54
c	1.0	1.50	2.40
d	1.0	1.80	2.10

2-26a *Selected preferred studio ratios.*

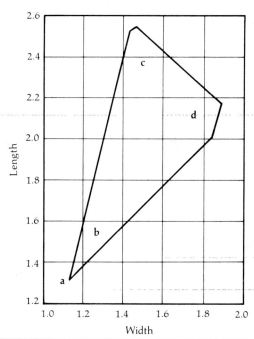

2-26b *Recommended ratios of studio dimensions. (Based on R. H. Bolt, "Note on Normal Frequency Statistics for Rectangular Rooms,"* Journal of the Acoustic Society of America 19 *(July 1946):130; L. W. Sepmeyer, "Computed Frequency and Angular Distribution of the Normal Modes of Vibration in Rectangular Rooms,"* Journal of the Acoustic Society of America 37 *(March 1965):413–423.)*

	Height	Width	Length
a	9 Ft.	10.1 Ft.	12.5 Ft.
b	9 Ft.	11.5 Ft.	13.8 Ft.
c	9 Ft.	13.5 Ft.	21.6 Ft.
d	9 Ft.	16.2 Ft.	18.9 Ft.
a	10 Ft.	11.4 Ft.	13.9 Ft.
b	10 Ft.	12.8 Ft.	15.4 Ft.
c	10 Ft.	15.0 Ft.	24.0 Ft.
d	10 Ft.	18.0 Ft.	21.0 Ft.
a	15 Ft.	17.1 Ft.	20.8 Ft.
b	15 Ft.	19.2 Ft.	23.1 Ft.
c	15 Ft.	22.5 Ft.	36.0 Ft.
d	15 Ft.	27.0 Ft.	31.5 Ft.

2-26c *Preferred studio dimensions using the ratios in* **2-26b**.

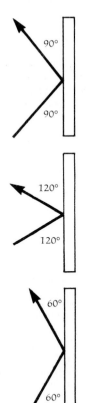

and the studio angled downward to help disperse the sound waves (see **2-29a, b, c,**). In acoustics, everything affects everything else, however, and a studio's shape has to be considered along with the materials used in its construction.

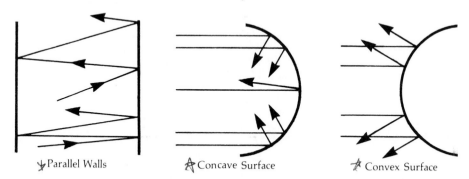

↘Parallel Walls   ↗Concave Surface   ↗Convex Surface

2-28 *The shape of a room's surface affects the direction of sound reflections. Two parallel surfaces opposite each other generate standing waves by reinforcing sound. Concave surfaces concentrate sound waves by converging them. A convex surface is more suitable because it disperses sound waves.*

2-27 *The angle of a sound's incidence is equal to the angle of its reflectance.*

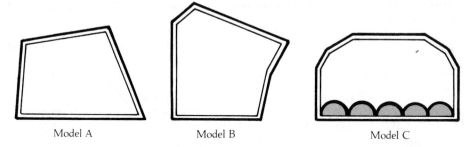

Model A   Model B   Model C

2-29a *Examples of studio shapes with nonparallel plane surfaces.*

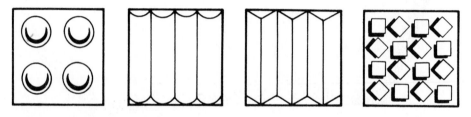

2-29b *Examples of studio walls with different surface shapes—spherical, cylindrical, serrated, and a combination of square and diamond.*

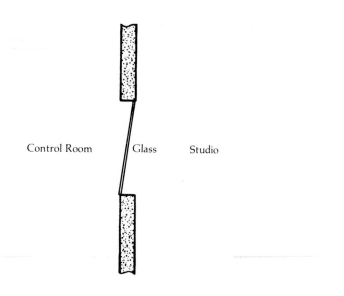

Glass between the control room and the studio is angled down toward the floor to avoid parallel wall surfaces.

CONSTRUCTION MATERIALS A studio must be isolated to prevent any sound from leaking in or out. Its shell usually consists of thick concrete blocks filled or covered with a sound-absorbent material such as sand, rock wool, or fiberglass (see **2-30**). Sometimes studios are "floated"—put on springs for added isolation (see **2-31**).

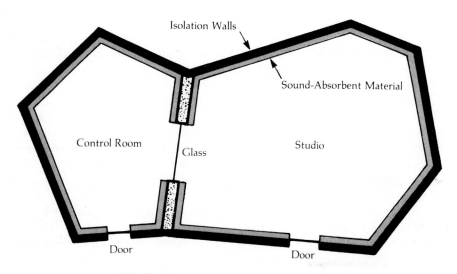

2-30 *Typical construction design of a studio shell.*

2-31 *Studio mounted on springs to increase isolation from outside sound.*

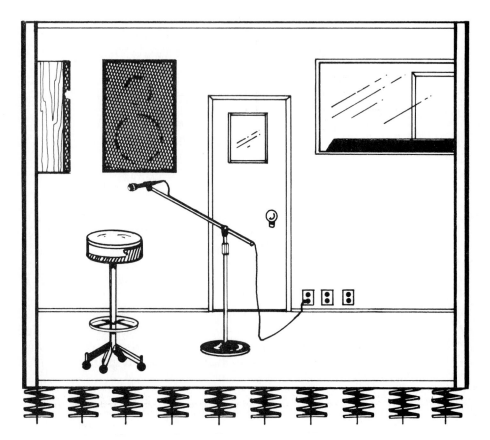

Once the shell has been constructed, the floor, the ceiling, and walls are built. They also consist of materials that help to control the acoustics inside the studio.

When sound hits a surface, one of three things happens, depending on the surface's material and mass. It is reflected, absorbed, or partially absorbed and partially reflected (see **2-32**). All surfaces absorb and reflect sound to some degree. On this basis they are given acoustical ratings: a sound absorption coefficient and a sound transmission classification.

The **sound absorption coefficient** indicates the percentage of sound a material absorbs. Generally, soft, porous materials absorb more sound than hard, nonporous materials; drapes, for example, have a higher absorption coefficient than glass.

A material's sound absorption coefficient must be considered along with the sound's **wavelength**—the distance between the beginning and end of one cycle of a sound wave. Low sounds have long, powerful wavelengths; then as frequencies go higher, wavelengths get shorter and weaker (see **2-33**). There-

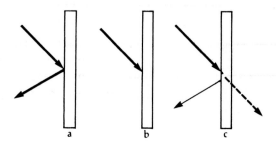

2-32 *When sound hits a surface, it is (a) reflected, (b) absorbed, or (c) partially reflected and absorbed.*

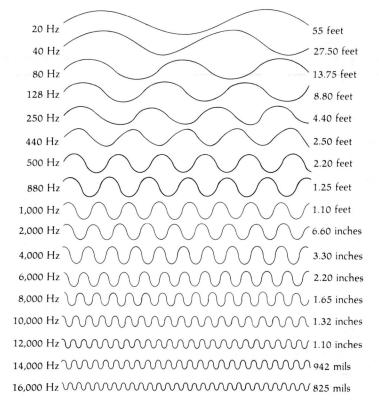

20 Hz		55 feet
40 Hz		27.50 feet
80 Hz		13.75 feet
128 Hz		8.80 feet
250 Hz		4.40 feet
440 Hz		2.50 feet
500 Hz		2.20 feet
880 Hz		1.25 feet
1,000 Hz		1.10 feet
2,000 Hz		6.60 inches
4,000 Hz		3.30 inches
6,000 Hz		2.20 inches
8,000 Hz		1.65 inches
10,000 Hz		1.32 inches
12,000 Hz		1.10 inches
14,000 Hz		942 mils
16,000 Hz		825 mils

2-33 *Selected frequencies and their wavelengths.*

fore, sound absorption coefficients are dependent on frequency (see **2-34**).

✰ The **sound transmission classification** (STC) is a measure of the transmission loss of sound as it goes through a mass of material, such as a wall or a door. It is based on the difference between the noise level outside a room and the desired noise level inside a room. For example, if the outside noise level is 100 dB and the inside (studio) noise level is to be no higher than 20 dB, the studio walls require an STC of 80 dB. If the outside noise level is 70 dB and the studio noise level should be no higher than 30 dB, the studio walls require an STC of 40 dB.

2-34 *(Below) Sound absorption coefficients of commonly used materials.*

Materials	125 Hz	250 Hz	500 Hz	1,000 Hz	2,000 Hz	4,000 Hz
Brick, unglazed	0.03	0.03	0.03	0.04	0.05	0.07
Brick, unglazed, painted	0.01	0.01	0.02	0.02	0.02	0.03
Carpet, heavy on concrete	0.02	0.06	0.14	0.37	0.60	0.65
Same on 40-oz. hairfelt foam rubber	0.08	0.24	0.57	0.69	0.71	0.73
Same with impermeable latex backing on 40-oz. hairfelt or foam rubber	0.06	0.27	0.39	0.34	0.48	0.63
Concrete block, coarse	0.36	0.44	0.31	0.29	0.39	0.25
Concrete block, painted	0.10	0.05	0.06	0.07	0.09	0.08
Fabrics						
Light velour, 10-oz. per sq. yd.	0.03	0.04	0.11	0.17	0.24	0.35
Medium velour, 18-oz. per sq. yd.	0.07	0.31	0.49	0.75	0.70	0.60
Heavy velour, 18-oz. per sq. yd.	0.14	0.35	0.55	0.72	0.70	0.65
Floors						
Concrete	0.01	0.01	0.01	0.02	0.02	0.02
Linoleum, asphalt, rubber, or cork tile on concrete	0.02	0.03	0.03	0.03	0.03	0.02
Wood	0.15	0.11	0.10	0.07	0.06	0.07
Glass						
Large, heavy plate	0.18	0.08	0.04	0.03	0.02	0.02

Sound transmission classifications vary with the type and mass of materials in a barrier. A 4-inch concrete block has an STC of 48 dB, indicating that it will stop up to 48 dB of sound. An 8-inch concrete block has an STC of 52 dB, which makes it 4 dB better at stopping sound than the 4-inch block (see **2-35**). The sound transmission classification is dependent on frequency; however, estimates of STC are usually based on 500 Hz.

Sound studios must have the optimum proportion of absorbent to reflective materials to ensure that all sound waves, regardless of length, are properly diffused. Announce booths and control rooms, which must be rela-

Materials	125 Hz	250 Hz	500 Hz	1,000 Hz	2,000 Hz	4,000 Hz
Glass, continued						
Ordinary window glass	0.35	0.25	0.18	0.12	0.07	0.04
Gypsum panels, ½-in. thick	0.29	0.10	0.05	0.04	0.07	0.09
Marble or glazed tile	0.01	0.01	0.01	0.01	0.02	0.02
Openings						
Stage, depending on furnishings				0.25–0.75		
Deep balcony, upholstered seats				0.50–1.00		
Grills, ventilating				0.16–0.50		
Plaster	0.01	0.01	0.02	0.03	0.04	0.05
Plywood paneling, ¼-in. thick	0.28	0.22	0.17	0.09	0.10	0.11
Water surface, as in a swimming pool	0.008	0.008	0.013	0.015	0.020	0.025
Audience, seated in upholstered seats	0.60	0.74	0.88	0.96	0.93	0.85
Unoccupied cloth-covered	0.49	0.66	0.80	0.88	0.82	0.70
Unoccupied leather-covered	0.44	0.54	0.60	0.62	0.58	0.50
Chairs, metal or wood, occupied	0.15	0.19	0.22	0.39	0.38	0.30
Person						
Adult				4.2		
Youth				3.8		
Child				2.8		

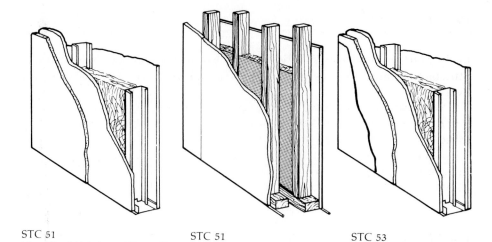

STC 51
Metal Stud-Unbalanced Drywall

STC 51
Staggered Wood Stud-Drywall

STC 53
Metal Stud-Veneer Plaster

2-35 *Sound transmission classifications of common barriers.*

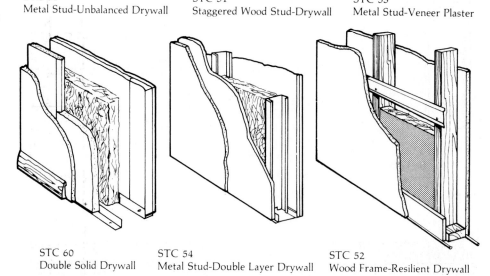

STC 60
Double Solid Drywall

STC 54
Metal Stud-Double Layer Drywall

STC 52
Wood Frame-Resilient Drywall

STC 52
Gypsum Tile-Plaster

STC 50
Wood Stud-Veneer Plaster

STC 49
Metal Stud-Plaster

tively nonreflective, usually have a high proportion of sound absorbency. Studios that must be "live" tend to have a high proportion of sound reflectiveness.

Some studios are able to vary acoustics with movable panels or louvers that change the ratio of reflected to absorbed sound (see **2-36**). Other studios make acoustic adjustments by using portable acoustic screens called *baffles* or *gobos* (see **2-37**). These baffles have either one reflective and one absorbent side, or two sides that are reflective or absorbent.

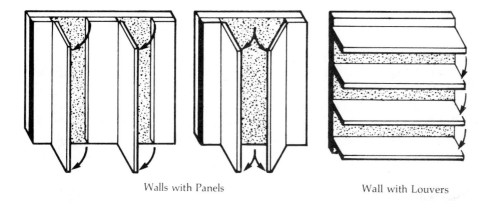

Walls with Panels   Wall with Louvers

2-36 *Movable wall panels and louvers are used to vary studio acoustics.*

2-37 *Movable baffles showing absorbent and reflective surfaces.*

Summary

1. Two types of rooms are usually found in a sound facility: a control room and a performance studio.

2. A control room houses the equipment that combines, processes, and routes sound from its source to its destination. It generally contains a microphone, turntables, reel-to-reel and cartridge tape recorders, a console, signal processors, and loudspeakers.

3. Depending on the medium, control rooms may be used for broadcasting, producing, postproduction editing, rerecording, and mixing.

4. Performance studios, where talent performs, vary in size from one-person announce booths to large studios where major productions are filmed or videotaped.

5. The master control is a highly technical room where signals from control room(s) are fed for final processing before being sent to the transmitter and then to broadcast.

6. Inputs and outputs in a sound facility are either hard wired—connected to each other, thus restricting the signal flow to the components that are wired—or wired to a central routing terminal called the patch panel, making multiple signal paths possible. Patch cords plugged into jacks connect the routing circuits.

7. The signal paths that are used most often are wired together at the terminals of the patch panel. This normals these routes and makes it unnecessary to use patch cords to connect them. It is possible to break normal and create other signal paths by patching.

8. A signal destined for broadcast travels from the control room to the master control and then to the transmitter, where it is superimposed on a carrier wave, and then to the antenna. From there, the signal is beamed to the home receiver.

9. Sound in a room reaches the listener in three stages: as direct sound, as early reflections (echo), and as late reflections (reverberation). Combined, these stages carry information about a sound's pitch, loudness, timbre, direction, and spatial environment.

10. The dimensions of a sound room—height, width, and length—should not be equal or exact multiples of each other or else certain frequencies will be reinforced and color the sound.

11. The shape of a studio and the shapes within it should be irregular to help break up sound, thereby preventing unwanted echoes, standing waves, and poor sound diffusion.

12. When sound hits a surface, it is reflected, absorbed, or partially absorbed and reflected.

13. Material used in studio construction is given either a sound absorption coefficient to indicate how much sound it absorbs, or a sound transmission classification to indicate transmission loss as sound passes through it.

3

Consoles

If the control room is the heart of a sound studio, then the mixing **console** or **board** is the nerve center. At the console, signals flowing from microphones, turntables, and tape recorders are amplified, mixed, balanced, and routed to broadcast or recording.

At first glance, most consoles look threatening, with their panel of buttons, switches, knobs, and lights. But all consoles, both simple and complex, work on the same theoretical principles. Once you understand these principles, you can learn to operate a console in a fairly short time.

Consoles: Why They Look That Way

For the sake of illustration, imagine that no console exists and one must be designed to suit the needs of a small radio station. Assume the station has the following equipment: two microphones, one for the disc jockey in the control room and one for the newscaster in the studio; two turntables; two reel-to-reel tape recorders for prerecorded programs; and two cartridge tape recorders for spot announcements. The design problem is threefold: (1) to get the signals from each sound source to inputs on the console, (2) to combine these inputs at some point into a single output that can be conveniently routed to broadcast, and (3) to provide a way to hear the resulting signals.

MICROPHONE INPUTS Let's begin with the microphones. The **microphone** (mike, for short) changes sound into electric energy. That energy, however, is too weak to go very far. Because it needs a power boost to get anywhere, the first component on the console should be a **preamplifier** (preamp, for short)—a device that boosts the power of low-level signals to usable proportions (see **3-1**).

LOUDNESS CONTROL Solving one problem often creates another. A preamplifier boosts power at a constant rate and has no way of varying the mike's level of output (loudness). The device that regulates the amount of power coming from a preamp is called a **potentiometer**, or *pot* (rhymes with "hot"). A pot is also known as an **attenuator, fader, gain control,** or **volume control.** A pot controls the amount of power that comes from the preamp either by rotating or by sliding up or down (see **3-2a, b**).

ON-OFF SWITCH Sometimes even when a pot is turned down all the way, sound leaks through. An on-off switch at each pot can activate or cut the signal flow. With the devices described so far, the microphone's output power can be amplified, controlled, and turned on or off (see **3-3**).

Mic 1   Mic-Level
              Preamp

3-1 *Microphone output feeds to a microphone preamplifier for power boost.*

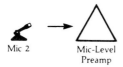

Mic 2   Mic-Level
              Preamp

3-2a *A console with rotary faders.*

3-2b *Sliding fader.*

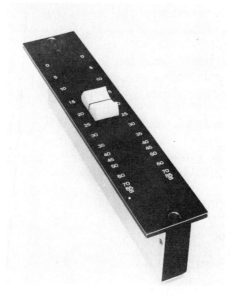

3-3 *Block diagram and console with pots and on-off switches added.*

3-4a *(Right) Block diagram with turntables and turntable preamps, pots, and on-off switches added.*

3-4b *(Far right) Console with turntable controls added.*

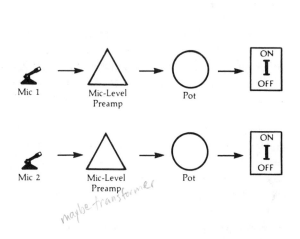

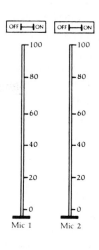

maybe transformer

OTHER INPUTS Turntables, like microphones, are low-level power sources and require preamplification. Many professionally used turntables have pre-amps but still need an additional power boost at the console (see **3-4a, b**). Generally they do not need as much as a microphone, however.

Tape recorders—reel-to-reel and cartridge—are high-level sound sources: that is, they contain more powerful amplifiers than those in low-level sound sources. Tape recorders still require preamps at the console, however, although not so powerful as those used for microphones and turntables. Tape recorders are wired to the console preamps in the same way that microphones and turntables are (see **3-5a, b**). Because various pieces of equipment have different output levels, each input on the console is electrically matched to take a particular component: mike to mike preamp, turntable to turntable pre-amp, tape recorder to tape recorder preamp, and so on.

OUTPUT With the equipment described so far it is possible to feed sound from microphones, turntables, and tape recorders to their own separate in-puts at the console, control their loudness, and turn their signal feed on and off. But there is no way to (1) combine their signals, (2) send their signals out of the console, (3) measure the amount of signal passing through each chan-nel that has its loudness regulated by a pot, and (4) hear the sound.

To solve the first two problems, each signal can be combined and then fed in a single output from the console (see **3-6a**). For these signals to be fed into one output line, there must be a mixing network to combine them electri-cally. Since this network results in some loss in the strength of these signals, the output line needs an amplifier and a pot (see **3-6b**). This pot regulates the combined loudness of all channels, so it is appropriately called the **master pot** (see **3-6c**).

VOLUME UNIT METER Although signals feed in and out of the console, there is still no way to determine how strong (loud) they are. If they are too strong, they will overload the output channel and generate distortion; if they are too weak, they will decrease the signal-to-noise ratio. Listening to the signals does not solve the problem because they are in the form of electric energy; besides, determining what is loud, soft, or just right is too subjective a judg-ment to be reliable. An instrument is needed that objectively measures the electric energy flowing through the console. The instrument most commonly used in this country is the **volume unit (VU) meter** (see **3-7**). When the VU meter is wired to the output of the master pot, it can measure the total power of the signal leaving the console (see **3-8a, b**).

The VU meter is uniquely suited to the sound medium. Unlike most de-vices that measure voltage, the VU meter responds to changes in electric energy the same way that the human ear responds to changes in acoustic energy. It "perceives" average sound intensity rather than momentary peaks

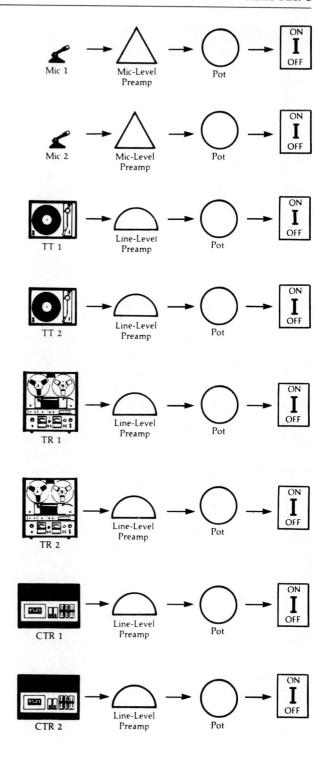

3-5a *Block diagram with reel-to-reel and cartridge tape recorders, preamps, pots, and on-off switches added.*

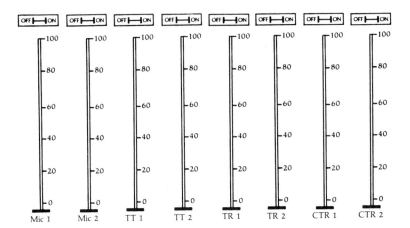

and dips. Its unit of measurement is the **volume unit,** which is closely related to the ear's subjective impression of loudness.

Two calibrated scales are on the face of the VU meter: a percentage of modulation scale and a volume unit scale. A needle, the volume indicator, moves back and forth across the scales, pointing out levels. Some consoles use light-emitting diodes, also called plasma displays, instead (see **3-9**). Both the needle and the light-emitting diodes respond to the electric energy passing through the VU meter. If the energy level is excessively high, the volume indicator will **pin**—slam against the meter's extreme right-hand side—or the diodes will flicker. Pinning can damage the VU meter's mechanism, thus rendering the volume indicator's reading unreliable.

The **percentage of modulation** scale is used mostly in broadcasting. It indicates the amount of signal passing through a channel relative to its capacity. If the VU meter indicates 50 percent of modulation, it means that half the channel capacity is being used. If it reads 100 percent of modulation, it means that the channel's full capacity is being used and any more signal will cause loudness distortion.

Usually any sound below 20 percent of modulation is too quiet or **in the mud,** and levels above 100 percent of modulation are too loud or **in the red.** (The scale to the right of 100 percent is red.) As a guideline, the loudness should "kick" between 60 and 100 percent of modulation, although the dynamics of sound make such evenness hard to accomplish. Usually the best that can be done is to **ride the gain**—adjust the pots from time to time so that, on average, the level stays between 60 and 100. It is normal for the level to move momentarily above or below these points, however.

3-6a *Block diagram with sound sources combined into a single output.*

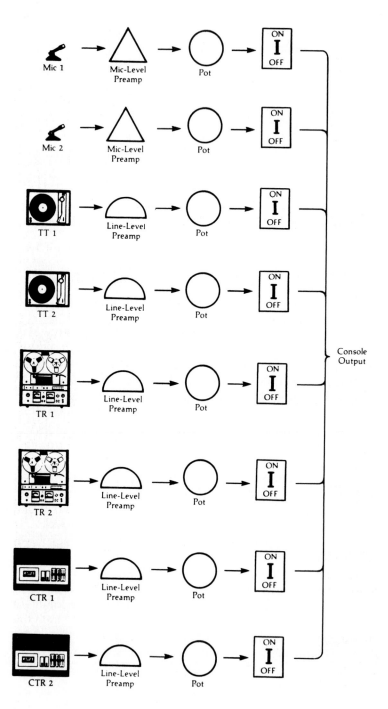

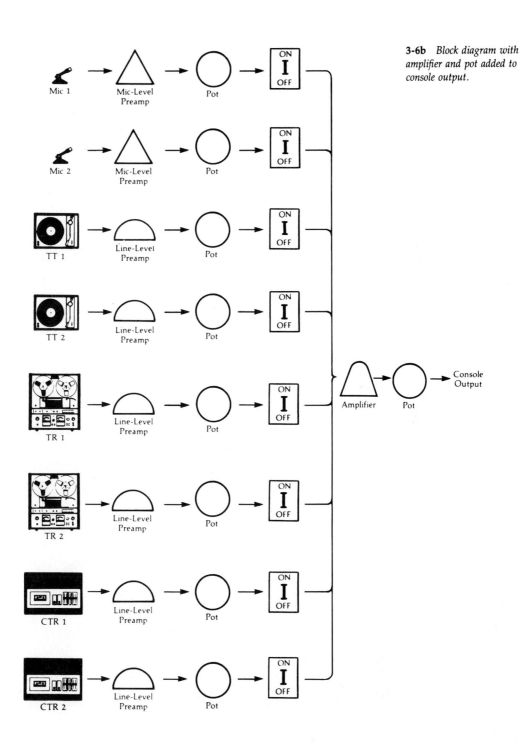

3-6b *Block diagram with amplifier and pot added to console output.*

3-6c *Console with master controls added.*

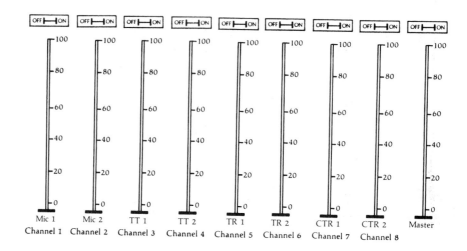

3-7 *Volume unit (VU) meter.*

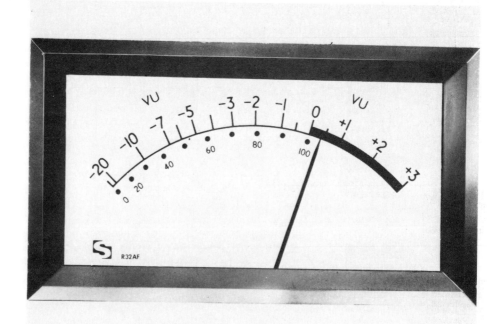

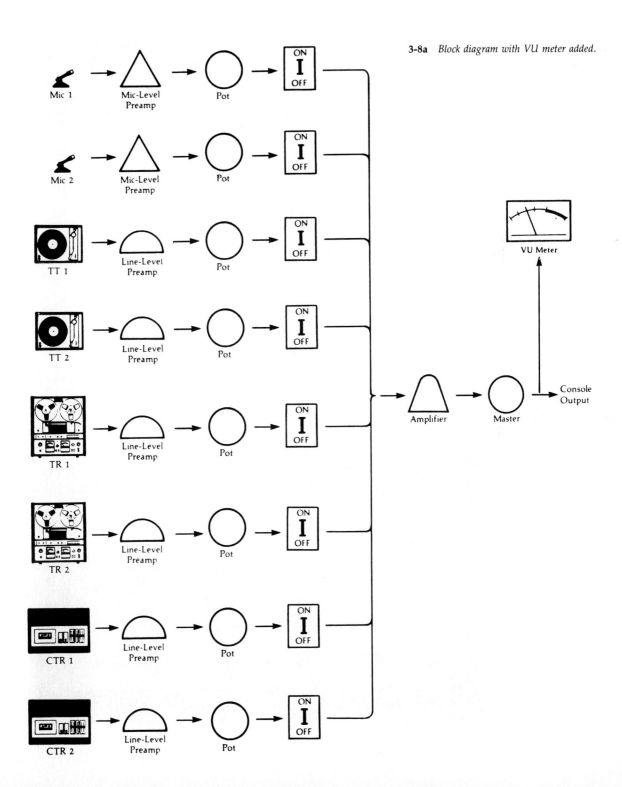

3-8a *Block diagram with VU meter added.*

3-8b *Console with VU meter added.*

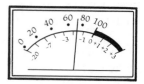

VU Meter

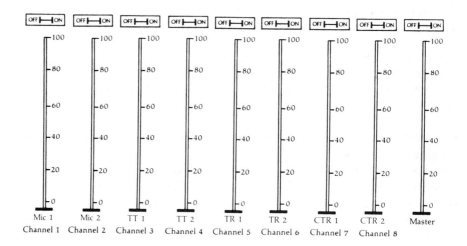

Mic 1 | Mic 2 | TT 1 | TT 2 | TR 1 | TR 2 | CTR 1 | CTR 2 | Master
Channel 1 Channel 2 Channel 3 Channel 4 Channel 5 Channel 6 Channel 7 Channel 8

3-9 *VU meter with light-emitting diodes.*

3-10 *Peak program meter.*

The operator should ride the gain with a light, fluid hand and not jerk the pots up and down or make adjustments at the slightest dip or peak in loudness. Changes in level should be smooth and imperceptible because abrupt changes are disconcerting to the listener.

The volume unit scale is used mostly in music recording for exact referencing. The numbers on the VU scale correlate with those on the percentage scale; that is, −10 VU is slightly more than 25 percent of modulation, −2 VU is equal to 80 percent, and 0 VU is equal to 100 percent.

PEAK PROGRAM METER Another instrument used for measuring loudness is the **peak program meter** (ppm)—a device that indicates peaks in level rather than averages (see **3-10**). It is used in Europe, and many think it gives a more realistic reading of a signal's actual level of loudness than the VU meter. The argument is that although humans may not hear momentary peaks in loudness, the electronics do. Therefore, the peak program meter is better insurance against signal distortion. Also, the ppm is calibrated in decibels, not volume units. Many newer consoles have both VU and ppm meters.

MONITOR SYSTEM We now know that the electric energy of a signal passing through the console can be measured and read, but there is still no way to hear the sound. Perhaps the easiest approach is to take another output line from the master pot and wire it to a loudspeaker. To power the signal and control its loudness, another amplifier and pot are added to the console. Since the loudspeaker in a sound studio is often called the **monitor,** this new pot is called the monitor pot (see **3-11a, b**).

There may still be one small problem with the monitor system. If the monitor is close to the microphone when the mike is turned on, its signal will feed through the speaker and back into the mike. This can continue round and round, causing a high-pitched squeal known as **feedback.** To prevent this, a **mute** is put on each mike's on-off switch so that when it is turned on, the signal to the loudspeaker is automatically cut. To hear the sound when the mike is on, it is necessary to use earphones (see **3-12**).

HOW CONSOLES WORK It is now possible to take output signals from any sound source, feed them into separate console inputs, and amplify, balance, mix, measure, hear, and route them. For example, you may start a record on turntable 1 feeding pot 3, and then want to announce its title, over the music, from mike 1 feeding pot 1. Turn on pot 3, start the record, and raise the pot so the loudness level of the music averages between 60 and 100 percent of modulation. At an appropriate point in the music, lower pot 3 so the music does not drown out your announcement. At about the same time, turn on pot 1 and raise its loudness level higher than the sound on pot 3. In the balance of these two sounds, the announcement is in the aural foreground and the music is in the background. You have to balance these sounds by listening to them in the earphones; the VU meter, remember, reads the combined levels

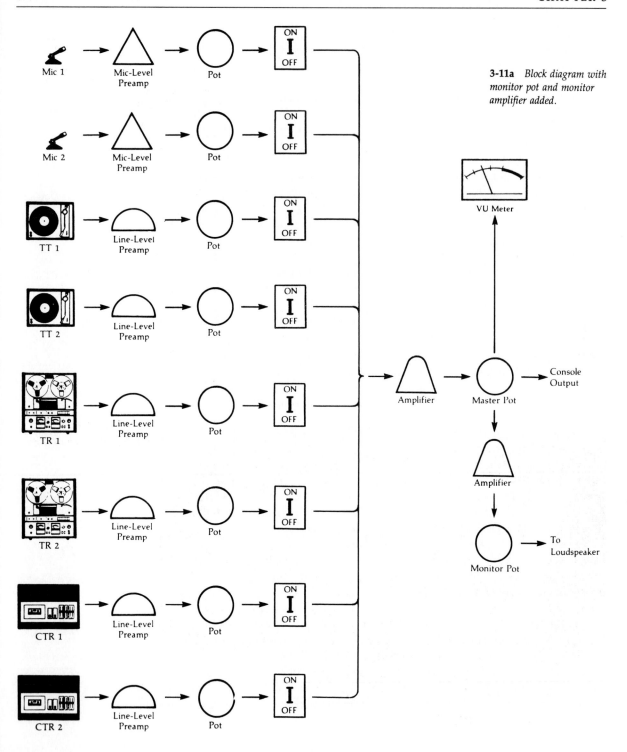

3-11a *Block diagram with monitor pot and monitor amplifier added.*

3-11b *Console with monitor controls added.*

VU Meter

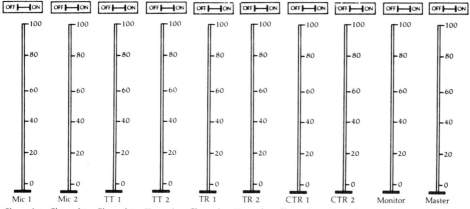

| OFF ⊢─⊣ON | OFF ⊢─⊣ON | OFF ⊢─⊣ON | OFF ⊢─⊣ON | OFF ⊢─⊣ON | OFF ⊢─⊣ON | OFF ⊢─⊣ON | OFF ⊢─⊣ON | OFF ⊢─⊣ON | OFF ⊢─⊣ON |

Mic 1 | Mic 2 | TT 1 | TT 2 | TR 1 | TR 2 | CTR 1 | CTR 2 | Monitor | Master

Channel 1   Channel 2   Channel 3   Channel 4   Channel 5   Channel 6   Channel 7   Channel 8

3-12 *Earphones plugged into console earphone jack.*

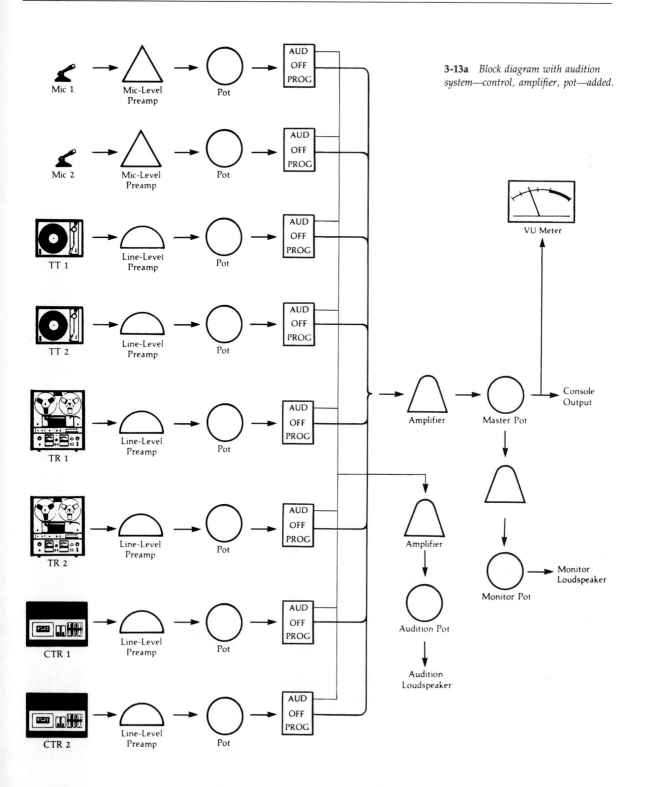

3-13a *Block diagram with audition system—control, amplifier, pot—added.*

Mic 1 — Mic-Level Preamp — Pot — AUD / OFF / PROG

Mic 2 — Mic-Level Preamp — Pot — AUD / OFF / PROG

TT 1 — Line-Level Preamp — Pot — AUD / OFF / PROG

TT 2 — Line-Level Preamp — Pot — AUD / OFF / PROG

TR 1 — Line-Level Preamp — Pot — AUD / OFF / PROG

TR 2 — Line-Level Preamp — Pot — AUD / OFF / PROG

CTR 1 — Line-Level Preamp — Pot — AUD / OFF / PROG

CTR 2 — Line-Level Preamp — Pot — AUD / OFF / PROG

VU Meter

Amplifier — Master Pot — Console Output

Amplifier — Monitor Pot — Monitor Loudspeaker

Audition Pot — Audition Loudspeaker

VU Meter

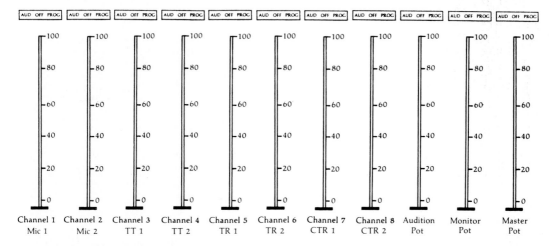

3-13b *Console with audition controls added.*

of electric energy passing through the output channel. After the announcement, continue to feed the music by raising pot 3 to its original level and turning off pot 1. All sound is routed out of the console at the master pot.

AUDITION SYSTEM   Now, with the music on the air, you want to prepare the next record for broadcast. There is no way to preview the record without putting it on the air, however, since there is only one routing system and it feeds to the master pot. Another routing system—an **audition** system—is needed.

One way to assign the audition system to a channel is to change the two-position on-off switch over each pot to three positions: (1) on or **program,** routing signals to the master pot; (2) off; and (3) audition (or **cue**), routing signals to the separate audition system. This audition system would require separate feeds from each pot to another output line with an amplifier, master audition pot, and loudspeaker (see **3-13a, b**). No VU meter is necessary because sound from the audition system is not recorded or broadcast. However, a VU meter is useful to preset levels. In order not to confuse the program sound with the audition sound, the program monitor and the audition monitor should be placed in different locations.

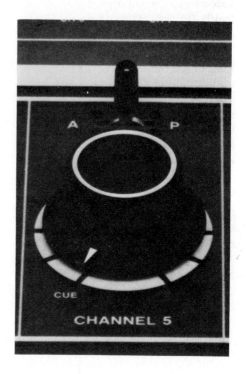

3-14 *Channel fader with cue control.*

3-15 *Unnecessarily large console.*

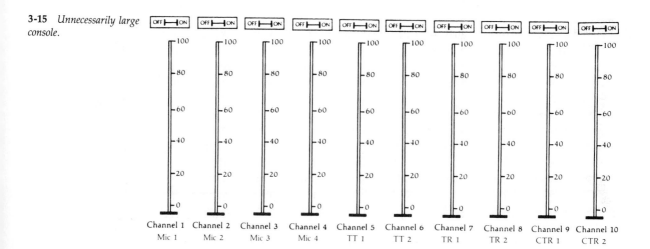

Some consoles have two independent audition (cue) systems: one activated from the channel on-off switch and one activated from the rotating pot (see **3-14**). By turning the pot far enough counterclockwise, it can be switched into cue.

Now that the console has two routing systems—an external or program system that sends signals on to broadcast or recording, and an internal or audition (cue) system that feeds signals to the studio—you can preview program material. To audition the record on turntable 2 through pot 4 while the record on turntable 1 is on the air, switch pot 4 to audition (some consoles label this "cue") and turn it up. Now you can hear the record from turntable 2 through the audition speaker at the same time the on-air signal is feeding through the program speaker.

The console just designed has eight inputs and one master output and will serve a small sound facility. Larger sound facilities may require more inputs and outputs for additional microphones, telephone talk shows, live music recording, network programs, video and film sound, broadcasts done away from the studio, and so on.

By applying the theory of our console design to accommodate larger audio operations, the appropriate number of preamps, pots, and switches can be added to build a bigger console (see **3-15**). You can see in 3-15, however, that the result could be a console either too large for many stations or too unwieldy for one person to operate. Another modification is needed. (Mixing consoles used in music recording and film sound sometimes do require more

VU Meter

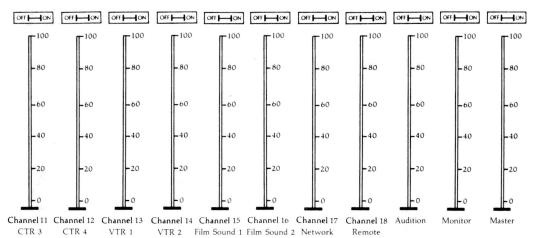

Channel 11 Channel 12 Channel 13 Channel 14 Channel 15 Channel 16 Channel 17 Channel 18 Audition Monitor Master
CTR 3   CTR 4   VTR 1   VTR 2   Film Sound 1 Film Sound 2 Network Remote

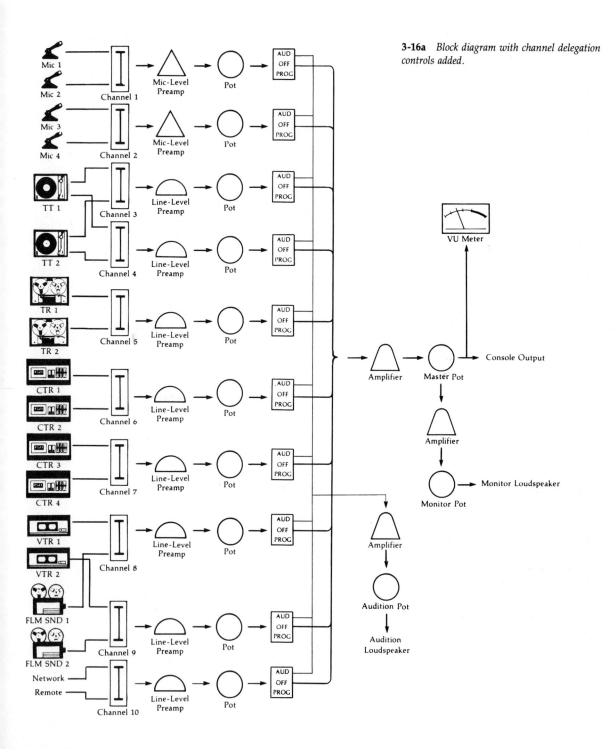

3-16a *Block diagram with channel delegation controls added.*

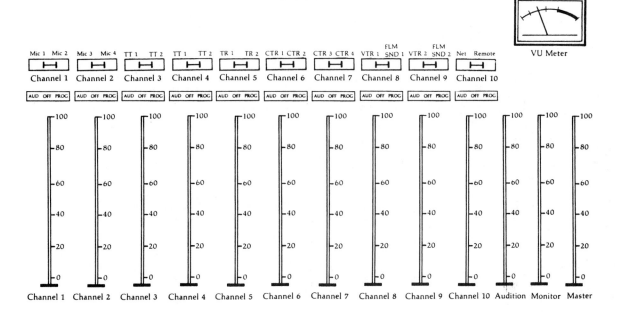

3-16b *Console with delegation controls added.*

than one operator. These consoles are impractical for most broadcasting stations.)

DELEGATION SWITCH Assume that our console has to handle two additional microphones, two cartridge tape recorders, two video tape recorders (VTRs), two film sound projectors, a network and a remote input. Since we want to add inputs without significantly increasing the size of the console, and since it is unlikely that all sound sources will be used at once, even in the busiest studio, certain functions can be doubled up. Instead of one mike for channels 1 and 2, use two for each channel; divide the four cartridge recorders between channels 6 and 7; put the two VTRs and two film sound sources on channels 8 and 9; and so on. Now two signal sources are assigned to each channel. To make sure they do not feed at the same time, connect them first to a **delegation switch.** As the term suggests, this switch delegates which of the two sound sources assigned to a given channel will be selected for routing to program or audition (see **3-16a, b**). The delegation control gives consoles greater capability without adding unnecessarily to their size.

The console just designed is a **monophonic** (*mono*) mixing console—a console with one master output channel.

Types of Consoles

Consoles can be grouped into two categories: (1) those used mainly for broadcast, and (2) those used for complex multichannel recording. Most broadcast consoles are either monophonic—with one master output channel, like the one just designed, or **stereophonic** (*stereo*)—with a tandem master output channel that carries two signals at once (see **3-17**). There are also dual-channel mono and stereo consoles with two separate master (program) routing systems (see **3-18a, b**).

Multichannel consoles have from 4 to 32 output channels (see **3-19**). Although they are used mainly for music, TV, and film sound recording, they are being used increasingly in average-size broadcast operations.

3-17 *Stereo console.*

3-18a *Example of a dual-channel mono console.*

3-18b *Example of a dual-channel stereo console.*

3-19 *Examples of multichannel consoles. (Bottom right: Harrison Modular Automated Post Production Console PP-1.)*

BROADCAST CONSOLES Broadcast consoles, both mono and stereo, have the same basic components as the console designed earlier in this chapter. Delegation switches route sound sources to certain channels; channel selector switches route sound sources to program or audition, or shut them off; individual pots control the loudness levels flowing through each channel; master and audition pots control the overall loudness level of the master and audition systems; and a VU meter(s) measures the electric energy flowing through the master channel.

MULTICHANNEL CONSOLES   The multichannel recording console was designed to give the recordist greater control over shaping the sound of each aural element. It is more elaborate than the broadcast console, but it has the same three basic functions: input, output, and monitor (see **3-20** and **3-21**).

Input Section   The input section receives signals from the microphones, tape recorders, and other devices, processes them, and then routes them to the output section. The input section consists of individual modules, each of which handles one signal. An input module usually contains microphone and line selectors, equalizer and filter, bus delegation, pan pot, reverb send, solo mute, and sliding fader.

Microphone and Line Selectors   Two types of power sources feed into input modules: low level, such as mikes, and high level, such as tape recorders. The microphone and line selector controls delegate which power source enters the input module. Each selector control has a preamplifier that boosts the power of the low- and high-level sources in different proportions; the low get more of a boost than the high. This is why mikes should not be plugged into line-level inputs, or line-level sources into mike inputs. To do so would make the microphone signal barely audible and distort the signal from the high-level source.

Multichannel consoles also have a control to adjust signals that enter the microphone or line inputs at too high or too low a level. The control is called a **pad, trim,** or **sensitivity,** and it is either built into or separate from the selectors. It prevents high-level signals from overloading other modules in the signal flow, and boosts low-level signals to sufficient strength for distribution through the console.

Equalizer and Filter   An **equalizer** is a device that alters a sound's frequency response by boosting or attenuating selected frequencies. A **filter** alters frequency response by cutting off frequencies above, below, or at a preset point. These signal processors add greatly to a console's capability to shape sound. (For a discussion of equalizers and filters, see Chapter 11.)

Bus Delegation   In audio, a channel that combines the outputs of several other channels is called a mixing network. The output of the mixing network is the **bus.** At each input module, delegators can assign a signal to any bus; each input module usually has one delegator for each bus.

Pan Pot   A **pan pot,** which is short for *panoramic potentiometer,* is a loudness control that can shift the balance of sound to any point between two master channels (or four if it is a quad pan pot). When you move it from right to left, or left to right, the sound between two loudspeakers moves laterally in the same direction (see **3-22**).

Reverb Send   For a sound to reverberate, it has to be sent, hit a reflective surface, and return. Multichannel consoles have **reverb send** and **reverb**

3-20 *Multichannel console with sixteen inputs and eight outputs.*

return functions built in. Each input module contains a reverb send control. It feeds sound to a separate reverb unit, which is not part of the console. This unit then returns the reverberant sound to a return control at another part of the console. (Reverberation devices are discussed in Chapter 11.)

Solo Mute   Feeding different sounds through several channels at once can create an inconvenience if you want to hear one of them briefly. It is not necessary to shut off or turn down all the channels except the one you want to hear, however, because each input module has a **solo mute** button. Pushing it automatically cuts off all other channels feeding the monitor system; it has no effect on the program system. More than one solo mute can be pushed to audition several channels at once and still mute the unwanted channels.

Sliding Pot   Each channel has a sliding pot to vary a signal's loudness.

Output Section   The output section receives signals fed from the input modules, routes them through the buses and then out to the monitor section and tape recorders. The input section can feed any combination of signals to any one or more of the buses.

3-21 *Control functions of the input, output, and monitor control modules.*

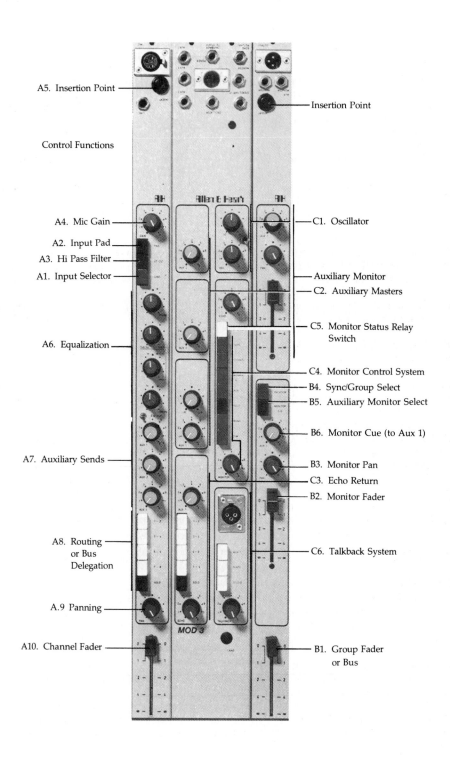

A5. Insertion Point

Insertion Point

Control Functions

A4. Mic Gain

C1. Oscillator

A2. Input Pad

A3. Hi Pass Filter

A1. Input Selector

Auxiliary Monitor

C2. Auxiliary Masters

C5. Monitor Status Relay Switch

A6. Equalization

C4. Monitor Control System

B4. Sync/Group Select

B5. Auxiliary Monitor Select

B6. Monitor Cue (to Aux 1)

A7. Auxiliary Sends

B3. Monitor Pan

C3. Echo Return

B2. Monitor Fader

A8. Routing or Bus Delegation

C6. Talkback System

A.9 Panning

A10. Channel Fader

B1. Group Fader or Bus

A1. Input Selector Feeds mic or line level signal to channel.

A2. Input Pad Attenuates mic signal by 20 dB and line signal by 12 dB.

A3. Hi Pass Filter Eliminates input overload caused by rumble or vibration.

A4. Mic Gain By varying the gain of the mic preamplifier the correct signal level may be obtained within the channel hence minimizing noise and distortion. 40 dB of gain is available. Line input gain may be optimized by a pre-set potentiometer allowing any source to be ideally matched.

A5. Insertion Point A stereo jack socket provides a send and return circuit at 0 dBm for the use of special effects such as the Pro Limiter.

A6. Equalization The selected signal may be corrected by the following controls. Hi frequency shelving, mid range sweep frequency and low frequency shelving. A cut switch is provided for A-B equalization monitoring.

A7. Auxiliary Sends Three auxiliaries are provided and these may be used for foldback or echo sends as required.

A8. Routing Each input channel may be fed to any of 8 group outputs by means of mix-buses wired into the console chassis. In the mixdown mode buses 1 and 2 feed the stereo master output. A PFL (solo) button feeds a separate bus which may be selected by the monitor section of the mixer and enables the engineer to listen to individual channels during a session without affecting the main signal levels.

A9. Panning The channel may be panned between odd and even buses in order to create stereo groups. It is normal practice for example to record the drum mix 'in place' onto two tracks of the tape recorder.

A10. Channel Fader Controls the level of the input signal being fed to the mix buses.

B1. Group Fader Controls the signal level feed to each track of the tape recorder. The signal is also fed to the meter system and via an insertion point for limiting etc. Output faders 1 and 2 also provide the master stereo mixdown which may be selected to appear on meters 1 and 2.

B2. Monitor Fader Provides an independent mix for the engineer in the control room. This is essential as the main output levels are determined by the required recording level, not the listening level and are not therefore suitable for monitoring.

B3. Monitor Pan Each fader may be panned left or right in the monitor mix in order to simulate the final perspective. The monitor mix may be either the group outputs, the tape machine output, or when overdubbing—a combination of the two. A combination of the master monitor selector (C5) and the sync buttons (B4) determine the signal appearing at the monitor fader.

B4. Sync/Group Select Determines the status of the monitor channel when overdubbing. It allows ouput group monitoring when the main monitor mix is off tape.

B5. Auxiliary Monitor Select Switches tape monitoring of tracks 1–8 to auxiliary monitor faders and allows monitoring and metering of tracks 9–16 on monitor faders 1–8 in a 16 track studio. In 8 track studios this function may be used for monitoring of stereo tape machines or other external equipment.

B6. Monitor Cue (to Aux 1) Provides foldback of the monitor mix (pre-fade) in order that the musician may hear sync tracks while overdubbing. Output groups may also be sent to foldback which tends to save time when recording as individual input channel foldback need not be set.

C1. Oscillator Provides calibration tone for the setting of desk and tape machine levels. Both frequency and level are fully variable.

C2. Auxiliary Masters Control level to echo and foldback as required.

C3. Echo Return Allows stereo echo return to be routed to main mix-buses. Useful when recording tracks with echo or when subgrouping in mixdown. An independent control sends echo to the foldback mix (aux 1).

C4. Monitor Control System Controls the status and level of the monitor mix. Every important section of the recording system may be fed to the monitor speakers and an independent echo return is provided for 'wet' monitoring.

C5. Monitoring Status Relay Switch Provides single button switching of the monitor mix from onto to off tape monitoring hence giving instant level and quality comparison. This important switch also changes the meter status so that A-B metering is also available at the push of a button.

C6. Talkback System In order to communicate with studio, musicians and also to identify tape tracks a microphone socket is built into the module. A switch bank allows talkback routing and a level control is also provided. The monitor speakers are automatically dimmed to suppress feedback and increase intelligibility. Any low impedance dynamic mic may be used.

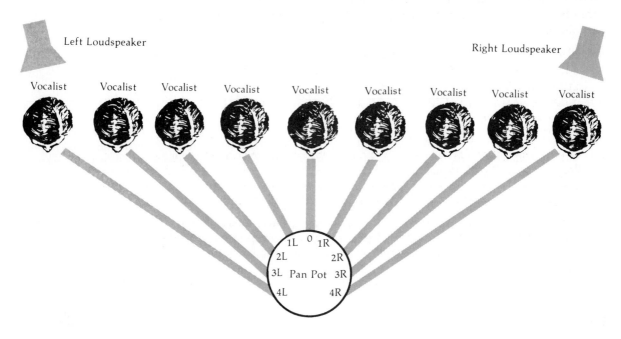

3-22 *Pan pot's effect on sound placement.*

Regardless of how many buses receive signals, they are all eventually mixed into one, two, or four master channels. Therefore, many consoles have several masters to facilitate mono, stereo, and quadriphonic (four channel) mixes. On these consoles, the buses that take their feed directly from the input section are called submasters.

Monitor Section   The monitor section takes signals from the submaster and master buses and feeds them to the VU meters, loudspeaker matrix, and foldback system so they can be measured and heard.

VU Meters   Multichannel consoles have two groups of VU meters: those for each individual channel and those for each submaster and master bus. Some multichannel consoles have both VU and peak program meters.

Loudspeaker Matrix   The loudspeaker or monitor matrix is a control panel that is used to assign sound from a channel(s) to a loudspeaker(s).

Foldback System   **Foldback** is the term used for the earphone system. Foldback delegation switches are on each input channel and sometimes on the loudspeaker matrix as well. They feed sound from the input section, individually or in any combination, to earphone jacks in the studio and control room.

Other Features of Multichannel Consoles Multichannel consoles usually have other features such as: slate/talkback, oscillator, patch panel, and phase reversal, discussed in Chapter 6.

Slate/Talkback Most consoles have a talkback to communicate with persons in the studio. Multichannel consoles also have a **slate** feature that automatically feeds to the recording tape anything said through the talkback. It is a convenient way to transcribe information about the name of the recording, the artist, the number of the cut (*take*), and so on.

Oscillator An **oscillator** is a signal generator that produces pure tones or sine waves (sound waves with no harmonics or overtones) at selected frequencies. On a console it is used to (1) calibrate the console with the tape recorder so their VU meters indicate the same levels, and (2) put reference tone levels on tape recordings (see Chapter 14).

Patch Panel The patch panel on a multichannel console usually has inputs and outputs from just the console's components. It is not intended to replace the control room patch panel but to be used as a supplement to it.

Summary

1. The mixing console or board amplifies, mixes, balances, processes, and routes signals to broadcast or recording.
2. Five types of consoles are: monophonic (mono), stereophonic (stereo), dual-channel mono, dual-channel stereo, and multichannel.
3. Consoles have three basic functions: input, output, and monitor.
4. In mono and stereo consoles, which are usually used for broadcast, input signals feed to (a) the selector delegation control, (b) the preamplifier, if their power is low level, then to (c) the pot, (d) the channel selector control, (e) the program (or audition) master pot, (f) the VU meter, (g) the monitor loudspeaker, and (h) broadcast or recording.
5. The volume unit (VU) meter measures the amount of electric energy flowing through the console. The meter has two scales: percentage of modulation and volume units.
6. The VU meter responds to average sound intensity, unlike another popular meter, the peak program meter, which responds to peaks in loudness.
7. The loudness level on a VU meter should average between 60 and 100 percent of modulation (about -4 to 0 VUs). If the loudness remains at levels too much higher or lower, the sound will be distorted or too quiet.
8. The input section of a multichannel console is made up of modules containing: microphone and line selectors, equalizer and filter, bus delegation, pan pot, reverb send, solo mute, and sliding pot.

9. The output section, which receives signals from the input modules, contains submaster and master buses that route signals out to the monitor section and to the tape recorders.

10. The monitor section consists of VU meters (or ppm meters), loudspeaker matrix, and foldback system.

11. Multichannel consoles have other features such as a slate/talkback, oscillator, and patch panel.

4

Turntables

Turntable operation is simple and easy to learn. Of all the equipment in the sound chain, however, it is one of the two most likely to cause trouble; the tape recorder, discussed in Chapter 10, is the other. They have a number of parts that require extremely fine adjustment, and rough handling can throw them out of alignment or damage them. Even dust and dirt can adversely affect their performance. Virtually any problem in a turntable or tape recorder is serious, since they are the sources of almost all reproduced sound.

The turntable is a **transducer**—a device that converts one form of energy into another. It converts the mechanical energy impressed in the record grooves into electric energy. Professional turntables differ from the familiar phonograph and home turntables in that they are heavy-duty and housed in a sturdy cabinet to prevent them from vibrating (see **4-1a,b,c**). Although pro-

4-1a *(Far left) Turntable mounted in a cabinet.*

4-1b *(Left) Example of an elaborate professional turntable and cabinet.*

4-1c *Broadcast Studio turntable. This model has automatic back-cueing (see p. 76).*

4-2 *Typical professional turntable with parts labeled.*

fessional turntables come in a variety of designs, they consist of the same basic parts: on-off switch, plate, drive system, speed control, tone (or pickup) arm, stylus, cartridge, and filter (see **4-2**).

The Parts of a Turntable and Their Function

ON-OFF SWITCH   This switch turns the power to the motor on or off.

PLATE   The **plate** is what the record sits on. It is a large, heavy, flat metal disc covered by felt or rubber.

DRIVE SYSTEM   The **drive system** turns the plate.

SPEED CONTROL   The **speed control** is like a gear shift; you move it to select the speed at which the plate spins. Most turntables have at least two speeds: 45 rpm (revolutions per minute) and 33⅓ rpm; many turntables also have 78 rpm for records made before the invention of long-playing formats. Some turntables have another position—neutral—which takes the drive system out of gear. In neutral, the plate spins freely (see **4-3**).

For idler wheel drive–type turntables, it is a good idea to put the speed control into neutral when the turntable is not in use. Idler wheel drive turntables consist of a shaft—the idler—connected to, and driven by, a motor. When the motor is turned on, the idler begins to spin. The top of the idler has stepped ridges that determine the speed at which the plate rotates. To spin the plate, the idler must engage a **pressure pad**—a free-moving rubber disc that is set spinning when it is moved against the idler. As the pressure pad engages the idler, it also butts against the side of the plate, driving it at the preset speed (see **4-4**).

4-3   *Speed control in neutral.*

4-4 *Pressure pad engaging the idler at the ridge for (**a**) 33$\frac{1}{3}$ rpm, (**b**) 45 rpm, and (**c**) 78 rpm.*

If the turntable is left in gear when not in use, the constant pressure of the idler against the rubber on the pressure pad could create an indentation in the rubber. This would cause the plate to bump each time it hit that point and jar the needle in the record **groove**.

TONE (OR PICKUP) ARM   The **tone** (also called **pickup**) **arm** houses the stylus and cartridge, which pick up and transduce sound from the record grooves. The tone arm is carefully balanced for the following reasons: (1) so its weight does not put too much pressure on the stylus and, hence, the record groove, (2) so the stylus sits properly in the record groove, and (3) so the stylus tracks across the record freely. Too much weight would cause distortion of the sound and ruin the stylus and the record. If the pickup arm is too light, however, the stylus will not track in the grooves and skips across the record.

> • Too much pressure will distort
> • Too little pressure will not track properly

The tone arm should be handled with great care not only because it is carefully balanced but also because the wires leading from the cartridge to the console are on its underside and could be loosened or broken. Most tone arms have small extensions to make handling easier and safer (see **4-2**).

STYLUS   The **stylus** (or needle) consists of an assembly carrier that has a small, compliant strip of metal on one end housing a precut tip of hard material (usually diamond) that fits into the record groove (see **4-5**). The other end fits between the coils of wires in the cartridge. The signal from the record begins its trip to reproduction by vibrating the stylus, which then carries these vibrations to the cartridge.

Styli come in several sizes depending on the amount of use they will get, the weight of the pickup arm, and the type of records played. The first two considerations have too many variables for discussion here. For the third, there is a general guideline: 78 rpm records require a larger stylus than 45 or 33⅓ rpm discs because they have wider grooves. If you use a stylus made for so-called microgroove records on 78's, it will be ruined; if a stylus designed for 78 rpm records is used on 45's or 33⅓'s, it will ruin the records.

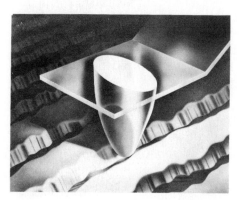

4-5 *Stylus tracking in modulated record grooves—grooves impressed with sound.*

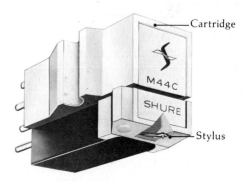

4-6 *Cartridge with stylus.*

CARTRIDGE The **cartridge** is the actual transducing element in the turntable. It converts the mechanical vibrations picked up by the stylus into electric energy (see **4-6**). All high-quality cartridges are designed with the same performance goals in mind: (1) to reproduce the signal as faithfully as possible, (2) to keep the stylus in contact with the record groove's walls, (3) to keep any distortion inaudible, and (4) to generate sufficient power for the signal to reach the amplifier. Certain cartridges, however, work better than others with particular pickup arms. If the cartridge and pickup arm are incompatible, you may hear either more or less bass and overly crisp highs.

FILTER Some turntables are equipped with a filter, which is usually built into the amplifier, to compensate for differences in frequency responses between records made in different countries. Records produced in the United States and Japan have a different high-frequency emphasis than records produced in Europe. The former conform to the RIAA (Recording Industry Association of America) standard reproducing characteristics, and the latter to the reproducing characteristic recommended by the CCIR (Comité Consultatif International Radio or International Radio Consultative Committee). CCIR uses more high-frequency boost than RIAA. To compensate for this difference, the filter can adjust records produced with the CCIR curve by reducing the high-frequency emphasis. Without the filter, records produced in Europe and played in this country would sound hissy.

Cueing

When playing records at home, perhaps you have noticed the pause between the time the stylus starts tracking and the first sound. In informal situations, these pauses are an accepted part of playing records, but in broadcasting they create "dead air." To reduce the time between the start of a record and the first sound, broadcasters **cue** the record.

You cue a record by placing the stylus in the wide, unmodulated grooves on the outside of a record or between the cuts. Then either (1) put the speed control into neutral, turn the on-off switch to "off," rotate the plate clockwise until you hear the first sound, and select the speed; or (2) turn the on-off switch to "off," select the speed, and rotate just the record clockwise. Since the speed gear is engaged, the plate will not spin. The felt or rubber mat on the plate allows the record to move freely.

Once you hear the first sound, gently backtrack the record into the un-modulated groove; the distance depends on the speed of the record. Professional turntables are built to start up quickly, so you should not have to backtrack very far. Generally, at 33⅓ rpm, backtrack about one-eighth of a turn; at 45 rpm, backtrack one-fourth of a turn; and at 78 rpm, backtrack half to three-fourths of a turn (see **4-7**). With the speed control in gear, just turn on the power; the record and the sound will start almost at once.

Starting the plate from "Stop" is one way to begin playing a record; another way is to **slip cue** it. Once you hear the first sound and backtrack the

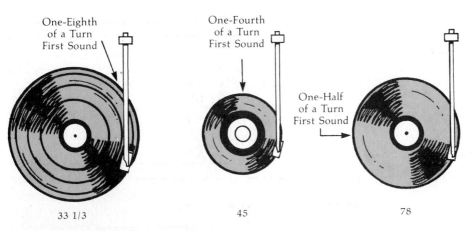

One-Eighth of a Turn First Sound

One-Fourth of a Turn First Sound

One-Half of a Turn First Sound

33 1/3

45

78

4-7 *Suggested degrees of backtracking to avoid wowing in records that spin at different speeds (the precise cue point depends on the quickness of the turntable's pick up).*

4-8 *Slip cueing a record.*

record, put your finger on the record to keep it in place and turn on the motor to start the plate spinning. When it is time, release the record and it will pick up at full speed. The advantage of slip cueing is that you get a tighter cue; the disadvantage is that it ties up one of your hands (see **4-8**).

Locating Record Grooves

To play a record or cut from the beginning, you can find the start of the sound by (1) locating the relatively clear space just before, or between, the group(s) of closely packed grooves (see **4-9**), (2) placing the stylus there, and (3) cueing it.

Many times in production, however, you have to locate special music or sound effects for a drama, documentary, or commercial. Either you do not know exactly where it is on the record, or it is located within a particular cut—such as a drum roll that is part of a march, a cheer that is part of the sound of a crowd, a quiet musical passage between two loud ones, or a couple of beeps and a boop that are part of a piece of electronic music.

You will notice that on the surface of a record, the grooves have light or dark shadings. The lighter, thinner grooves show where the quieter sounds are; the darker, wider ones indicate the location of the louder passages (see **4-10**). If you have some idea of a sound's relative loudness, you can quickly audition a record by moving the stylus from one likely spot to another. Understandably, the term for this technique is spotting.

4-9 *When cueing a record or record cut, look for the grooves before the record cut and place the stylus there. Then locate the first point of sound.*

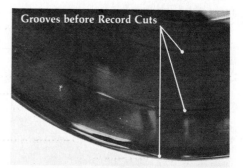

4-10 *Close-up of a 33⅓ rpm record.*

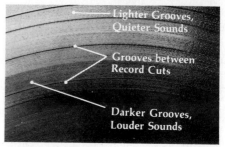

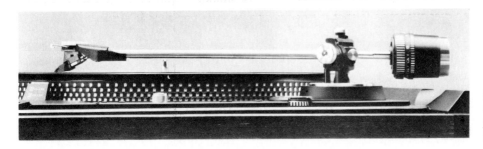

4-11 *Strobes on the side of a turntable plate to adjust for 45 rpm and 33⅓ rpm at 50 Hz and 60 Hz.*

Wow

One of the most common problems in record reproduction is **wow**—variations in pitch that sound like an off-speed recording. Wow, which is more noticeable with lower-pitched sounds, is caused when a plate does not spin at exactly the right speed; when the spindle hole in the record is slightly off center or too large; when the record is warped; or when the sound starts before the record reaches full speed.

You can check to determine whether a turntable is off-speed and by how much with a **strobe** (see **4-11**). A strobe is a device that is used to adjust rotating objects by making them appear stationary. As the strobe spins, look at the markings for the speed you are checking. If the markings seem to remain stationary, the turntable is spinning at the correct speed. If the markings appear to spin forward or backward, the turntable is off-speed. The faster the markings spin, the more off-speed is the turntable.

If a record is defective, there is almost no way to correct the problem. Sometimes you can flatten warped records by putting a specially designed weight on the label. In professional audio, however, it is not worth taking the chance and possibly upsetting a broadcast or recording session. Replace warped and worn discs.

Turntable and Record Care

In most sound studios, the technical staff performs routine equipment maintenance. However, the production staff can do a great deal to help with equipment care by taking some simple precautions. Here are a few.

1. Although the stylus may be diamond, it will wear and it should be replaced regularly. A worn stylus not only damages records but also inhibits good sound reproduction.

2. Do not touch the stylus with your finger. Skin is oily and the oil can coat the needle, causing dust and dirt to stick to it. Dust and dirt on the stylus will wear out the record grooves more quickly. If sufficient amounts collect on the stylus, sound quality will be noticeably degraded.

3. To clean the stylus use a very light brush, and brush from the back to the front only.

4. Be gentle when handling the balanced tone arm. If it is unbalanced, the result will be accelerated record wear and poorer sound fidelity.

As for record care, dust, dirt, smoke, fingerprints, and scraping one record against another or against a rough surface all shorten record life and lower the sound quality. In the hectic surroundings of most professional operations, it is difficult to treat records as you would at home; it is not impossible, however, and is worth the effort.

Summary

1. The turntable is a transducer that converts mechanical energy on records into electric energy.

2. The professional turntable is heavy-duty but vulnerable. If its parts are not properly and routinely balanced and cleaned, the quality of the sound reproduction suffers.

3. The parts of a turntable consist of an on-off switch; a plate on which the record is placed; a drive system which drives the plate; a speed control, which sets the rotation of the plate at 33⅓, 45, or 78 rpm; a pickup or tone arm, which houses the cartridge; a cartridge, which is the actual transducer and also houses the stylus; a stylus, which picks up the mechanical vibrations from the record grooves; and a filter, which reduces the noise from scratchy records and makes the European CCIR recording curve compatible with the American RIAA curve.

4. Cueing is a technique used to eliminate "dead air" between the time a record starts spinning and the first sound.

5. To locate or spot a cue point that is not at the beginning of a disc or between cuts, look for the lighter grooves to indicate the location of quieter sounds, or the darker grooves to indicate the location of louder sounds.

6. Wow is caused when records are warped, when the hole in the label is off center or too large, when the plate is not spinning at a constant speed, or when the sound starts before the plate is spinning at full speed.

7. Attention to turntable and record care is essential to good sound reproduction. The tone arm should be properly balanced, and the stylus and record surface should be kept clean and untouched.

Ⅰ. Microphones

Perhaps the best way to emphasize the importance of the microphone is to say that without it (except for the electronic instruments) audio in media would not exist. Just about everything that is recorded or broadcast starts with a microphone.

A. Defined

The microphone is a transducer that converts acoustic energy into electric energy. Although all mikes perform the same basic function, different types have special capabilities that suit them for the varied aesthetic demands of broadcasting, recording, and film sound. For example, in television, if a microphone is in the picture, it should be good looking but not call attention to itself; outdoors, a mike must be resistant to wind sound; and when distance is a factor, a mike must isolate the sound source and still provide acceptable quality. These special requirements make microphone selection a critical and ever-present creative challenge. When you choose a microphone, you should know four things:

1. What type it is.
2. What its directional characteristics are.
3. What it sounds like. *frequency response*
4. What it looks like (for television). *cost*

B. Purchasing criteria

C. ## Types of Microphones

We have noted that microphones convert acoustic energy into electric energy. The device that actually does the transducing is mounted in the mike head and is called the *element*. Each type of microphone gets its name from the element it uses. There are five types, three normally used by professionals:

2.

81

(1) **moving coil**, (2) **ribbon**, and (3) **condenser** (or **capacitor**),* and two used by nonprofessionals: (4) **carbon** and (5) **crystal** (or **ceramic**). The difference between a professional and a nonprofessional microphone is the sound quality they produce.

HIGH- AND LOW-IMPEDANCE MICROPHONES   After a microphone changes acoustic energy into electric energy, the electric energy flows through a circuit as voltage. Whatever resistance that voltage encounters in the circuit is called **impedance**. Less resistance means lower impedance, and equipment with lower impedance usually gives better sound quality.

Low-impedance microphones have two advantages over high-impedance mikes. Because there is less resistance to the signal flow, low-impedance mikes are much less susceptible to hum and electric noise, such as static from motors and fluorescent lights. They can also be connected to long cables without increasing the noise. It is mainly for these reasons that professionals use low-impedance mikes (and equipment).

High- and low-impedance equipment are incompatible and produce sound distortion if they are connected. If you have to connect high- and low-impedance equipment, you must use a **transformer**—a device that matches impedances, thus making the different sound sources compatible (see **5-1**).

TYPES OF LOW-IMPEDANCE MICROPHONES   Of the three types of low-impedance microphones—moving coil, ribbon, and condenser—the *moving coil* is the most widely used. The transducing element consists of a coil of wire attached to a diaphragm suspended in a magnetic field (see **5-2**). When sound waves hit the diaphragm, they move the coil, which gives the element its name. As the coil moves in the magnetic field, voltage is induced within the coil; the voltage is the electric energy equivalent of the acoustic energy that first caused the diaphragm to vibrate.

This design has several advantages over ribbon and condenser microphones. It is (1) less expensive, (2) less subject to overload from high loudness levels and wind, (3) more rugged, and (4) capable of being used outdoors.

Ribbon microphones replace the diaphragm and moving coil with a corrugated metal ribbon suspended in a magnetic field (see **5-3**). As the ribbon vibrates from the pressure of the sound waves, voltage is induced. The ribbon design makes these microphones quite sensitive, particularly the older mod-

---

*The term **dynamic** is often used to describe moving-coil microphones. Actually, dynamic microphones are a class of mikes that transduce energy electromagnetically. This classification also includes ribbon types, sometimes called *velocity* microphones. To avoid confusion, we will designate a microphone's type by its element, not its classification, although in actual use it probably would be more convenient to use the term *dynamic* synonymously with *moving coil*.

Condenser mikes, classified as electrostatic, should be called *capacitor* mikes, since their transducing element is a capacitor. However, they used to be called condenser mikes and the name has remained in popular usage.

5-1 *Line-matching transformer.*

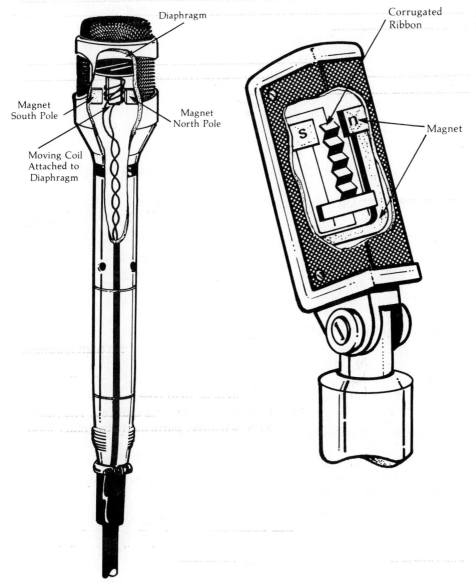

Diaphragm

Corrugated
Ribbon

Magnet
South Pole

Magnet
North Pole

Moving Coil
Attached to
Diaphragm

Magnet

5-2 *(Far left) Element of a moving-coil microphone.*

5-3 *(Left) Element of a ribbon microphone.*

els (see **5-4**). Strongly blown sounds or sudden, loud changes in sound pressure can damage the ribbon. New models are more durable but they, too, should be used with care (see **5-5**). Despite their delicacy, ribbon microphones are still used because they give sound a mellow and warm quality.

Condenser microphones operate on a principle different from that of the moving coil and ribbon types. They transduce energy using voltage (electrostatic) variations instead of magnetic (electromagnetic) variations. The condenser design consists of two parallel metal plates or electrodes separated by a small space (see **5-6**). The front plate is the diaphragm, the only moving part in the mike head, and the back plate is fixed. Together these plates or electrodes form a *capacitor*—a device that is capable of holding an electric charge. As acoustic energy moves the diaphragm back and forth in relation to the fixed back plate, the voltage changes, varying the signal. The signal, however, is low level and requires a preamplifier (usually mounted in the mike head) to boost it to a usable strength.

5-4   *(Right) Older model of ribbon microphone.*

5-5   *(Below) Newer model of ribbon microphone.*

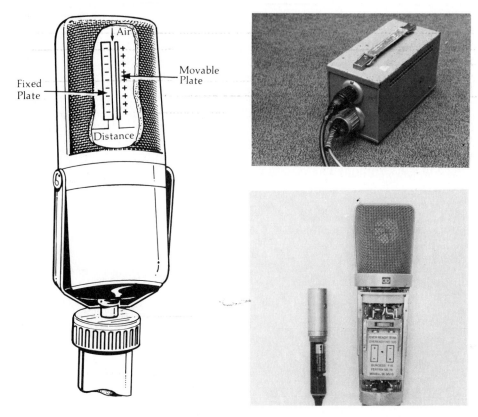

Fixed Plate

Air

Movable Plate

Distance

5-6 (Far left) Element of a condenser microphone.

5-7 (Above left) External power supply for an older tube-type condenser microphone.

5-8 (Left) Battery locations in two electret condenser microphones.

Since the capacitor and preamplifier require voltage to operate, all condenser microphones must have a separate power supply. The older, tube-type condensers came with a bulky, external power supply that fed both condenser and preamp (see **5-7**). Today, most condenser mikes are manufactured with the element permanently charged. These so-called **electret** condensers still require a power source for the preamplifier, but with their simpler design, electrets can use small batteries to supply the preamp's power (see **5-8**).

Electret condensers also can take power from a **phantom power supply** which eliminates the need for batteries altogether. Phantom power supplies can be installed in the studio microphone input circuits, thereby providing voltage the instant a mike is plugged in, or they can be portable.

The electrostatic design of professional condenser microphones generally produces the highest-quality sound of any type of microphone but at a cost, since condensers are also the most expensive microphone type. Although many condensers are too sensitive for use outdoors, some models can stand up to the demands of remote broadcasting and recording.

Usually too sensitive to use outdoors

Directional Characteristics

A fundamental rule of good microphone technique is that a sound source should be **on-mike**—at an optimal distance from the microphone and directly in its **pickup pattern.** Pickup pattern refers to the direction(s) from which a mike hears sound. Depending on the design, a microphone is sensitive to sound from (1) all around—**omnidirectional**; (2) its front and rear—**bidirectional**; or (3) its front only—**unidirectional** (see **5-9**).

The fundamental pickup patterns are omni- and bidirectional, and in the early days of radio these were the only patterns available. When the unidirectional microphone came along, it was actually an electronic hybrid of the omni- and bidirectional designs (see **5-10**). This helps to explain why the unidirectional microphone has certain response limitations.

5-9 *Pickup patterns: (a) omnidirectional, (b) bidirectional, and (c) unidirectional or cardioid.*

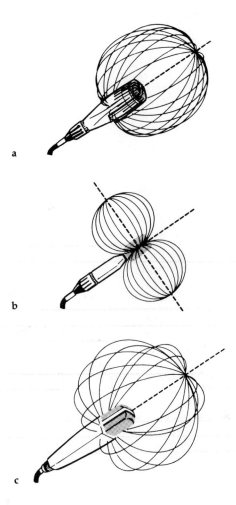

Omnidirectional Pattern   Bidirectional Pattern   Resultant Pattern

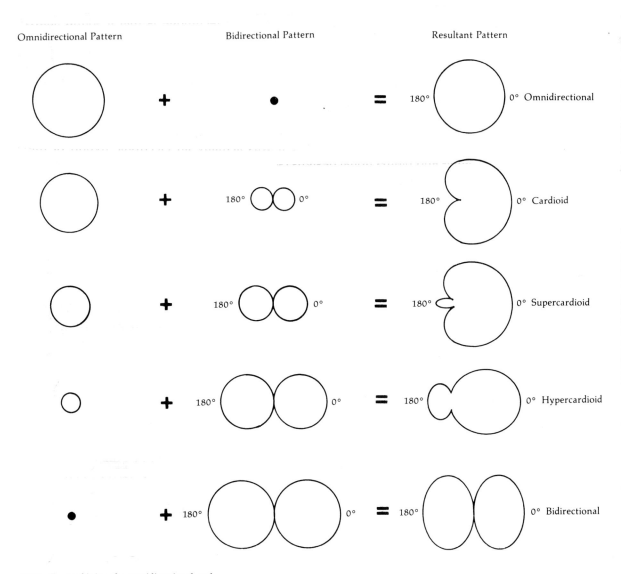

5-10 *By combining the omnidirectional and bidirectional designs, various pickup patterns are created.*

Once the unidirectional pattern (called **cardioid** because of its heart shape) was developed, variations were not long in coming. Now there are more highly directional patterns known as **super-, hyper-,** and **ultracardioid** (see **5-11**). The diagrams **5-9, 5-10,** and **5-11,** show basic microphone directionalities. The precise pattern varies slightly from mike to mike. To get a better idea of a microphone's pickup pattern, its polar response diagram should be studied.

POLAR RESPONSE DIAGRAMS   As an aid to microphone selection, manufacturers provide specification sheets ("spec" sheets, for short) that display, among other things, a microphone's **polar response pattern**—a graph of the microphone's directional sensitivity (see **5-12**). The graph consists of concentric circles, usually divided into segments of 30 degrees, to depict directionality.

5-11 *Pickup patterns: (a) supercardioid, (b) hypercardioid, and (c) ultracardioid.*

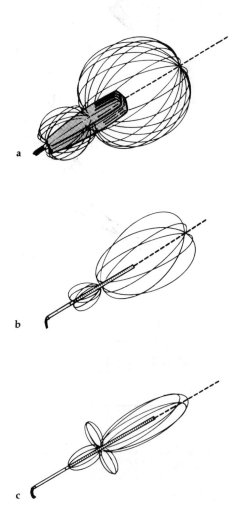

Reading inward or outward, the circles represent sound levels; the interval between each circle is 5 dB.

The omnidirectional polar pattern shows that sound is picked up from all directions at almost the same level (see **5-13**). The bidirectional polar pattern indicates maximum sensitivity to sound coming from the front and rear (0 and 180 degrees) (see **5-14**). Sensitivity decreases when moving toward the sides. Sound that reaches the mike at roughly 50, 130, 230, and 310 degrees is reduced by 5 dB; sound at 60, 120, 240, and 300 degrees is reduced by 10 dB; and at 90 and 270 degrees, there is almost no microphone response.

The cardioid polar pattern illustrates response from, in effect, one direction, with maximum sound rejection at 180 degrees (see **5-15**). Variations in the cardioid pattern are even more acutely unidirectional; super- and hyper-cardioid polar patterns show narrower areas of acceptance at the front with

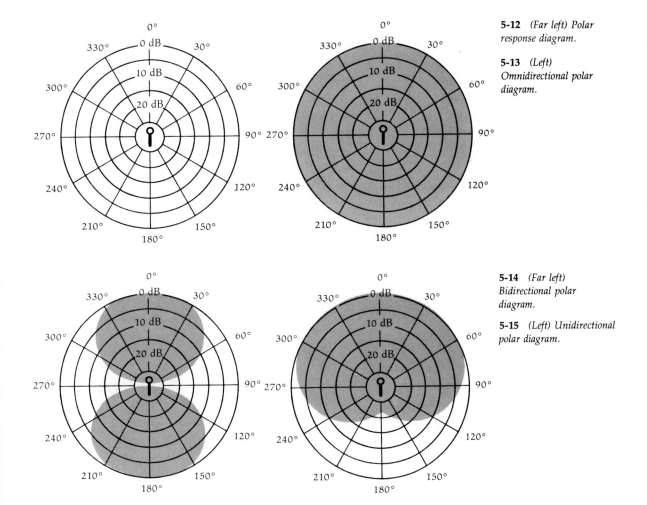

5-12 *(Far left) Polar response diagram.*

5-13 *(Left) Omnidirectional polar diagram.*

5-14 *(Far left) Bidirectional polar diagram.*

5-15 *(Left) Unidirectional polar diagram.*

maximum rejection at the sides (see **5-16** and **5-17**). Since they pick up and reject sound at almost the same points, there is often confusion about the differences between super- and hypercardioid mikes. The supercardioid mike has good sound rejection at both the sides and rear, however; the hypercardioid is more highly directional and has better side rejection but poorer rear rejection.

An even more directional response has been designed into the ultracardioid microphone (see **5-18**). It has a narrower angle of acceptance than the hypercardioid but similar rejection characteristics at the sides; however, rear rejection is poorer because the rear lobe gets larger as the angle of acceptance at the front gets narrower.

MULTIDIRECTIONAL MICROPHONES Microphones with a single directional response have one fixed diaphragm (or ribbon). By using a switchable dia-

5-16 *(Right) Supercardioid polar diagram.*

5-17 *(Far right) Hypercardioid polar diagram.*

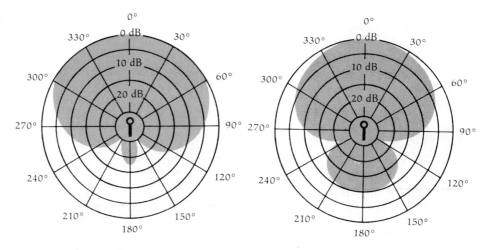

5-18 *Ultracardioid polar diagram.*

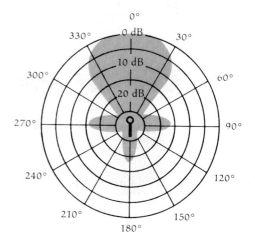

phragm or two diaphragms, microphones can be made **multidirectional** (see **5-19**).

SYSTEM MICROPHONES   Another way to make a mike multidirectional is to use a **system microphone**—interchangeable heads or capsules with different pickup patterns that can be mounted onto a common base (see **5-20a, b**). Since these multidirectional systems are usually condensors, the power supply and preamplifier are in the base and the mike capsule simply screws into the base. Any number of directional capsules—omni- and bidirectional, cardioid, super-, hyper-, and ultracardioid—can be used with a single base.

When using a directional microphone or microphone system, remember that, in general, the lower the frequency, the less is the mike's directional sensitivity. Sometimes this will not show up on a polar response graph.

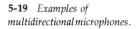

5-19 *Examples of multidirectional microphones.*

Omnidirectional Head

Cardioid Head

Powering Module Amplifier

Mini-Shotgun Head

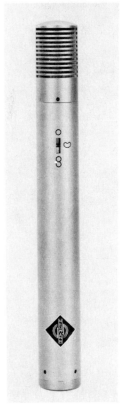

5-20a *Example of a system microphone.*

5-20b *System microphone with accessories.*

Frequency Response: The Sound of a Microphone

In addition to the element, type, and directional characteristics of a microphone, you should also know how the mike sounds or, more precisely, how it affects sound. Most professional microphones are designed with a wide, flat response; that is, at a given level, they reproduce most audible frequencies at equal amplitude (see **5-21**). Theoretically, therefore, the best mikes should sound about the same; they do not, however. Each microphone colors sound in a unique way. For example, an Electro-Voice RE15 and RE16 have somewhat similar **frequency responses** on paper (see **5-22**), yet their sounds are

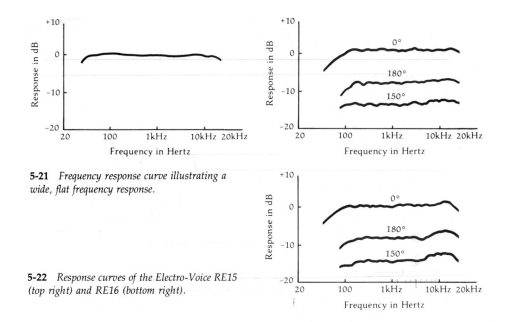

5-21 *Frequency response curve illustrating a wide, flat frequency response.*

5-22 *Response curves of the Electro-Voice RE15 (top right) and RE16 (bottom right).*

different. The sound of the RE15 is richer than the RE16, but the RE16 is brighter than the RE15. This is not to say that one mike is better than the other—just different.

With such subtle differences and so many good models, choosing a mike can be confusing, and there are some who complain about the absence of a standard. Because of the many different aesthetic demands in audio and the variety of personal tastes, the variety of tonal colors that microphones can provide is really an advantage. If you want, say, a slight boost between 500 and 1,000 Hz to define a trumpet sound better, a reduced high-frequency response for a mellower string sound, or enhanced frequencies at 4,000 and 5,000 Hz for added presence, you can choose a mike with the appropriate response characteristics. Also, consider how routine sound would be if all microphones had a similar frequency response.

Special Response Features of Microphones

PROXIMITY EFFECT AND BASS ROLL-OFF We noted that unidirectional microphones hear sound from one direction. Ports at the side and/or the rear of the mike allow sound from unwanted directions to enter the mike, where it is canceled (see **5-23**). (This is why you should never cover the ports with the hand or with tape.) The unidirectional design, however, has one problem, called **proximity effect**: the closer you put a unidirectional mike to a sound

5-23 *Examples of ports on unidirectional microphones.*

source, the more disproportionately loud the bass becomes. (Over the years, design changes have eliminated proximity effect in some unidirectional microphones.) Although you may sometimes want to enhance the lower frequencies of a voice or an instrument, usually you want close miking without increased bass response.

To meet this need, most unidirectional microphones have a feature known as **bass roll-off,** which functions like a limited in-mike equalizer (see **5-24**). When turned on (switch in / position), the roll-off attenuates bass frequencies several decibels from a certain point and below, depending on the microphone, thereby neutralizing any proximity effect.

5-24 *Example of a bass roll-off control and its effect on bass response.*

Due to its effect on sound, bass roll-off can be used to reduce or eliminate low-frequency studio noise or rumble from an air conditioner, subway, or construction. A particularly bass voice may be annoying, even at an optimal mike-to-source distance, so rolling off some bass can eliminate the voice's boominess without adversely affecting its timbre. Outdoor recording is often plagued by low-frequency noise, and using the bass roll-off to eliminate the noise is common practice.

Since bass roll-off is so versatile, it has become a common feature on many microphones, even on those with no proximity effect. Also, the bass roll-off concept has been extended in some models so that you can choose different degrees of roll-off (see **5-25** and **5-26**).

Proximity effect is sometimes desirable—for example, when the sound of a bass drum or bass guitar could use more bottom or when a thinly textured voice needs more solidity. If you need more bass response than a standard unidirectional microphone can provide, you can use unidirectional mikes with an extended proximity effect (see **5-27**).

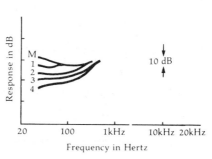

5-25 *Microphone with four-position roll-off and its effects on bass response.*

5-26 *Microphone with five-position roll-off and its effects on bass response.*

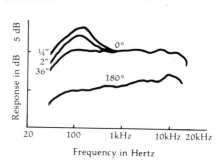

5-27 *Microphone with extended proximity effect built in, and its response curve.*

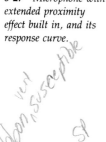

<u>OVERLOAD</u> All microphones will <u>distort if sound levels are too high</u>—a condition known as **overload**—but some mikes handle it better than others. <u>Moving-coil microphones are least vulnerable to distortion caused by excessive loudness due to their rugged design and construction.</u> They can take high levels of loudness without internal damage. Do not use ribbon mikes when there may be overload, however, for you risk damaging the element.

Condenser microphones have somewhat the same problem. They are delicate, and overload can damage the element and preamplifier. Unlike the ribbon mike, however, some condensers have a built-in pad positioned just before the preamp. By switching the pad into the mike system, it can reduce a signal several decibels before it reaches the preamp, thus eliminating loudness distortion (see **5-28**).

A pad and a bass roll-off are not the same. A bass roll-off attenuates only the low frequencies and is found on all three types of professional microphones. <u>A pad,</u> which is found on many condenser mikes, <u>reduces the level of the microphone's entire frequency range</u> (see **5-29**).

5-28 *(Right) −10-dB pad control.*

5-29 *(Far right) Effect of a −10-dB pad on frequency response.*

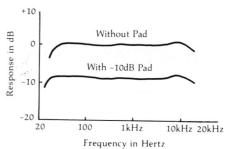

<u>POP FILTERS AND WINDSCREENS</u> Loudness is only one cause of microphone distortion. Others are <u>blowing sounds</u> caused by wind and breathing, and <u>transients</u>—sounds that begin with a sudden attack such as popping from speech and then quickly decay. These sounds are often unaffected by attenuation and require either a built-in **pop (blast) filter** or an externally mounted **windscreen** to neutralize them (see **5-30a, b, c**). (Another way to minimize distortion from blowing sounds or popping is through microphone placement. This is discussed in Chapters 6 and 7.)

— more effective
— can get closer to source

A pop filter is most effective against blowing sounds and popping. It allows you to place a mike so that it almost touches the sound source without fear of distortion.

Pop Filter

5-30a *Built-in pop filter.*

5-30b *Various windscreens for conventional microphones.*

5-30c *Windscreens for shotgun microphones.*

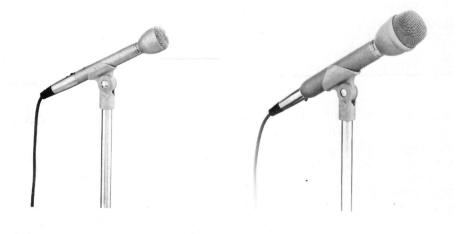

5-31 *Both the Electro-Voice 635A (right) and RE50 (far right) have omnidirectional pickup patterns and similar frequency responses. Their main difference is the RE50's built-in pop filter.*

External windscreens reduce the distortion from blowing and popping but rarely eliminate distortion from particularly strong sounds. They also slightly affect response, somewhat reducing the crispness of the high frequencies.

Pop filters are mainly found in moving-coil microphones, particularly unidirectional models, because they are more susceptible to wind noise than omnidirectional mikes. The elements in all ribbon and some condenser microphones make it hard to place a pop filter inside the mike head without seriously affecting response. Not all moving-coil models have pop filters, however, since they increase cost and can affect response. To provide an alternative, some manufacturers design two similar microphones, one with and one without a pop filter (see **5-31**).

Special-Purpose Microphones

APPEARANCE: MICROPHONES IN THE PICTURE   A microphone's looks were never a problem until television was invented. Then it became clear that a microphone that is seen on camera must not only have the appropriate directional characteristics and sound response but be good-looking as well. It would not be good show business to use a microphone because of its exquisite sound if it also blocked an actor's face, or to ask a singer to hold a shotgun mike because it had the appropriate directional pattern. Television mikes must satisfy both aural and visual requirements.

The first TV microphone created primarily for looks was the small and unobtrusive **lavalier microphone** (see **5-32**). Still smaller models are called **tie-tac** or lapel lavaliers (see **5-33**).

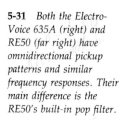

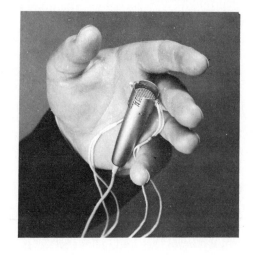

5-32 *(Right) Lavalier microphone with windscreen.*

5-33 *(Far right) Tie-tac lavalier microphone.*

Lavaliers have two things in common: (1) they are omnidirectional, and (2) they have a built-in high-frequency boost. The omnidirectional pickup is necessary because a speaker does not talk directly into the mike but across it, since the mike is mounted under the chin; a unidirectional response would pick up only part of the sound. Also, as a speaker talks, the chin cuts off many of the higher frequencies. The built-in high-frequency boost compensates for this loss (see **5-34**). If you hold a lavalier in front of your mouth, its response would be overly bright and hissy. Another reason not to use lavaliers in front of the mouth is their sensitivity to breathing and popping sounds; they have no pop filter, although windscreens come with many models.

Lavaliers are available in two types: moving coil and electret condenser. Generally the electrets are smaller and have better frequency response. They are also more expensive and somewhat less rugged.

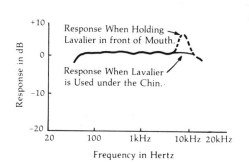

5-34 *Response curve illustrating the lavalier's built-in high-frequency boost.*

REACH: MICROPHONES OUT OF THE PICTURE Television created the need for a good-looking on-camera microphone, but it was in sound motion pictures that the need for an off-camera mike first became apparent. The problem was to record actors' voices without a microphone being visible. Of course, directors had many ingenious ways to hide a mike on the set; they tried flower pots, vases, lamps, clothing, and virtually anything that could conceal a microphone. These attempts only made more obvious the need for a microphone capable of picking up sound from a distance.

SHOTGUN MICROPHONES The solution was the **shotgun microphone** (see **5-35**). The basic principle of all shotgun mikes is that they cancel sound from all directions except a narrow angle at the front. This creates the illusion that they have greater reach. Actually, most microphones have extended reach. Omnidirectional, bidirectional, and cardioid mikes, however, pick up a diffused sound that includes the target sound plus the **ambience**—the acoustics of an environment that interact with the sound source (see **5-36**). Since the shotgun mike is either hyper- or ultracardioid, it can discriminate against unwanted ambience and lock in on the main sound source. However, some shotguns do this better than others, so be careful when you choose a shotgun mike, especially one for use in mediocre acoustic environments.

Another aspect of the shotgun's design is that many models sacrifice quality for apparently greater reach. The main response problem is that the shotgun becomes less directional at lower frequencies. This limitation is because of its inability to deal very well with wavelengths (see Chapter 2) that are longer than the length of its tube, called the *interference tube.*

If the tube of a shotgun mike is 3 feet long, it will maintain directionality for frequencies of 300 Hz and higher—that is, wavelengths of 3 feet and less. For 300 Hz and lower, the mike becomes less and less directional, canceling

handwritten margin notes:
- shotgun – highly directional mic
- ambience is sometimes
- Focusing – tends to amplify the sound up to 20 dB. (wildlife, football games)
- Parabolic mikes - DRAWBACKS: picks up unwanted surrounding sounds

5-35 *Shotgun microphone mounted on a boom.*

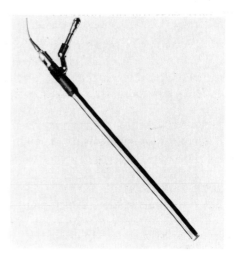

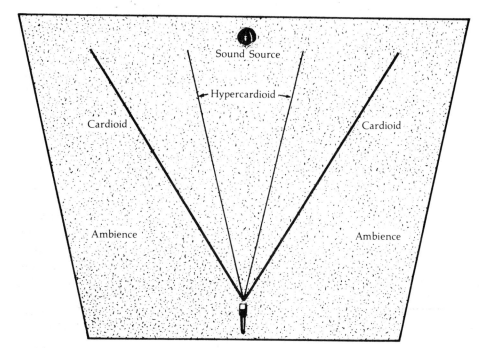

Sound Source

←—Hypercardioid—→

Cardioid

Cardioid

Ambience

Ambience

5-36 *The hypercardioid's narrower directional pattern focuses on the sound source and picks up less room ambience than microphones with wider directional patterns.*

less and less of the unwanted sound. This reduces the shotgun's overall sound quality and limits its use in situations where considerable low-frequency sound is present. As lower frequencies increase in power, directionality deteriorates and response becomes "muddy." Some shotgun mikes do have bass roll-off, however.

PARABOLIC MICROPHONES   Another microphone that is used for long-distance pickup, mainly outdoors, is the **parabolic** microphone. It consists of an omnidirectional microphone facing inward and attached to a parabolic reflector (see **5-37**). Instead of canceling unwanted sound, the parabolic dish, which is concave, concentrates the desired sound waves from the sound source and directs them to the microphone. As with the shotgun mike, the parabolic mike's low-frequency response deteriorates at wavelengths longer than the diameter of the parabolic dish.

WIRELESS MICROPHONE SYSTEM   Even shotgun and parabolic microphones reach just so far. When mike-to-source distances are quite long, you can use a **wireless microphone system**—also called **radio, FM,** and **transmitter** mikes (see **5-38a, b**). The wireless microphone system consists of any small, stand-

5-37 *Parabolic microphone with earphones for monitoring the sound.*

ard mike, such as a lavalier, attached to a battery-powered transmitter that sends its signal to a receiver. The transmitter is small enough to be carried in a pocket or taped to the body, and it operates on a designated frequency in the FM megahertz band—hence, the name FM microphone. Since there is no cord, the performer is free to move about almost anywhere within the transmitter's range, which can be from several feet to several yards, depending on the transmitter. Wireless microphones, however, are subject to interference from objects that are in the signal path between transmitter and receiver and from other transmitting sources like police, taxi, and CB radios.

HEADSET MICROPHONES Sports broadcasting has led to the development of the **headset microphone system**—a moving-coil mike with a built-in pop filter mounted to earphones (see **5-39a, b, c**). The microphone may be unidirectional to keep background sound to a minimum, or omnidirectional for added background color. The earphones carry two separate signals; the program feeds through one earphone and the director's cues through the other. An additional benefit of the headset system is that it frees the announcer's hands and frontal working space.

CONTACT MICROPHONES In Chapter 1, we discussed air as a conducting medium for sound waves. Actually, any molecular medium will conduct

Best for Sportscasters

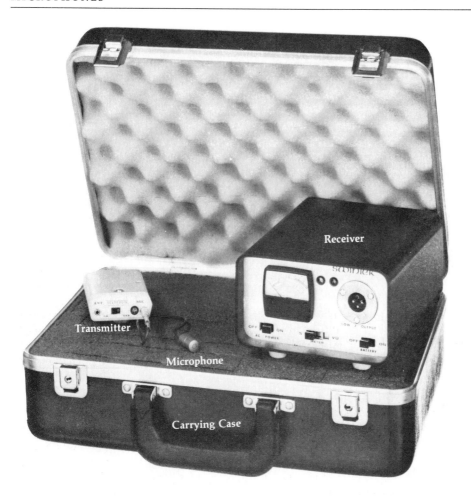

5-38a *Wireless microphone system consists of any conventional microphone connected to a transmitter, which sends the microphone's signal to a receiver. The receiver is connected to the console's microphone input.*

Receiver

Transmitter

Microphone

Carrying Case

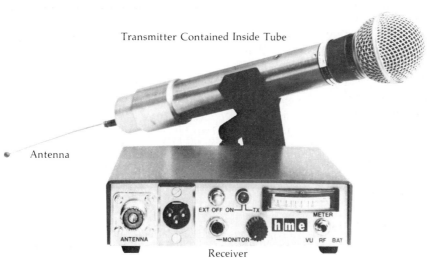

Transmitter Contained Inside Tube

Antenna

Receiver

5-38b *In a wireless microphone system, the transmitter can be self-contained. This microphone can be hand-held or used on a desk stand.*

5-39a *(Right) Headset microphone system with a unidirectional mike.*

5-39b *(Far right) Headset microphone system with an omnidirectional mike and a "cough" switch that is used to cut off the microphone if the performer has to cough or clear his throat.*

5-39c *Wireless headset microphone.*

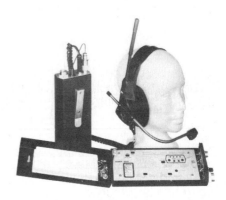

sound, and the greater the concentration of molecules, the better is the conductance. Water is a better conductor than air, and solids are better than water. The **contact microphone** picks up vibrations pulsing through solid objects. A contact mike attached to a vibrating surface of an object such as an acoustic bass, acoustic guitar, or the sounding board of a piano produces a close, direct sound that is almost devoid of reflections (see **5-40a, b, c**). Since contact microphones come with various impedances, make sure to select the low-impedance models for better sound response.

PZM MICROPHONES Most microphones pick up some proportion of direct to reflected sound, depending on their polar patterns. The **PZM** or **pressure**

zone microphone is designed to eliminate the time difference between direct and reflected sound waves by picking up all waves that reach the microphone indirectly and in phase, reinforcing their amplitude without distortion (see **5-41**). The PZM contains a pressure-calibrated electret transducer in a cantilever mounting. Its directional pattern is hemispheric and its response is spacious.

STEREO AND QUAD MICROPHONES **Stereophonic** and **quadriphonic microphones** are actually separate microphone capsules with electronically separate systems housed in a single case (see **5-42** and **5-43**). The stereo mike has two separate elements. The lower one is stationary, and the upper element rotates

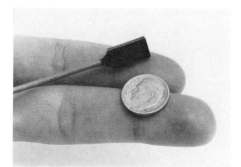

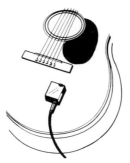

5-40a *(Far left) Example of a contact microphone.*

5-40b *(Left) A contact microphone mounted on the body of a sound source transduces the vibrations pulsing through the wood, metal, or other material into electrical energy.*

5-40c *This electromagnetic pickup has three sensors that slip into position behind the strings near the top of the piano and stick to the frame magnetically. Unlike contact or other microphones, the sensors record only string movement and are not dependent on vibrations of the sounding board.*

Can be set up position in whatever is needed

270 degrees to facilitate several different stereo pickup patterns. Most stereo mikes can be remote-controlled.

Quad mikes have four capsules arranged in pairs, one above the other. The upper capsule rotates and picks up sound from the right front and left rear; the lower capsule picks up sound from the left front and right rear. Quad mikes require special controls to coordinate the pickup patterns.

SOUNDFIELD MICROPHONE SYSTEM Another concept in simultaneous multidirectional sound pickup is the **soundfield microphone system**—a mike with four separate outputs with feeds that are controlled through a separate control unit (see **5-44a, b, c**). The mike can be set for monaural—

5-41 *PZM (pressure zone) microphone. (PZM is a trademark of Crown International, Inc.)*

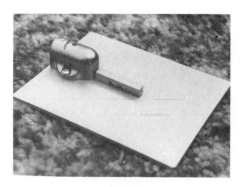

5-42 *(Right) Stereo microphone.*

5-43 *(Far right) Quadriphonic microphone.*

Microphone Capsule

Microphone Capsule

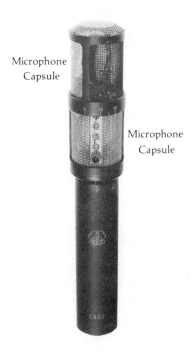

Microphone Capsule

Microphone Capsule

Microphone Capsule

Microphone Capsule

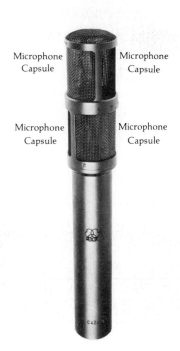

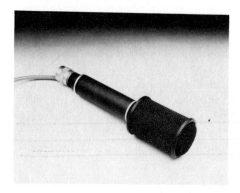

5-44a *Soundfield microphone.*

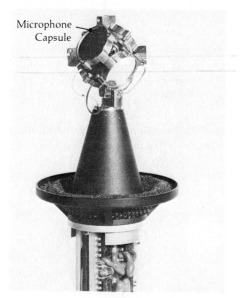

Microphone
Capsule

5-44b *Four rotating capsules of the soundfield microphone.*

5-44c *Control unit for the soundfield microphone.*

omnidirectional, bidirectional, cardioid, and hypercardioid—stereo, or quad pickup. The idea is to reproduce the ambience of an acoustic environment by creating an **ambisonic** or surround-sound sonic experience.

Microphone Accessories

MICROPHONE CABLE Microphone cable consists of either one or two wires (conductors and ground) surrounded by a metallic insulating screen and covered with rubber or plastic (see **5-45**). The twin-conductor cable, or **balanced line,** is preferred to the one-conductor cable, or **unbalanced line,** because it is less susceptible to electric noise and its impedance matches that of professionally used microphones.

When winding mike cable, be careful not to make the angle of the wrap too severe or it can damage the internal wires. It is also a good idea to secure the cable with a clasp especially made for this purpose to prevent it from getting tangled (see **5-46**).

MICROPHONE CONNECTORS All professional mikes and mike cable use a three-pronged male plug that fits into three conductor inputs of a female plug generally called **XLR connectors** (see **5-47**). Usually the female plug on the microphone cable connects to the mike and the male plug connects to the console (see **5-48**).

The female plug has a safety lock to prevent the connection from accidentally coming loose. When you connect the male to the female plug, listen for the click of the safety lock, which tells you the two are joined. When you disengage the connection, remember to release the safety lock first or you could pull out the entire plug and wiring.

[handwritten note in margin: Balanced is better: less susceptible]

5-45 *Microphone cables.*

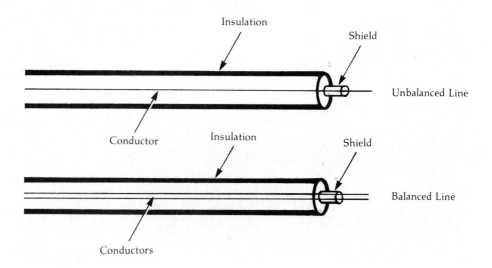

Insulation

Shield

Unbalanced Line

Conductor   Insulation   Shield

Balanced Line

Conductors

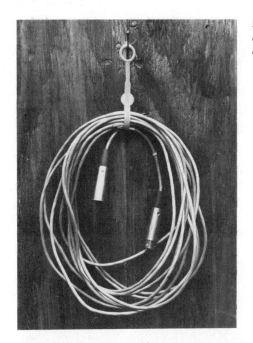

5-46 *To keep microphone cable intact and avoid damage to internal wires and connections, wind and secure it when not in use.*

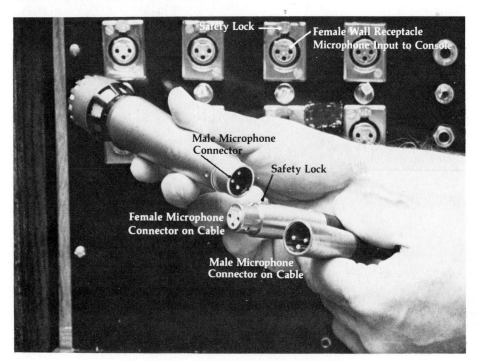

5-47 Microphone connectors.

5-48 *The female cable connector plugs into the male microphone connector; the male cable connector plugs into the female wall receptacle, which is connected to the microphone input on the console.*

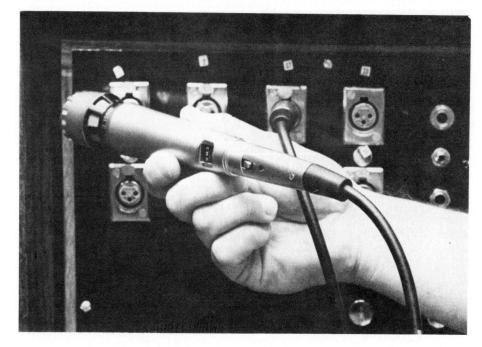

5-49 *Various types of microphone stands.*

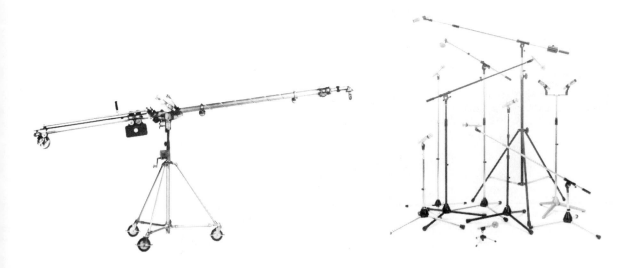

MICROPHONE STANDS Just as there are many types of microphones to meet a variety of needs, many types of microphone stands are available for just about every possible application (see **5-49**).

SHOCK MOUNTS Because solid objects are excellent sound conductors, the danger always exists that unwanted vibrations will travel through the mike stand to the microphone. To reduce noises induced by vibration, you can place the mike in a **shock mount**—a device that suspends and mechanically isolates the microphone from the stand (see **5-50**).

5-50 *Various types of shock mounts.*

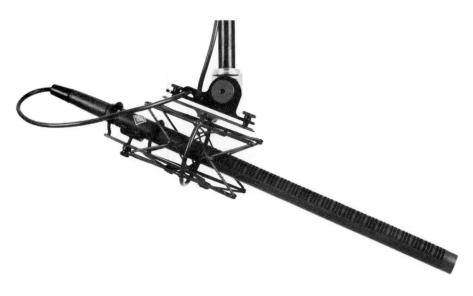

Selected Microphones: Their Characteristics and Uses

The purpose of this section is to display, for convenient reference, some commonly used microphones that are in production or readily available. There is no implication that these mikes are the "best" or that professional microphones not included are inferior. This section is intended as only a guide. Always *listen* to equipment before you make a decision involving sound.

Condenser

Microphone	Directional Pattern(s)	Characteristics	Uses
AKG 414	Omni Bi Cardioid Hypercardioid	Wide response but not a typically flat condenser-like curve; good low end, brisk midrange, but harsh on bright instruments; adds snap to dull sound; 10-dB pad; good rear rejection on hypercardioid.	Good on most vocals except high-pitched voices; very good on orchestral sections; excellent blending mike.
AKG 451 System, Preamp and Capsules		Preamp has two-position bass roll-off.	Interchangeable capsules make this system mike excellent on most instruments, especially cymbals and voices; adds edge or briskness, depending on the instrument; excellent for blending.
	Cardioid (CK1)	Wide, flat response.	

Microphone	Directional Pattern(s)	Characteristics	Uses
AKG 451 System, Preamp and Capsules			
	Cardioid (CK1S)	Rising response from presence range and up.	
	Omni (CK2)	Wide, flat response with slight high-end boost.	
	Cardioid (CK5)	Built-in pop filter and shock mount.	
	Hyper (CK8)	Boom mike with short interference tube.	

Microphone	Directional Pattern(s)	Characteristics	Uses
AKG 451 System, Preamp and Capsules			
	Shotgun (CK9)	Boom mike with long interference tube.	
Electro-Voice CS15	Cardioid	At mike-to-source distance of 2 feet has flat response to 3 kHz, then response rises through high end; pronounced proximity effect at 3 inches and closer; good rear rejection; blast filter; rugged.	Excellent for remotes and on voices; brightens sound at 2 to 3 feet; tight miking makes sound robust; also excellent on boom when mike-to-source distance is not more than 3 to 4 feet.

Microphone	Directional Pattern(s)	Characteristics	Uses
Neumann KM 86	Omni Bi Cardioid	Wide, flat response; good pickup at extended mike-to-source distances; susceptible to breathing and popping sounds; 10-dB pad.	Good on strings and larger ensembles; vocal is a problem; excellent blending mike.
Neumann KM 88	Omni Bi Cardioid	Wide, flat response, particularly good midrange and high end; bright sound; excellent distance pickup; 10-dB pad.	Excellent on orchestras, strings, guitar, and banjo.

Microphone	Directional Pattern(s)	Characteristics	Uses
Neumann U 47 fet	Cardioid	Newly designed version of the revolutionary classic U 47; extremely wide, flat response with slight dip at 3 kHz; rich sound; capsule isolated against shock; high overload level; added protection against wind and popping noises; bass roll-off; 10-dB pad.	One of the best vocal mikes; excellent on single instruments.
Neumann U 87	Omni Bi Cardioid	Classic mike; extremely wide, flat, rich response; bass roll-off; 10-dB pad; sensitive to breathing and popping noises.	Everything.
Neumann U 89	Omni Bi Cardioid Wide-angle cardioid Hypercardioid	Smaller version of the U 87 with several different features: capsule has greater isolation against dirt, humidity, and breathing sounds; high overload level; two-position bass roll-off; 10-dB pad.	Everything; size also makes it suitable for on-camera use in TV.

Microphone	Directional Pattern(s)	Characteristics	Uses
Schoeps Colette System Microphone	Omni Omni (speech) Cardioid Cardioid (speech) Hypercardioid Omni and cardioid Omni, bi, and cardioid	A first-rate line of microphones; excellent wide, flat response with added high-frequency boost in capsules recommended for speech; can take loud sound levels; extremely clean, natural, uncolored sound.	Excellent for voice, most musical instruments, ensemble sections, and blending.
Shure SM81	Cardioid	Wide, flat response; excellent rear rejection; three-position bass roll-off; 10-dB pad; slim, sleek, lightweight; rugged.	Good for drums, except bass drum, guitar, brass, and speech; good-looking for TV; can be used as boom in close mike-to-source situations.
Sony C-37P	Omni Cardioid	Classic mike, wide, flat, smooth response; four-position bass roll-off; 8-dB pad.	Excellent on strings, horns, guitar, banjo sections, and vocals.
Sony C-47	Omni Cardioid	Wide, flat, smooth response; takes edge off overly bright, harsh sound; four-position bass roll-off; high frequency roll-off.	Excellent on vocals and orchestra sections, especially strings.

Microphone	Directional pattern(s)	Characteristics	Uses
Electro-Voice CO85	Omni	One of the best lavaliers; wide response for this type of mike; no roll-off or pad and sensitive to handling and rustling noises (which are characteristics of most lavaliers).	Lavalier; best used, as intended, mounted on lapel, tie, etc., for speech.
Sony ECM-50	Omni	Perhaps most frequently used of all lavaliers; excellent, wide response.	(Same as CO85.) Also good as contact mike (wrapped in foam plastic) on acoustic bass, guitar, and piano.
Neumann KMR82	Hypercardioid	Unusually wide, flat response for a boom mike; rising characteristic between 5 and 10 kHz; high overload level; insensitive to wind and handling noises but should have windscreen outdoors; good rejection of incident sound; bass roll-off.	Boom and fish pole; good enough to use in critical long-distance music recording, either indoors or out.
Sennheiser 416	Supercardioid	New edition of the classic boom mike, the 415; unusually wide, flat response for this type of mike; rising response between 2 and 15 kHz; excellent rejection of incident sound.	Boom and fish pole; used almost everywhere for remote recording; excellent pickup at closer mike-to-source distances; also good enough for boom pickup of music.

Microphone	Directional Pattern(s)	Characteristics	Uses
Sennheiser 816	Hypercardioid	New edition of the classic 815, the long-reach version of the 415; sharp boost from 5 to 15 kHz; as good a rejection of incident sound as any mike available.	Boom and fish pole; virtually universal long-reach mike used for remotes.
AKG C-24	Stereo—variable	Vacuum tube condenser; superb life-like quality; excellent low-end response; can be remote-controlled; a classic in this small group of mike types. (No longer in production.)	Stereo recording.
Neumann SM 69	Stereo—variable	Has two separate mike systems, upper element rotates 270 degrees, and has nine patterns between omni and cardioid; can be remote-controlled. Excellent sound quality.	Stereo recording.
Sennheiser MKE 2002	Binaural	Two very high-quality, lavalier-size, condenser mikes mounted at both ends of a U-shaped frame, positioned just at the earlobes of an artificial head; theoretically, mikes duplicate actual spatial sound perception of humans.	Binaural recording.

Microphone	Directional Pattern(s)	Characteristics	Uses
AKG 424	Quad: Cardioid with lateral front and rear pickup	Four condenser cardioid capsules arranged in pairs above each other; upper capsule rotates and picks up right front and left rear; fixed capsule picks up left front and right rear.	Quadriphonic recording.

Moving Coil

Microphone	Directional Pattern(s)	Characteristics	Uses
AKG 222	Cardioid	Smaller version of the AKG 202 (see **7-31**); good clean response that stays flat to 90 degrees off axis, although level decreases 6 dB; excellent rear rejection; no proximity effect; pop filter, two-position bass roll-off; rugged.	Excellent on drums, cymbals, Leslies (cabinets with two loudspeakers, usually used to amplify organs), and other amplifiers; good on strings and wind instruments.
AKG 224E	Cardioid	One of the best moving-coil mikes around; wide, clean, bright response—"condenser" quality; virtually does not "hear" at 180 degrees off axis; no proximity effect; two-position bass roll-off.	Everything.

Microphone	Directional Pattern(s)	Characteristics	Uses
Electro-Voice DS35	Cardioid	Designed for extra bass boost at close mike-to-source distances; adds fullness and bottom to sound; pop filter; rugged.	Excellent for bass drum, bass, low end of piano, clarinet, tenor saxophone, and thin-sounding voices.
Electro-Voice RE15	Supercardioid	Wide, flat, yet distinctive response; enhances mid-range but less bright than the similar RE16; no proximity effect; excellent side-to-rear rejection; sensitive to popping; bass roll-off.	Excellent on snare and other drums, cymbals, piano, viola, and cello.
Electro-Voice RE16	Supercardioid	Similar to RE15 but has flatter, smoother response; bright, even high end; bass roll-off; pop filter; hum rejection; can take high sound levels; no proximity effect; rugged.	Excellent on amplifiers, Leslies, drums, cymbals, brass, guitar, and vocals; good-looking for TV.
Electro-Voice RE20	Cardioid	Another of the "condenser"-quality moving-coil mikes; extraordinary wide, flat, clean response; subject to proximity effect; bass roll-off; pop filter; very rugged.	Everything, except on camera. It is not a good-looking microphone.

Microphone	Directional Pattern(s)	Characteristics	Uses
Electro-Voice 635A and RE50	Omni	Similar mikes with good, clean responses; lack edge and brilliance; main difference: RE50 has pop filter; both very rugged.	Very good for practically anything where isolation is not critical; RE50 is virtually standard for on-location reporting.
Electro-Voice RE55	Omni	One of the best moving-coil omnidirectional mikes around; very smooth, wide, flat, almost flawless response; clean and bright.	Everything; particularly superb on piano and at reducing sibilance; good-looking for TV.
Sennheiser 421	Cardioid	Bright, clean, uncolored sound with rising response from 3 kHz; five-position bass roll-off; excellent rear rejection; high overload capacity.	Excellent on drums, cymbals, piano, brass, woodwinds, strings, and speech.
Sennheiser 441	Supercardioid	Similar to 421 with added equalization for midrange boost; internal shock mount; excellent side-to-rear rejection; very high overload capacity.	Same as 421 plus advantage of tight miking.

Microphone	Directional Pattern(s)	Characteristics	Uses
Shure SM 53 and SM 54	Cardioid	Natural-sounding response; particularly flat between 100 and 2,000 Hz; rising response from 2,000 Hz; built-in shock mount; hum rejection, bass roll-off; rugged; only difference: SM 54 has pop filter.	Excellent for studio and remote recording and TV; piano, guitar, drums (except bass drum), saxophones, amplifiers, Leslies, and vocals; can be used for close boom work.
Shure SM 58	Cardioid	Excellent frequency and transient response; rugged; has proximity effect; pop filter.	Widely used vocal mike; excellent for studio and live conditions.
AKG 110	Omni	Good, wide response; shock mounted; fairly large.	Lavalier.

Microphone	Directional Pattern(s)	Characteristics	Uses
Electro-Voice 649B	Omni	Good response, but range not as wide as other lavaliers; smaller than the similar 647A.	Lavalier.
Shure SM 11	Omni	One of the smallest lavaliers; wide response but low end begins rolling off at 400 Hz.	Lavalier.
AKG 900E	Hypercardioid	Wide response; excellent long-range pickup and side-to-rear rejection; problem with reverberant sound, which is the case with most shotguns; bass roll-off.	Boom and fish pole.

Microphones	Directional Pattern(s)	Characteristics	Uses
Electro-Voice DL42	Hypercardioid	Good response to 10 kHz; good for average mike-to-source distances.	Boom and fish pole.
Shure SM 5	Cardioid	Smooth response up to 10 kHz; excellent rear rejection, proximity effect; best when used at close to average mike-to-source distances.	Boom and fish pole; particularly good for speech and vocals.

Ribbon

Microphone	Directional Pattern(s)	Characteristics	Uses
Beyer M 160	Hypercardioid	Smooth response; can take higher sound pressure levels than most ribbons.	Excellent on brass, strings, and sections; good blending mike.

Microphone	Directional Pattern(s)	Characteristics	Uses
Shure 300	Bi	Flat response to 4 kHz; warm, mellow sound; pronounced proximity effect; subject to popping and overload; bass roll-off.	Excellent for any voice work —music or speech, horns, and woodwinds—so long as isolation is not a factor; very good blending mike.
Shure SM 33	Cardioid	Smooth, warm, and mellow; dulls bright sound; pronounced proximity effect; subject to popping but not as sensitive to overload as 300; bass roll-off.	Excellent for any voice (speech) work, horns, woodwinds, and strings.
RCA 77 DX	Omni Bi Uni	Classic ribbon mike; rich, warm, resonant response; extremely delicate and sensitive to overload; three-position bass roll-off.	Unsurpassed on strings, tympani, saxophones, horns, sections, and speech; not recommended for tight miking.

Summary

1. Microphones are transducers that convert acoustic energy into electric energy.
2. There are three types of professionally used microphones: moving coil, ribbon, and condenser.
3. Microphones pick up sound from essentially three directions: all around—omnidirectional; front and rear—bidirectional; and front—unidirectional.
4. The unidirectional, or cardioid, design has even narrower pickup patterns: supercardioid, hypercardioid, and ultracardioid.
5. There are also multidirectional microphones—mikes with more than one pickup pattern.
6. Many unidirectional mikes are susceptible to the proximity effect. To neutralize it, they are equipped with bass roll-off.
7. Ribbon and condenser microphones are sensitive to distortion from overload. Many condensers are equipped with a pad to reduce the overall sound level and avoid damage to the element.
8. Pop filters and windscreens are used to reduce distortion caused by wind and transients.
9. Microphones have been developed for special purposes: the lavalier to be unobtrusive; the shotgun, parabolic, and wireless mikes for long-distance pickup; the headset mike to keep background sound to a minimum by maintaining a close mike-to-source distance; and stereo and quad mikes for different spatial pickups.
10. The accessories used for professional microphones are standard: twin-conductor cables called balanced lines; XLR connectors; various types of stands for mike placement on desk, floor, and boom; and shock mounts to reduce vibrations reaching the microphone from the mike stand.

(1) Never use more mikes than necessary.
(2) Always follow the 3 to 1 rule. (in mono)
(3) Select correct microphone for each specific situation.
(4) Evaluate mike's quality periodically (maintenance
(5) Check mike cables for proper phasing
(6) Never use ribbon mike outside.
(7) Never blow or tap on the microphone.
(8) Panel discussions, interviews, etc. conducted at a hard-surfaced tabletop, the mike should be placed as close as possible to the tabletop.
(9) Never hold a cardiod mike around the shell (sound ports)
(10) Purchase mikes with the same ide of quality that you would give to other equipment.   (eye)

Ten commandments of microphone usage.

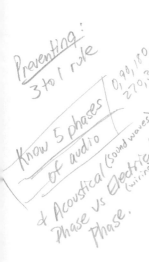

Preventing:
3 to 1 rule

0, 90, 180
270, 360

Know 5 phases
of audio

+ Acoustical (sound waves)
Phase vs Electrical (wiring)
Phase.

6

Miking Speech

No aspect of audio has more of an influence on sound shaping—or is more subjective—than microphone selection and placement. Since no two sound designers achieve their results in exactly the same way, there can be no hard and fast rules about selecting and positioning microphones.* The purpose of this chapter and the next, then, is to suggest guidelines for miking speech and music using as examples the types of productions you are most likely to encounter.

Phase: Acoustical and Electrical

ACOUSTICAL PHASE Before we begin a discussion of microphone technique, it is important to say something about **phase**—the time relationship between two or more sound waves at a given point in their cycles. Five phases constitute the cycle of a sound wave (see **6-1**). If the phases of sound waves coincide, the waves are *in phase*—they reinforce each other, thus adding to a sound's loudness (see **6-2a**). If these phases do not coincide, the waves are *out of phase*—they reduce a sound's loudness or cancel the sound altogether (see **6-2b**).

Phase is closely related to microphone placement. If sound sources are not properly placed in relation to microphones, sound waves could reach the mikes at different times in their cycles, therefore, out of phase. For example, sound waves from a performer who is slightly off center between two microphones will reach one mike a short time before or after they reach the

---

*Since audio in media involves several different functions, *sound designer* is used as a general, but indicative, term.

128

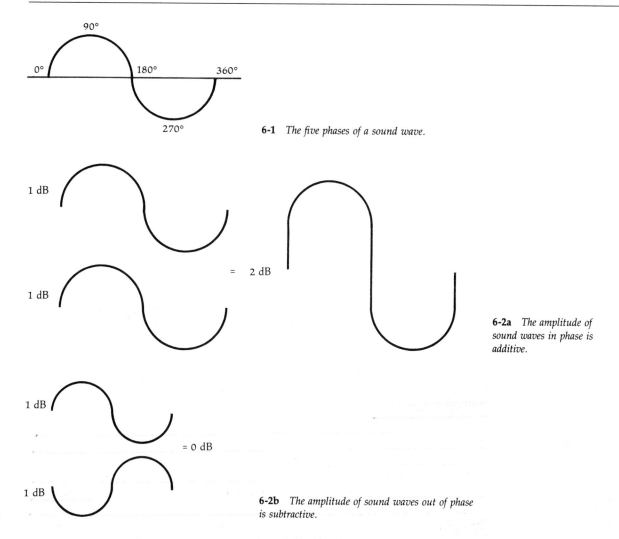

6-1 *The five phases of a sound wave.*

6-2a *The amplitude of sound waves in phase is additive.*

6-2b *The amplitude of sound waves out of phase is subtractive.*

other mike, causing some cancellation of sound. Perceiving sounds that are considerably out of phase is relatively easy; when you should hear sound, you hear little or none. Perceiving sounds that are only a little out of phase, however, is not so easy.

One way to avoid phase problems with microphones is to follow the **three-to-one rule**—place no two microphones closer together than three times the distance between one of them and its sound source. If one mike is 2 inches from a singer, the other nearest mike should be no closer than 6 inches; if one mike is 3 feet from an orchestra section, the other nearest mike should be no closer than 9 feet; and so on (see **6-3**).

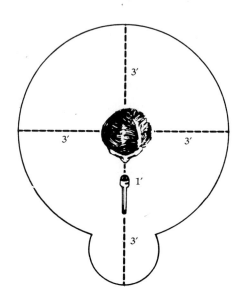

6-3 *Most phasing problems generated by improper microphone placement can be avoided by placing no two microphones closer together than three times the distance between one of them and its sound source.*

ELECTRICAL PHASE The difference between acoustical phase and electrical phase is that signals that are acoustically in phase are dependent on the behavior of sound waves, whereas signals that are electrically in phase are dependent on proper wiring.

The main cause of microphones being electrically out of phase is incorrect wiring of the microphone plugs. Male and female connectors have three pins: (1) a positive pin for high output, (2) a negative pin for low output, and (3) a ground. Mike cables house three coded wires. All mikes in the same facility must have the same number pin connected to the same color wire (see **6-4**). If they do not and are used at the same time, they will be electrically out of phase.

To check whether mikes are electrically out of phase, adjust the level of one pot for a normal reading as someone speaks into a mike. Turn down the pot and repeat the procedure with another mike and pot. Then open both mikes to the normal settings. If one VU meter reading decreases when the levels of both mikes are turned up, you have an electrical phase problem.

The obvious way to correct an electrical out-of-phase condition is to fix the equipment. If there is no time for that, however, most multichannel consoles have a phase reversal control that shifts out-of-phase signals by 180 degrees into phase (see **6-5**).

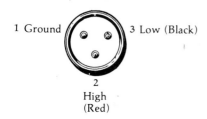

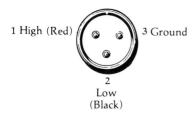

6-4 *If these two microphone connectors were used in the same studio at the same time on different microphones, the mikes would be out of phase.*

6-5 *Phase reversal control on a Neve console.*

Microphone Applications

From the standpoint of miking performers, regardless of the medium, in or out of a studio, productions are either *static*—requiring little or no movement within a small area, or *dynamic*—requiring broad movement across an extended area(s). Using these classifications as guidelines, we can divide microphone usage into two categories: *fixed* and *mobile*.

FIXED MICROPHONE MOUNTS For static productions, there are six ways to mount a microphone: (1) on a flexible, stationary boom (see **6-6**); (2) on a desk

Six fixed mounts:
① stationary boom
② desk stand
③ floor stand
④ attached to neck/clothing
⑤ overhead suspended
⑥ Hidden

Mobile mounts:
① Moving boom
② Hand Held
③ wireless

6-6 (Right) Stationary boom stand.

6-7 (Above) Desk stands.

6-8 Floor stands.

3 types

stand (see **6-7**); (3) on a floor stand (see **6-8**); (4) around the neck or attached to clothing (see **6-9**); (5) suspended from overhead (see **6-10**); and (6) hidden (see **6-11**).

MOBILE MICROPHONE MOUNTS In dynamic productions, microphones are: (1) mounted on a movable boom (see **6-12**), (2) hand-held (see **6-13**), or (3) wireless (see **6-14**).

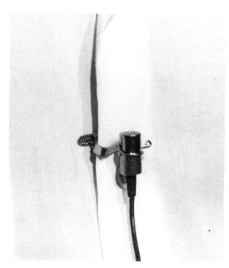

6-9 *Microphone clasp attached to clothing.*

6-10 *Hanging microphone.*

6-11 *Hidden microphone.*

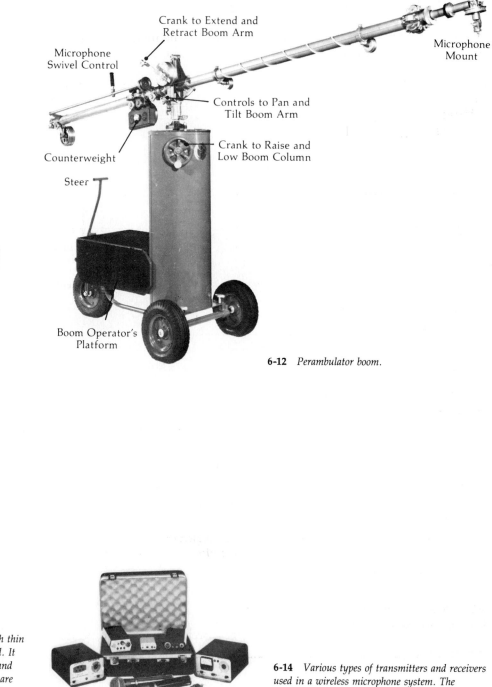

Crank to Extend and
Retract Boom Arm

Microphone
Swivel Control

Microphone
Mount

Controls to Pan and
Tilt Boom Arm

Counterweight

Crank to Raise and
Low Boom Column

Steer

Boom Operator's
Platform

6-12 *Perambulator boom.*

6-13 *Microphone with thin
tube is easily hand-held. It
is also shock-resistant and
has a pop filter, which are
essential in a hand-held
microphone.*

6-14 *Various types of transmitters and receivers
used in a wireless microphone system. The
transmitter is either carried on the person or
placed inside a special microphone handle.*

SUPER HYPER ULTRA (handwritten)

Omnidirectional versus Unidirectional Microphones

In most cases, when you are deciding what microphone mount to use, you will also be deciding whether to use an omni- or unidirectional mike. Sometimes choosing a particular microphone mount automatically commits you to a certain pickup pattern; all lavaliers are omnidirectional, and most boom mikes are hyper- or ultracardioid. If you have a choice between an omni- and a unidirectional mike, note that each has certain advantages and disadvantages, depending on the demands of a given situation.

Lavaliers = omni (handwritten)
Most booms = hyper/ultra (handwritten)

The Omnidirectional Microphone

Advantages	Disadvantages
Does not have to be held directly in front of the mouth to be in the pickup pattern	Does not discriminate against unwanted sound
Does not reflect slight changes in the mike-to-source distance	Is difficult to use in noisy environments
Gives a sense of the environment *ambience* (handwritten)	Has danger of feedback in reverberant locations
Is less susceptible to wind, popping, and handling noises	
Is not subject to the proximity effect	
Is less expensive	

Know (handwritten)

The Unidirectional Microphone

Advantages	Disadvantages
Discriminates against unwanted sound	Must be angled correctly to the mouth or the performer will be off-mike
Gives little or no sense of the environment (which could also be a disadvantage)	May be subject to the proximity effect
Significantly reduces the danger of feedback in reverberant locations	Is susceptible to wind and popping, unless there is a pop filter
	May be susceptible to handling noises
	Requires care not to cover the ports, if hand-held
	Is more expensive

corrected by bass-rolloff (handwritten)

Based on these differences, it is tempting to conclude that an omnidirectional microphone is superior to a unidirectional mike. In fact, unidirectional mikes are far more widely used, which is not to suggest that they are superior either, however. A microphone's suitability must depend on the given situation.

Sound and the Human Voice

KNOW!

The frequency range of the human voice is roughly 60 to 8,000 Hz, including overtones. It is not wide compared with that of some musical instruments (see the diagram inside the front cover), but its harmonic richness makes the human voice a highly complex musical instrument. A bass voice, for example, may have a range of only 60 to 500 Hz, but the frequency content alters considerably with the amount of voice effort used. Changes in loudness and intensity change pitch.

Loud speech boosts the midrange frequencies and reduces the bass frequencies, thus raising the overall pitch. Quiet speech reduces the midrange frequencies, lowering the overall pitch. If speech is played back at a level louder than it was originally recorded, as is possible in film, the bass frequencies will be disproportionately louder. If speech is played back at a quieter level than originally recorded, as is possible in TV, the bass frequencies will be disproportionately quieter. In both cases, the problem can be reduced through proper microphone selection and placement. If the problems exist after recording, adjustments in the loudness level or **equalization** will be necessary to restore the natural timbre of the voice.

accentuates — / antennuates

Radio: Static In-Studio Productions

6-15 *Performer using a microphone mounted on a flexible, gooseneck stand.*

SINGLE SPEAKER In radio, positioning a microphone in front of a seated performer—disc jockey, newscaster, talk-show host—is the most common miking placement. The mike usually is mounted on a small, flexible, stationary boom suspended in front of the talent (see **6-15**), or on a table stand (see **6-16**).

It is important in selecting and positioning the mike to keep sound that is reflected from room surfaces, furniture, and equipment from reaching the mike. The greater the ratio of indirect to direct sound, the more reverberant sound is in the aural space. A reflectant aural space is not conducive to the intimate performer-audience rapport that is fundamental to the sound of so much of today's radio.

6-16 *Performer speaking into a microphone mounted on a desk stand.*

To prevent sound reflections from reaching the microphone, a performer should work at a relatively close mike-to-source distance and use a unidirectional microphone. The directionality of the mike should depend on how much side-to-rear sound rejection is needed. Keep in mind, however, that the more directional the mike, the more restricted is the side-to-side movement.

"Voice" 60–8000 Hz

equalization accentuates/antennuates

[handwritten margin note at top: Ambience – background sound (reverb, noise, atmosphere)]

It is difficult to suggest an optimal mike-to-source working distance because voice projection and timbre vary from person to person. Here are some guidelines that may help.

1. Always stay within the microphone's pickup pattern.

2. Ride the voice level so that it averages between 60 and 100 percent of modulation; some stations like it between 80 and 100.

3. The weaker the voice, the closer the mike-to-source distance should be.

4. Working too close to a mike, however, creates sound that is devoid of ambience, oppressive, and unnatural.

5. Working too close to a mike emphasizes tongue movement, lip smacking, and teeth clicks.

6. Working too far from a mike diffuses the sound quality, creating spatial distance between performer and listener.

7. When the mike-to-source distance is doubled, the sound pressure level drops approximately 6 dB, thus reducing loudness by one-fourth. Conversely, cutting the mike-to-source distance in half increases loudness approximately 6 dB (see **6-17**). This is known as the **inverse square law**. The precise effect of this law depends on whether a sound source is in an open or enclosed space.

Sometimes a microphone is positioned to the side of or under a performer's mouth, with the performer speaking across the mike face (see **6-18**). Usually this is done to reduce popping and sibilance that often occur when the performer talks directly into a mike.

Speaking across a unidirectional microphone reduces these sounds by reducing the sound pressure that hits the diaphragm. Unless the mouth-to-

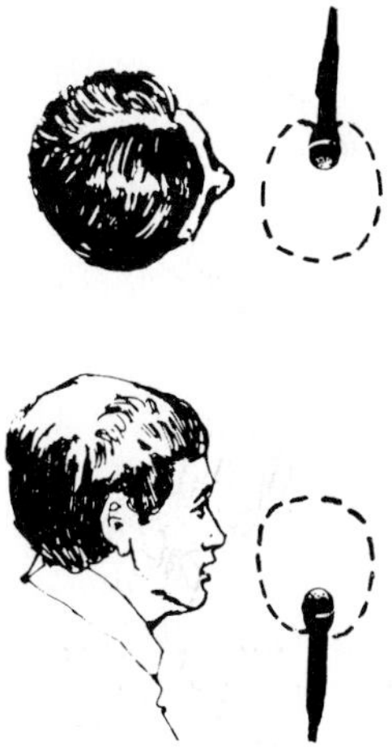

[handwritten margin notes:]
1. On mike
2. Modulation up
3. Closeness
4. Too close? devoid of amb
5. too close? up noise
6. Too far diffuse
7. Mike-to-source distance dbld
   = -6 dB, ¼th level drop

6-18 *Speaking across a unidirectional microphone may reduce popping and sibilance, but it also reduces the frequency response. Sound reaches the microphone from off axis.*

6-17 *Illustration of the inverse square law, which states that as the distance from a sound source doubles, loudness decreases in proportion to the square of that distance.*

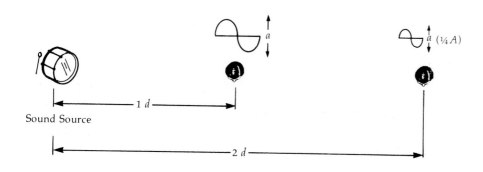

Sound Source

1 d

2 d

a

a (¼ A)

Mike heads should not be parallel to tabletop

mike angle is within the microphone's pickup pattern, however, talking across the mike degrades the response. To eliminate popping and reduce sibilance without degrading the response, (1) use a windscreen, (2) use a microphone with a built-in pop filter, or (3) point the mike at no more than a 45-degree angle above, below, or to the side of a performer's mouth (see **6-19**). If sibilance persists, try either a newer-model ribbon mike or a moving-coil mike with reduced high-end response. Both minimize the more piercing higher frequencies and produce a warmer, less harsh sound.

In positioning a mike, make sure that its head is not parallel to or facing the table top. Since the angle of a sound's incidence is equal to its angle of reflectance (see **2-34**), sound waves bouncing from the table will reflect back into the mike's pickup pattern, thereby reducing the sound quality (see **6-20a**). Any hard surface that is close to a mike, like a copy stand or window, should be angled so the sound waves do not reflect directly into the mike (see **6-20b**). If changing the microphone's angle presents a problem, cover the hard surface with a soft material to absorb some of the reflections, or use a microphone that can be placed on the table top (see **6-21a, b**).

The main difference between miking a performer for mono and for stereo broadcasting is that stereo requires two microphones instead of one. (The stereo mike is rarely used in radio because it is very expensive.) The same guidelines that apply to positioning one mike for a single speaker apply to positioning two mikes, with an additional consideration: the proximity of the microphones both to each other and to the performer. The mikes should be close to each other and at a slight angle to the performer, but the distance between the mikes should be less than the distance between the mikes and the performer (see **6-22**). To avoid phasing problems, center the performer between the microphones and do not spread the mikes too far apart.

6-19 *Speaking at a 45-degree angle into a unidirectional mike reduces popping and sibilance but not the frequency response, since the performer is still on axis.*

BROADCAST STANDARD: 50-15,000 Hz

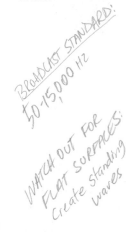

WATCH OUT FOR FLAT SURFACES: Create standing waves

6-20a *Indirect sound waves reflecting back into a microphone cause phase cancellations that degrade the response. To avoid this, a microphone should not be placed parallel to or more than a few inches from a reflective surface.*

6-20b *Placing a microphone at an angle to a reflective surface reduces indirect sound bouncing back into the mike.*

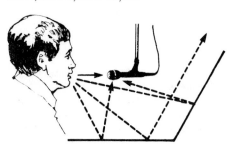

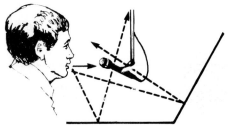

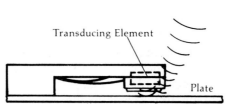

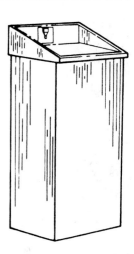

6-21a *This "Mike Mouse" by Electro-Voice can be placed directly on a table top or stage for sound pickup with no phase cancellation from waves bouncing back into the microphone. It consists of a specially designed windscreen and a microphone (in this picture, an RE15).*

6-21b *The PZM microphone avoids phase cancellations by picking up only concentrated, indirect sound waves. It can be placed directly on a table top (above) or mounted vertically (right).*

INTERVIEW When there is more than one speaker, you must first decide how many microphones are needed. In this day of the multichannel console and the multitrack tape recorder, the tendency is to use a mike for every sound source, whether or not it is necessary. You would be wise, however, to *try to use as few microphones as possible.* Each mike you add to a sound chain (1) adds more noise to the system, (2) creates more potential for phase problems, (3) gives the engineer another pot to operate, and (4) reduces the potential for a more life-like sound.

In a radio interview, there are two choices: use one microphone for both interviewer and interviewee, or give separate mikes to each. Using one bi-directional microphone is the easier and "cleaner" alternative, although it is not without its problems. Since there is only one pot controlling the microphone's loudness, it is not possible to compensate electronically for differences in loudness between guest and host.

If the difference between them is obvious but not great, the interviewer, who is usually a professional, can modulate his or her voice to match more closely the level of the interviewee's voice; or the louder speaker can sit farther from the mike and the quieter speaker can sit closer (see **6-23**). If the

Adding mikes to chain:
① More noise
② More potential phase problems
③ Another pot
④ reduces life like sound

6-22 *When speaking into microphones positioned for stereo pickup, a performer should be in front of and between them, and the distance between the mikes should be less than the distance between the mikes and the speaker. This reduces phasing problems and increases the overall sound level.*

6-23 *Microphone positioned closer to the speaker with the quieter voice and farther from the speaker with the louder voice to compensate for differences in loudness.*

6-24 *Directional microphones positioned with their dead sides opposite each other to prevent one speaker's sound from leaking into the other speaker's microphone.*

Cardioid/super cardioid dead sides opposite

Leakage—sound intended for one mike heard by another

difference between the voices is too great and cannot be balanced by adjusting the positions of the participants, there is little alternative but to use two microphones. Either cardioid or supercardioid will do, but they must be positioned so their dead sides are opposite each other to reduce phasing problems and **leakage**—sound intended for one mike being heard by other mikes (see **6-24**). Two hypercardioid mikes would also work in this situation, but there is a danger of reduced sound quality due to their somewhat poorer rear rejection.

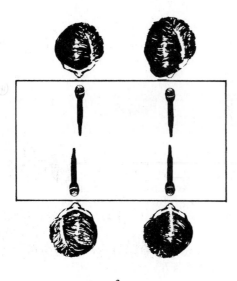

a

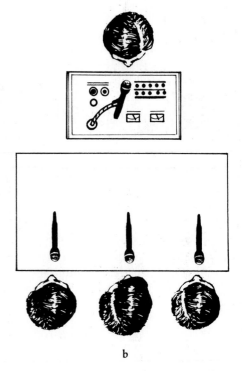

b

6-25 *Various miking arrangements for radio panel programs. Note that in **b**, the moderator is also operating the controls. The arrangement in **c** (facing page) could make it difficult to coordinate microphone levels. Part **d** (facing page) offers a better alternative to the miking in **c**, but to ensure balanced sound pickup, the panelists would have to be close to and equidistant from the microphone.*

PANEL In miking a radio program with more than two voices, such as a panel discussion, there are several alternatives depending on (1) the number of participants, (2) how they are positioned, and (3) the shape of the table at which they are seated (see **6-25**).

[handwritten margin note: ① Participants ② Position ③ Shape of table]

Radio: Active In-Studio Productions

MONAURAL RADIO DRAMA There may be some quarrel with placing radio drama in the category of active productions since the actors perform from relatively stationary positions around a microphone(s). Unlike the radio interview or panel, however, radio drama has dynamics that require the actors to position themselves in relation to the mike and to each other, and to change positions as the action warrants, to create aural space and perspective.

[handwritten margin note: ★ creating the right image in the listener's mind. "theater of the mind"]

Space and Perspective Radio drama has been called the "theater of the mind"; the stimulus of sound compels the listener to create mental images. The stim-

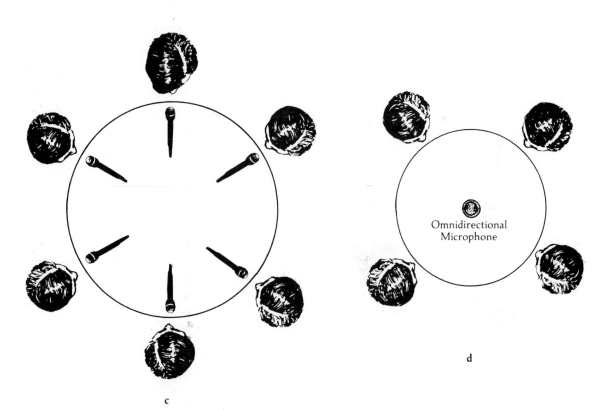

c

d

Space/Perspective:
① acoustically (interact sound/environ.
② Mechanically (artificial acoustics)

uli that trigger your imagination to "see" the "stage" with its actors, scenery, and action are words, music, and sound effects. But how do you "show" space and perspective—the size of a room around the actors, someone leaving the room, the distance between one person calling upstairs to another, or the intimacy between lovers?

In a studio, basically two methods are used to create space and perspective: (1) acoustically, through the interaction of sound and environment, and (2) mechanically, through the use of devices that provide artificial acoustics (see Chapter 11).

Single-Microphone Technique   The preferred technique for creating space and perspective acoustically is to group actors around one microphone and have them play to the mike as if it were the ear of the audience (see 6-26). To establish aural perspective, position the actors at appropriate distances relative to the mike and to each other, as the action of the play dictates.

If an actor is close to the mike, the audience perceives the sound as near or the space as small; if an actor is farther from the mike, the sense of distance increases and the space becomes larger. If a man and woman are on-mike playing opposite each other in a scene that calls for them to be fighting, position the man farther from the microphone than the woman to compensate for the (usually) more powerful male voice. If they are equidistant from the mike, the man will sound closer than the woman and the audience's perspective will be from his position (see 6-27). Even in a subdued scene, like a love scene, position the actors at distances from the microphone relative to the strengths of their voices; otherwise, the audience's point of view will be with the louder voice.

Maintaining space and perspective does not always mean keeping voice levels balanced. If a scene requires one character to call to another from a

6-26 *Grouping actors around one microphone is a typical miking technique used in radio drama.*

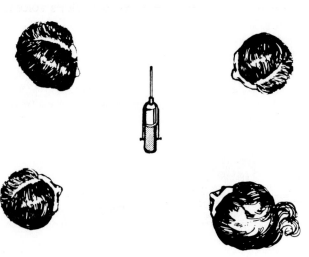

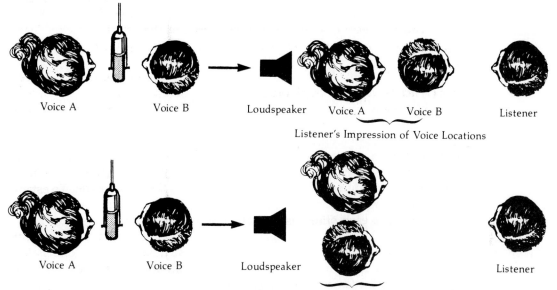

Voice A   Voice B   Loudspeaker   Voice A   Voice B   Listener

Listener's Impression of Voice Locations

Voice A   Voice B   Loudspeaker   Listener

Listener's Impression of Voice Locations

distance, perspective is created by placing the actor who is supposed to be closer on-mike, and the one who is supposed to be farther **off-mike** (see **6-28**).

If movement is involved, such as someone leaving or entering a room, there are three ways to create the effect: (1) by moving from the live to the dead side of a bidirectional microphone, or vice versa; (2) by turning in place toward or away from the mike; or (3) by walking toward or away from the mike.

Fading the pot up or down will also create the effect of coming or going, but not as well as having the actors do it. The difference between the two techniques is that using the pot fades not only the actor's voice level but also the room's acoustics. When a person enters or leaves a room, the space does not change; only the person's movement within it changes.

Once you determine the proper aural balances, it is a good idea to mark or tape the studio floor so the performers will know exactly where to stand and how far to move. Marking the studio floor also assists in traffic control around a microphone when several performers are in a scene and have to give and take on-mike position.

6-27 *To balance two voices with different loudnesses, position the stronger voice farther from the microphone. This keeps them in proper aural perspective relative to the listener.*

6-28 *If one actor is supposed to be farther away than another, position them at the microphone that way to establish proper perspective in relation to the listener.*

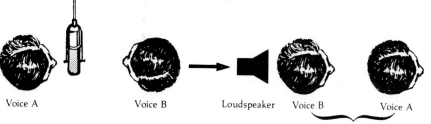

Voice A   Voice B   Loudspeaker   Voice B   Voice A

Listener's Impression of Voice Locations

Listener

Varying Acoustics   Earlier we suggested placing an actor off-mike to produce the effect of talking from a distance. But what if a studio has normal reverberation time (for speech) and the play calls for a performer to talk from a distance across an acoustically live office setting? You can establish perspective by moving the actor off-mike, but creating a more reverberant space is another matter.

As a guideline, here are four basic acoustic conditions and how to recreate them in a speech studio.

1. *Considerable reverberation and long decay time.* This combination creates the acoustics of a concert hall, castle, or large church. Most speech studios do not have the capability to produce such acoustics. They can be generated, however, by adding mechanical reverberation from an echo chamber or reverb system (see Chapter 11).

2. *Considerable reverberation and short decay time.* This produces the type of reverberation you hear in a tiled bathroom, a barroom (as opposed to a cocktail lounge), or an open office area. You can reproduce these acoustics by enclosing an average to small space with reflectant baffles. A separate bidirectional microphone, in addition to the main microphone(s), to pick up the reflections may also help create the desired effect.

3. *Little reverberation and long decay time.* This is the sound of a living room with rugs and drapes, a cocktail lounge, or a conference room. You can reproduce these acoustics by adding live surfaces to normal announce-type studios.

4. *No reverberation.* This is what it sounds like in the country. It can be produced by adding absorbent surfaces to an announce-type studio to deaden its acoustics even more.

Microphone Selection and Mounting   Perhaps the best microphone to use for the single-mike technique is a multipattern condenser. Condensers not only provide extremely wide, flat response, but they also give the human voice a rich, realistic timbre. Ribbon microphones are good for voice, but they lack the high-frequency response that gives sound its life-like quality.

As for moving-coil microphones, several models have excellent voice response but almost all are either omni- or unidirectional. Since radio performers usually are grouped around the microphone (in the single-mike technique), the most commonly used pickup patterns are omni- and bidirectional. It is easier to set up one multipattern microphone than to change mikes every time the situation requires.

The preferred microphone mount for radio drama is the boom. It gives actors easy access to the mike, there is no floor stand to get in their way, and there is less chance of sound conductance from movement across the studio floor.

Multimicrophone Technique With the advent of modern recording, some directors in radio drama have begun to take advantage of the flexibility that the multichannel console and multitrack tape recorder afford. Each performer can be miked separately to allow greater sound control during recording; then the various performance tracks are combined after recording—that is, in postproduction.

Although added sound control is an advantage of this technique, there are also disadvantages. It is more difficult to obtain natural spatial relationships and perspective between performers and the environment, it reduces the opportunity for talent to interact, and it requires a postproduction session to blend the various tracks into one (mono) or two (stereo) tracks.

Deciding whether to use the single- or multimicrophone technique in radio drama should depend on your aesthetic philosophy and the complexity of the script. All in all, however, single-microphone production, although old-fashioned, produces a more realistic sound shape.

STEREO RADIO DRAMA Much of what we have said about monaural radio drama applies to stereo drama as well. The main difference is that with mono, aural space has one dimension—depth—whereas with stereo, it has two dimensions—depth and breadth (see **6-29a, b**).

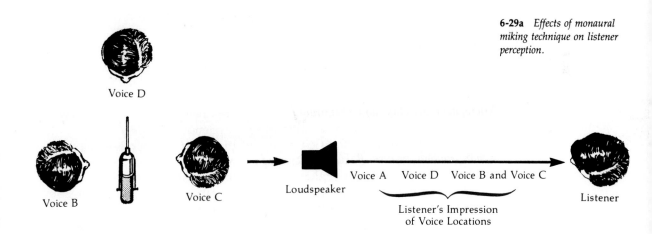

6-29a *Effects of monaural miking technique on listener perception.*

Voice D

Voice B   Voice C   Loudspeaker   Voice A Voice D Voice B and Voice C   Listener

Listener's Impression of Voice Locations

Voice A

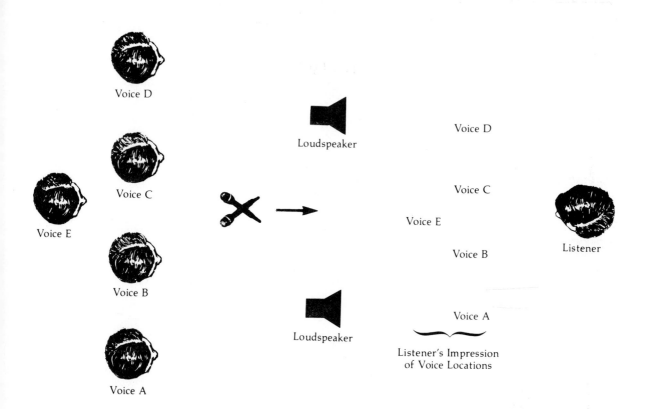

Voice D

Voice C

Voice E

Voice B

Voice A

Loudspeaker

Loudspeaker

Voice E

Voice D

Voice C

Voice B

Voice A

Listener

Listener's Impression
of Voice Locations

6-29b *Effects of stereo miking technique on listener perception.*

Cardioid: leakage eliminates other sound

① Spread out
② Strongest in center

Miking Stereo Drama   Three microphone techniques used to produce stereo perspective in radio drama are: (1) crossing two cardioid mikes—a technique known as **coincident miking**, (2) using a stereo mike, and (3) using the multi-microphone approach and combining the various sound sources into two channels during postproduction. In either of the first two techniques, the angle at which you position the mikes (or mike capsules) is the key to creating a realistic stereo image. Assuming there are no acute acoustic problems, the inclusive angle usually recommended for a balanced stereo field is 90 degrees; at least that is a good starting point.

Across its breadth, stereo space has five points: left, left center, center, right center, and right. Since the audience is usually assumed to be in the center, the so-called stereo seat, and the center is also where the main action usually takes place, that is where the sound should be loudest. As action plays left or right of center, the sound should gradually reduce in loudness. Therefore, a balanced stereo field in radio drama has a center that is closer to the audience than the sides. If the microphones (or capsules) are at too wide an angle, the level of loudness at the center will be lower than the levels to the left and right, thus creating an aural stage with the unnatural dimensions of a center dominated by its sides (see **6-30**). If the angle of the two microphones is too narrow, the center of the stereo field will be disproportionately larger than the sides (see **6-31**).

Another technique sometimes used in stereo miking is to space two cardioid microphones several feet apart. This **spaced-pair** technique is not recommended for radio drama, however. In radio drama, the actors are playing to a fixed point, so the phase relationships of the sound waves reaching the microphones are roughly analogous to the way the waves would reach your ears if you were at the same positions as the mikes. Separating the microphones will result in any sounds that are not exactly dead center reaching the mikes at different times. This will imbalance the stereo image and perhaps create more serious phase problems. This is more of a problem when a few people, sometimes changing positions, are involved, as in drama, than it is in

reaches the mikes at different times

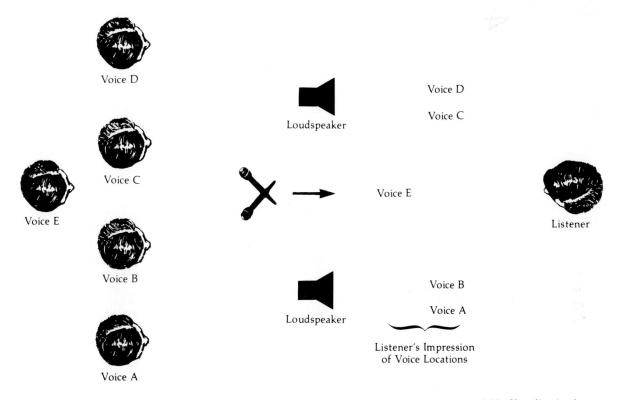

6-30 *How directional microphones set at too wide an angle affect listener perception.*

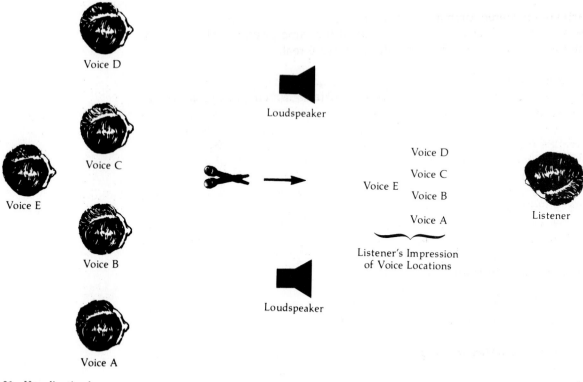

6-31 *How directional microphones set at too close an angle affect listener perception.*

music where performers are often stationary; there is also more flexibility in positioning several instruments across a stereo field (see Chapter 7).

 Perspective Stereo radio drama also differs from monaural drama in the way performers create perspective. To produce the illusion of someone walking from left to right, an actor cannot simply walk in a straight line across the stereo pickup pattern. If that happened, the sound at the center would be disproportionately louder than the sound at the left and right, and the changes in level would be too abrupt. To create a more realistic effect, an actor has to pass the microphones in a semicircle, always staying the same distance from the mikes.

If a script calls for a conversation among several actors in various parts of a room, they cannot be grouped around a microphone—some closer, some farther—in stereo drama as in monaural drama. To maintain the stereo perspective, each actor should be in about the same position, relative to one another, as they would be if the situation were real.

BINAURAL RADIO DRAMA The mike technique that produces perhaps the most realistic spatial effect is the **binaural** [also known as *artificial head* or *dummy head* (Kunstkopf) stereo]. Although stereo is more realistic than mono, it still does not reproduce sound the way humans actually hear it. Our ears are separated by our head; stereo recording separates the mikes but places nothing between them. Therefore, the phase relationship of sound waves as humans hear them—binaurally—is quite different from the phase relationship of sound waves that reach a stereo microphone or a coincident pair of cardioid mikes.

To produce a binaural recording, you have to use a specially designed artificial head with an onmnidirectional condenser microphone at each ear (see **6-32**). A few radio drama workshops have experimented with binaural sound since the late 1960s and have achieved some remarkable effects with aural space and perspective. Binaural recording is still essentially experimental, however, because it is difficult for the listener to perceive directionality, and earphones are necessary to get the full effect of binaural sound.

QUADRIPHONIC RADIO DRAMA Also in the experimental stage is **quadriphonic** radio drama—four-channel sound. Although quad has been around for a while, it is still experimental because there have been regulatory problems in standardizing a broadcast quad reproducing system.

In binaural, you must use headphones

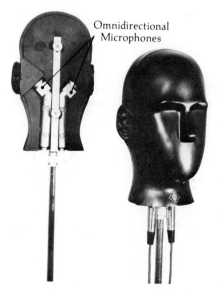

Omnidirectional
Microphones

6-32 *The so-called dummy head—two omnidirectional condenser microphones mounted in "ear" cavities—reproduces binaural sound. To hear the binaural effect, it is necessary to listen with earphones.*

6-33 *(Right) In miking for quad radio drama, one technique is to place the microphones in the middle of the action.*

6-34 *(Far right) Listening to quadriphonic sound, the listener's perspective is from the middle of the action.*

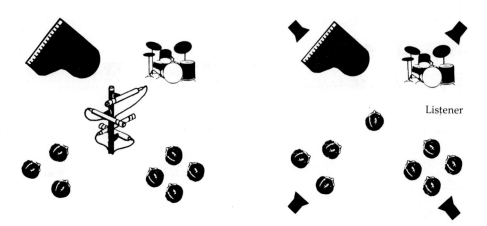

Listener

[handwritten margin note: discorceptive?]

[handwritten margin note: Lavalier cords? Hide it Secure it]

Quadriphonic sound attempts to reproduce the aural space in front and in back of the listener. The two most common miking techniques used to record quad radio drama are to place four cardioid microphones at 90-degree angles to one another (see **6-33**) and to use one quadriphonic mike. In quad radio drama, as in stereo, actors should be positioned at the mike(s) as they would be if the action were really taking place. The audience's perspective is from the middle of the action instead of front and center to it as with stereo (see **6-34**).

Television: Static In-Studio Productions

Five factors influence microphone technique in television: (1) whether the mike is in or out of the picture, (2) how much picture content is in the frame, (3) the number of people in the picture, (4) where they are situated, and (5) the extent of their movement.

NEWS AND TWO-PERSON INTERVIEW PROGRAMS   In news and two-person interview programs, the participants are usually seated at a desk or in an open set. The mike almost universally used in these situations is the lavalier. It is unobtrusive and easy to mount; its sound quality with speech is good (using a moving-coil mike) to excellent (using a condenser); and its omnidirectional pickup pattern ensures that a performer will stay on-mike regardless of how much his or her head moves to one side or the other.

To make these mikes more unobtrusive, many directors prefer to hide as much of the mike cord as possible underneath the performer's clothing (see

6-35 (Far left) Directors concerned with making a lavalier unobtrusive often hide the microphone cord underneath clothing. Many directors think this is unnecessary, since microphones in a shot have become an accepted part of many types of programs.

6-36 (Left) Belt clips are sometimes used to tie down a lavalier's microphone cord to keep it from rubbing against clothing or distracting the viewer.

6-35). If you do this, use a belt clip to (1) keep the microphone in position, (2) isolate it from the rest of its cord, and (3) reduce the sound of clothes rustling, which the cord often picks up through conductance (see **6-36**).

Many directors, however, are not concerned about how much of the mike cord shows. They think the audience accepts it as a natural part of the picture and is not disturbed by it.

Sometimes the mike itself is hidden underneath clothing. This is usually not a good idea because clothing inhibits certain frequencies from reaching the mike and thereby degrades the sound quality. Also, the mike is even more sensitive to the sound of clothes rustling than the cord.

In light of the concern to keep mikes unobtrusive, you may wonder why some newscasters wear two lavaliers (see **6-37**). In these instances, the microphones are condensers, and one is simply for backup in case the power supply of the on-air mike fails.

Since the lavalier and its mike cord can pick up rubbing sounds from movements, you have to be careful when miking a performer, such as a weathercaster, who walks within a small set. The performer should use a belt clip, leave enough play in the mike cord so it scrapes across the floor as little as possible, and avoid sudden, wrenching motions. If the mike cord is put underneath a pant leg or dress to keep it out of sight, it is a good idea to tape it to the thigh to reduce rustling sounds. This precaution should be taken when a performer is on camera a long time and moves about a good deal.

Normally the boom is not used for news and two-person interview programs. It requires another crewperson to operate and, hence, is more expensive. It also creates another task for the lighting director, who must make sure that no boom shadow falls across the set. In newscasts, shots that show the entire set are usually too long to hide a boom; and with news sets as wide as they are today, it would be difficult to move the boom fast enough to cover verbal interplay between newscasters.

From time to time, you see a mike mounted on a desk stand in front of a performer (see **6-16**). This technique is used much less often today than it was a few years ago due to the lavalier's many advantages. If, however, you do use the desk stand, remember to do the following.

Two — one for backup

6-37 Two condenser lavaliers mounted on one specially designed clasp. One microphone is used as backup for the other in case the power supply fails.

1. Mount a unidirectional microphone on it to avoid picking up noises from cameras, technical crew, and others moving about the studio.

2. Select a good-looking mike that does not call attention to itself.

3. Place the stand to the performer's left or right (right is preferred because it usually balances the frame better) so that sound waves do not hit the mike head-on. This reduces the possibility of picking up popping and sibilance, and the performer's hand and script movements are less restricted.

4. Make sure the mike-to-source angle is correct so the talent is not off-mike.

5. Use a mike with a built-in shock mount so unwanted noises are not picked up from hands, legs, or shoes hitting the desk.

PANEL AND TALK PROGRAMS Set design influences microphone technique in that it determines where people sit, stand, or move on a set. Most panel and talk programs on the air use basically the same type of set arrangement: guests sit in a line diagonal to and facing the principal(s)—host, moderator, or main guest. If the participants sit relatively close to the principal(s), you can cover the sound pickup with a few mikes. If more than two groups of participants are separated by several feet, then you may have to use individual microphones, since the set may be too wide to conceal a boom (see **6-38**). The

6-38 *The proximity of the performers to each other and the size of the set often dictate the microphone technique used.*

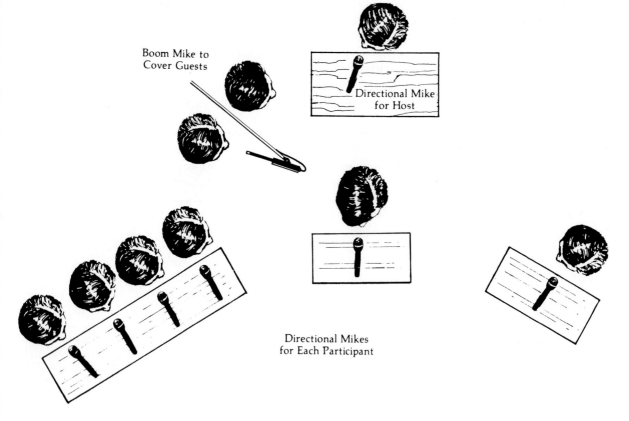

Boom Mike to
Cover Guests

Directional Mike
for Host

Directional Mikes
for Each Participant

choice between using a boom or individual mikes usually depends more on the size and arrangement of the set than on the number of people sitting in it. A good boom operator can comfortably handle up to four people sitting in a row or a semicircle.

Operating the Boom Since the boom is so much a part of TV audio, it is important to say something about its operation. Whenever one boom covers two or more people in conversation, the boom operator has to make sure that none of the program's content is inaudible or off-mike.

A good boom operator (1) quickly learns the speech rhythms and inflections of the people talking; (2) listens to their conversation; (3) anticipates the nonverbal vocal cues that signal a change in speaker; and (4) when the change occurs, moves the mike from one speaker to another, quickly and silently.

In static productions, there is little need to move anything but the mike itself. In active productions, however, moving the boom arm and extending and retracting it are also important to good boom operation. We discuss more about this aspect of boom operation later in the chapter in the section on miking TV drama.

Using Individual Microphones When several feet separate participants seated at a desk or split them into more than two groups, the best alternative is to mike everyone with cardioid, supercardioid, or hypercardioid desk mikes mounted on either stands or small, flexible booms. The directional pattern you use depends on how much side-to-rear sound rejection is necessary.

Lavaliers are usually not used. Since their pickup pattern is omnidirectional, they will pick up overlapping sound from speaker to speaker (if several people are participating), as well as more studio noise. Also, the desk top may look a bit bare.

The advice to use as few microphones as possible is impractical to follow here; each participant needs a mike. If you ask two panelists to share one mike, each would have to move toward it when speaking and back when not. This could be disconcerting to the panelists and distracting to the viewing audience.

When you use individual microphones on desk stands, check to make sure that the following are true.

1. The mikes look good.
2. The mikes are small so they do not take up too much of the picture or block any faces.
3. The angle and height of each mike are relatively uniform.
4. The mike points in the direction to which the participants speak (see **6-39**).

In panel or talk programs, several participants are sometimes seated around a large table. Desk mikes would create a clutter, and although

6-39 *If several desk mikes are lined a row, they should be at approximately the same height and faced in the direction to which the participants are speaking. The arrangement is good looking, and the sound pickup is uniform.*

6-40 *Using boom microphones instead of individual mikes to cover a round-table discussion reduces phasing problems, keeps the table clear for papers and other materials, and keeps rustling and table-bumping sounds to a minimum.*

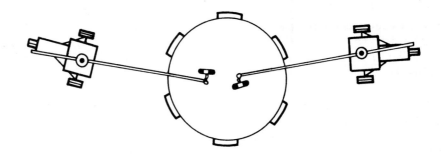

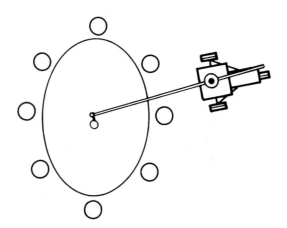

6-41 *Using an omnidirectional microphone in this situation would place the speakers at both ends of the table off-mike compared with the two speakers at the center of the table.*

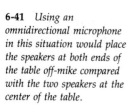

lavaliers are a possibility, the danger of phase problems due to the positioning of the participants may preclude their use.

One approach is to use two booms, one to cover the left side of the table and the other to cover the right (see **6-40**). Try to use cardioid microphones rather than the typical hypercardioid boom mikes because the cardioid's wider acceptance pattern and usually better rear rejection ensure more uniform sound pickup. Another advantage of the cardioid mike's wider pickup pattern in this situation is that if the boom operator is late in changing from one speaker to another, or if a few participants speak at once, there is a better chance of not losing the sound. If the mike-to-source distance is more than 3 to 4 feet, however, you need the hypercardioid boom mike.

Although it may seem to be a likely alternative, do not use an omnidirectional microphone suspended over the center of the table. It cannot discriminate against unwanted sounds or compensate for different spatial distances between the speakers and the mike (see **6-41**).

Miking the Host, Moderator, or Special Guest In panel and talk shows, the host, moderator, or special guest usually sits apart from the other participants since he or she conducts the program or is the star. Since this person sits separately at a desk or in an open set, there are three miking possibilities: lavalier, boom, or desk stand. The one to use depends on the set and how animated the individual is.

If the set is small and the individual does not move a great deal, either a lavalier or a desk mike will work. If the host is active, however, which is likely to be the case in entertainment-type talk shows, the boom is probably the best bet. There are several miking techniques used in panel and talk programs (see **6-42a, b**).

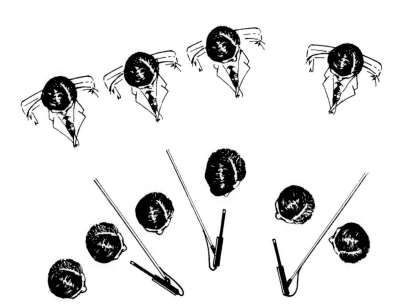

6-42a *In a talk show that involves only a few people who are stationary, lavaliers are probably the most convenient microphones to use.*

6-42b *In a talk show that involves several people who may move around the set, booms are probably most convenient to use. The host in this arrangement could wear a lavalier; but if everyone did, the mike cords could get in the way.*

Miking the Audience   Some talk shows take place before an audience whose reactions are integral to the program's excitement. Since audience sound is also critical to game shows, we discuss this important aspect of microphone technique in the next section.

Television: Active In-Studio Productions

GAME SHOWS   In terms of microphone technique, television game shows appear to present demands similar to TV panel and talk programs. The productions call for miking a group(s) of people sitting in a row or opposite one another, conversing with the principal performer or guest. But further comparison ends here because in game shows, (1) the host is usually not stationary but moves about the set interacting with the participants, (2) verbal response is less predictable and often overlapping, and (3) the sets are wider. Therefore, the usual concerns about how many mikes to use and whether they should be in or out of the picture are irrelevant. To pick up all the sound, each participant has to have a mike; there is too much verbal interplay over too much distance to cover with booms. Several different sets and mike techniques are used on game shows (see **6-43a, b**).

In miking game shows, the participants are miked with unobtrusive unidirectional microphones that have built-in pop filters or shock mounts. The master of ceremonies (M.C.) uses an omnidirectional mike, either hand-held or a lavalier.

By now the reasons for using unidirectional mikes should be clear. They pick up the sound source they are aimed at and little else, and they reduce overall ambient noise levels. Since the M.C. walks around with an omnidirectional mike, the chance of phase problems is reduced, and with loudspeakers in the studio, feedback is reduced as well. The unidirectional mikes are mounted on small, flexible, gooseneck stands for easy adjustment to the height of each participant.

An omnidirectional mike is suitable for the M.C. because it allows more flexibility in varying the mouth-to-source distance without appreciably affecting the levels of loudness; unidirectional mikes are more likely to reflect changes in loudness. Also, the M.C. can hold the mike comfortably in a position perpendicular to his or her mouth and still be on-mike; unidirectional mikes must be held at a less comfortable angle in front of the mouth if a performer is to be on-mike, which could also block part of the face. Omnidirectional mikes are less susceptible to breathing sounds, to wind sound if they are whisked through the air, and to handling sounds; and omnidirectional mikes are not subject to proximity effect.

Many M.C.'s use hand-held mikes because lavaliers inhibit their mobility, but hand-held mikes make it more difficult for the M.C. to hold question cards and other program paraphernalia. Using a lavalier with a wireless microphone system solves both problems.

P.90-91

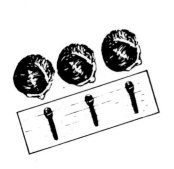

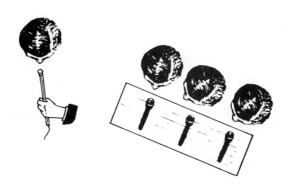

6-43a *Here each contestant has a directional desk microphone. Should a contestant stand up and walk to the host, the two can share the host's mike, which is usually a "wand" microphone—a lavalier mounted on an extension tube. If contestants remain stationary, the host can also use a lavalier clipped on, plugged in or wireless. In any case, the host is free to move around the set.*

6-43b *In this unique arrangement, guests who sit in the cubicles are miked with directional microphones. Since the cubicles are enclosed, a directional loudspeaker is mounted in the upper right-hand corner of each so the guests can hear each other, the contestants, the host, and the audience. To prevent feedback the microphones have extremely good rear rejection and the loudspeakers are mounted behind the mikes. The contestants have directional mikes; the host has a lavalier or hand-held mike. (The loudspeakers are not visible to the audience.)*

Sometimes sound coming from the audience sitting too close to the set or from the musical accompaniment is too loud. In these instances, the M.C. should either hold the omnidirectional mike closer to his or her mouth or use a unidirectional microphone.

Miking the Audience The audience is as much a part of game shows (and some talk shows) as the stars and contestants. Their applause, laughter, and other reactions are critical to a program's spontaneity and excitement. If audience response is to be part of the program, however, the audience must hear what is happening on stage and the home viewers must hear the audience. This requires both mounting loudspeakers near the audience so they can hear the program audio and miking the audience so the people at home can hear them. If microphones and loudspeakers are in the same vicinity, you must be

Know where speakers are in relation to the audience?

6-44 *Typical microphone-loudspeaker arrangement allows the audience to hear the program sound and the audience sound to be picked up. Placing the mikes in front of and with their dead sides facing the loudspeakers reduces the chance of feedback. Loudspeakers should be directional and played at moderate levels.*

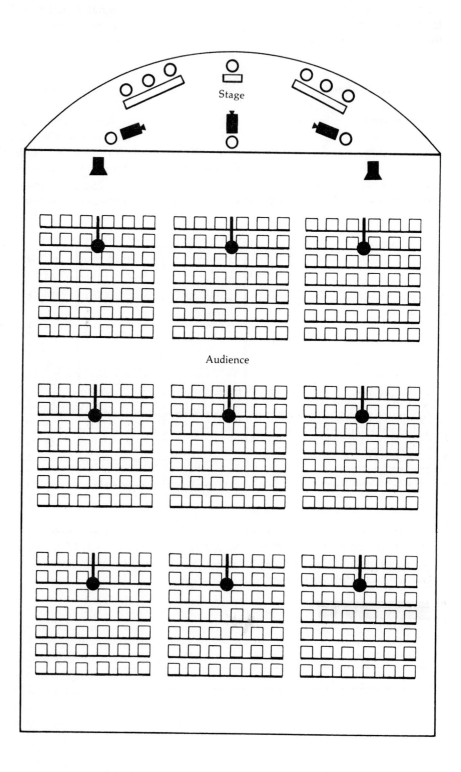

careful of feedback—that high-pitched howl from a signal rapidly feeding from a mike to a loudspeaker, around and around. To avoid feedback, place the dead side of a directional microphone facing the live side of a loudspeaker (see **6-44**). If the loudspeaker is too loud, however, this technique will not prevent feedback or sound coloration. Therefore, low-level public address (P.A.) loudspeakers are often used for studio audiences instead of the familiar high-fidelity loudspeakers.

The studio audience should sound relatively close and uniform so the viewer feels part of the action, and no single voice or group of similar sounding voices (that is, high-pitched cackle, children, men, etc.) should predominate. One way to achieve these ends is to mount unidirectional microphones several feet above the audience and distribute the mikes equally throughout the studio (see **6-45**). Sound designers who prefer a warm-sounding audience sound should use ribbon mikes.

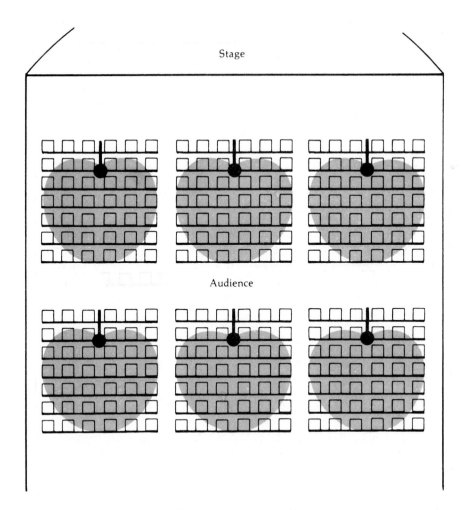

6-45 *Audience microphones distributed throughout the studio to ensure uniform sound pickup.*

Milking the Audience Audiences usually react in two ways, by laughing and applauding. The sound intensity of these reactions is different, so you have to ride the gain on the audience level. Since applause is louder than laughter, the guideline is to decrease the loudness level of the applause and increase the level of the laughter when they occur at the same time. If laughter occurs separately, the level should be increased. If this is done skillfully, it can heighten the infectiousness of the laughter, thus adding to the impact of a funny line or joke. This is known as **milking the audience.**

DRAMA The challenge in miking television drama (including situation comedy), as it is in radio drama, is to establish an aural environment and to maintain aural perspective among the actors, the setting, and their position in it. In radio, you accomplish this by positioning actors at various distances from a stationary microphone without regard for appearance. But in TV, seeing the actors in a setting is fundamental to creating dramatic illusion; a mike in the picture would destroy that illusion. The performers are also in motion much of the time, so a mike has to be mobile and be able to pick up sound at long range. Since the one microphone that can satisfy these needs is the boom, mike selection is just about predetermined in TV drama.

Blocking The important miking decisions in television drama are logistical. They are to (1) plot the best microphone positions and angles for each scene in a production to ensure optimal aural balance; (2) keep the boom out of the lighting pattern so its shadow does not fall across the set; (3) make sure that the boom does not get in the way of the actors; (4) make sure that the boom can move freely; and (5) if an audience is present, try to keep cameras and boom out of their sight line as much as possible. (Studios do have large TV screens, but it is to the program's advantage for an audience to feel that they are part of a live event, especially with comedy.)

In drama, miking decisions are made in the preproduction planning stages when you **block** the program—work out the movements of actors, cameras, and sound boom(s). Blocking begins with a **floor plan**—a diagram, drawn to scale, showing where scenery, cameras, microphones, and actors will be positioned.

One boom microphone can usually handle the action on a set providing the actors are not more than 6 to 10 feet from the mike when they speak (see **6-46**). If a set is large and performers interact across greater distances, or if there is too much action for one boom to cover, two booms and sometimes hidden or hanging mikes are used (see **6-47**).

It is also necessary to think about the boom mount when you block. It is large, bulky, and difficult to move quickly over extended distances, especially when cameras, cables, and set furniture are in the way. It is easier to leave the boom mount in place and swing, extend, or retract the boom arm to cover the action (see **6-48**).

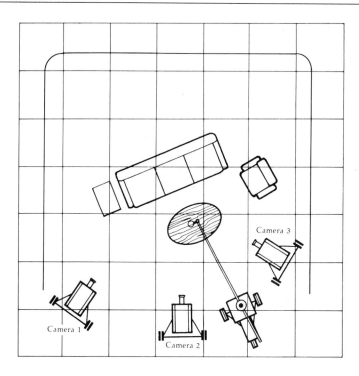

6-46 *Floor plan (not to scale) showing boom and camera placement to cover action in a small set.*

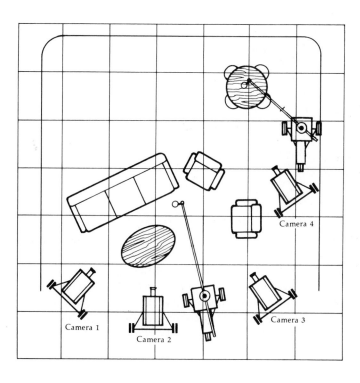

6-47 *Floor plan (not to scale) showing boom and camera placement to cover action in a large set.*

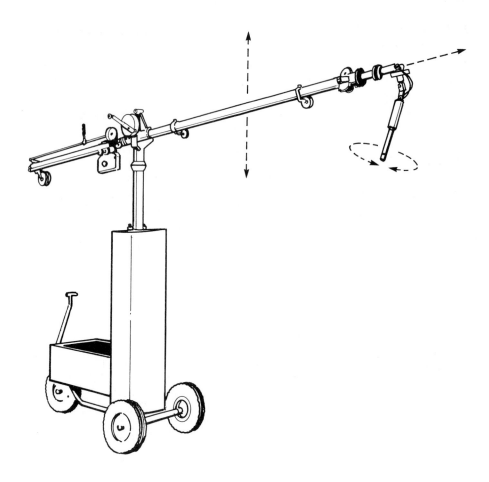

6-48 *On most booms used in TV and film, the boom arm extends and retracts, moves up and down, and side to side, and the microphone mount swivels 360 degrees.*

One thing a floor plan does not show is how to keep the microphone out of the picture. In TV and film, there are basically five shots: long shot (LS), medium long shot (MLS), medium shot (MS), medium close-up (MCU), and close-up (CU) (see **6-49**). Unless you are careful, a boom mike positioned so that it is out of the picture in a close-up could show up in a longer shot (see **6-50a, b**). Because shots change so quickly, planning and good boom operation are very important. Here are three suggestions.

1. Position the boom toward the front of the set, not to the side. From the side it is difficult to judge the microphone's height in relation to the cameras, since they are usually positioned in an arc around the front of the set. Also, placing a boom at the side limits its reach into the playing area; sets often have walls that are at 90-degree angles and it is difficult to get around them.

2. Frame each shot to determine how close you can bring the microphone to the performer without the mike showing up in the picture.

3. Use earphones and feed the program sound to one ear and the director's cues to the other ear. This makes it easier to become familiar with the actors' lines and the shot changes, which facilitates quick and precise mike movement from one actor and height to another. Earphones also make it possible to maintain proper sound balance.

Perspective The challenge in operating a boom is to maintain aural perspective while keeping the boom mike out of the picture and the actors in the pickup pattern at the same time. To create a realistic setting, sound and picture must work together; the aural and visual perspectives should match. If you see two actors talking in the same plane, you should hear them at relatively the same loudness; if you see one actor close up talking to another actor farther away, the actor who is closer should sound louder.

Volume should be relative to distance (zooming)

6-49 *Five basic fields of view in visual composition.*

Long Shot (LS)

Medium Long Shot (MLS)

Medium Shot (MS)

Medium Close-up (MCU)

Close-up (CU)

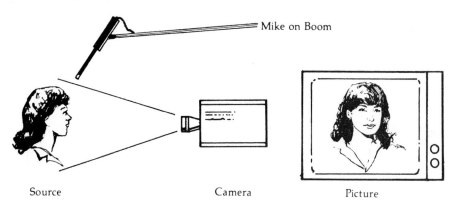

Mike on Boom

Source   Camera   Picture

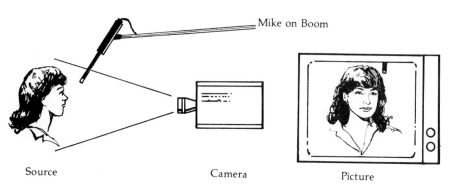

Mike on Boom

Source   Camera   Picture

6-50 *(Top) The mike-to-source distance has been adjusted so the boom does not show in the picture. (Below) If the shot changes to a wider angle and the mike-to-source distance is not increased, the microphone will show up in the picture.*

*Person closer
Should sound
louder*

Actors in the Same Plane   The easiest way to pick up actors talking in the same plane, and to maintain their aural relationship, is to position the microphone equidistant between them and close enough so they are on-mike (see **6-51a**). If one actor walks a short distance away from the group, the blocking will have determined how far the boom can follow and still keep the actor on-mike yet be close enough to get back in time to cover the others (see **6-51b**).

Actors in Different Planes   During a scene, it is typical for shots to change from, say, a MS of a group with actor 1 talking, to a close-up of actor 1, to a close-up of actor 2 responding, to another MS of the group, to a close-up of actor 3 talking, and so on. To keep visual and aural perspective consistent, the sound in the MS should not be quite so loud as the sound in the CU. There are a few ways to handle this.

Sometimes the aural changes are taken care of naturally. For example, to keep the boom out of the picture in a medium shot compared with a close-up, it has to be higher and therefore farther from the actors. In a long shot compared with a medium shot, the mike has to be higher and farther still. The aural difference in the mike-to-source distance, reflected by the acoustic change in the loudness level and the ratio of direct to indirect waves, will match the visual difference in the audience-to-source distance.

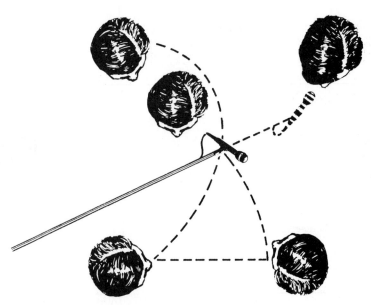

6-51a *If two performers are on the same plane, the easiest way to boom-mike them is to place the microphone equidistant between them and swivel it back and forth*

6-51b *If performers are on different planes and move about in relatively close proximity to the microphone, position the boom so it can reach each person with a minimum of movement.*

Another way to change the aural perspective is to use the pot; increasing loudness brings sound closer, and decreasing it moves sound farther away. This technique is not recommended in studios that have a lot of ambience, however. Although set designers try to plan sets with good acoustics, they can do little about a TV studio that is live. In this case, increasing the level of loudness would also increase the ambience (see Chapter 14).

Regardless of the visual perspective, the audience must hear the actors clearly. As we have said, someone close up should sound louder than someone farther away, but only to a certain extent. An actor in a close-up shot should not sound "on top of the audience," and the audience should not have to strain to hear an actor in a long shot. The mike also has to be close enough to an actor so that it does not pick up too much ambience. You have to "cheat" a bit with mike placement to reduce the unwanted reflections so that the difference in loudness levels is obvious but not disconcerting.

Suppose a scene calls for two actors to talk across a room, front to back. First, the distance between them has to be within the microphone's range. Second, the mike should be between them but closer to the actor in the foreground (see **6-52**). Third, if further changes in the loudness level are necessary, you can increase the range of the boom arm to get the mike closer, change the actors' positions, or, if the acoustics allow it, ride the gain. If the actors are too far apart to cover with one boom, use two (see **6-53**). Remember, within the

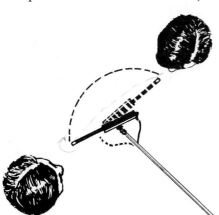

6-52 *If two performers are on different planes and close enough to be covered by one boom, the microphone should be placed between the performers, but mike-to-source distance should reflect viewer-to-source distance. In other words, the person who is closer should be louder.*

6-53 *If two performers are on different planes and too far apart to be covered by one boom, two booms should be used. To compensate for the difference in the performers' viewer-to-source distances, the fader should be used to establish loudness levels and set perspective.*

same scene and locale, differences in levels of loudness should be apparent but not marked. Do not worry about the discrepancy between the visual and aural perspectives. If the audio sounds realistic enough, the psychological effect of the picture's perspective should make up for the difference between the two.

Hidden Microphones **Hidden microphones** are sometimes used in TV (and film) drama when an actor is stationary for a period of time or when it is difficult to get a boom into an area. Suppose the performer at the rear of the set in **6-53** does not have to move much. Instead of going to the trouble of using a boom, you can hide a unidirectional microphone inside a prop that is close to the actor, taking care not to obstruct the mike's live side (see **6-54**). Make sure, however, that the frequency response of the hidden mike is similar to that of the other mike(s) being used, or else the aural differences could be distracting. The mike levels should be balanced to maintain the proper perspective.

Hanging Microphones **Hanging microphones** help in situations where using the boom is difficult or unnecessary. If two people are standing at a

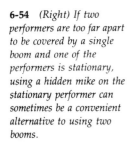

6-54 *(Right) If two performers are too far apart to be covered by a single boom and one of the performers is stationary, using a hidden mike on the stationary performer can sometimes be a convenient alternative to using two booms.*

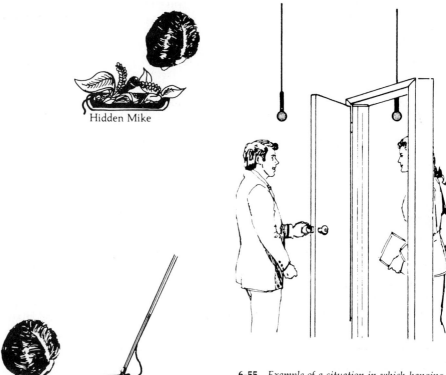

Hidden Mike

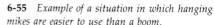

6-55 *Example of a situation in which hanging mikes are easier to use than a boom.*

doorway talking, the door frame may make it hard to cover the shot with a boom. By mounting hanging mikes, you can pick up the conversation and maintain loudness levels and perspective at the same time (see **6-55**).

Sometimes a hanging mike is used in active dramatic situations because it is more convenient than the boom. This is not a good idea, however. Although it may be possible to maintain aural perspective as the actors move about the set playing to a fixed mike, this technique severely limits the types of shots you can take. A mike hung near enough to obtain good sound pickup in a close-up shot will be in the picture in a medium shot or a medium long shot. Furthermore, if the mike is omnidirectional, it will pick up too much ambience; if it is unidirectional, the actors will be off-mike if they move more than a few feet from the microphone.

Despite this, some productions are so active that the easiest way to cover the action is to hang a few omnidirectional microphones. The set, however, should be as dead as possible without being oppressive; perspective should not vary greatly; and the mikes have to be far enough apart to avoid phasing, yet close enough to avoid "holes" in the evenness of the pickup. Even so, it is usually necessary to equalize the sound either during production or in post-production.

We said at the beginning of this chapter that it is difficult to be specific about microphone technique since individual tastes and productions vary so much. The key to solving any sound problem is to start with basic principles and, through experimentation, apply those that work best in a given situation. To put it another way: be flexible.

Film

Although film and television productions differ in many ways, they are similar when it comes to miking studio drama. The techniques used in blocking and boom operation apply to both media.

Summary

1. Acoustical phase refers to the time relationship between two (or more) sound waves at a given point in their cycles. Electrical phase refers to the relative momentum of two electric quantities in a circuit. When these waves or quantities are in phase—roughly coincident in time or momentum—their amplitudes are additive. When these waves or quantities are out of phase—not coincident in time or momentum—their amplitudes are reduced.

2. Miking performers for speech usually involves using fixed microphone mounts for static productions, mobile microphone mounts for active productions, and either omni- or unidirectional microphones.

3. Regardless of the microphone mount or the microphone's directional pattern, the mike-to-source angle must be such that the performer is within the microphone's pickup pattern; otherwise, sound quality suffers.

4. The frequency range of the human voice is not wide compared with that of other instruments. Due to its harmonic richness, however, its timbre changes as loudness and intensity change, thus making microphone selection and placement challenging.

5. Mike-to-source distance creates aural space and perspective: the closer the mike-to-source distance, the smaller the space and the more intimate the sound; the farther the mike-to-source distance, the larger the space and the less intimate the sound.

6. In monaural sound, which is one-dimensional, microphone placement should create the proper front-to-back perspective. In an interview or panel program, the participants should sound like they are coming from the front of the space. If one microphone is used, the weaker voices should be closer to the mike and the stronger voices farther away if all are to sound like they are coming from the same place at the front of the monaural space. If individual microphones are used, which is the preferred technique, the levels of loudness for the participants must be similar if the sound is to seem like it is coming from the front of the monaural space.

7. In drama, if one performer is calling to another and they are supposed to be some distance apart, the one who is supposed to be closer should sound like he is coming from the front of the aural space and the one who is farther away should sound like he is coming from the rear of the aural space.

8. In stereo sound, which is two-dimensional, microphone placement should create the proper front-to-rear and side-to-side perspective. Two microphone heads are required for stereo, and they should be at roughly a 90-degree angle for drama. If they are at too wide an angle, the stereo perspective will be too wide; if they are at too narrow an angle, the stereo perspective will be too narrow.

9. In radio, any microphone can be placed anywhere without regard for appearance. In television, if a microphone is in the picture, it must be good looking and positioned so that it does not obscure the performer's face. If it is not in the picture, it must be mounted close enough to the performer so the sound is on-mike.

10. A boom is usually used when mikes must be out of the picture. Often one boom mike must cover more than one performer. To provide adequate sound pickup, the boom operator must anticipate when one performer is about to stop talking and another to start in order to move the boom at the right time to the right place.

11. If an audience is present, it must be miked to achieve an overall sound blend and prevent one voice or group of voices from predominating.

12. In TV drama, it is essential to block the action to ensure that the microphone(s) can pick up all the sound from a relatively close mike-to-source distance. A microphone should be able to move freely with the action without getting in the way of either the performers or the cameras.

13. Successful selection and placement of microphones involve applying basic guidelines, using your "ear," and being willing to experiment.

Miking Music

Two methods:
① stereo
② Multi-mike

When the sound designer is trying to capture the nuances of sound—timbre, tonal balance, blend, and so on—miking live music is perhaps the most demanding challenge. The ways to shape the sound of music are as infinite and individual as music itself. Since there can be no firm rules about microphone technique, and artistry in mike technique never compensates for lack of artistry in musicianship, you must trust your creative judgment and your ear.

Basic Techniques of Miking Music

Choosing technique: (4 factors)
① Environment to be created
② Complexity of music/arrangement
③ Type of music
④ All musicians recording at same time or not?

Two basic techniques of miking live music are: *stereo miking*—using two microphones (or capsules) to record an entire ensemble—and *multiple miking*—using one microphone to record each sound source or group of sound sources in an ensemble. The technique you choose depends on several factors: the spatial environment you wish to create, the complexity of the music and arrangement, the type of music, and whether all the musicians record at the same time.

Stereo Miking

Techniques:
① focal point of sound pickup
② excellent acoustics

Stereo miking attempts to reproduce the aural experience that audiences receive in live concerts, whether the recording is made in a studio or in a concert hall. There are different techniques of stereo miking, but they all assume two things. (1) The mikes should be at the focal point of the sound pickup—positioned to hear the sound as you would if you were in the center of the audience or if you were the conductor. (2) The acoustics have to be excellent—the optimal proportion of direct to indirect sound relative to the music being played.

COINCIDENT MICROPHONES   The coincident or crossed pair, also known as **X-Y miking,** was discussed in Chapter 6. Some points are worth repeating, however, since they also apply to music recording.

The coincident pair should be cardioid microphones of the same make and model to ensure similar response from all directions. They should be at an angle, usually 90 degrees, so the pickup of sounds in the center is louder than the pickup to the left and right of center (see **7-1**). This is analogous to the aural balance perceived by a person sitting in the center of an audience. Too narrow an angle reduces the breadth of the stereo field, compressing the spatial dimension of the ensemble (see **7-2**); too wide an angle creates a "hole in the middle" of the stereo image, with sounds on the left and right disproportionately stronger than those in the center (see **7-3**). The wider the angle, the greater is the hole in the middle.

In stereo miking music, there are two other guidelines. (1) The angle of the microphones may be widened to 135 degrees, depending on the breadth of the ensemble. (2) The closer a coincident pair is to an ensemble, the wider is the stereo image.

Another approach to coincident miking uses bidirectional microphones instead of cardioids. The results are somewhat like binaural sound but without the degree of spaciousness, the sound localization problem, or the need for earphones during playback.

When you cross the bidirectional mikes, point one to the left and one to the right at roughly a 90-degree angle, then route one mike to the left loudspeaker and the other to the right loudspeaker. The sound quality is spacious, and there is an excellent sense of an ensemble's breadth (see **7-4**).

[handwritten margin notes: Coincident = XY (Cardioids) crossed pair (usually 90°); Guides for stereo ① Angle up to 135 ② closer = wider; Also can use bidirectional instead of cardioid]

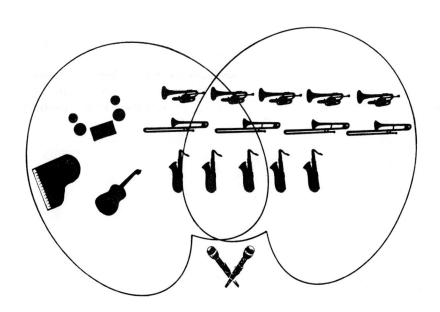

7-1 *Crossed directional microphones set at an optimal angle in relation to the breadth of the sound source reproduce a balanced stereo field—a center that is louder than the sides and a left-to-right spread that complements the ensemble's dimension. (The space between loudspeakers also affects breadth in stereo reproduction.)*

7-2 *If directional microphones are crossed at too narrow an angle, the sound will seem compressed toward the center and lack left-to-right dimension.*

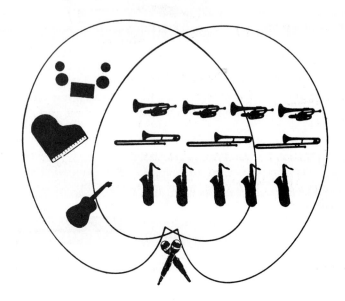

7-3 *Directional microphones positioned at too wide an angle reproduce a stereo image with the sound level greater at the sides than in the center. If the microphone angle is very wide, the sound level in the center of the stereo field will be so low that it creates what seems like a "hole in the middle."*

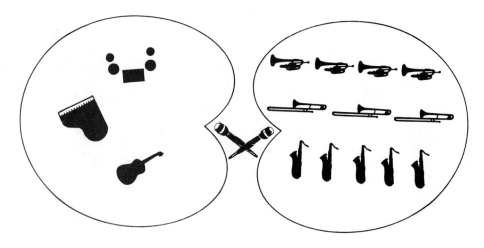

SPACED MICROPHONES   Another way of positioning two mikes for stereo recording is to space them (see **7-5**). The distance between the mikes depends on the size of the ensemble and the size of the room. For a singer, a distance of 6 inches may be sufficient; however, a symphony orchestra may need a spread of several feet. The advantage of the spaced pair over the coincident pair is that it results in a more spacious sound. The disadvantage is that if the distance between the mikes is not correct, phasing problems may result.

M-S MIKING   Still another variation of coincident miking is the **M-S** (middle-side) technique. This requires one cardioid and one bidirectional mike arranged so that the cardioid pickup pattern faces the sound source and the figure-8 pattern faces sideways, picking up the extreme left and right sounds (see **7-6**). The two advantages of the M-S technique are: (1) the stereo image is usually quite spacious because the bidirectional microphone picks up many indirect reflections, and (2) the cardioid pickup alone may be used for monaural reproduction. A disadvantage of the M-S approach is that it requires a technician to wire the microphones into a matrix system that combines their outputs (adding and subtracting) to reproduce the stereo field (see **7-7**).

BINAURAL SOUND   As we said in Chapter 6, binaural sound is an extraordinary sonic experience because it comes closest to reproducing sound as humans hear it. Since listening to binaural sound requires earphones and it is

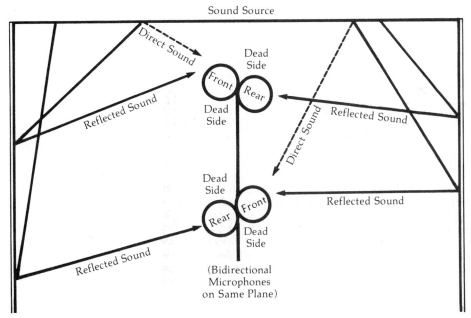

7-4   *Crossed bidirectional microphones reproduce a spacious stereo image due to the significantly greater ratio of indirect to direct sound received and the left-to-right separation created by the facings of the microphones' dead sides.*

7-5 *In spacing directional microphones for stereo pickup, the distance between them is usually dependent on the breadth of the ensemble.*

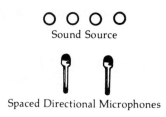

Sound Source

Spaced Directional Microphones

a

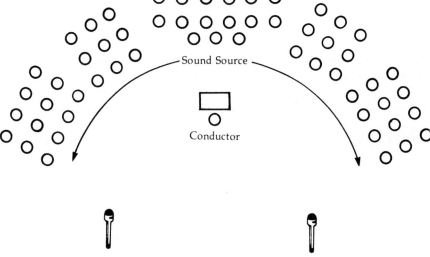

Sound Source

Conductor

Spaced Directional Microphones

b

7-6 *(Below) The M-S microphone technique uses a directional mike aimed at the sound source to pick up mainly the direct sound, and a bidirectional mike aimed at the sides to pick up the indirect reflections.*

Sound Source

Cardioid—Middle
Microphone

Bidirectional—Side
Microphone

(Microphones Are on
the Same Plane)

often difficult to tell from which direction the sounds are coming, however, binaural recording is still mainly experimental.

This may be changing. Commercial recordings have been made that use other microphones in addition to the artificial head. The sound, although not truly binaural, has more breadth and depth than straight stereo and does not require earphones for listening. Furthermore, researchers have been working on ways to reproduce sound binaurally without the need for earphones and with a more realistic sense of directionality.

To record music binaurally, position the artificial head with its microphones where you want the listener to be in relation to the music—in the so-called stereo seat. If possible, put the head on top of a seated mannequin

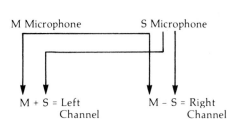

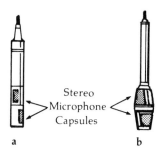

7-7 (Far left) Generalized diagram of the wiring in the M-S microphone matrix.

7-8 (Left) The capsules in **a** are set for a wide stereo pickup; the capsules in **b** are set for a narrow stereo pickup.

rather than on a table or chair, so the reflections of the sound waves are more realistic.

STEREO MICROPHONE Using the stereo microphone is the obvious and perhaps easiest stereo miking technique. It requires centering the microphone in the studio or hall, positioning it far enough back and high enough to pick up the optimal proportion of direct to indirect sound, and adjusting the angle of the capsules to create the desired stereo field. The angle of the capsules relative to the size of the ensemble and room will most likely determine placement (see **7-8**). Stereo mikes are not used often because they are very expensive.

Multimicrophone Technique

Despite the advantages of stereo miking, not much of today's music is recorded that way. Many recordists are quite willing to sacrifice the more realistic sense of sonic space for greater control in recording the nuances of each musical element. This means using the **multimicrophone technique**—putting a mike on practically each instrument or group of instruments in an ensemble. Reverberation, spatial positioning, and blend—all natural functions of stereo miking—are lost in multimicrophone recording and must be added artificially in the postrecording session called the **mixdown**. To understand the implications of the multimicrophone technique, let's set up and mike a pop music recording session using a group consisting of drums, electric bass guitar, acoustic lead guitar, piano, and vocal.

SETTING UP The first thing to do in a recording session is to position the musicians. Assume this production calls for miking each instrument and recording them all at once. This requires that the musicians be far enough apart to avoid phase problems and reduce leakage—picking up sounds from one instrument on another instrument's microphone. Using the three-to-one rule should take care of most acoustic phase problems. For reducing leakage: (1)

7-9 *Musicians isolated from each other to prevent sound from one instrument leaking into the microphone of another instrument, yet still be able to maintain visual contact. It is possible, in this arrangement, that the acoustic guitar sound will leak into the piano mikes, and vice versa. Supercardioid mikes on both instruments—to reject sound from the sides and rear, the piano lid—blocking sound coming from the front guitar baffle, and the guitarist's body—blocking the piano sound coming from the back of the studio, should minimize leakage.*

use unidirectional microphones and place them so their dead sides are pointed to the other instruments; (2) use acoustic baffles to separate the instruments; and (3) use the isolation booth(s) that most recording studios have for instruments with sound levels that are very high (for example, drums and amplifiers) and for sound sources that must be recorded with absolutely no leakage (vocals). For one way to arrange the group, see **7-9**. Although positioning the musicians to avoid phasing and leakage is important, they should be able to see each other for cueing and other visual communication; they usually play better that way, too.

(Another technique used to eliminate leakage is **overdubbing**—recording each instrument at a different time on a different tape track. Overdubbing is discussed in Chapter 14.)

MIKING DRUMS Perhaps no other instrument provides as many possibilities for microphone combinations, and therefore as much challenge, as the drums. Several different components make up a drum set—at least a bass drum, floor tom-tom, medium tom-tom, snare drum, hi hat cymbal, and two

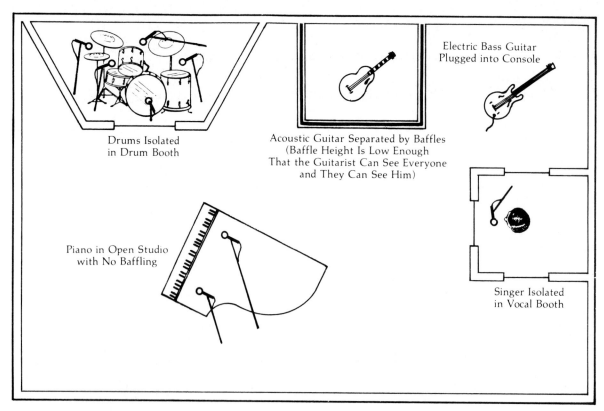

Drums Isolated
in Drum Booth

Acoustic Guitar Separated by Baffles
(Baffle Height Is Low Enough
That the Guitarist Can See Everyone
and They Can See Him)

Electric Bass Guitar
Plugged into Console

Piano in Open Studio
with No Baffling

Singer Isolated
in Vocal Booth

Overhead Cymbals

Medium Tom-Tom

Hi Hat
Cymbal

Snare Drum

Floor Tom-Tom

Bass (Kick) Drum

7-10   *Typical drum set.*

overhead cymbals (see **7-10**). They must be miked to sound good individually and blend as a unit.

There are many ways to mike drums (see **7-11** to **7-16**). The approach you
take will depend on (1) how much sound control you want, and (2) the type of
music you are recording. Explaining how to deal with sound control is relatively easy: the more components you want to regulate, the more mikes you
use. Achieving a particular drum sound for a certain type of music involves
many variables and is more difficult to explain.

Generally, in rock and roll and contemporary music, producers like a
tight drum sound for added punch and attack. Since this usually requires
complete control of the drum sound, they tend to use several microphones for
the drums. In jazz, however, many styles are loose and open; hence, producers are more likely to use fewer drum mikes—two or three, rarely more
than four—to achieve an airier sound.

Another factor that affects the drum sound is *tuning*—adjusting each
drum skin for pitch and liveness. The tighter the skin, the higher is its pitch
and tighter its sound. It is worthwhile to remember, however, that a good

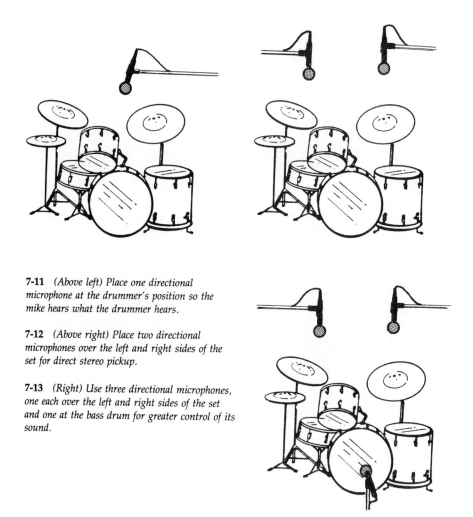

7-11 *(Above left) Place one directional microphone at the drummer's position so the mike hears what the drummer hears.*

7-12 *(Above right) Place two directional microphones over the left and right sides of the set for direct stereo pickup.*

7-13 *(Right) Use three directional microphones, one each over the left and right sides of the set and one at the bass drum for greater control of its sound.*

drum sound begins with the musicianship of the drummer and the quality of the drum set.

To treat the subject of miking the drums in more detail, let's assume our group is recording a contemporary pop tune and the preference is to mike each instrument in the set.

MIKING THE BASS DRUM   The bass drum (also called the *kick drum*) is the foundation of the drum set because it provides the bottom sound that, along with the bass guitar, supports the other musical elements. Since it produces high levels of sound pressure and steep transients, most producers mike the bass drum with a moving-coil microphone to avoid overload and distortion. They also put padding around the inside of the drum to reduce unwanted vibrations and rattle (see **7-17**).

As for mike placement, the common technique is to cut a hole in the front skin of the drum or remove it entirely and place the mike inside. This usually gives the sound of the bass drum more punch. Pointing the mike perpendicular to the back drum skin produces a fuller sound (see **7-18a**), and pointing it toward the side of the drum picks up more of the instrument's overtones (see **7-18b**).

When using the multiple miking technique on the drums, the mikes should be directional to increase sound separation and reduce leakage from

7-14 (Above left) Use four directional microphones, three as suggested in **7-13** and the fourth either on the snare drum or between the snare and the hi hat cymbal. This gives greater control of the snare and the hi hat.

7-15 (Above right) Use five directional microphones, four as suggested in **7-14** and the fifth between the two tom-toms for added control of the tom-toms.

7-16 (Left) Keep the two directional microphones for the overhead cymbals and put a separate directional mike on each of the other components.

7-17 *Foam rubber pads are placed in a bass drum to reduce vibration and rattle.*

7-18a *(Right) A directional microphone pointed at the drum skin produces a fuller sound.*

7-18b *(Far right) A microphone pointed to the side of the drum produces more of the drum's overtones.*

the rest of the drum kit. Nevertheless, the proximity of the drum mikes makes some leakage and signal phasing inevitable.

MIKING TOM-TOMS Tom-toms come in a variety of sizes and pitches. Typical drum sets have two toms: the low-pitched, fuller-sounding floor tom and the higher-pitched, sharper-sounding medium tom (see **7-19**).

Although toms produce transients (all drums do), they are not so strong as those the bass drum produces; therefore, you can mike them with moving-coil, condenser, or the newer ribbon mikes. Placement, as always, depends on the sound you want. Generally, the mike is placed from 1 to 10 inches above the tom and is aimed at the center of the skin. It is usually mounted just over the edge of the rim to avoid interfering with the drummer's sticks (see **7-20**).

The mike-to-source distance usually depends on the low-frequency content of the drum sound itself. If it has little low-frequency content, place a unidirectional mike that is susceptible to the proximity effect close to the drum skin to boost the lower frequencies.

MIKING THE SNARE DRUM Of all the components in a drum set, the snare usually presents the biggest problem in miking. Most producers prefer a crisp snare drum sound. Miking the snare drum too close tends to produce a lifeless sound, whereas miking it too far away tends to pick up annoying overtones, ringing, and leakage from the other drums.

7-19 *(Far left) Medium tom-tom (left) and floor tom-tom (right).*

7-20 *(Left) Miking a floor tom.*

Another problem is that the snare drum sometimes sounds dull and thuddy, more in the range of a tom-tom. In this instance, the problem is most likely the drum itself. Two ways to add crispness to the sound are to (1) use a mike with an extended high-frequency response, and (2) equalize it at the console. A third alternative, and perhaps the best, is to replace the drum.

Moving-coil or condenser microphones work well on the snare drum; the moving-coil mike tends to give it a harder edge, and the condenser mike tends to make it sound richer or crisper. To find the optimal mike position, begin at a point 6 to 10 inches from the drum skin and aim the mike so its pickup pattern is split between the skin and the side of the drum (see **7-21**). This picks up the sounds of the snares and the stick hitting the skin. To get the slight delay of the snares' snap, use two mikes: one over and one under the drum (see **7-22**).

MIKING THE HI HAT CYMBAL The hi hat cymbal produces two sounds: a clap and a shimmer. Depending on how important these accents are to the music, the hi hat either shares the snare drum's mike or has a microphone of its own. If it shares, place the mike between the hi hat and the snare and adjust the sound balance through placement of the mike (see **7-23**). The hi hat, like the snare, can take either a moving-coil or a condenser microphone.

If the hi hat has a separate mike, the two most common positions for it are over the center stem, about 4 to 6 inches above it, with the mike pointing straight down (see **7-24**), and off the edge (see **7-25**). Miking too close off the

7-21 *(Right) Miking a snare drum.*

7-22 *(Far right) Miking a snare drum over and under.*

7-23 *Miking the hi hat cymbal and the snare drum.*

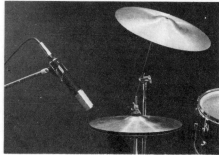

7-24 *(Far left) Miking over the hi hat cymbal.*

7-25 *(Left) Miking at the edge of the hi hat cymbal.*

center produces ringing, and miking off the edge may pick up the rush of air produced each time the two cymbals clap together (see **7-26**).

MIKING OVERHEAD CYMBALS Two types of overhead cymbals are the ride, which produces ring and shimmer, and the crash, which has a splashy sound. In miking either cymbal, the definition of the characteristic sounds must be preserved. To this end, condensers usually work best; and for stereo pickup, they should be either in a coincident pair or spaced (see **7-27**).

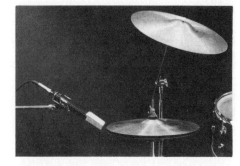

7-26 *A microphone aimed at the point where the cymbals clap may pick up the rush of air as they come together.*

7-27 *A crossed pair (right) and a spaced pair (far right) of directional microphones to pick up the sound of the overhead cymbals and blend the sound of the drum set.*

The overhead microphones should also blend the sounds of the entire drum set. They should be at least a few feet above the cymbals. If they are too close to the cymbals, the drum blend will be poor and the cymbals may produce an annoying gonging sound.

Beware of cheap cymbals, which you can usually spot by their tinny ring. If you cannot replace them, which is recommended, try putting a thin cloth pad or masking tape on the cymbal to reduce its tinniness. This technique is also useful for reducing ring and tinny sounds on other drums (see **7-28**).

7-28 (Far left) Pad on the skin of a snare drum to reduce vibrations.

7-29 (Left) A transformer connected from the electric guitar to the console to match their impedances.

MIKING THE ELECTRIC BASS GUITAR Basically, two techniques are used to re-cord an electric bass guitar (or any electric instrument): (1) plugging it into an amplifier and placing a mike in front of the amp's loudspeaker, and (2) **direct insertion** (D.I.)—plugging the guitar directly into the mike input on the con-sole. With direct insertion, you need a transformer (see **5-1**) connecting the guitar to the console to match their impedances (see **7-29**).

Although this chapter deals with microphone technique, it is important to know the differences between miking an amp and going direct. Deciding which method to use is a matter of taste, practicality, and convenience.

Miking an Amplifier Loudspeaker

Advantages	Disadvantages
Adds interaction of room acoustics to sound	Could leak into other mikes due to its loudness or long bass waves
Creates more potential for different sound textures and louder sound pres-sure levels	Could be noisy due to electric problems with amp

Direct Insertion

Advantages	Disadvantages
Has a cleaner sound	Has a drier sound—no indirect reflec-tions
Allows more sound control	
Eliminates leakage	Requires a transformer, which adds another electronic device to the sound chain

In miking an amp loudspeaker, the moving-coil type is most often used. It can handle high levels of sound without overloading, and when used for the bass guitar, it is less susceptible to vibration and conductance caused by the instrument's long wavelengths. If sound pressure levels are not loud and mike-to-source distance is not close, a condenser or the newer, more rugged ribbon mikes produce excellent response. Both types of microphone tend to give the bass sound added warmth and resonance.

As for placement, the closer a mike is to an amp loudspeaker, the greater is the ratio of direct to indirect waves and, hence, the tighter the sound. If you aim the microphone directly at, and on an axis with, the amp's loudspeaker cone, the sound will be brighter (see **7-30a**). If the mike is aimed off center to the speaker cone, the sound will be fuller (see **7-30b**).

In their continuing effort to achieve new sounds, some producers record both amp loudspeaker and direct insertion feeds simultaneously. This technique combines the drier, unreverberant sound of direct insertion with the acoustic coloring of the amplified sound.

MIKING THE ACOUSTIC GUITAR The bulwark of today's pop music is the guitar—acoustic and electric, 6 strings and 12 strings; its potential for tone colors is enormous. Many factors affect a guitar's sound: how the instrument is made; a player's technique; what the strings are made of; whether they are plucked with fingers, or metal or plastic picks; and, of course, the microphone and where you put it. The instrument is so flexible that almost any type and model of mike yields a sound that is satisfactory to someone.

Generally, aiming a mike at the center of an acoustic guitar's hole produces the most balanced sound in terms of frequency response (see **7-31**). To get more high- or low-frequency accent, angle the mike either up toward the low strings or down toward the high strings.

The proper mike-to-source distance depends on how tight or open a sound you want. The farther a mike is from an instrument, the more open is the sound. If you do close-mike the guitar, be careful of (1) interfering with the guitarist's movements, and (2) having too much bass response from the proximity effect of some cardioid microphones.

7-30a (Right) Aiming a directional microphone at the loudspeaker produces a brighter sound.

7-30b (Far right) Aiming a directional microphone at an angle to the loudspeaker produces a fuller sound.

7-31 *(Far left) Aiming a microphone at the center of the guitar hole produces a sound with balanced highs, middles, and lows.*

7-32 *(Left) If fret sounds are a problem, placing the dead side of a super- or hypercardioid microphone opposite the guitar's neck reduces their loudness without interfering with the overall frequency response.*

A natural part of the guitar's sound is the screechy, rubbing noises called *fret* sounds caused by the guitarist's fingering. Some guitarists are more heavy-handed than others. This usually brings to a head the problem of whether the fret sounds, which are a natural part of the guitar sound, should be part of the recording. Personal taste is the determining factor. If you do not care for the fret sounds, use a super- or hypercardioid mike placed at a slight angle to the neck of the guitar (see **7-32**). This puts the mike's dead side facing the frets. Make sure the mike's angle is not too severe or else the sound from the guitar will be off-mike.

Another technique is to use a contact microphone mounted either near the bridge or on the body of the instrument. This gives the guitar sound added resonance.

MIKING THE PIANO The piano is another instrument that offers almost unlimited possibilities for sound shaping. Unlike many other instruments, however, the character of the piano sound is dependent on the quality of the piano itself. Mike technique and signal processing cannot change a piano's voicing from dull to bright, from thin to rich, or from sharp to smooth, but they can alter a piano's existing sound. There are several common miking techniques for the piano (see **7-33a, b, c, d**).

MIKING VOCALS Although the human voice has a comparatively limited frequency range, it places a severe test on any microphone. The voice can produce great variations in **timbre**—tone color; **dynamic range**—subtle and extreme changes in loudness; and **plosives** and **sibilants**—annoying popping and hissing sounds.

Timbre In choosing a vocal mike, the most important consideration is the singer's timbre—how edged, velvety, sharp, mellow, or resonant the voice sounds. The microphone should enhance a voice's attractive qualities and

7-33a *Two directional microphones, one pointed at the piano's sounding board mainly to pick up direct sound and another a few feet away facing the raised hood to pick up reflections from the hood, produce a full sound that is also open and, if acoustics are suitable, spacious.*

7-33b *One directional microphone above and facing the high strings and one directional microphone above and facing the low strings, recorded on separate tracks, produce stereo sound with more discrete high and low frequencies.*

7-33c *Positioning microphones just above the hammers adds the "kiss" of hammer and string to the piano sound. In this particular arrangement, a ribbon microphone picks up the low-frequency sounds to enhance their warmth, and a microphone with a transparent aural quality picks up the high-frequency sounds to enhance their clarity.*

7-33d *A microphone positioned in a sound hole (middle) produces a full, close sound.*

minimize the unattractive. For example, if a voice sounds mellow, a ribbon mike may enhance the mellowness, but if a voice sounds low-pitched, the ribbon mike could muddy its quality. If a voice sounds too sharp or edged, the ribbon mike would smooth the sound, but a moving coil or condenser could make the voice sound more cutting. A condenser may add richness to a voice that is soft and has little projection; and a moving-coil type may help to thin out a voice that sounds too full.

Generally, assuming there are no serious problems with tone quality, most producers prefer to use condenser microphones for vocals because they add richness to the sound and they can better handle the complicated pattern of overtones in the human voice.

Dynamic Range   Controlling the dynamic range—the quietest to loudest levels a sound source produces—is another tricky problem. Well-disciplined singers can usually control wide fluctuations in the dynamic range themselves. Many singers, however, cannot; their voices barely move the needle on the VU meter during soft passages and pin it during loud ones. In miking these vocalists, a producer has three alternatives: (1) ride the level, (2) adjust the vocalist's microphone position, or (3) put an electronic limit on the sound and prevent it from going above a preset level (see Chapter 11).

Riding the level works but it requires an engineer's full attention, and this may be difficult considering everything else that goes on in a recording session. Also, less gifted singers may handle dynamic range differently each time they sing, which means that riding the level becomes coping more than aiding.

Limiting the voice electronically controls the dynamic range in the sense that the loudest sounds will not go above a preset level; however, it has no effect on the quiet sounds. Since limiting tends to cut off the very high frequencies, producers prefer to use microphone technique to adjust for irregularities in a vocalist's dynamic range.

One technique is to place the singer at an average distance from the mike relative to the loudest and softest passages sung; the distance depends on the power of the singer's voice and the song. From this average distance, you can direct the singer how close to move to the mike during quiet passages and how far for the loud ones. The success of this technique depends on the vocalist's microphone presence—the ability to manage the song and the movements at the same time.

Breathing, Popping, and Sibilance   The closer to a microphone a performer stands, the greater is the chance of picking up unwanted breathing sounds: popping sounds from p's, b's, and t's, and sibilance from s's. If the singer's vocal projection or the type of music permits, increasing the mike-to-source distance significantly reduces these noises. Windscreens also help, but they tend to reduce the higher frequencies. Other ways to reduce popping and sibilance are to have the singer work slightly across mike but within the pickup pattern, or to position the mike slightly above the singer's mouth (see **7-34**). If leakage is no problem, using an omnidirectional mike permits a closer working distance since it is less susceptible to breathing, popping, and sibilant sounds. The sound will not be intimate, however, since an omnidirectional microphone picks up more indirect sound waves than a directional mike.

7-34 *Positioning the microphone slightly above a performer's mouth is a typical miking technique used to cut down on unwanted popping, sibilants, and breathing sounds.*

MICROPHONE TECHNIQUES FOR OTHER COMMONLY USED INSTRUMENTS Now that you have an idea of how to mike a few selected instruments, see **7-35** to **7-48** for some general guidelines for miking other commonly used instruments or families of instruments.

7-35 *Miking a violin or viola several feet above the instrument, aimed at the strings between the f-holes, tends to produce an open, natural sound.*

7-36 *To produce a scratchy fiddle sound, place the microphone closer to the f-holes but not close enough to interfere with the bowing.*

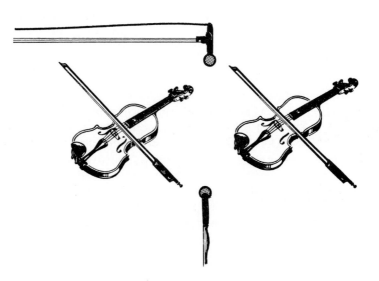

7-37 *To enlarge a violin or viola sound, place one microphone several feet over the instrument(s) and one microphone under the instrument(s). This tends to make one instrument sound like a few and a few sound like several.*

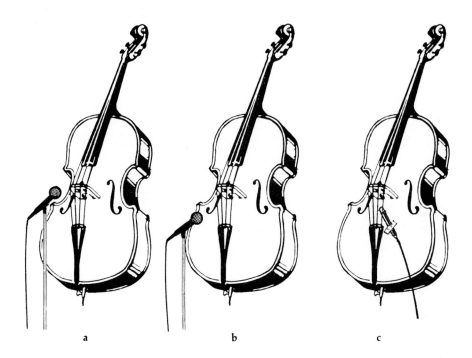

7-38   *Three ways to mike a cello or bass are:* (**a**) *off the bridge to produce a brighter sound;* (**b**) *off the f-hole to produce a fuller sound; and* (**c**) *behind the strings, near the bridge, taped to the body of the instrument to produce a richer, more resonant sound.*

7-39   *Miking a mandolin off the bridge* (**a**) *tends to produce a brighter sound. By aiming the microphone at the velum* (**b**), *the sound tends to become richer.*

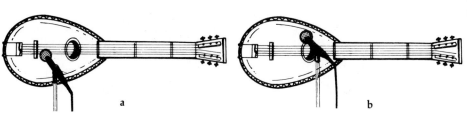

7-40 (Above) Miking a flute and piccolo over the finger holes picks up most of the sounds these instruments emit and does not pick up the breathy sounds that miking the mouthpiece produces. Some producers feel that these sounds are part of the instruments' overall aural character, however, and mike the mouthpiece to produce a thinner, textured sound.

7-41 (Above right) Clarinet and oboe are miked over the finger holes since most of the sounds come from this part of the instruments. In miking the keys of any instrument, avoid close mike-to-source distances, otherwise the sound of the moving keys will be heard.

7-42 (Right) Mike alto, tenor, and baritone saxophones off the bell but not too close, or else the mike will hear the blowing and spit sounds.

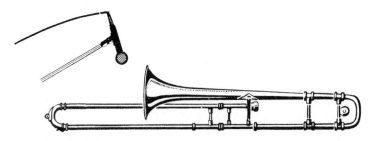

7-43 (Left) Mike trumpets, trombones, baritones, and tubas off the bell, being careful to avoid close mike-to-source distances so the blowing and spit sounds are not heard.

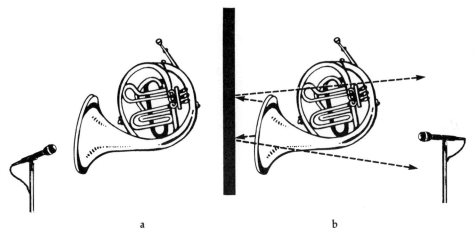

7-44 *Two ways to mike a French horn are (**a**) directly off the bell, and (**b**) by picking up the sound reflections from a baffle. Since the bell of the French horn faces away from an ensemble, in stereo miking, the musician would have to sit with his or her back toward the players for the bell to be on-mike. Placing a baffle several feet from the bell should carry the sound to the mike, along with the room acoustics, in sufficient proportions.*

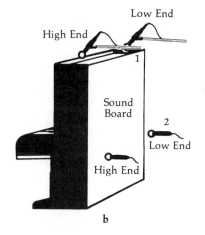

7-45 *When miking an upright piano for mono (**a**), position a microphone over an open top, 1, or behind the sound board, 2. For stereo (**b**), position two microphones, one for low-end pickup and the other for high-end pickup, over an open top, 1, or behind the sound board, 2. (Mikes also can be placed inside the piano.)*

7-46 *A Leslie loudspeaker cabinet, often used to amplify an electric Hammond organ, contains a high-frequency loudspeaker (the tweeter) in the upper portion and a low-frequency loudspeaker (the woofer) in the lower portion. The loudspeakers rotate creating a tremolo effect. One way to mike a Leslie is with two directional microphones, one to pick up the highs and the other to pick up the lows. The greater the mike-to-source distance, the less the chance of picking up the rotor sounds, and the better the sound blend.*

7-47 *Mike-to-source distances vary with the vocalist and the music. Generally, pop singers require closer working distances (**a**) than classical singers (**b**) due to differences in loudness and sound throw.*

Depends upon the type of music

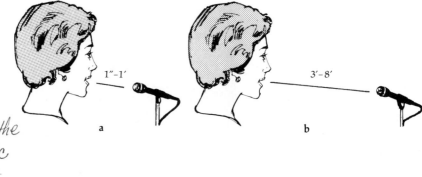

1"–1' a 3'–8' b

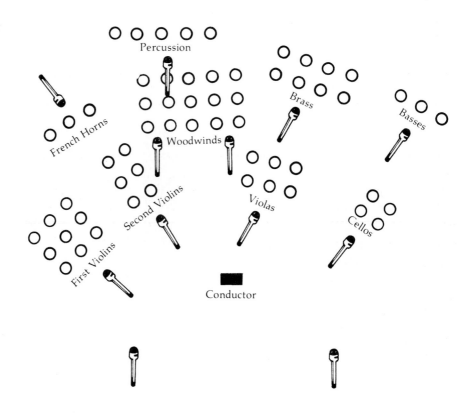

Percussion
Brass
French Horns
Basses
Woodwinds
Second Violins
Violas
Cellos
First Violins
Conductor

7-48 *In miking a symphony orchestra for recording in a studio, the sound of each section and the overall sound should be under separate controls. (Sometimes microphones are placed within sections for added control and better blend.) All microphones are directional.*

MULTIPLE MIKING VERSUS STEREO MIKING Although multiple miking is used more than stereo miking, each technique has its advantages and disadvantages.

Stereo Miking

Advantages	Disadvantages
More closely reproduces the way we hear in an acoustic environment	Requires adjustment of the musicians, not the mikes, to accomplish the music blend
Requires fewer mikes, hence, fewer pots to control, and reduced electronic noise	Requires a retake by all musicians for a mistake by one, since all instruments are recorded at once
Can record entire ensemble at the same time	Makes it difficult to isolate instruments for solos
May spark performance from interaction because everyone plays at once	Requires a recording environment with excellent acoustics

Multiple Miking

Advantages	Disadvantages
Allows virtually complete control over each element in the recording	Makes it difficult to create the nuances of each sound's interaction with the acoustic environment
Increases separation of sound sources	Requires artificial production of acoustics and spatial placement
Usually means multitrack recording, thus: musicians can be recorded separately, a few musicians can do the work of several, and a mistake by one musician does not always require rerecording the entire ensemble	Increases phasing problems

Music in Television

Several different types of TV productions use live music, including variety, concert, and some talk programs. Three basic considerations are involved in miking all of them: (1) whether the musicians are seen on camera, (2) the acoustics, and (3) the type of music.

MUSICIANS ON OR OFF CAMERA   Getting the best possible sound is the primary goal of every sound designer, particularly when music is involved. If the musicians are seen on camera, however, it can be disturbing to an audience to have them blocked by, and the picture cluttered with, microphones. Mikes have become an accepted part of the TV picture, but unless they are selected and positioned with care, they can ruin a shot.

Fortunately, a variety of mikes produce excellent sound and are also good looking. Even windscreens now come in various colors.

If musicians are off camera, mike them in any way with little concern for appearance. Keep in mind that if there is a conductor, the musicians have to be able to see him or her.

Whether musicians are on or off camera, you will most likely use unidirectional mikes to cut down not only on leakage but on feedback as well. Many large studios and theaters have loudspeakers so the audience can hear the music blend better. Singers sometimes need loudspeakers to hear the music blend when they are not near the accompanying ensemble. With loudspeakers and microphones in the same vicinity, unidirectional mikes are almost a necessity to avoid feedback.

ACOUSTICS   The types of studios used for large-scale TV productions, particularly with an audience present, are acoustically adequate for speech but sometimes not so for music. Therefore, most sound designers use the multimicrophone technique instead of the one- or two-microphone approach. Sound control is much better, and, even if the acoustics are excellent, much of today's popular music requires multiple miking.

TYPE OF MUSIC   The type of music can influence TV miking. Classical music audiences may not care to see a symphony orchestra, or string quartet for that matter, draped with microphones. They are used to hearing music in excellent acoustic settings where mikes are not necessary to carry the sound. Their objection is not so much that mikes are in the picture but rather that mikes are being used at all.

This is one reason concert broadcasts originate from concert halls and not from studios. In controlled acoustic environments, the sound designer can hang a few mikes to achieve a natural sound blend and also keep the mikes out of the picture.

On the other hand, popular music usually requires a mike for each sound source plus electronic enhancement. It would be impractical to use only a few mikes to pick up, say, a rock ensemble, since it would change the entire character of the sound.

TECHNIQUES FOR MIKING MUSIC IN TELEVISION   For some of the common techniques used in miking music for television, see **7-49** to **7-56**.

7-49 *A singer using a hand-held directional microphone should hold it at about a 45-degree angle to the mouth to stay within the pickup pattern but not block the face (**a**). Hand-held omnidirectional mikes can be held at chest level (**b**). A hand-held microphone should contain a pop filter and be shock-resistant, easy to hold, and good looking.*

7-50 *(Far left) Mike a guitarist who plays and sings with two directional microphones: one to pick up the voice and the other to pick up the guitar.*

7-51 *(Left) A singer-pianist requires one microphone to pick up the vocal and another microphone to pick up the instrument.*

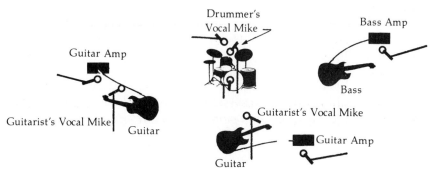

7-52 *Pop (top) and rock (bottom) ensembles usually require a directional microphone on each sound source and at least three to four mikes on the drums.*

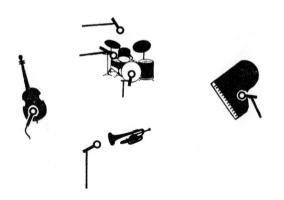

7-53 *Miking a jazz ensemble.*

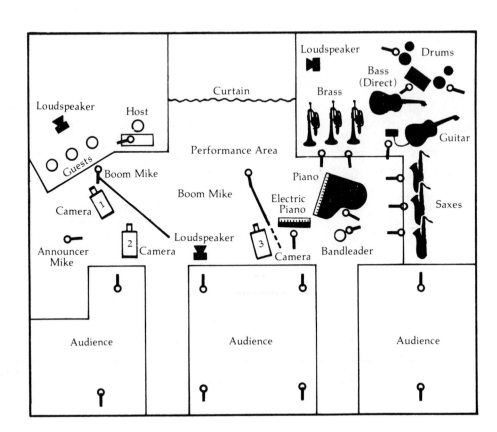

7-54 *Putting it all together: miking for a talk/variety program. All mikes are directional.*

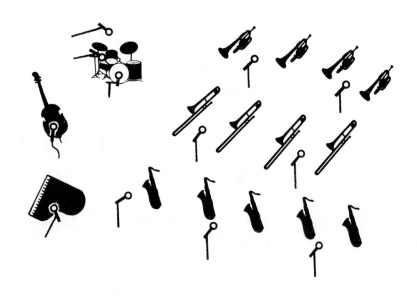

7-55 *Miking a jazz (or dance) band. Notice how directional microphones are placed between pairs of trumpets, trombones, and saxophones for balanced sound pickup. The odd third mike to the left of the saxophone section is placed to pick up the leftmost sax. Placing two mikes in the sax section would split the sound of one saxophone between two mikes.*

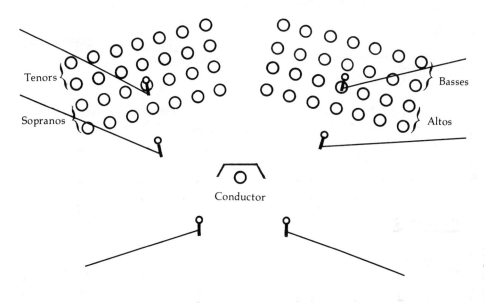

7-56 *In miking large choruses, section microphones and blending microphones usually produce the most controlled and balanced sound.*

Music in Film

The microphone technique used in recording music for film is similar to the techniques used in recording studios: ensembles are miked using individual microphones on instruments or groups of instruments. Since the ensemble is not in the picture, it is no concern whether microphones block players from view or clutter the stage.

Summary

1. Two basic approaches to miking live music are: (a) stereo miking—using two microphones (or capsules) to pick up the sound of an ensemble—and (b) multiple miking—using a separate microphone for each sound source or group of sound sources in an ensemble.
2. Stereo miking can be accomplished by using a coincident or crossed pair of unidirectional microphones (also called X-Y miking), a spaced pair of unidirectional microphones, the middle-side (M-S) approach, or a stereo microphone.
3. Since multiple miking involves miking most of the instruments in an ensemble, it means that (a) microphones should be no closer together than three times the distance from any mike to its sound source to avoid phasing problems; (b) mike-to-source distances are usually close, thus reducing the interaction of music with acoustics and requiring the addition of artificial reverberation; and (c) each sound source usually requires a separate channel to control better the various microphone inputs.
4. If two or more musicians in a recording session are using separate microphones and if controlling leakage is important, baffles or isolation booths are used to keep the sound of one instrument from leaking into the microphone of another instrument.
5. No one technique is better than any other in miking music. Microphone selection and positioning depend on many factors: the music, the musician, the quality of the instrument, the acoustics, the blend, and so on. Generally, however, the closer the mike-to-source distance, the fuller and more intimate is the sound; the farther the mike-to-source distance, the more diffused and spacious is the sound.
6. Some electric instruments, such as the guitar, bass, and Hammond organ, can be recorded either by miking their amplifier loudspeaker or by direct insertion—plugging the instrument into the console.
7. Recording a vocalist is a severe test for any microphone, since the mike must be able to handle the nuances of a vocalist's timbre and dynamic range, as well as any breathing, popping, and sibilant sounds. Mike selection and placement depend on voice quality, style of music, and microphone presence.

8. Microphone placement for a music performance on TV depends on a combination of factors: whether the musicians are on camera, the acoustics, and the music. Generally, small ensembles playing popular music require more microphones, regardless of the acoustics, than large ensembles playing classical music or jazz. In both cases, however, unidirectional microphones are almost always used.

8

Monitor Loudspeakers

Each component in the sound chain is important, but no matter how good the components are, when you listen to their product, you hear only what the **loudspeaker** can reproduce. To put it another way, the quality of every sound you evaluate is based on what you hear from the loudspeaker. The tendency, however, is to underestimate the importance of the loudspeaker, perhaps because it is the last link in the sound chain and there may be a subconscious correlation between last and least. This attitude is aesthetically fatal.

The point seems straightforward: always use the best loudspeaker. But which is best? Is it the most expensive, the largest, the loudest, the one with the widest, flattest frequency response, or the one suitable for symphonic music or AM radio? Although a loudspeaker is critical to any audio operation, choosing the best one for your needs is anything but straightforward. It involves several decisions; each influences later decisions and each is mainly subjective.

In deciding which loudspeaker is "best," you should look at four factors: (1) the loudspeaker's frequency and transient response and loudness potential in relation to your needs, (2) the compatibility of the loudspeaker sound with the room sound, (3) loudspeaker placement and sound dispersion, and (4) the operator's monitoring position in relation to the loudspeaker.

Types of Loudspeakers

Like the microphone, the loudspeaker is a transducer, but it works in the opposite direction. Instead of changing acoustic energy into electric energy, it changes electric energy back into acoustic energy. Also, like the microphone,

202

the loudspeaker uses moving coils, ribbons, or capacitors as transducing elements. Unlike microphones, however, which are readily available and commonly used in all three types, the overwhelming majority of loudspeakers in use are moving coil. Ribbons and condensers are rare.

The **moving-coil loudspeaker** is so popular because it can deliver excellent sound quality in rugged and variously priced designs. The **ribbon speaker** is extremely delicate and usually reproduces the powerful lower frequencies badly. The **condenser loudspeaker**, although capable of reproducing a more spacious sound, is less sensitive than the moving-coil type and more expensive.

Loudspeaker Systems

All the audio components in a sound system handle electric, magnetic, or mechanical energy; only the loudspeaker produces sound. It is the one component that must be able to reproduce both the long wavelengths of the powerful low frequencies and the short wavelengths of the weak high frequencies.

Theoretically, a loudspeaker that is large enough to handle the bass sound waves should be able to reproduce the treble waves as well. In fact, this is not the case. A loudspeaker that is large enough to generate low-frequency sound waves is too big to disperse the delicate high frequencies efficiently. Conversely, a speaker capable of dispersing the shorter waves is too small to handle the longer wavelengths.

To illustrate the problem, most radio and television receivers, as well as 8- and 16-mm film projectors, contain a single speaker; even many stereo radios and phonographs contain only one loudspeaker in each of the two loudspeaker enclosures. Since a single speaker cannot cope with the entire range of audible frequencies, a compromise is made. The long and short wavelengths are sacrificed for the medium wavelengths that a single loudspeaker can reproduce more efficiently. Therefore, regardless of a recording's sound quality, a receiver with just one loudspeaker cannot reproduce it with full frequency response. (As we note later, this imposes certain restrictions on selecting studio loudspeakers and monitoring.)

This is the reason the **two-way loudspeaker system** was created. The two-way system uses two speakers, informally called the **woofer** and the **tweeter**, inside a single cabinet (see **8-1**). The woofer reproduces the lower frequencies, and the tweeter handles the higher frequencies.

Before the low and high frequencies reach the woofer and tweeter, they must be separated. This is accomplished by a device called the **crossover network**. The actual point, or frequency, where the bass and treble divide is called the **crossover frequency.** Depending on the size of the loudspeaker unit, the crossover frequency is usually between 500 and 1,500 Hz (see **8-2**).

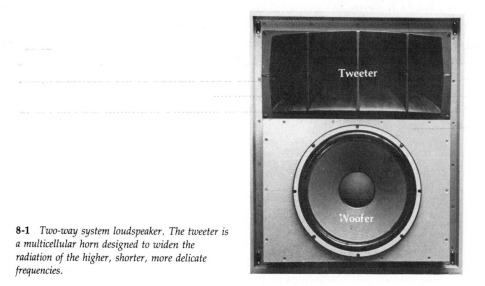

8-1 *Two-way system loudspeaker. The tweeter is a multicellular horn designed to widen the radiation of the higher, shorter, more delicate frequencies.*

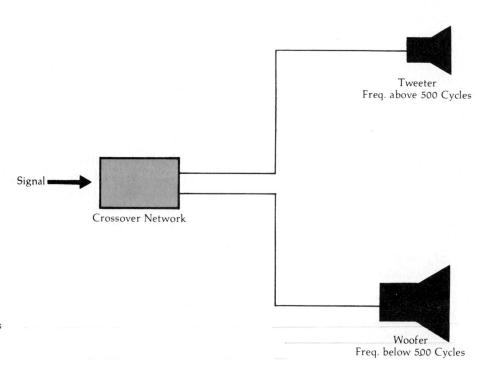

8-2 *The crossover network in a two-way system divides the high and low frequencies, usually somewhere between 500 and 1,500 Hz. It sends the highs to the tweeter and the lows to the woofer.*

Although the two-way system dominates the market, it has limitations in situations that demand highly sensitive sound reproduction. The main limitation is that there is only one speaker for the low frequencies and one for the highs. The solution to the problem is familiar: use more than two loudspeakers and divide the frequency spectrum further into **three-way** and **four-way** systems (see **8-3a, b**).

The three-way system divides the treble instead of the bass range, since short wavelengths are more directional and harder to disperse. The crossover point between the bass and low treble or midrange is around 500 Hz. For the midrange and high treble, the point is roughly 6,000 Hz, again depending on the size of the cabinet (see **8-4a**). At 6,000 Hz and above, most sound consists of overtones with wavelengths that are not only short but also weak. A separate loudspeaker with additional power can better disperse these difficult frequencies without affecting the strong wavelengths of the midrange.

The four-way system uses two loudspeakers for the bass, dividing at around 300 Hz, and two loudspeakers for the treble, dividing at about 6,000 Hz (see **8-4b**).

8-3a *A three-way system loudspeaker.*

8-3b *A four-way system loudspeaker.*

Lower Midrange

Treble

Tweeters

Upper Midrange

Woofers

Bass

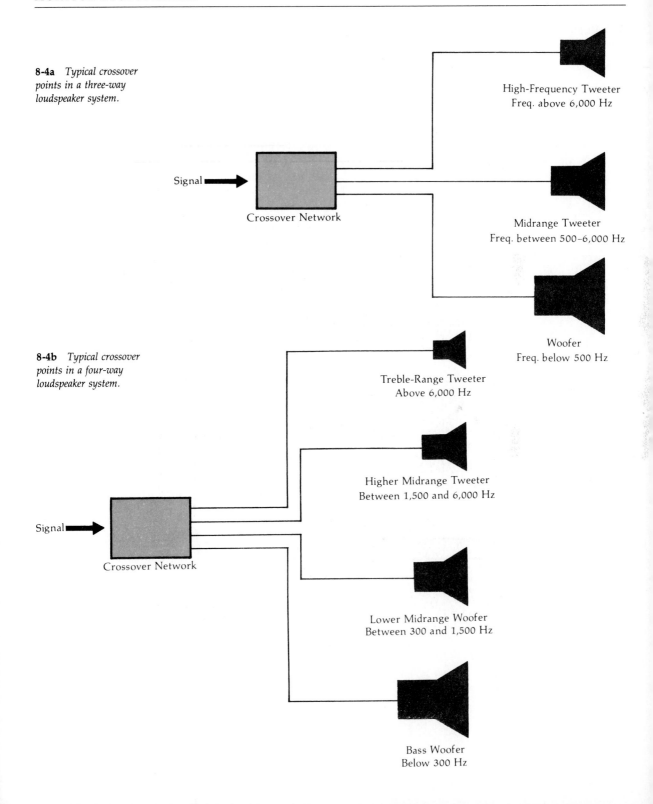

8-4a *Typical crossover points in a three-way loudspeaker system.*

High-Frequency Tweeter
Freq. above 6,000 Hz

Signal →

Crossover Network

Midrange Tweeter
Freq. between 500–6,000 Hz

Woofer
Freq. below 500 Hz

8-4b *Typical crossover points in a four-way loudspeaker system.*

Treble-Range Tweeter
Above 6,000 Hz

Signal →

Crossover Network

Higher Midrange Tweeter
Between 1,500 and 6,000 Hz

Lower Midrange Woofer
Between 300 and 1,500 Hz

Bass Woofer
Below 300 Hz

Loudspeaker Selection

Loudspeakers are like musical instruments in that they produce sound. They are not like purely mechanical-electric components such as microphones or electronic components such as consoles, which can be objectively tested and rationally evaluated. No two loudspeakers ever sound quite the same. Comparing the same make and model loudspeakers in one room only tells you what they sound like in that acoustic environment; in another room, they may sound altogether different. Furthermore, a loudspeaker that satisfies your taste may be unappealing to someone else's taste. Thus, it is extremely hard to suggest guidelines for selecting a studio monitor. One aspect of loudspeaker selection that may be useful to discuss, however, is the relationship between the sound produced in the studio and the sound reproduced through the audience's receiver/loudspeaker.

Each medium has a particular response capability (see 8-5). The same is true for the components that reproduce the sound from each medium (see 8-6). For example, TV audio can carry the entire range of audible frequencies. You may have noticed during a televised music program, however, that you see certain high- and low-pitched instruments being played but you hear them only faintly or not at all. Overhead cymbals are one example. Generally, their response range is between 300 and 15,000 Hz (including overtones), but

8-5 *Frequency responses of various reproducing systems.*

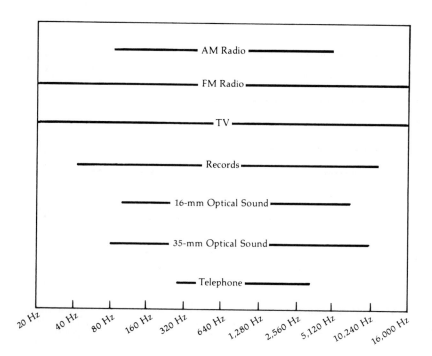

they usually begin to gain good definition between 4,500 and 8,000 Hz, which is well within the frequency of television transmission. The highest response of many home TV receivers is about 6,000 Hz, though, which is below a good part of the cymbals' range.

Assume you wish to boost the cymbal frequencies that the home TV receiver can barely reproduce. Unless you listen to the sound over a monitor comparable in size and response to the average TV speaker, you cannot get a sense of what effect the boost is having (see **8-7a**).

Unlike television sound, optical film sound is limited in frequency response not only by the speaker in the projector but also by the medium itself (see **9-14**). Suppose a film calls for the sound of distant thunder. If you record and equalize that sound on a good studio monitor, you may be tempted to boost the very low frequencies to make the thunder sound louder and boomier. When that sound is transferred to a 16-mm optical film track, however, the frequencies below about 100 Hz are lost (35-mm optical is somewhat better). Furthermore, the speaker usually found in a 16-mm projector has limited low-frequency response at roughly 300 Hz and below (see **8-7b**). Unless you take these two factors into consideration when recording and equalizing, the thunder effect may be considerably diminished or lost. High frequencies are also difficult to produce in 16-mm optical sound since the frequency response does not extend much beyond 8,000 Hz.

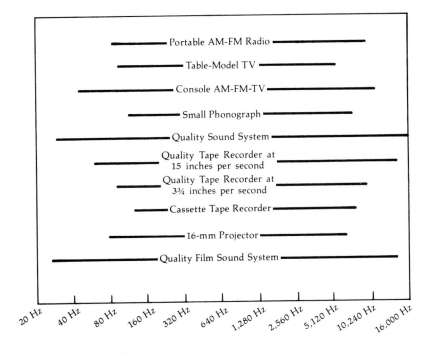

8-6 *Frequency responses of various receiver/loudspeaker systems.*

8-7a *Typical single-system loudspeaker found in many table-model TV receivers. Note the difference between the size of the loudspeaker and the size of the screen.*

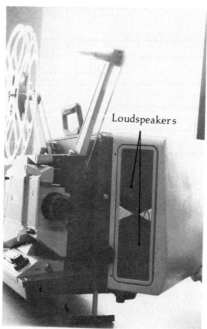

Loudspeakers

8-7b *Although this 16-mm film projector has two loudspeakers, they are not much larger than the loudspeaker in **8-7a**. Therefore, sound reproduction still will be essentially midrange.*

✳ Perhaps the medium hardest to adjust for is records. So many different types and qualities of stereos and radios exist that it is hard to produce a record that sounds good on all of them. For example, many AM radio stations broadcast with limited frequency response and power. To sound decent on such stations, records may need midrange enhancement, particularly in the presence range. On a speaker with a wide, flat response, however, this boost could make the sound harsh and annoying.

Due to the differences between the potential sound response of a medium and its actual response after processing, transmission, and reception, it makes sense to choose at least two types of studio monitors. One should provide both wide, flat response and a broad range of sound levels, and the other should have response and loudness that reflect what the average listener hears. Many recording studios use three sets of monitors to check sound: (1) low-quality loudspeakers with only midrange response and limited power output, such as those in portable and car radios and cheap phonographs; (2) average-quality loudspeakers with added high and low response, such as moderately priced phonographs and component systems; and (3) high-quality loudspeakers with a very wide, flat response and high output capability.

Monitor Placement

Although it is important that studio monitors produce a broad and balanced sound, to be useful as a reference the sound must also be adequately dispersed. In addition to hearing sound directly from the loudspeaker, you also depend on the indirect reflections from the walls, ceiling, and floor.

An important influence on your perception of sound is the intensity with which sound waves reach your ears, and this intensity is related directly to the placement of the loudspeaker. Generally, loudspeakers are located in one of four places: (1) well toward the middle of a room; (2) against or flush with a wall; (3) at the intersection of two walls; or (4) in a corner at the ceiling or on the floor (see **8-8**). Each of these positions affects the sound's loudness and dispersion differently.

A loudspeaker mounted in the middle of a room radiates sound into what is called a *full sphere* (or *full space*), where, theoretically, the sound level at any point within a given distance is the same (see **8-9**). If a loudspeaker is placed against a wall, the wall concentrates the radiations into a *half-sphere,* thereby increasing the sound level by 6 dB. With loudspeakers mounted at the intersection of two walls, the radiation angle is concentrated still more into a *one-quarter sphere,* thus increasing the sound level another 6 dB. Loudspeakers placed in corners at the ceiling or on the floor radiate in a *one-eighth sphere,* generating the most concentrated sound levels in a four-walled room. A significant part of each increase in the overall sound level is due to the loudness

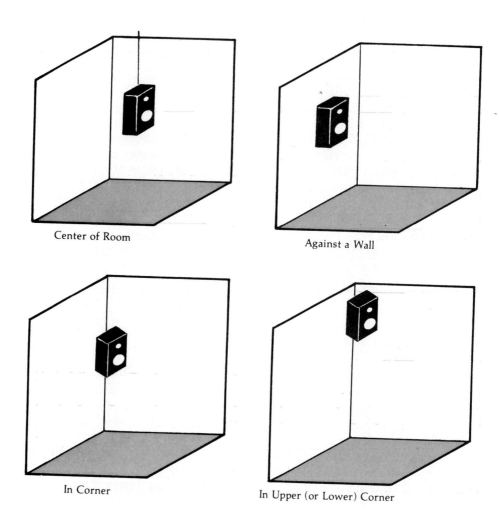

Center of Room

Against a Wall

In Corner

In Upper (or Lower) Corner

8-8 *Four typical loudspeaker locations in a room.*

increase in the bass (see **8-10**). One of these monitor positions is not necessarily better than another; proper placement depends on your needs and personal taste. The most important point here is that there is a relationship between the location of the loudspeakers and the sound you hear.

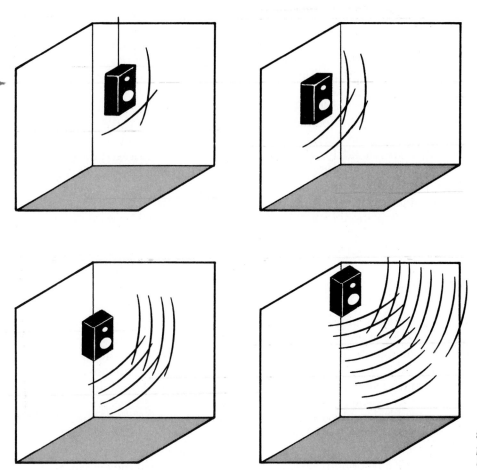

8-9 *Effects of loudspeaker placement on overall loudness levels.*

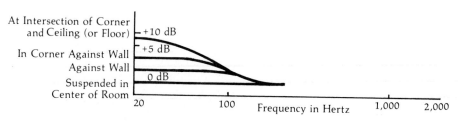

At Intersection of Corner
and Ceiling (or Floor)   +10 dB

In Corner Against Wall   +5 dB
Against Wall
Suspended in   0 dB
Center of Room

20   100   1,000   2,000
        Frequency in Hertz

8-10 *The effects of loudspeaker placement on bass response.*

Adjusting Monitor Sound to Room Sound

No room produces a totally wide, flat response. Even a studio designed for acoustic control colors sound in some way. In one studio, acoustics may boost 500 Hz, 4 dB and attenuate 4,300 Hz, 5 dB; in another studio, the frequency response may drop off 10 dB at 10,000 Hz. The sound of any loudspeaker, no matter where it is placed in a room, is colored by the acoustic anomalies of that room.

To neutralize these effects, sound is fed through an equalizer before reaching the monitor loudspeaker. The equalizer is adjusted to compensate for idiosyncrasies in the room response. In the studio that boosts 500 Hz, 4 dB and attenuates 4,300 Hz, 5 dB, the frequencies are equalized by attenuating 500 Hz, 4 dB and boosting 4,300 Hz, 5 dB to make the response flat. Where the frequency response drops off 10 dB at 10,000 Hz, frequencies at 10,000 Hz and above are boosted to form the desired response curve.

Equalizing monitor loudspeakers does not correct gross deficiencies in monitor design or studio acoustics, however. Before you do any equalizing, it is important to start with a compatible room-loudspeaker relationship.

Monitoring

After you choose and place the monitor loudspeakers, it becomes important where you listen and at what levels. This is even more crucial with stereo than with mono. Sit about 3 to 10 feet from the speaker(s), depending on its size; the larger the speaker, the farther back you should sit. With monaural sound, sit in front of the speaker; and with stereo, sit in front of and equidistant between the speakers. If you sit to the left or right of center, one speaker will sound louder than the other, and the spatial placement of elements within a recording will seem off center.

Sometimes you may be properly situated between two speakers, yet the signal is still left- or right-heavy. This usually means that the loudspeakers are out of phase; the cones from one are moving out—generating sound waves—while the cones from the other are moving in—creating a vacuum. When loudspeakers are out of phase, it is usually because the connections are not wired properly (see **8-11a, b**). If you think a sound is out of phase because of improperly wired speakers, check the VU meters. If they show a similar level, then the speakers are out of phase.

 In listening to monitor loudspeakers, be aware of how loud or soft they are, especially when recording or mixing down. The principle of equal loudness (see Chapter 1) indicates that if you process sound at loud monitor levels, the highs and lows will be disproportionately soft or disappear altogether if that sound is heard at low level. Conversely, if you process sound at a low monitor level, that sound will have too much bass and treble if it is played back at loud levels.

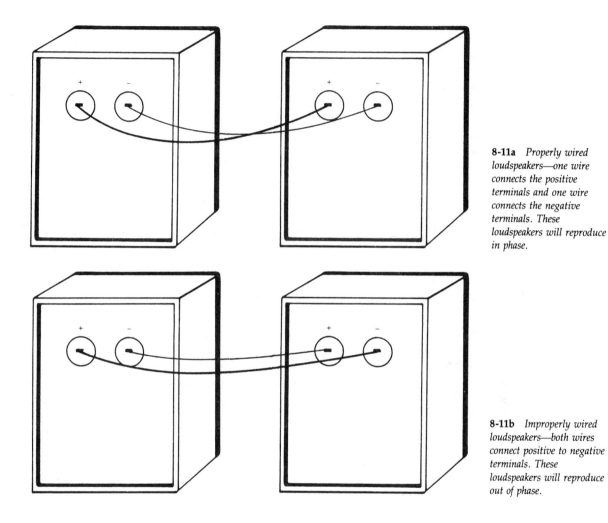

8-11a *Properly wired loudspeakers—one wire connects the positive terminals and one wire connects the negative terminals. These loudspeakers will reproduce in phase.*

8-11b *Improperly wired loudspeakers—both wires connect positive to negative terminals. These loudspeakers will reproduce out of phase.*

Summary

1. Loudspeakers are transducers that convert electric energy into sound energy.
2. There are three types of loudspeakers: moving coil, ribbon, and condenser. The moving coil is the type most often used.
3. Loudspeakers that attempt to cover the entire spectrum with a single cone cannot reproduce high and low frequencies very well; they are essentially midrange instruments.

4. For improved response, many monitor loudspeakers have two-way systems: one to handle the low frequencies and one for the highs. Within each monitor, there are two speakers: a woofer and a tweeter.

5. Some loudspeakers have three- and four-way systems. In the three-way system, the treble is divided; in the four-way system, both the treble and the bass are divided.

6. Each medium that records or transmits sound, such as AM radio, TV, or optical film, and each loudspeaker that reproduces sound, such as a studio monitor or home receiver, has certain response characteristics and loudness capabilities. For optimal results, sound should be produced with an idea of how it will be reproduced.

7. Loudspeakers are usually positioned toward the middle of a room, against a wall, at the intersection of two walls, or in a corner at the floor or ceiling.

8. Each loudspeaker position affects sound dispersion and loudness. A loudspeaker in the middle of a room generates the least concentrated sound; a loudspeaker at the intersection of a ceiling or wall generates the most.

9. The more enclosed a loudspeaker is, the louder its bass response will be; a corner loudspeaker generates more bass than a wall loudspeaker. To a certain extent, frequencies that are too loud or too quiet can be equalized flat to a room's acoustics.

10. When monitoring sound, the operator should sit 3 to 10 feet from the loudspeaker, depending on its size and loudness. The larger and louder the loudspeaker, the farther back the operator should sit.

11. When monitoring stereo, the operator should sit in front of and equidistant between the loudspeakers; otherwise the sound will be imbalanced to the left or right.

9

Tape and Film

Of all the links in the recording chain, magnetic tape and film are perhaps the ones most taken for granted, no doubt because they are so familiar and easy to obtain. This attitude is a mistake, however, when you consider that tape and film make it possible to store creative output. Indeed, these materials are to mechanical-electronic media what paper is to print media. Thus, it is as important for you to understand the properties of tape and film stock as it is for the printer to know the properties of paper stock.

Physical Properties of Audio Tape

MATERIALS Audio tape is a thin plastic ribbon consisting of: (1) hard, needle-like particles composed of iron (ferric) oxide; (2) a plastic base material that supports the oxide; and (3) a back coating to reduce slippage and buildup of magnetic charges (see **9-1**). Some tape is made with chromium dioxide and some with pure metal particles instead of iron oxide. These tapes are discussed later in the chapter.

Iron Oxide and Magnetism Tape recording is possible because of the ability of the **iron oxide** particles to store electromagnetic impulses. Certain metals are magnetized when exposed to a field of force such as magnetic or electric current. Soft metals do not retain magnetization after the field of force is re-

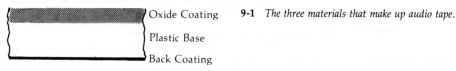

Oxide Coating

Plastic Base

Back Coating

9-1 *The three materials that make up audio tape.*

moved, but hard metals like iron do. In tape recording, the force field, which is electric current, flows to the record head of the tape recorder and polarizes the iron particles on the tape—arranges them into patterns—as they pass across the head. The arrangement of these polarized particles is the magnetic equivalent of the original sound.

Plastic Base   Two types of plastic materials are used for the tape's backing: (1) **polyester,** also called **mylar,** and (2) **cellulose acetate.**

Compared with acetate, polyester is stronger and more stable, it is less affected by temperature extremes and humidity, it stores better over longer periods, and it is more supple. Why, then, is acetate used at all? Polyester has one significant drawback: it stretches under too much tension or when used too often. Once a tape is stretched, so is the recording. Acetate is more brittle, and when too much tension is applied, it will snap cleanly; therefore, the tape can be spliced back together.

Researchers have tried to produce a tape that has the characteristics of polyester but does not stretch. The tape is actually prestretched and is called *tensilized*. This procedure simply reverses the problem with polyester, however. Tensilized tape shrinks under heat, and a shrunken recording is as useless as a stretched one.

Most professionals feel that the advantages of polyester far outweigh its one main disadvantage. They overcome the stretching problem by obtaining only the highest-quality tape, making sure that tape recorders have the proper tension when spooling, and using new tape for each project.

DIMENSIONS   Two physical dimensions of magnetic audio tape are thickness and width. Knowing a tape's thickness helps to determine: (1) how much tape can be spooled onto a reel, (2) how long it will play, and (3) how vulnerable a magnetic signal on one layer of tape will be to a magnetic signal on an adjacent layer. PRINT THROUGH

Thickness   Most audio tape comes in four thicknesses, measured in **mils**—thousandths of an inch: 1½, 1, ½, and ¼ mil. (These measurements are taken from the plastic base. Actually the plastic base plus the iron oxide are slightly thicker.) A tape's thickness determines how much can be spooled onto a given size of reel. For example, the most common reel sizes are 5, 7, and 10½ inches (see **9-2**). A 7-inch reel holds 1,200 feet of 1½-mil tape, 1,800 feet of 1-mil tape, or 3,600 feet of ¼-mil tape. The more tape that is on a reel, the longer is the playing time (see **9-3**).

One-quarter-mil tape may look like the best buy, but not for professionals. Broadcasters and recordists prefer 1½-mil tape for two reasons: (1) it is thickest, most durable, and therefore least likely to crease, snap, or stretch; and (2) the chance of **print-through** is considerably less. Print-through usually occurs in storage, when an encoded signal from one layer of tape affects the encoded signal of an adjacent layer. When the tape is played back, you

9-2 *The most common reel sizes are 10¹/₂-inch, 7-inch, and 5-inch.*

Reel Size (in inches)	Tape Thickness (in mils)	Tape Length (in feet)	Playing Time (in minutes): 15 IPS	7½ IPS	3¾ IPS
5	1½	600	7½	15	30
5	1	900	11¼	22½	45
7	1½	1,200	15	30	60
7	1	1,800	22½	45	90
7	½	2,400	30	60	120
10½	1½	2,400	30	60	120
10½	1	3,600	45	90	180

9-3 *Recording times for reel-to-reel tape.*

can hear both signals, one strongly and one faintly. The sound is not unlike two radio stations on the same frequency, with one broadcasting from nearby and the other from far away. The thicker the tape, the less chance of sound "spilling" from layer to layer. Other factors that affect print-through are discussed later in this chapter.

¼-Inch Tape

9-4 *One-channel monaural recording.*

¼-Inch Tape

9-5 *Two-channel stereo recording.*

Width Before the days of multitrack recording, magnetic audio tape came in one width—¼ inch. Recordings were one-channel—monaural—and the signal filled almost the entire width of the tape (see **9-4**). When stereo or two-channel recording was used, ¼-inch tape still sufficed; each stereo channel was recorded on ⅛ inch of the tape (see **9-5**). The reduced width of the signal also reduced the signal-to-noise ratio, but for many audiophiles the added spatial dimension of stereo more than compensated for the slight loss in quality. As multitrack technology developed, it became clear that to record 4, 8, 16, or 24 channels, wider tape would be necessary. Now magnetic audio tape is available in ⅛- (for cassettes), ¼-, ½-, 1-, and 2-inch widths (see **9-6**).

By the way, do not confuse *channel* with *track;* these terms are not synonyms. A **channel** feeds one signal through the record head to the tape. The signal path the channel makes on the tape is the **track**. See **9-7** for a graphic explanation of the relationship between channel and track.

9-6 *Reel-to-reel audio tape is available in* ¹/₄*-,* ¹/₂*-, 1-, and 2-inch widths.*

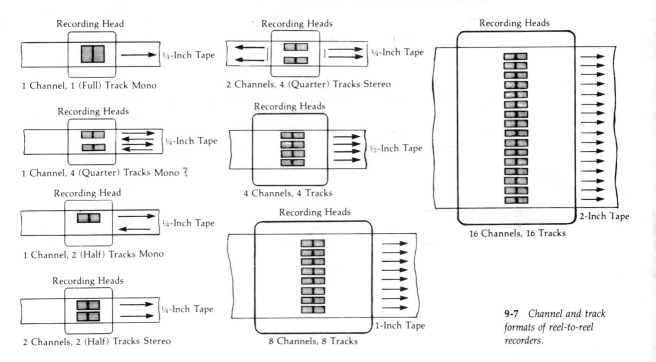

Recording Head
¼-Inch Tape
1 Channel, 1 (Full) Track Mono

Recording Heads
¼-Inch Tape
2 Channels, 4 (Quarter) Tracks Stereo

Recording Heads
2-Inch Tape
16 Channels, 16 Tracks

Recording Heads
¼-Inch Tape
1 Channel, 4 (Quarter) Tracks Mono ?

Recording Heads
½-Inch Tape
4 Channels, 4 Tracks

Recording Head
¼-Inch Tape
1 Channel, 2 (Half) Tracks Mono

Recording Heads
1-Inch Tape
8 Channels, 8 Tracks

Recording Heads
¼-Inch Tape
2 Channels, 2 (Half) Tracks Stereo

9-7 *Channel and track formats of reel-to-reel recorders.*

Magnetic Properties of Audio Tape

Much of the tape used in electronic media has been designed to provide particular response characteristics. For example, the type normally used to record popular music is **high-output tape** capable of handling higher levels of loudness than standard tape, whereas **low-output tape** is used to preserve program material for long periods of time. Low-output tape cannot handle loud levels, so the chance of ruining the material because of print-through is reduced.

Several measures are used to determine how suitable a tape is for a particular recording. Three ways to determine a tape's ability to retain magnetic information are to know: (1) how strong a force field must be to saturate (magnetize) the tape completely, (2) how well the tape retains magnetization once the force field is removed, and (3) how great an output level the tape can reproduce. The terms used to describe these measures are *coercivity, retentivity, and sensitivity.*

COERCIVITY **Coercivity** indicates the magnetic force (current) necessary to erase a tape fully, which is also an indication of what it takes to magnetize a tape fully. Coercivity is measured in **oersteds**—units of magnetic force—and it tells a technician how much current should flow between the erase and record heads of the tape recorder and the tape to ensure optimal tape saturation. (This adjustment, known as *biasing*, is discussed in Chapter 10.) Tapes that are used professionally have different oersted measurements, usually between 280 and 380. Once a tape recorder has been "biased" for one type of tape, another type may not respond so well.

RETENTIVITY **Retentivity** refers to a tape's ability to hold magnetization after the current has been turned off. Retentivity is measured in **gauss**—a unit of magnetic density. A higher gauss rating means greater retentivity, which, in turn, indicates that a tape has a greater potential output level. Greater is not necessarily better, however; again, that depends on what you are recording and why.

[handwritten margin note: ability to hold magnetization (rated by gauss) higher is greater]

SENSITIVITY Sensitivity is similar to retentivity in that it indicates the highest output level a tape can deliver; however, sensitivity is measured in decibels and the test must be made against a reference tape. If the maximum output level of a reference tape is 0 dB and the output of the tape you are testing is +3 dB, that means your tape is capable of handling 3 dB more loudness before it saturates—becomes fully magnetized.

Special-Purpose Tape

We have said that many recordings require a special tape made to satisfy a particular response requirement. Perhaps the two most common types of special-purpose tapes are low print-through and high output. There is *low-noise* tape, but it is not a special type as much as it is a response characteristic of any high-quality tape with a finely grained oxide coating.

LOW-PRINT-THROUGH TAPE As the name suggests, **low-print-through tape** reduces the chance of magnetic information on one tape layer transferring to another tape layer. If you intend to store recordings for any length of time, this is the tape to use. Low-print-through tape has low retentivity and low sensitivity; it cannot handle high energy levels without becoming saturated. If the signal energy on a tape is reduced, the chance that it will print through is also reduced. Three other factors also increase the possibility of print-through: heat, excessive spooling, and thin tape.

HIGH-OUTPUT TAPE Since very high levels of loudness became an inherent part of popular music, there has been a need for recording tape that could combat noise buildup on multitrack machines. A high-output tape was developed by increasing the coercivity and sensitivity of the iron oxide to a point where it could take a few decibels more signal than most standard tape before saturation. Due to its greater capacity to retain more magnetic energy, however, high-output tape is more susceptible to print-through.

Tape Defects

Most tape defects are the product of inferior manufacturing, and it is false economy to try to save money by purchasing such tape. To make the point emphatically: *Do not use cheap tape!*
   The following are several results of using cheap tape (see **9-8**).

1. *Dropout*—sudden, irregular drops in sound level caused by poor distribution or flaking of the oxide coating

2. *Clinching*—slippage between the tape layers due to loose packing

3. *Ridging*—a bulge or depression, seen after winding, caused by a deformed layer(s) of tape

4. *Adhesion*—one tape layer sticking to another because it has a tendency to absorb humidity

5. *Cupping*—stiffness in the tape due to poor binding of the plastic base to the oxide

6. *Curling*—tape that twists when it hangs due to a problem in the binding between plastic and oxide

Each of these defects adversely affects the sound quality.

Know

9-8 *Five common problems caused by poorly made tape.*

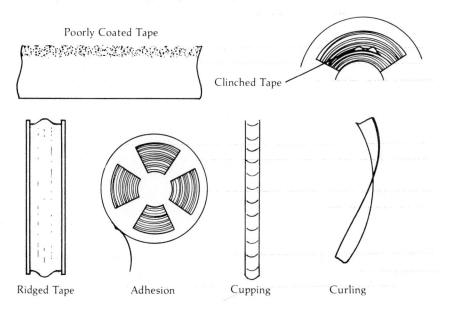

Poorly Coated Tape

Clinched Tape

Ridged Tape   Adhesion   Cupping   Curling

Storage

If you intend to keep a recording for any length of time, take the following precautions against alteration of the magnetically encoded signal.

1. Use low-print-through tape.

2. Store the tape in a controlled environment, between 60 and 75 degrees Fahrenheit and 40 and 60 percent humidity.

3. Wind the tape **tails out**—with the end of the recording on the outside of the reel. Then if print-through does occur, the weaker signal will be transferred into, instead of before, the stronger signal, thus masking the print-through.

4. If the tape is in long-term storage, try to wind and rewind it at least once a year as an added precaution.

Cartridge Tape

Cartridge tape ("cart," for short) is actually a continuous loop of standard 1½-mil, ¼-inch polyester tape housed in a plastic cartridge. The tape is highly lubricated to ensure smooth, nonabrasive winding, since the same relatively short length of tape is used over and over again. Standard-size carts come in various lengths from 10 seconds to 10½ minutes, and they have 75 inches to 400 feet of tape (see **9-9**). Larger cartridge casings hold up to 30 minutes of tape (see **9-10**).

Most cartridge tape has average coercivity and sensitivity and, therefore, standard output level. A high-output cartridge tape is also available that can take up to 6 dB more loudness than standard cartridge tape (see **9-11**). Many broadcasters, particularly AM radio stations that play rock and roll, are con-

9-9 *(Right) Cartridge tape.*

9-10 *(Far right) Thirty-minute cartridge tape.*

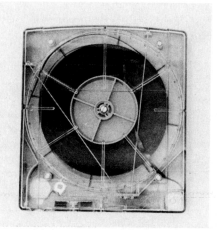

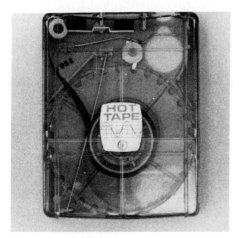

9-11 *So-called hot tape designed to reproduce greater loudness levels.*

tinuously looking for ways to improve the intensity of their sound. Since many of these stations dub records and commercials onto carts, high-output carts give them another way to increase the sound level.

Cassette Tape $1\frac{7}{8}''$ IPS

Cassette tape is a miniaturized combination of the reel-to-reel and cartridge designs (see **9-12**). Because of its small size, light weight, and portability, it is extremely convenient and possible to use virtually anywhere. The cassette has revolutionized the sound industry.

Due to the size of both tape and recorder, however, most cassettes are not yet capable of producing broadcast-quality sound. A cassette tape is also difficult to splice. Professionals, particularly in news, use them for remote recording but usually dub the cassette to a reel-to-reel or cart tape for broadcast.

One reason for the cassette's mediocre sound quality is the tape's dimensions. Most cassette tape is either ½ or ¼ mil thick and ⅛ inch wide. Regardless of the grade of oxide coating, there is simply not enough surface, track width, or stability to encode a strong output signal with an acceptable signal-to-noise ratio and frequency response.

In an attempt to overcome these problems, some cassette tape is made with chromium dioxide, cobalt-treated oxide, or pure metal particles. (All cassettes have polyester backing.) **Chromium dioxide** tape delivers an improved frequency response and higher sound levels, but its very high coercivity (roughly 500 oersteds) requires special circuitry. It also tends to wear down faster the soft metal type of tape recorder head. Cobalt-treated tape also gives

Iron sharpeneth Iron

9-12 *Cassette tape.*

a better response than standard iron oxide tape, but although it does not need special circuitry, it is still too unstable for professional use.

A more recent development is **metal-particle tape**, which has a magnetic surface of pure metal instead of oxide compounds. It gives the best frequency response, the most favorable signal-to-noise ratio, and the highest output level of any cassette tape available (its coercivity is 1,000 oersteds). It is possible to hear the improved sound on most cassette recorders. It does require specially designed heads and circuitry to take full advantage of the tape's sonic superiority, however, and several cassette recorders so designed are available. Most cassette tapes used to reproduce music on the air are metal-particle tapes.

Cassette tape comes in prepackaged cartridges of 30-, 40-, 45-, 60-, 90-, 120-, and 180-minute lengths—that is, using both sides of the tape. You can determine the length of time for one side by dividing the total time in half. The 30- to 60-minute tapes are ½ mil; the 90- to 180-minute tapes are usually ¼ mil. Try not to use any ¼-mil tape. In addition to its fragility and poor response, it tends to have slippage problems winding in fast forward and rewind.

Video Tape

The magnetic and physical properties of **video tape** are similar to those of audio tape: a plastic base backing coated with magnetically sensitive iron oxide particles; available in ½-, ¾-, 1-, and 2-inch widths; 1½ and 1 mil thick; and in reel-to-reel, cartridge, and cassette formats (see **9-13**). The magnetic particles on video tape are either transverse or slanted, however, which is

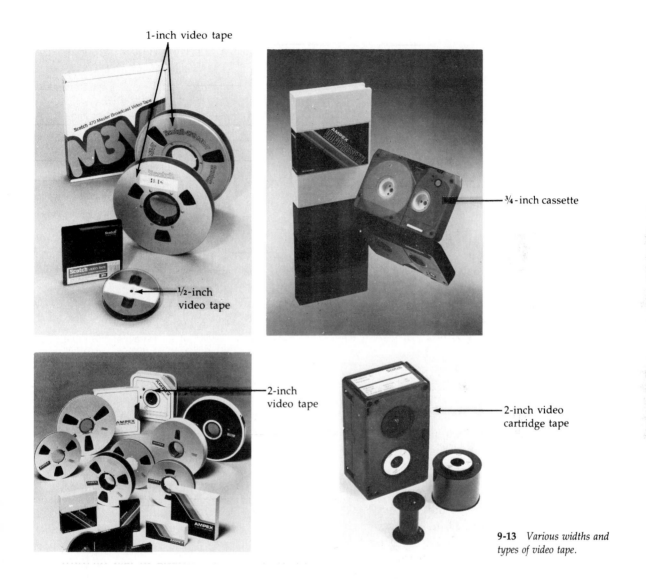

1-inch video tape

¾-inch cassette

½-inch video tape

2-inch video tape

2-inch video cartridge tape

9-13 *Various widths and types of video tape.*

better for recording video than for recording audio. The magnetic particles on audio tape are aligned horizontally, which is better for recording sound.

Film

PROPERTIES AND WIDTHS Picture **film** consists of a clear plastic base material coated with **emulsion**—tiny particles of light-sensitive silver halide that undergo a chemical reaction when struck by light.

9-14 *Various film stock formats.*

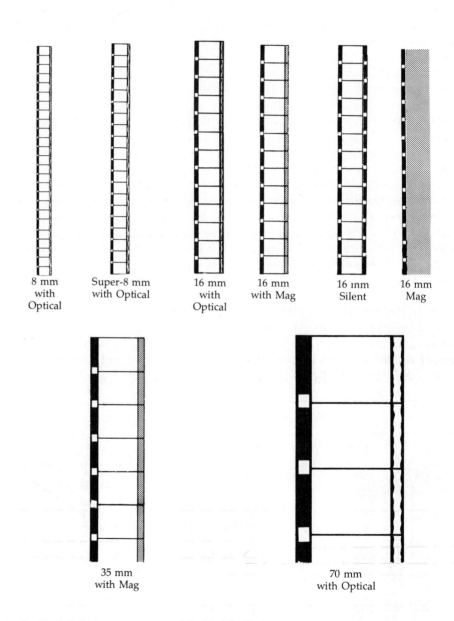

8 mm with Optical • Super-8 mm with Optical • 16 mm with Optical • 16 mm with Mag • 16 mm Silent • 16 mm Mag

35 mm with Mag

70 mm with Optical

Picture film comes in five different formats that are labeled according to width: 8 mm, super-8 mm, 16 mm, 35 mm, and 70 mm (see **9-14**). The larger the width, the better are the image and sound quality. Generally, 70 mm is used in wide-screen feature films and played only in theaters, 35 mm is used in feature films and played in theaters and network television, 16 mm is used by most (non-Hollywood-type) film makers and TV stations (that is, those TV stations still using film), and super-8 mm by amateur film makers. The 8-mm format has become less popular since super-8 mm gives a picture area that is 50 percent larger for little additional cost.

TYPES OF FILM There are three basic types of film: silent, sound, and magnetic. **Silent film,** which carries no sound information, consists of the picture area and two columns of sprocket holes (except 8 mm), one on each edge of the film. **Sound film**, which carries both picture and sound, replaces the sprocket holes on one edge of the film with an audio track that is either in the optical or magnetic stripe format. **Magnetic film** is similar to audio tape in that it contains all sound and no picture and it has the same magnetic characteristics. However, magnetic film is the same size as regular film stock, and it contains sprocket holes. Magnetic film is opaque and comes either fully coated with iron oxide (also called **full coat**) or with several **magnetic stripes** of iron oxide (see **9-15**).

OPTICAL SOUND TRACK There are two ways to shoot sound film. One is to expose the picture separately on silent film stock and record the sound separately on audio tape, in sync with the picture. This is called **double-system sound recording** (see Chapter 12). After filming, the sound on the audio tape is transferred to magnetic film—full coat or multistripe—so that picture

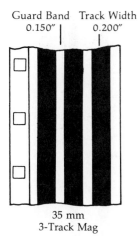

Guard Band   Track Width
   0.150″ | 0.200″

35 mm
3-Track Mag

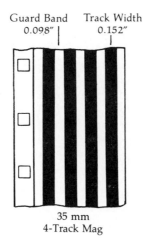

Guard Band   Track Width
   0.098″ | 0.152″

35 mm
4-Track Mag

Guard Band   Track Width
   0.060″ | 0.100″

35 mm
6-Track Mag

9-15 *Types of multistripe magnetic film.*

and sound are in the same operational format. They are sent to the film lab this way.

At the lab, the sound and picture are combined onto a new roll of film stock, and in the process the audio is reproduced photographically into an optical track. When the film is played on a projector, the sound head reads the patterns of photographic information and changes them into electric energy. At the projector's speaker, the electric energy is changed into sound.

MAGNETIC STRIPE SOUND TRACK   The second way to shoot film is to record the sound and picture together on the same roll of film stock. This is called **single-system sound recording** (see Chapter 12).

Recording sound directly onto film requires a special film with a magnetic stripe running along one of its edges. The magnetic properties of the stripe are similar to those of audio tape, and, like audio tape, you can record directly onto it. For playback, the projector must have a special head to read the magnetic stripe.

For sound quality, magnetic stripe is superior to optical. The optical format is by far more commonly used, however, since double-system recording is an easier and more controlled way to shoot film, it is easier and more accurate to edit, and most projectors are equipped to play optical sound. (It is possible to record single-system optical sound, but this format is no longer used in production.)

DOLBY STEREO OPTICAL SOUND   Since optical sound is so widely used and other, better-quality formats are slow in coming, efforts have been made to improve it. One successful attempt has been to change the sound from mono to stereo and use Dolby noise reduction (see Chapter 11).

An optical track has two sides. Recording a separate channel on each side creates stereo sound (see **9-16**). Then, by processing the whole track through

9-16 *Optical mono and stereo film sound tracks.*

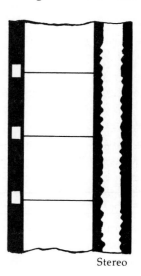

Mono

Stereo

the Dolby noise reduction system, not only the sound's dimension but also its quality improves considerably.

Another advantage to this system is that projectors equipped to play the standard mono optical track can still play film with Dolby stereo. Instead of reading both sides of the optical track as stereo, however, the sound head reads them as mono.

Video Tape versus Film

In broadcasting, video tape is fast replacing film. Once you have the necessary equipment, video tape is cheaper, easier, and more convenient to use. The picture and sound are ready for playback immediately after shooting, editing is computerized, picture quality is better for TV, and audio quality on video tape is better than optical sound on fllm. Film is not in danger of becoming extinct, however, at least not until someone discovers how to project video tape onto a large, wide screen without the considerable loss in quality that now results, and how to reproduce stereo TV sound through a large loudspeaker system.

Summary

a back coating ... and

1. Most recording tape is composed of a thin, plastic ribbon of polyester or acetate and needle-like particles of iron oxide that can be magnetized.

2. The differences between polyester and acetate tape are that polyester tape is stronger, more stable, less affected by hot and cold temperatures and humidity, and stores better over longer periods of time. It also stretches. Acetate tape's main advantage is that it breaks cleanly and can be spliced back together.

3. Audio tape comes in four thicknesses: 1½, 1, ½, and ¼ mil. Professionals prefer 1½-mil tape because it is least likely to crease, snap, or stretch, and it reduces the chance of print-through.

4. Audio tape has five widths: ⅛, ¼, ½, 1, and 2 inches to accommodate the single and multitrack formats used in recording today.

5. There are several measures of a tape's ability to reproduce sound. Three are coercivity—the magnetic force it takes to saturate a tape; retentivity—how well a tape retains magnetic information once the force field is removed; and sensitivity—how much output level a tape can reproduce.

6. Some tape is made for special purposes. Low-print-through tape has lower retentivity and sensitivity so it can handle lower energy levels, thus reducing the chance of magnetic information transferring from one tape layer to another. High-output tape has higher coercivity and sensitivity and, therefore, is capable of reproducing higher output levels.

7. Cheap tape can have several defects, which may cause dropout, clinching, ridging, adhesion, cupping, and curling. All adversely affect sound quality.

8. Store tape tails out in a controlled environment of 60 to 75 degrees Fahrenheit and 40 to 60 percent humidity.

9. Cartridge tape is a continuous loop of highly lubricated, standard, 1½-mil, ¼-inch tape. Carts come in lengths from 10 seconds to 30 minutes.

10. Cassette tape is reel-to-reel tape in an enclosed cartridge. It is ½ or ¼ mil thick, ⅛ inch wide, and comes in several lengths from 30 to 180 minutes.

11. Due to a cassette's dimensions, its sound quality is not yet acceptable for broadcast. In an effort to change that, tapes made with chromium dioxide, cobalt-treated oxide, and metal particles have been developed to widen the frequency response and increase the output level and the signal-to-noise ratio.

12. Video tape has the same magnetic and physical properties as audio tape except that the magnetic particles are either transverse or slanted, which makes the tape more conducive to recording video than audio. Audio tape has the magnetic particles in horizontal alignment, which is better for recording sound.

13. There are three types of film: silent, sound, and magnetic.

14. Sound film comes in an optical format, in which the sound is put on the film photographically, and in magnetic stripe, which is like audio tape and runs down the side of the film in a thin strip.

15. Although sound from an optical format is not as good as that from magnetic stripe, most projectors are equipped to play it and, hence, optical sound is more widely used.

16. Magnetic film is the same size and shape as regular film but is used only for sound; it contains no picture.

10
Tape Recorders

Most of what you hear and see in media today comes from a tape recording. Radio stations tape much, if not all, of their program material: music, commercials, and information. Television stations tape record almost all their sound and picture for broadcast. In film, sound usually is taped before it is transferred to film stock. Before most phonograph records become records, they are tape recordings. In short, the tape recorder is indispensable to media production and broadcasting.

Audio Tape Recorders

Audio **tape recorders** have three essential elements: (1) the tape transport system, (2) magnetic heads, and (3) record and playback amplifiers. You may consider the recording tape as a fourth element.

Tape Transport System

Tape transports have different features, but they are all designed to pull the tape across the magnetic heads at a constant speed and tension without causing fluctuations in the tape movement. In a typical **open-loop tape transport**,* a tape is prepared for record or play by placing it on the feed reel, threading it past the tape guide, across the head assembly, and between the capstan and pinch roller, through another tape guide to the take-up reel (see **10-1**).

---

*There is also a **closed-loop system** (also called *isolated,* or *iso* for short). Its main advantage over the open-loop system is better tape support around the head assembly (see **10-2**).

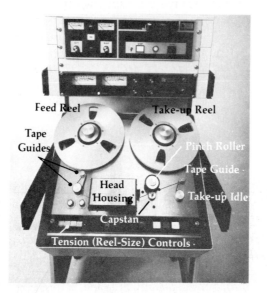

10-1 *(Right) Tape recorder with the open-loop transport system.*

10-2 *(Far right) Tape recorder with the closed or isolated loop system.*

CAPSTAN AND PINCH ROLLER The heart of the transport system is the **capstan**—a precision drive shaft that regulates the tape speed. When you put the machine in "Play," the tape is forced against the motor-driven shaft by the **pinch roller.** The pinch roller is rubber, and as the spinning capstan comes into contact with it, the capstan drives the roller and the roller pulls the tape.

FEED AND TAKE-UP REELS Both the feed and take-up reels are also driven by motors. Electric current feeding these motors controls the tension on each reel so that (1) tape will not spill as it is pulled by the capstan and pinch roller, and (2) tape maintains optimal contact with the heads without stretching.

TENSION (REEL-SIZE) CONTROL Although electric current to the feed and take-up motors keeps the tension on the reels constant, it does not control differences in tension created when tape winds from one size reel to a different size reel. Therefore, most professional recorders that are designed to take different size reels have a **tension** or **reel-size switch** so the tape wind from reel to reel is neither too taut nor too loose, regardless of tape distribution and reel sizes (see **10-3a, b**).

TAKE-UP IDLER Some tape recorders have a spring-loaded control called the **take-up idler.** It is designed to perform three functions. First, as a safety on-off lever, it activates and deactivates the tape transport system; the actual on-off switch is for the power. If a tape breaks, the idler releases, thereby stopping the tape transport and preventing the tape from spilling off the reels (see **10-4**). Second, the tape guide on the idler arm ensures even stacking of the tape as it winds onto the take-up reel. Third, it cuts down on machine wear and tear. If the transport is not in use, it can be shut off by releasing the idler arm without turning off the entire recorder.

TAPE GUIDES **Tape guides** are used to position the tape correctly on the heads as it winds from the feed to the take-up reel.

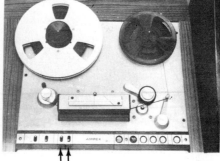

10-3a (Far left) Arrows point to reel-size adjustments set for 7-inch hubs on the feed and take-up reels.

10-3b (Left) Arrows point to reel-size adjustments set for a 10$\frac{1}{2}$-inch hub on the feed reel (left) and a 7-inch hub on the take-up reel (right).

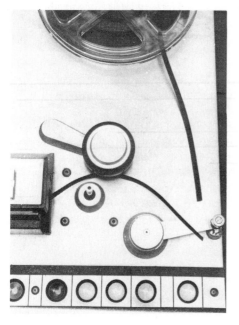

10-4 When a tape breaks, the take-up idler is released, thus stopping the transport system and preventing the tape from spilling off the reel.

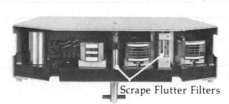

Scrape Flutter Filters

Scrape Flutter Filter

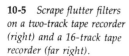

10-5 *Scrape flutter filters on a two-track tape recorder (right) and a 16-track tape recorder (far right).*

Wow and Flutter

Constant tape movement and tension are critical to acceptable recording. If a problem develops with some part of the tape transport system, the sound may take on **wow** or **flutter**. Wow and flutter are actually similar in that they are caused by irregular motion in the tape transport; wow refers to distortion in the lower frequencies and flutter to distortion in the higher frequencies.

Some recorders come with **scrape flutter filters** (see **10-5**) to reduce high-frequency distortion, which is more likely to occur than low-frequency distortion. Scrape flutter filters are installed between the heads to reduce the amount of unsupported tape, thereby restricting the degree of tape movement as it passes across the heads.

Tape Speeds

Six speeds are used in tape recording: $^{15}/_{16}$, $1\frac{7}{8}$, $3\frac{3}{4}$, $7\frac{1}{2}$, 15, and 30 ips (inches per second). The faster the speed, the better is the sound quality or signal-to-noise ratio (see Chapter 1).

Professionals usually use $7\frac{1}{2}$ ips as a common speed when distributing or airing tape recordings, but they commonly work at 15 or 30 ips for improved sound quality and ease of editing. In any case, do not use speeds lower than $7\frac{1}{2}$ ips. To give you an insight into the relationship between speed and sound quality, a top-quality professional tape recorder may have a frequency response to 20,000 Hz at 15 ips, at $7\frac{1}{2}$ ips response may reach 15,000 Hz, and at $3\frac{3}{4}$ ips it may only go as high as 10,000 Hz. Also, faster speeds make it easier to edit tape (see Chapter 13). The more tape that passes across the heads per second, the more spread out the sound is on the tape.

Tape Transport Controls

Several different controls operate the tape transport system (see **10-6**):

On-Off Switch—turns the electric power to the tape recorder on or off.

Selectable Speed Control—most professional recorders operate at more than one speed. This control selects the speed.

Variable Speed Control—some two-speed recorders have a control that adjusts the tape speed to a rate that is ±5 to 20 percent of the machine's two set speeds. This **variable speed control** comes in handy when you want to change the pitch of a sound for special effect.

10-6 *Tape transport controls.*

Play—engages and starts the tape transport.

Record—activates the record head. To avoid accidental erasure, it usually will not work unless you also press the "Play" button.

Rewind and Fast Forward—disengages the capstan/pinch roller to permit winding or rewinding the tape at high speed. In either mode, tape lifters hold the tape away from the heads to avoid unnecessary wear to both tape and heads, and to mute the annoying high-pitched squeal that comes when running the tape at high speed.

Stop—stops the feed and take-up reels and disengages the pinch roller from the capstan.

Edit Control—allows you to spool off unwanted tape without having to use a take-up reel. For **edit control,** press "Edit" to disengage the take-up reel while allowing the tape transport to continue functioning.

Magnetic Heads

The heads of a tape recorder are small electromagnets—coils of extremely fine wire wrapped around laminated cores of either very soft metal or ferrite, a hard ceramic-like material. These magnetic heads are transducers; they convert electric energy into magnetic energy during recording or magnetic energy back into electric energy during playback.

Most professional tape recorders have three heads: erase, record, and playback (see **10-7**). A good way to identify them is to remember that the erase head is always closest to the feed reel, the record head is in the middle, and the playback head is closest to the take-up reel. Some machines have two heads, combining the record and playback functions. These recorders still have the playback head closest to the take-up reel. Some recorders have four heads: either erase, record, four-track playback, and two-track playback (see **10-8**); or an erase head, a sync head to the left or right of the record head, and a playback head (see **10-27**). Again, these playback heads are nearest to the take-up reel.

10-7 *Audio tape recorder with three magnetic heads.*

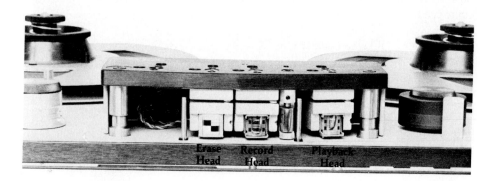

Erase Head   Record Head   Playback Head

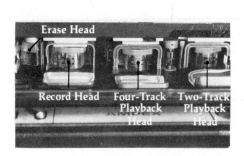

10-8 *(Far left) Audio tape recorder with four magnetic heads.*

10-9 *(Left) Good-quality bulk eraser.*

BIAS Before we discuss the function of each magnetic head, it is necessary to explain bias. The iron oxide on recording tape is nonlinear—the magnetic particles will not align to conform exactly to the signal that reaches the tape from the erase and record heads. Something is needed to line up the magnetic properties of the oxide—to align the particles as the audio current directs. To solve the problem, the erase and record heads feed a high-frequency current, called the **bias current,** to the tape. The current has a frequency between 100,000 and 200,000 Hz—many times higher than the limits of human hearing but strong enough to affect the polarity of the oxide particles so they respond and conform to the audio signal.

The exact frequency of the bias current is critical. Loss of high end frequencies result if it is too high, and sound distorts if it is too low. Certain bias frequencies work better with some tapes than with others. Since engineers set the bias for a particular type of tape, you should know which type it is before using a tape recorder.

ERASE HEAD The **erase head** is activated during recording. Its function is to neutralize the polarities of the oxide particles—to remove sound from the tape with a high-frequency bias current before the tape passes across the record head.

BULK ERASERS Another way to erase tape is with a **bulk eraser** (also known as a **degausser**)—a large magnet that can erase an entire reel at once (see **10-9**). It is quick and easy to use, but the following precautions should be taken.

1. The tape (and your watch) should not be near it when it is turned on, or they could become magnetized.

2. Rotate the tape over the demagnetizer slowly, do not scrape it too hard across the surface, and make sure the passes include both sides of the entire reel, otherwise residual magnetism will remain on the tape.

3. When you finish, take the tape away from the eraser before you turn it off.

4. Make sure you know what the use-time of the demagnetizer is; some of them tend to heat up quickly and will burn out if left on too long.

RECORD HEAD The **record head** transduces electric energy into the magnetic force that magnetizes the tape. It carries two signals; the record bias current and the audio current—the signal that was transduced from the original acoustic sound.

PLAYBACK HEAD The **playback head** transduces the recorded magnetic field back into electric energy.

HEAD CARE Magnetic heads require very careful treatment. The slightest change in their alignment, any accumulation of dust, dirt, or oxide particles, scratches, wear, or overmagnetizing will adversely affect sound quality.

ALIGNING THE HEADS Although an engineer usually aligns the heads, you should be aware of what adjustments are made and some problems that can result when the heads are out of alignment. There are five adjustments (see **10-10**).

    Zenith—the vertical angle of the heads. If the top or bottom of a head is tilted and one end applies greater pressure to the tape than the other, it causes the tape to skew—ride up or down on the head.

    Height—to make the heads present themselves to the tape at exactly the right height. Otherwise, the result could be signals that are only partially recorded or reproduced, crosstalk between tracks, more noise, or poor erasure.

    Tangency—the pressure of the head against the tape. The farther forward the head, the greater is the pressure. Too little or too much pressure noticeably degrades a signal.

10-10 *Five alignment adjustments made to a magnetic head.*

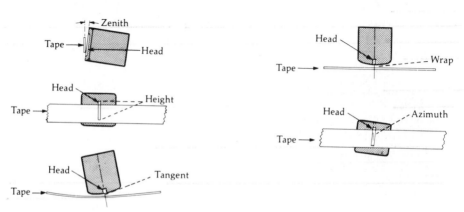

Wrap—the angle at which the tape curves around the head. Without firm tape-to-head contact, there is sound dropout.

Azimuth—adjustment of the head exactly perpendicular to the tape. Heads that are not in azimuth alignment record and reproduce out-of-phase signals.

It is difficult to visually spot heads that are out of alignment, but you can hear many of the problems caused by unaligned heads. Most studios have a routine schedule of preventive maintenance that includes head alignment. If you are getting poor sound from a tape recorder, have an engineer check the heads. As for the other aspects of head care, you can handle them yourself.

DEMAGNETIZING THE HEADS Before you use a tape recorder, make sure the heads are free from any magnetization that may have been left from previous use. When heads build up enough permanent magnetism, they can partially erase a recording; higher frequencies are particularly susceptible. Recordings so affected sound "muddy"; they often lack presence and brilliance.

You can easily demagnetize heads with any of several inexpensive demagnetizers available (see **10-11**). Select one that does not produce too strong a magnetic field, however, or it can permanently magnetize a head instead of demagnetize it. Also, turn the demagnetizer on and off away from the heads, otherwise the surge or cut in power could leave remnant magnetization on the heads. Make sure, too, that the demagnetizer does not touch or scrape the heads, or they could be scratched and permanently damaged.

CLEANING THE HEADS Dust, dirt, and oxide particles collect on the heads and tape guides even in the cleanest studios. Some of these particles are abrasive, and when the tape picks them up and drags them across the heads, they can scratch both the oxide and the heads. If these particles build up sufficiently, sound quality suffers noticeably.

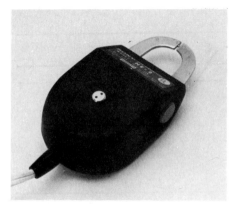

10-11 *Head demagnetizer.*

The best preventive maintenance is to clean the heads and tape guides each time you use a tape recorder. Cotton swabs and an approved head cleaner or easy-to-obtain and inexpensive isopropyl alcohol will do. Use one cotton swab for each head and guide, two if the cotton turns brown, and swab the head gently. Special head cleaner is available, but it may be too potent for some heads and dissolve part of the material. Check with a technician if you are in doubt.

Amplifiers

RECORD AMPLIFIER The record amplifier receives all audio input to the tape recorder and converts it to the current that flows to the record head.

PLAYBACK AMPLIFIER The playback amplifier takes the current from the playback head and converts it into voltage, which is then sent to the output of the tape recorder.

Features of Audio Tape Recorders

TRACKS AND TRACK WIDTHS Professional reel-to-reel audio tape recorders come in 1-, 2-, 4-, 8-, 16-, 24- and 32-channel/track formats (see **10-12a**). Each channel records and plays back a single track. The amount of surface on each head (or **headstack** as it is called on 4-, 8-, 16-, 24-, and 32-track machines) used for recording or playback varies with the size of the head (see **10-12b**). Between each head is a **guard band** that reduces considerably the chance of magnetic information from one head affecting the magnetic information on an adjacent head (see **10-13**).

SELECTIVE SYNCHRONIZATION (SEL SYNC) Multitrack recorders were developed to permit greater control of the sound sources during recording and playback by making it possible to assign each one to its own track. Multitrack recorders also make it possible to record various sound sources at different times by overdubbing—recording new material on open tracks and synchronizing it with material on tracks already recorded. The technology that facilitates this production technique was developed by Ampex (the innovator was guitarist Les Paul) and is called by the copyrighted term **sel sync (selective synchronization)**.

Under normal conditions, if you recorded, say, instrumental accompaniment and a vocal at different times, the vocalist would have to listen to the recording (through earphones) to synchronize the words to the music. A distance of a few inches separates the record and playback heads, however, thus creating a delay between the music as it is heard and the lyrics as they are sung and recorded (see **10-14**). To eliminate this delay, sel sync converts the record head into a playback head for the previously recorded tracks and plays

10-12a *Examples of tape recorders: (far left) 2-track, (left) 4-track, (bottom, far left) 8-track, (bottom, left) 24-track.*

10-12b *Examples of 1-, 2-, 4-, 8-, 16-, 24-, and 32-track headstacks. The 32-track headstack (bottom right) is for a digital 1-inch audio tape recorder.*

10-13 *Standards for track and guard band widths set by the National Association of Broadcasters (NAB).*

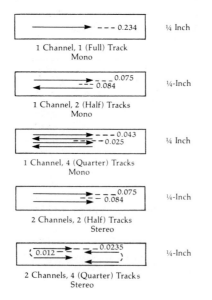

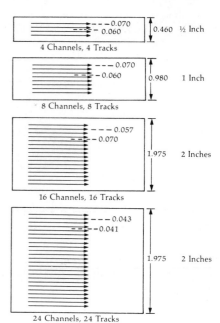

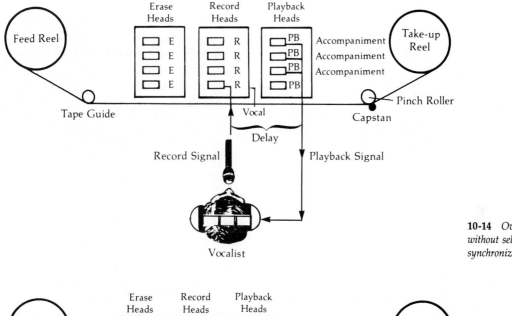

10-14 *Overdubbing without selective synchronization (sel sync).*

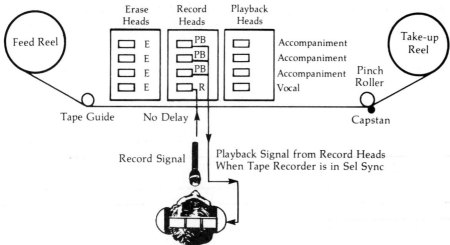

10-15 *Overdubbing with sel sync.*

them in sync with the new material being recorded (see **10-15**). (Also see the section on overdubbing in Chapter 14.)

TIMING Most tape recorders manufactured today are equipped with either a **footage counter** (see **10-16**) or a **tape timer** (see **10-17**). They provide an easy way to locate recorded material.

Footage counter is actually a misnomer because it does not indicate how many feet of tape pass across the heads. What turns the counter is either the

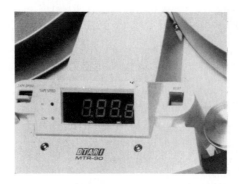

10-16 *(Right) Footage counter.*

10-17 *(Far right) Tape timer.*

10-18 *(Right) Tape timer with light-emitting diode display.*

10-19 *(Far right) Search-to-cue control with memory to store commands.*

feed reel or one of the tape guide rollers. The footage reading is really a count of the number of revolutions of the feed reel or tape guide roller. Nevertheless, it is a convenient, if imprecise reference and better than nothing.

An actual tape timer is wound by a tape guide roller with revolutions that are synchronized to inches per second. Tape timers read out in hours, minutes, and seconds, and may be displayed by light-emitting diodes (see **10-18**).

SEARCH-TO-CUE   Even with timing devices, locating specific cue points on a tape can be time-consuming. Some recorders have a **search-to-cue** function that allows you to program cue points so that in rewind or fast forward the recorder will automatically stop at the preset point (see **10-19**).

Analog versus Digital Recording

The method of tape recording used since the late 1940s has been **analog**—encoding magnetic information that has a direct relationship to the original acoustic and electric information; that is, the wave form of the signal on tape resembles that of the original sound (see **10-20**). Although the sound quality of analog recording has improved dramatically over the years, the tape medium is still the main inhibitor to bringing recorded sound closer to the quality of live sound.

Dynamic range is the ratio between the quietest and loudest sounds a sound source emits. Acoustically, dynamic range is measured in dB-SPL, with 0 dB-SPL as the threshold of hearing and 120 dB-SPL as the threshold of pain (see Chapter 1). Tape recording, at best, however, can deliver up to only 65 or 70 dB-SPL of dynamic range—about half of what is possible acoustically. This is why nothing on tape has come near the quality of live sound.

In an effort to improve the dynamic range of tape, **digital recording** has been developed. Using computer technology, the digital process converts signals into coded pulses that are recorded on the tape; the pulses do not resemble the wave form of the original signal (see **10-21**). They are actually bits or samples of the original information and, hence, take up less room on the tape as they are encoded.

Digital tape recorders contain special circuitry to encode tape with these pulses (see **10-22**). Standard speeds vary from manufacturer to manufacturer; one recorder may operate at 15 ips and another at 45 ips. The tape widths used are ¼ inch, ½ inch, and so on. Digital recording is so free of noise that several more tracks can be recorded on a tape than with analog recording. For

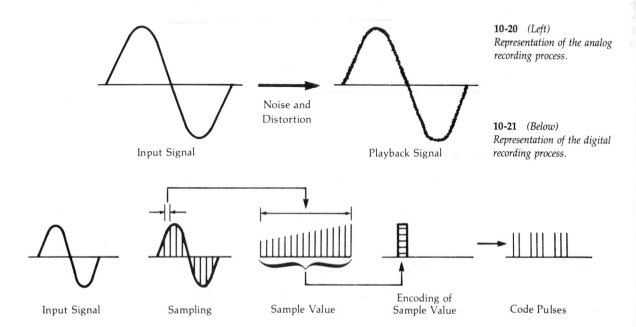

Input Signal   Noise and Distortion   Playback Signal

10-20 (Left)
Representation of the analog recording process.

10-21 (Below)
Representation of the digital recording process.

Input Signal   Sampling   Sample Value   Encoding of Sample Value   Code Pulses

10-22 *A 32-track, 1-inch, digital tape recorder.*

example, 1-inch tape can take 32 tracks. Operationally, the transport and controls of digital recorders are similar to those of analog recorders.

Digital recordings have virtually no noise, **crosstalk**—track-to-track leakage—print-through, flutter, or loudness variations. They have an expanded dynamic range to 90 dB-SPL. One relatively serious problem with digital recording, however, is that the texture of the sound has a characteristic hardness or unnatural clarity. The problem is analogous to that of the synthesizer, which makes an unmistakable electronic sound no matter how "human" or natural musicians try to make it sound. Also, questions have been raised about digital sound's psychophysical effect in causing stress. Regardless of these difficulties, however, the digital format is revolutionizing recording and is fast becoming the state-of-the-art.

Cartridge Tape Recorders

The first major departure from reel-to-reel recording was the **cartridge tape** (see **9-10**) and the special machine needed to play it (see **10-23**). They were developed in 1958 to speed up and simplify the threading, recording, cueing, and playing of short program materials such as spots, news actualities, and jingles. Now many stations dub records onto carts for easier handling, to cut down on record wear, and to facilitate tighter production.

The operation of the cartridge system is uncomplicated. The tape is wound loosely around a hub so it can be easily pulled from the center of the reel. The tape feeds in a continuous loop around the tape guides that are in the cartridge casing. When the cart is pushed into the recorder and locked in place, the hole in the bottom, upper right-hand side of the cart sits over the pinch roller. When the machine is put into "Play" (or "Start"), the pinch roller engages the capstan, pulling the tape across the heads and rotating the roll as it does so (see **10-24a, b**).

10-23 *Cartridge tape recorders from left: stereo record/playback unit; three-cartridge playback unit; stereo record unit.*

Since the tape is continuous, there is no need for feed and take-up reels or for a "Rewind." Until recently there was no "Fast Forward" either. Sometimes, however, several separate bits of material are recorded on a single cart and "Fast Forward" speeds cueing (see **10-25**).

What makes the cartridge system possible is the **cue tone**—a pulse that tells the continuous **tape loop** when to stop. The record head puts the pulse on the tape, and the playback head senses it. The heads are designed so that

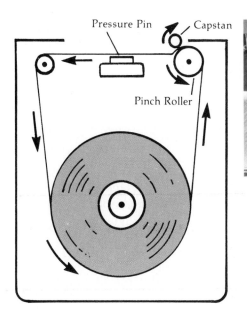

Pressure Pin   Capstan

Pinch Roller

Capstan   Pinch Roller

10-24a *(Far left) The capstan and pinch roller engage the cartridge tape to keep the tape winding at a constant speed.*

10-24b *(Left) When the cartridge tape recorder is in play, the pinch roller and the capstan are engaged.*

10-25 *Cartridge record/playback unit with fast forward control.*

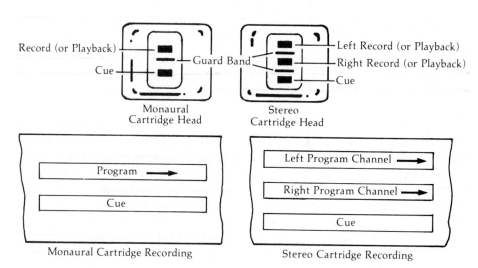

Record (or Playback) ⎯ Guard Band ⎯ Cue

Monaural Cartridge Head

Left Record (or Playback) ⎯ Right Record (or Playback) ⎯ Cue

Stereo Cartridge Head

Program ⎯→

Cue

Monaural Cartridge Recording

Left Program Channel ⎯→

Right Program Channel ⎯→

Cue

Stereo Cartridge Recording

10-26 *Head and track formats for mono and stereo cartridge tape recorders.*

the cue tone is a function of record and playback (see **10-26**). As you can see in **10-26**, <u>carts recorded in mono cannot be played on stereo cart machines, and vice versa.</u> Eight-track cartridge recorders are also available, but they are not used in broadcasting.

To give you an idea of how the cue tone works, assume you are recording a 30-second spot on a 40-second cart. (Always use a cartridge that runs slightly longer than the material.) After loading the cart, push "Record" to put the machine into the record mode. <u>This automatically puts the cue tone on the tape.</u> Push "Play" (or "Start") to start the tape spinning and recording. On some cart machines, the cue tone is put on the tape when "Record" is pushed; <u>on other cart machines, it is put on the tape when "Play" is pushed.</u> Make sure to <u>begin the material you are recording just after you start the cart</u>

machine, otherwise when you play back the cart, the material will not start when the tape does and there will be some dead air.

Once the tape starts, it will wind 30 seconds for the spot, continue for another 10 seconds until it reaches the cue tone, and then stop, recued. Either the machine will automatically switch off the record mode or you will have to do it manually. Once that is done, the tape is ready for playback.

Keep in mind that each time you hit the "Record" or "Play" button when the machine is in the record mode, it puts a pulse on the tape. Therefore, it is important to be careful during recording or you may have unwanted cue tones that will stop the cart at the wrong place(s).

Cartridge tape recorders have either record and playback heads, or just record or playback. Thus, carts cannot be erased by rerecording; they must be bulk erased each time you reuse them.

Cassette Tape Recorders

The cartridge tape system was developed mainly for broadcasting to speed and simplify tape handling and operation. However, it was obvious that a tape that is enclosed and ready for immediate use, that can be easily inserted in a tape recorder and removed regardless of how much tape is on the reels, that is small, and that can be handled without being sullied had potential beyond broadcasting. It took only five years from the development of the cartridge tape before the cassette was introduced in 1963.

The cartridge was impractical for wide use because the recorder was bulky and heavy, the running time of the tape was limited, and the cost was high. The cassette improved upon the cartridge concept in three ways. (1) The tape is in the reel-to-reel format, which allows more tape on the reel and hence more playing time. (2) Cassettes have a narrower tape size (1/8 inch) and slower speed (1 7/8 ips), which makes it possible to have a recorder that is small and lightweight. (3) Cassettes operate on both AC current and batteries.

Since its development, the **cassette tape recorder** has revolutionized tape recording. Now it is possible to take a recorder practically anywhere with little physical or logistical inconvenience; to record up to 180 minutes of material on tape that is smaller than a 3 by 5 card; and to store these tapes in a small amount of space.

For the professional, however, two problems limit the cassette's use: comparatively poor sound quality and difficulty in editing. When a cassette recording is used for broadcast, it is usually dubbed onto a reel-to-reel or cartridge recorder.

The operating principle of the cassette combines the reel-to-reel and cartridge concepts. The main difference between the cassette and other recorders, besides the size and sound quality, is the track format. Cassettes are available in mono and stereo; two tracks for mono, and four or eight for stereo. Unlike those on standard stereo recorders, the pairs of stereo tracks on a cassette recorder are adjacent rather than alternate.

In an effort to upgrade the sound quality of cassettes, machines have been built that record and play the tape at 3¾ ips. Indeed, this results in increased frequency response, output level, and signal-to-noise ratio. There are three problems with these cassette recorders, however: (1) the tape speed is not compatible with that of most other cassette recorders, (2) many are not portable, and (3) they are comparatively expensive. Since the development of metal-particle tape and the special circuitry to play it, the sound quality of cassettes has improved to the point where many FM radio stations are using them in their music programming.

High-Quality Portable Tape Recorders

Since so much field recording is done in broadcasting and film, high-quality portable reel-to-reel tape recorders are standard equipment. A portable recorder should be relatively small, lightweight, and able to run on a self-contained battery supply. It should also be rugged, comparatively trouble-free, and capable of some signal processing to overcome some of the sound problems frequently encountered in remote recording (see **10-27**).

10-27 *The Nagra 4.2 audio tape recorder and most of its features.*

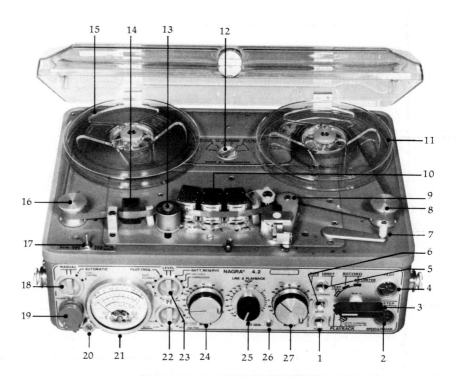

Video Tape Recorders

Audio and video recording are similar in that sound and picture are converted into electric and then into magnetic information, and encoded on the iron oxide coating of the tape. During playback, these steps are reversed. Although the process of audio and video recording is the same, there is little similarity in the way they are accomplished.

The reason for the difference is the amount of information that has to be processed in video tape recording. With sound recording, the only concern is the audible part of the frequency spectrum, 20 to 16,000 Hz. Taping a color picture involves the visible part of the frequency spectrum, however, which runs into the millions of hertz. To record and play back at these frequencies, a video tape would have to spin at more than 1,000 ips to record a picture of acceptable quality. This would require about 8,330 feet of video tape per minute.

To solve the problem, instead of the tape moving faster against the stationary heads, the tape moves at the usual 7½ or 15 ips but against video heads that rotate at 14,400 rpm. All video tape recorders (VTRs) have rotating video heads; however, there are two different ways in which these heads record a picture: (1) by transverse scanning, and (2) by helical or slant track scanning.

Nagra 4.2 Operation Controls

1 Power Selector	15 5" Supply Reel (7" reels can also be used with lid open)
2 Speed and Power Indicator	
3 Principal Function Selector	16 Tension Roller
4 Pilot Indicator	17 Rewind and Fast Forward Switch
5 Tape/Direct Switch (Line and Phones)	18 Manual/Automatic Microphone Selector
6 Tape/Direct Switch (Meter)	19 Headphone Jack
7 Pinch Wheel and Tape Guide Control Lever	20 Headphone Volume
8 Tension Roller	21 Meter
9 Capstan and Pinch Wheel	22 Low-Frequency Roll-off Attenuator
10 Record, Pilot, and Playback Heads	23 Meter Switch
11 5" Take-up Reel (7" reels can also be used with lid open)	24 Mike 1 Input Level Control
	25 Line Input Level Control and Playback
12 Speed and Tape Selector	26 Reference Signal Generator Switch
13 Roller Filter and Strobe Disc	27 Mike 2 Input Level Control
14 Erase Head	

TRANSVERSE SCANNING: THE QUADRUPLEX FORMAT Transverse scanning, so called because the video information is encoded across the tape in almost straight up and down patterns, is more commonly referred to as **quadruplex** or **quad recording** since it uses four rotating video heads to record and play the video. Because it usually results in better picture and sound quality, most of the video tape broadcast is in the quad format, although it is expensive and sometimes cumbersome to work with.

Tape Tracks   The quad VTR, which uses only 2-inch video tape, puts down four different tracks (see **10-28a, b**).

10-28a *Examples of quadruplex video tape recorders.*

10-28b *Track format for quadruplex video tape recording.*

Audio Track

Video Track

Cue Track (SMPTE Code)
Control Track

2-Inch Tape

1. The video track, which contains the picture information, takes up most of the tape.

2. The audio track contains the program's sound; some VTRs have two audio tracks, which can be used as separate mono tracks or as stereo.

3. The **cue track** is another audio track, but it is of such poor sound quality that it is usually used to record the director's cues, verbal notes, or most often, a code that identifies each video frame with a number, thus allowing easy retrieval of any picture during editing (see the discussion of the SMPTE code in Chapter 13).

4. The **control track** consists of pulses that synchronize video playback. These pulses also indicate the beginning and end of each video frame, which is essential in video tape editing. The control track is analogous to the sprocket holes on film, which synchronize playback of the picture.

Tape Heads   There are four heads on most quad VTRs. (1) The master erase head erases old video during the recording of new video. (2) The video head-wheel assembly houses the four rotating video heads that record and play the picture. (3) The audio and cue erase heads erase old sound information during the recording of new audio and cue information. (4) The audio and cue record-play heads record and reproduce program and cue audio (see **10-29**).

The video and audio heads operate independently. Therefore, a quad VTR can record and play back in three modes: (1) video and audio together, (2) video only, and (3) audio only. This has obvious advantages in dubbing and editing; you can change or move audio from one point in the tape to another without affecting the video, and vice versa (see Chapter 13).

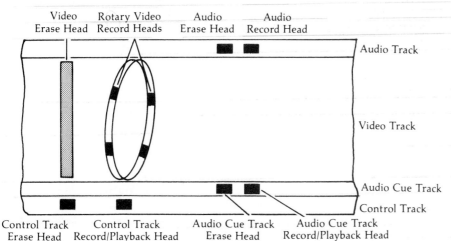

Video   Rotary Video   Audio   Audio
Erase Head   Record Heads   Erase Head   Record Head

Audio Track

Video Track

Audio Cue Track

Control Track

Control Track   Control Track   Audio Cue Track   Audio Cue Track
Erase Head   Record/Playback Head   Erase Head   Record/Playback Head

2-Inch Tape

10-29 *Video tape head locations on a quad video tape recorder.*

Sound Quality   The frequency response of the best quad VTRs is 50 to 12,000 Hz, which is good but not excellent. There are two reasons why the sound quality of quad is somewhat lacking. The first reason is that the magnetic particles on audio tape are arranged longitudinally for optimal sound reproduction; on quad video tape, however, they are arranged transversely for optimal picture reproduction. This difference in the alignment of magnetic particles adversely affects the audio in favor of the video. The second reason is that the width of the audio track on quad VTRs is less than ⅛ inch.

The inability of quad VTRs to produce better-quality sound is not a major concern right now and probably will not be until another more significant TV audio problem is solved: the sound quality of home receivers. A typical TV loudspeaker has a frequency response between 100 and 8,000 Hz, far below the capability of TV sound. This is changing, however, with the advent of improved loudspeakers in TV receivers and stereo TV.

SLANT TRACK SCANNING: THE HELICAL FORMAT   Slant track scanning is so called because, unlike quad, the video information is encoded across the tape on a slant. This format is also known as **helical recording** due to the somewhat spiral shape of the tape when it is threaded around the head assembly; the Greek word for spiral is *helix* (see **10-30**). Also, unlike quad, which plays only 2-inch tape, different types of helical VTRs can play 2-, 1-, ½-, or ¼-inch reel-to-reel video tape, or ¾-inch cassette video tape; the larger the width, the better is the sound and picture quality.

Tape Heads and Tape Tracks   Most helical VTRs have one or two video heads mounted on a rotating drum called the *head drum*. They also have stationary heads for the audio and cue tracks, and the capability to reproduce video and audio separately or simultaneously. Newer 1-inch helical VTRs have several rotating heads, not only for video but also for such functions as *automatic system tracking* (AST), better known as *slo mo, picture and shuttle* so a picture can be seen during fast forward and rewind, and *record head read* to enable monitoring directly from the record head during taping. The track arrangement varies with the VTR (see **10-31a, b, c**).

Tape Speed   Quad VTRs run at either 7½ or 15 ips, but helical VTRs run at several different speeds, all less than 15 ips. The better slant track recorders have playing speeds of almost 10 ips; however, some models run as slow as 5 ips.

Sound Quality   Paradoxically, helical recording has the potential to produce better sound quality than quad because its scanning format—slant track—brings the magnetic particles closer to the longitudinal alignment of audio tape. The sound quality of the newer 1-inch machines comes very close to quad (see **10-32**). Most helical format VTRs, however, particularly those less than 1 inch, have inferior audio systems and audio tracks between ⅛ and ¹⁄₁₆ inch wide (depending on the head width), hence, the inferior signal-to-noise ratio.

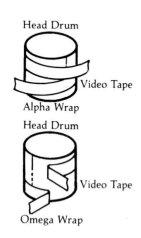

Head Drum

Video Tape

Alpha Wrap

Head Drum

Video Tape

Omega Wrap

10-30 *Two ways video tape winds around the video head drum in helical recording. Alpha and omega wraps get their names from the Greek letters their configurations resemble.*

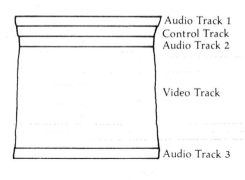

Audio Track 1
Control Track
Audio Track 2

Video Track

Audio Track 3

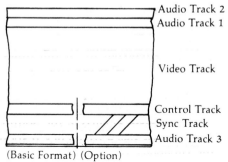

Audio Track 2
Audio Track 1

Video Track

Control Track
Sync Track
Audio Track 3

(Basic Format) (Option)

10-31a *(Far left) The Type B video tape track format used on 1-inch helical VTRs with the alpha wrap design.*

10-31b *(Left) The Type C video tape track format used on 1-inch helical VTRs with the omega wrap design. This format is now standard for 1-inch helical VTRs.*

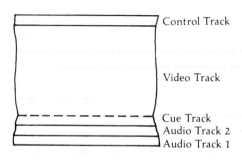

Control Track

Video Track

Cue Track
Audio Track 2
Audio Track 1

10-31c *The two video tape track formats used on ¾-inch cassette VTRs: the U-Matic series, which uses an audio track as a cue track, and the BVU series, which has a separate cue track.*

10-32 *Type C 1-inch helical video tape recorder.*

Quad versus Helical Video Tape Recording

Although quad has been superior to helical recording in picture and sound quality and has been the standard for years, the newer 1-inch helical VTR with the Type C format is supplanting quad. It generally has superior picture quality and more sound capability with three audio tracks, although not better sound quality.

The helical format has other advantages over quad. It is less expensive and easier to work with; its size facilitates on-location production and paved the way for **electronic news gathering** and **electronic field production** (see Chapter 12); and it can reproduce an image in slow motion (slo mo) and single frame (freeze frame). The quad design needs a special accessory to accomplish these effects.

The helical format has disadvantages, too. Its several different formats are not interchangeable, whereas all quad tapes are. And, except for the newer 1-inch designs, picture and sound quality is not as good as that of quad and, too often, much worse.

Summary

1. The three essential sections of a tape recorder are the tape transport system, the magnetic heads, and the record and playback amplifiers.

2. The transport system consists of the feed and take-up reels to hold the tape while it is unwinding and winding; a capstan and pinch roller to pull the tape across the heads at a constant speed; a tension control to prevent the tape from layering unevenly; and the take-up idler to stop the transport if the tape breaks.

3. A number of controls operate the transport: the power switch, selectable and variable speed control, play, record, stop, fast forward, rewind, and the tape edit release.

4. An important function of the transport system is to restrict tape movement as it passes across the heads and thus prevent wow—low-frequency distortion—and flutter—high-frequency distortion.

5. Tape recorders run at various speeds, $^{15}/_{16}$, $1\frac{7}{8}$, $3\frac{3}{4}$, $7\frac{1}{2}$, 15, and 30 ips. The faster the speed, the better is the sound quality.

6. Most professional tape recorders have three heads: erase, record, and playback. Tape heads are electromagnets made of either soft iron, which will wear down, or ferrite, a harder, more durable, ceramic-like material.

7. Because the iron oxide particles on tape respond to magnetization non-linearly (they cannot make sense of the information carried by the input signal), the erase and record heads have a high-frequency bias current that linearizes the magnetic information so it can be encoded on the tape.

8. The position of the heads is critical and any change in their alignment—tilt, height, tangency, wrap, or azimuth—adversely affects sound quality.

9. Heads should be cleaned and demagnetized before use.

10. A multitrack tape recorder has a headstack that contains 4, 8, 16, 24, or 32 separate tracks, allowing individual control of each recorded element.

11. Multitrack machines also have sel sync, which temporarily changes selected tracks on the record head into the playback mode. This permits various elements in a recording to be taped at different times.

12. The format used since modern tape recording began has been analog, which can reproduce a dynamic range of about 65 dB-SPL, half of what humans can hear live. A new format—digital recording—can deliver up to 90 dB-SPL so far, and without many of the noise problems common to the analog format.

13. Cartridge tape recorders play a continuous tape loop, which winds until it reaches a cue tone and then automatically stops, recued. Carts eliminate threading and cut down the time it takes to cue and play tape.

14. Since cart machines have no erase head, cartridge tapes must be bulk erased before they are reused.

15. Cassette recorders are lightweight, small, highly portable machines that make recording possible virtually anywhere. Although their size and format have inhibited sound quality, improvements in cassette tape and recorders are increasing the dynamic range and signal-to-noise ratio.

16. Video tape recorders (VTRs) come in two formats: quadruplex and helical.

17. The quad VTR has four heads: master erase, video record and play, audio and cue erase, and audio and cue record and play. They put on the tape a video track, audio track, cue track, and control track.

18. The helical VTR has one or two video heads, an audio and a cue head. They put on the tape basically the same four tracks as those of quad VTRs.

11

Signal
Processing

Most sound sources produce complex tonal structures consisting of a fundamental—the lowest, most powerful frequency a sound source can produce; harmonics—the tonal multiples of the fundamental; and overtones—the rest of a sound's components (see **11-1**). These elements give sound its timbre, or textural uniqueness. The **sound envelope** also contributes to the uniqueness of a sound. It consists of the **attack**—the first sound emitted after a sound source is struck, plucked, bowed, blown, or has spoken; the **sustain**—how long a sound stays at full loudness; and the decay—how long it takes a sound to go from full loudness to silence (see **11-2**). As long as nothing alters any of these components appreciably, you hear a sound pretty much the way it is produced.

11-1 *Representation of the interactions of the fundamental, harmonics, and overtones of a sound wave.*

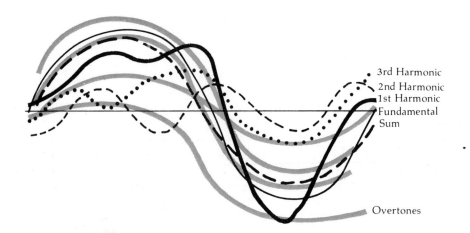

3rd Harmonic
2nd Harmonic
1st Harmonic
Fundamental
Sum

Overtones

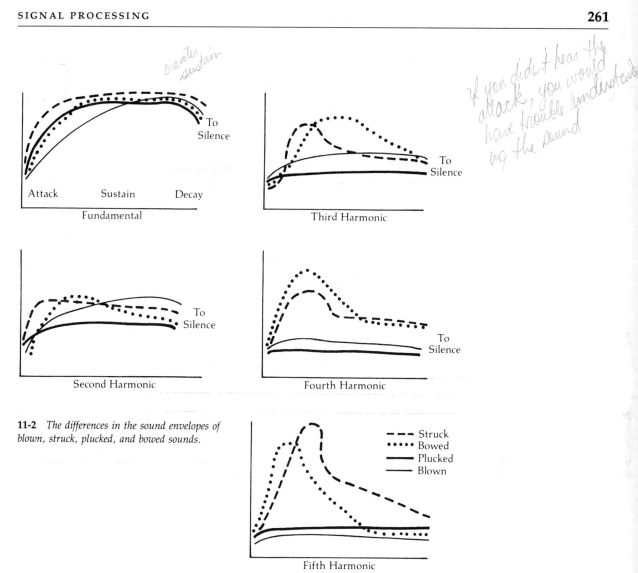

greater sustain

If you didn't hear the attack, you would have trouble understanding the sound

11-2 *The differences in the sound envelopes of blown, struck, plucked, and bowed sounds.*

Many things can happen to a sound, however. It can be bent, delayed, strengthened, weakened, doubled, repeated, flipped, squeezed, or expanded. This may suggest that a lot can happen to interfere with a sound's tonal purity, but actually, the opposite is true. The more ways you are able to modify sound, the greater is your ability to produce an individual sonic statement. That is why most recordists today use **signal processing**—altering the shape, size, length, and quantity of sound waves through mechanical and electronic devices generally called *signal processors*. Specifically, these processors are called the *equalizer, reverberation unit, digital delay, phaser, flanger, limiter-compressor, expander,* and *noise reducer.*

amplifies or attenuates certain frequencies

selects frequency that you want to equalize

band

Equalizers

Perhaps the best known and most often used signal processor is the equalizer—an electronic device that alters the frequency response (1) by increasing or decreasing the loudness level of a selected frequency, or (2) by filtering (cutting off) frequencies above, below, or at a certain point. The equalizer is so useful that it is a standard feature on multichannel consoles. Three types of equalizers are the selectively variable (see **11-3**), continuously variable or parametric (see **11-4**), and graphic (see **11-5**) equalizers.

SELECTIVELY VARIABLE EQUALIZER   The selectively variable equalizer, the type usually found on multitrack consoles, has sets of concentric controls (to save space) that equalize frequencies in the low, middle, and high ranges. The bottom ring chooses the frequency, and the upper one increases or decreases the level of that frequency. Although the frequency you equalize is the one most affected by whatever change you make in the loudness, it is not the only one affected.

11-3 *Selectively variable equalizer.*

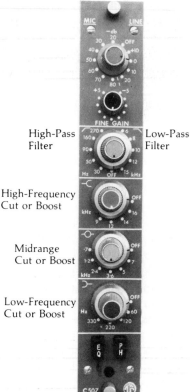

High-Pass Filter

Low-Pass Filter

High-Frequency Cut or Boost

Midrange Cut or Boost

Low-Frequency Cut or Boost

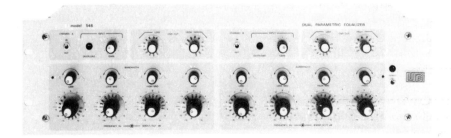

11-4   *Parametric equalizer.*

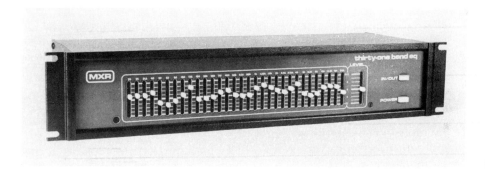

11-5   *Graphic equalizer.*

Each selectively variable equalizer has a preset **bandwidth**—the range of frequencies adjacent to the one selected for equalizing that is also modified— and **bandwidth curve** (see **11-6**). If you boost, say, 250 Hz a total of 18 dB, the bandwidth of frequencies also affected may go to as low as 80 Hz on one side and up to 2,000 Hz on the other. The peak of the curve is 250 Hz—the frequency that is boosted the full 18 dB. The adjacent frequencies are boosted also but to a lesser extent, depending on the bandwidth's curve. Since each selectively variable equalizer has a different fixed bandwidth and bandwidth curve, it is a good idea to study the manufacturer's specification sheets before you use one.

PARAMETRIC EQUALIZER   The main difference between a selectively variable and a **parametric equalizer** is that the parametric has continuously variable bandwidths; you can change the curve by making it narrower or wider (see **11-7**). This provides greater flexibility in controlling the equalizing.

[handwritten annotations in margin:]
range of frequencies affected by the setting

or continuously variable

✳ changes → bandwidths and frequencies

11-6 *(Right) Various frequencies boosted and attenuated 18 dB and their preset bandwidths.*

11-7 *(Far right) A parametric equalizer allows adjustment of the bandwidth from wide to narrow.*

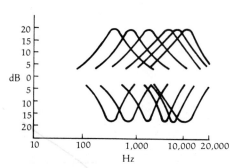

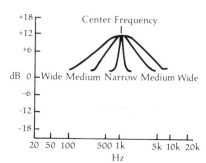

GRAPHIC EQUALIZER The **graphic equalizer** consists of sliding, instead of rotating, controls that boost or attenuate the selected frequencies. It is called *graphic* because the positioning of these controls gives a graphic display of the frequency curve set. Although you can shape the curve, each frequency does have a bandwidth.

FREQUENCY SETTINGS The number of frequencies on equalizers varies; usually the more expensive the equalizer, the greater is the number of settings. Generally, the frequencies are in full-, half-, and third-octave intervals. If the lowest frequency on a full-octave equalizer is 50 Hz, the other frequencies ascend in octaves: 100 Hz, 200 Hz, 400 Hz, 800 Hz, 1,600 Hz, and so on, usually to 12,800 Hz. A half-octave equalizer ascends in half-octaves. If the lowest frequency is 50 Hz, the intervals are at or near 75 Hz, 100 Hz, 150 Hz, 200 Hz, 300 Hz, 400 Hz, 600 Hz, and so on. A third-octave equalizer would have 50 Hz, 60 Hz, 80 Hz, 100 Hz, 120 Hz, 160 Hz, 200 Hz, 240 Hz, 320 Hz, 400 Hz, 480 Hz, 640 Hz, and so on. Obviously, the more settings, the better is the sound control.

FILTERS An equalizer may also contain a filter—a control that cuts off frequencies above, below, or at a preset point. The two most commonly used filters are **high-** and **low-pass filters** (see **11-8**).

Suppose, in a recording, that there is a bothersome rumble between 35 and 50 Hz. By setting a high-pass filter at 50 Hz, all frequencies below that point are cut off and the band of frequencies above it continues to pass—hence the name "high-pass" filter.

The low-pass filter works on the same principle but affects the higher frequencies. If there are annoying scratches in a record, you can get rid of them by setting a low-pass filter at, say, 10,000 Hz. This cuts the frequencies above that point and allows the band of frequencies below 10,000 Hz to pass through.

Sometimes there is confusion about the difference between attenuating and filtering, since both reduce the level of loudness. There are two differences. (1) Attenuation affects only the selected frequency and the frequencies adjacent to it, whereas filtering affects all frequencies above or below the selected frequency. (2) Attenuation allows you to vary the rate of the drop in the loudness level; with a filter, however, the drop is preset and precipitous (see **11-9**).

(1) Adjacent freqs.
(2) The amount of drop

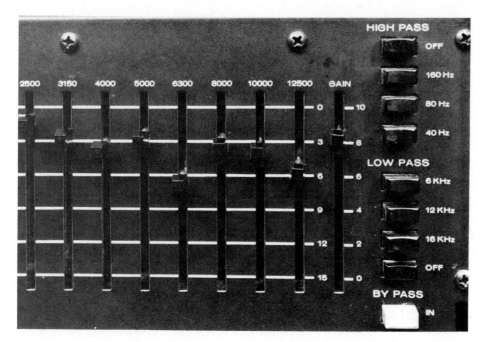

11-8 *High- and low-pass filters on a third-octave equalizer.*

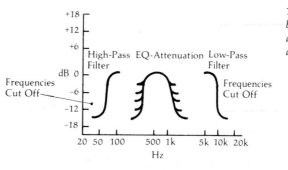

11-9 *Differences between the effects of high- and low-pass filtering and attenuating.*

11-10 *(Above) Notch filter.*

11-11 *(Right) A notch filter can tune out, or tune in, an extremely narrow bandwidth with little effect on adjacent frequencies. In this illustration, 60 Hz is being attenuated 18 dB.*

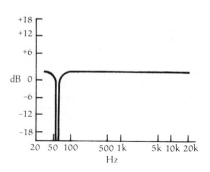

NOTCH FILTER   A **notch filter** is a specialized filter used mainly for corrective purposes (see **11-10**). It can tune out an extremely narrow bandwidth. For example, a constant problem in audio is AC (alternating current) hum. That hum has a frequency of 60 Hz. A notch filter can remove it without appreciably affecting adjacent frequencies (see **11-11**).

Reverberation

Another often used signal processor is the reverberation (reverb) unit—a device that artificially reproduces different time delays of sound to recreate the aural dimensions of various sizes of rooms. Reverberation, you will recall, is the repeated reflections of a sound. Those reflections and the time it takes them to decay help to define acoustically the size of an enclosed space.

There is a common principle basic to all reverberation systems. If you think of what it takes to produce an echo, it is easy to understand. To produce an echo, a sound has to be sent, hit a reflective object, and then bounce back to, roughly, its starting point. In the parlance of audio, the sound sent is <u>**dry**</u>—without reverb—and the sound returned is <u>**wet**</u>—with reverb.

Actually, as defined, there is a difference between echo and reverb. Echo is one or, at most, a few repetitions of a sound (or signal); reverb is many repetitions. To produce either, the dry sound must be sent, reflected, and returned wet.

Four types of reverberation systems are: (1) the so-called acoustic echo chamber, which is more accurately an acoustic reverb chamber; (2) plate and foil reverb; (3) electronic digital reverb, and (4) spring reverb. The echo chamber is the most natural and realistic of the four because it works on acoustic sound in an acoustic environment. The other systems use mechanical-electronic devices that act on signals to create reverb.

<u>ACOUSTIC ECHO CHAMBER</u> The acoustic **echo chamber** is a room with hard, <u>highly sound-reflective surfaces</u> and usually <u>nonparallel walls</u> to avoid standing waves (see **11-12**). It contains a <u>unidirectional microphone</u> (two for stereo)   *Most natural* and a <u>loudspeaker placed back to back</u> to minimize the amount of direct sound the mike(s) picks up. The dry sound feeds from the console through the loudspeaker, reflects around the echo chamber, is picked up by the mike(s), and is fed, wet, back into the console for further routing. Decay times can be varied by changing the levels of the signal being sent to the chamber, or by using movable acoustic baffles (see **11-13**).

Although an acoustic echo chamber is the most realistic reverb system, it is also the most expensive. It must be a good-sized room (too small a room is poor for bass response) with specially treated surfaces, it must be isolated, and it must contain professional quality microphone(s) and loudspeaker. Ar-

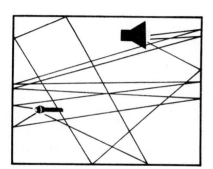

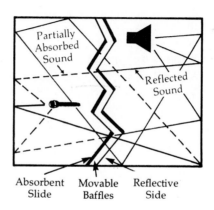

Partially Absorbed Sound

Reflected Sound

Absorbent Slide   Movable Baffles   Reflective Side

11-12 *(Far left) In an acoustic echo chamber, sound feeds from a loudspeaker, bounces around the chamber off highly reflective walls and into a microphone. The dead sides of the microphone and loudspeaker are opposite each other to avoid feedback.*

11-13 *(Left) Using movable baffles with absorbent and reflective sides in various arrangements can alter the acoustics in an echo chamber.*

ranging the baffles to produce appropriate reverb times can also be time-consuming and, therefore, costly. If you can afford it, however, the acoustic echo chamber is worth the investment.

PLATE REVERBERATION   The reverberation plate is a mechanical-electronic device consisting of a large, thin, steel plate suspended under tension in an enclosed frame (see **11-14a**). A moving-coil driver, acting like a small speaker, vibrates the plate, thus transducing the electric signals from the console into mechanical energy. A contact microphone (two for stereo) picks up the plate's vibrations, transduces them back into electric energy, and returns them to the console. The multiple reflections from the vibrating plate create the reverb effect.

Most plate reverb systems have a control to vary the reverb times; better units have more time settings. Usually the reverb times range from about 1 second (the reverb time in a live studio), to about 3 seconds (the reverb time in a large hall), or longer. With a plate, reverb times are modified by damping—reducing the number of oscillations.

FOIL REVERBERATION   Foil reverberation operates on the same principle as plate reverb. The main difference is that the foil reverb unit replaces the steel plate with gold foil (see **11-14b**).

ELECTRONIC DIGITAL REVERBERATION   The electronic digital reverberation unit replaces the plate/foil concept with analog and digital electronic processing (see **11-14c**). The input signal is converted from analog to digital information, processed, and then reconverted to analog information. The unit also has a memory system. An electronic digital reverb unit is capable of producing delay, echo, extremely long reverb, stereo phasing (see the later section on phasing and flanging), and the "chorus effect"—varying the arrival times of sounds from different sources.

- Very Precise
- Fairly Natural Sounding

11-14a   *(Right) Reverberation plate.*

11-14b   *(Far right) Gold foil reverberation unit.*

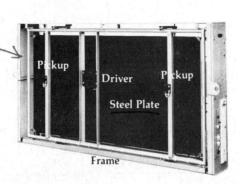

11-14c *Electronic digital reverberation unit.*

SPRING REVERBERATION The spring reverb unit is also a mechanical-electronic device. It is the smallest and least expensive reverb system manufactured. Several types of spring reverbs are available, but their operating principle is the same: the dry signal activates a driver that vibrates coiled springs; then a contact pickup senses the motion and feeds the wet signal from the springs to the console. Controls on the reverb unit vary the reverb time (see **11-15**).

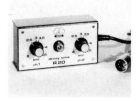

11-15 *A better-quality spring reverb unit showing the inside, spring assembly, and decay times on the remote control.*

Read ch. 4 No quiz

There is a wide difference in the quality of spring reverbs, but generally their sound tends to be tinny, artificial, and not as clean as that from the two other systems. Their main advantages are small size and low cost.

Delay

Not repeated, but long delay in reproducing

Delay is often confused with echo and reverb since their effects sound similar. Echo and reverb are created by the number of reflections in a sound, whereas delay is created by the time difference between sound reflections (see **11-16**). Two ways to produce delay are by using a tape recorder and digitally.

TAPE DELAY To produce tape delay, you need a tape recorder with separate record and playback heads that are live at the same time. The console (or sound source) feeds the signal to the record head. As the tape passes to the playback head a split second later, the signal is reproduced and returned to another channel, usually at the console. The signal path then continues round and round; the speed determines the amount of delay (see **11-17**). The slower the delay, the more deliberate and discernible is the repeat. As the speed of the delay increases, the sound becomes more cascading and spacier.

At 3¾ ips, the delay is roughly half a second, assuming the record and playback heads are the typical 2 inches apart. At 7½ ips, the delay is one-quarter of a second; at 15 ips, it is one-eighth of a second; and at 30 ips, it is one-sixteenth of a second. You can obtain many interesting effects by changing these fixed times using a variable speed recorder.

You can create a variety of sound intensities by coordinating the loudness controls on the console and tape recorder, since different levels of loudness also change the sonic character of delay. Make sure to coordinate these settings, however, because in most reverb and delay systems, the "return" is noisier than the "send." It is common practice to set the level of the "returns" lower than the level of the "sends."

In addition to the electronic noise a signal generates as it passes through the channels, the tape produces noise. As the number of repeats in the delay increases, the signal-to-noise ratio decreases. For these reasons, tape delay, although it produces a variety of effects for almost no extra cost, is not a particularly clean way of creating delay.

DIGITAL DELAY Digital technology has provided an easier, more flexible, noise-free electronic device to produce delay. Digital delay performs the same function as tape delay, but it requires no tape, has no moving parts, and depending on the quality of the unit, has little adverse effect on the frequency response or signal-to-noise ratio (see **11-18**). It provides continuously variable delay times, which increase in number with the more expensive units.

The operation simply involves sending a dry signal from the console to the input of the digital delay unit, setting the delay time, and then returning

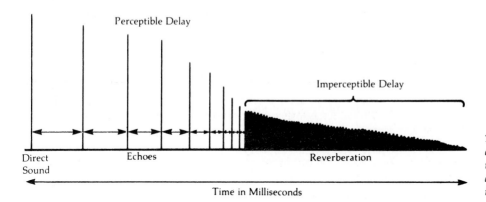

11-16 *Delay is the time difference between sound reflections; some differences are perceptible and some are imperceptible.*

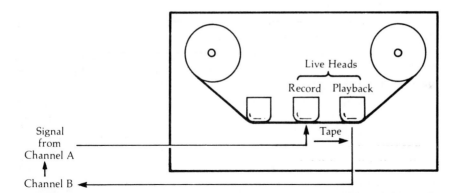

11-17 *To produce tape delay manually, feed a signal through one channel to a tape recorder that is in the record and playback modes at the same time. When the signal reaches the playback head, feed it to another channel, then back again to the original channel, the tape recorder, the second channel, and round and round.*

11-18 *Digital delay.*

the wet signal to the console. In the process, the unit changes the original analog signal to digital at the input and changes it back again at the output.

Another advantage of digital delay is its ability to generate very slight delays—so slight that they are almost imperceptible to the human ear. The effect, called **doubling,** is similar to the effect of overdubbing sound from the same source again and again. Since it is almost impossible to repeat a performance exactly the same, and since the number of indirect reflections increases with each take, the slight time differences between each recording make one performer sound like many. They also add spaciousness to a sound.

Phasing and Flanging

Another effect that can be produced by varying the time differences between sound waves is **phasing**—splitting a signal and slightly delaying one part to create controlled phase cancellations. The sound is difficult to describe, but it is something like pulsating, wavering tremolo, or the undulating sound produced by talking or playing an instrument underwater.

Two ways to produce phasing are (1) manually using tape recorders, and (2) electronically with a device called a *phaser.* The effect was first discovered in experiments with time delay using tape recorders. The same signal was fed to two different machines and recorded simultaneously. The playback from both was fed to a single output, but one playback was delayed, usually by applying some pressure to the flange of the supply reel to slow it down. (This is where the term **flanging** comes from—a word often used synonymously with phasing.) As both playback signals were mixed, one was slightly out of

11-19 *Electronic phaser.*

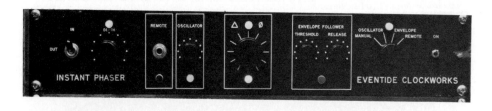

11-20 *Electronic flanger.* (Instant Flanger *is a trademark of Eventide Clockworks.*)

phase with the other, thereby producing the cancellations that created the phasing effect. This effect was enhanced by reversing the phase of one of the signals.

Today, two types of electronic devices, *phasers* and *flangers*, produce a variety of effects by cancelling or delaying signals without using tape recorders (see **11-19** and **11-20**). Operationally, a phaser combines a direct signal with the same signal after it passes through a phase shifter; a flanger combines a direct signal with the same signal after it has been slightly delayed and as its delay time is being continuously varied.

Compressors and Limiters

In Chapter 10, we discussed dynamic range, comparing a human's ability to perceive an extremely wide range of sound levels with the inability of analog recording to reproduce any more than half that range. There are two reasons for this limitation. First, the tape medium can handle only a certain amount of information before reaching its "threshold of pain" and becoming saturated. Second, at its "threshold of hearing," the tape's noise level is often as loud as the information. Before the development of certain signal processing devices, the only way to control the program level was to ride the gain—manually control loud sound surges to prevent them from going into the red and raising the level of quiet passages to lift them out of the mud.

Today, most recordists use electronic devices called the *compressor* and the *limiter* to keep a signal automatically within the dynamic range that tape can handle. The compressor is an amplifier whose output level decreases as its input level increases. The limiter is an amplifier whose output level stays the same regardless of its input level. Since limiting is an extreme form of compression, these functions are commonly combined in a single unit (see **11-21**).

COMPRESSOR   The **compressor** is like an automatic fader; it keeps the sound above the inherent noise level of tape and below its saturation point while preserving the relative dynamics of quiet to loud. Compressors usually have four controls, and each one affects the other: compression ratio, threshold, attack time, and release time.

11-21   *Limiter-compressor.*

The **compression ratio** establishes the proportion of change between the input and output levels. The ratios are usually variable and, depending on the compressor, there are several selectable points between 1.5 to 1 and 9 to 1. If you set the compression ratio for, say, 2 to 1, it means that for every 2-dB boost of the input signal, the output will increase by 1 dB; at 5 to 1, a 5-dB boost of the input signal increases the output by 1 dB. This is how sound with a dynamic range that is more than a tape can handle is brought to usable proportions.

The **compression threshold** is the level of loudness at which the compression ratio takes effect. You set it based on your judgment of where compression should begin. For an idea of the relationship between compression ratio and threshold, see **11-22**. There is no way to predetermine what settings will work best for a given sound at a certain level; it is a matter of listening and experimenting.

Attack time is the length of time it takes the compressor to react to the signal being compressed. Attack time can enhance or detract from a sound. If it is long, it can help to bring out the bass and drums, but if it is too long, it can miss or overshoot the beginning of the compressed sound. If the attack time is too short, the response can be so percussive that it produces popping or clicking sounds. When it is controlled, however, a short attack time can heighten transients and add a crisp accent to sound. Again, set attack time by using your ear.

Release time (or recovery time) is the length of time it takes a compressed signal to return to normal. It is perhaps the most critical variable in compression because it controls the moment-to-moment changes in the level and, therefore, the overall loudness. Generally, the purpose of the release time function is to make the variations in loudness level caused by the compression imperceptible. Longer release times are usually used with music that is slower and more legato, and shorter release times for sound that is fast. This is not to suggest a rule; it is only a guideline.

Various release times produce various effects. Some enhance sound; others degrade it.

11-22 *(Right) The relationship of various compression ratios to a fixed threshold point.*

11-23 *(Far right) The difference between the effects of limiting and compressing.*

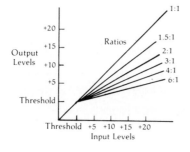

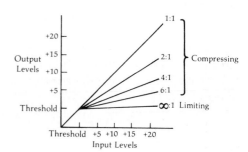

11-24 *A de-esser.*

1. A fast release time combined with a close compression ratio makes a signal seem louder than it actually is.

2. If the release time is too short and the ratio is wide, the compressor pumps or breathes. You actually hear it working as a signal rapidly returns to normal after it has been compressed and quickly released.

3. A longer release time smooths a fluctuating signal.

4. Combining a longer release time with a short attack time gives the signal some of the characteristics of a sound going backward. This effect is particularly noticeable with transients.

5. Too long a release time creates a muddy sound and could cause the gain reduction triggered by a loud signal to continue through a soft one that follows.

LIMITER   The **limiter** is a compressor with a compression ratio of 10 to 1 or greater. It puts a ceiling on the loudness of a sound at a preset level (see **11-23**). Regardless of how loud the input signal is, the output will not go above this ceiling. This makes the limiter useful in situations where high sound levels are constant, or where a performer cannot prevent loud sounds from going into the red.

The limiter has a preset compression ratio, anywhere between 10 to 1 and infinity, but a variable threshold; the threshold sets the point where limiting begins. Attack and release times, if they are not preset, should be relatively short, especially the attack time. A short attack time is usually essential to a clean-sounding limit.

Unlike compression, which can have little effect on the frequency response, limiting can cut off high frequencies. Also, if you severely limit a very high sound level, the signal-to-noise ratio drops dramatically.

DE-ESSER   Some compressors are equipped with a filter to help control the stronger, more annoying high-frequency sounds such as "s," "z," "ch," and "sh." The filter, called a **de-esser**, handles the highly sibilant signals without affecting the rest of the sound (see **11-24**).

USES OF COMPRESSION AND LIMITING   Compressors and limiters have several applications. A few of them are listed here.

1. <u>Compression minimizes the wide changes</u> in levels of loudness caused when the talent varies the mike-to-source distance.

2. <u>Compression smooths the variations in attack and loudness of instruments with wide ranges or wide sound pressure levels,</u> such as the guitar, bass, trumpet, French horn, and drums. It can also smooth percussive sound effects such as jangling keys, breaking glass, and crashes.

3. <u>Compression improves speech intelligibility in a tape recording that has been rerecorded, or dubbed, several times.</u>

4. <u>Compression can improve the signal-to-noise ratio if the compression ratios are close. Wider ratios add more noise.</u>

5. <u>Compression creates the effect of moving a sound source back in relation to the noncompressed sound sources.</u> This may or may not be desirable depending on the overall spatial balance.

6. <u>Limiting prevents high sound levels,</u> either constant or momentary, <u>from saturating the tape.</u>

7. The combination of <u>compression and limiting</u> is often used by AM radio stations to <u>prevent distortion from loud music and to bring out the bass sounds.</u> This adds <u>more power</u> to the sound, thus making the station more obvious to someone sweeping the dial.

Here are some general guidelines to use in applying compression to selected instruments. They should not be followed, however, without listening and experimenting.

Drums—a long to medium attack time reduces the percussive effect. A short release time and wide ratio create a bigger or fuller sound.

Cymbals—medium to short attack and release times and an average ratio reduce excessive ringing.

Guitar—short attack and release times and a wide ratio increase the sustain.

Keyboards—a medium to long attack time, a medium to short release time, and a wide ratio give a fuller sound.

Strings—short attack and release times and an average ratio add body to the sound.

Vocals—medium to short attack and release times and an average ratio reduce sibilance.

Expanders

An **expander**, like a compressor, affects dynamic range (see **11-25**). But whereas a compressor reduces it, an expander increases it. Like a compressor, an expander has variable ratios and is triggered when sound reaches a set threshold level. However, the ratios on an expander are the inverse of those on a compressor: 1 to 2, 1 to 3, and so on. At 1 to 2, each 1 dB of input expands to 2 dB of output; at 1 to 3, each 1 dB of input expands to 3 dB of output. Since an expander is triggered when a signal falls below a set threshold, it can be used as a **noise gate** to reduce or eliminate unwanted low-level sounds, such as room ambience, rumble, and sound leakage from one microphone to another.

Assume, for example, that you have two microphones, one for a singer and one for an accompanying piano. When the singer and pianist are performing, the sound level will probably be loud enough to mask unwanted low-level noises. But if the pianist is playing quietly and the vocalist is not singing, or vice versa, the open, unused microphone may pick up these noises.

An obvious solution to this problem is to turn down the pot when a microphone is not being used, cutting it off acoustically and electronically. But this could become hectic for a console operator if there are several sound sources to coordinate. A better solution would be to set the expander's threshold level at a point just above the quietest sound level that the vocalist (or piano) emits. When the vocalist stops singing, the loudness of the sound entering the microphone falls below the threshold point and shuts down, or *gates*, the mike.

The key to successful noise gating is in the coordination of the threshold and ratio settings. Since there is little difference between the low level of a sound's decay and the low level of noise, you have to be wary that in cutting off noise, you do not cut off program material also. Always be careful when you use an expander. Unless it is set precisely, it will adversely affect response.

11-25 *Expander—noise gate.*

Tape Noise

Of all the links in the sound chain, tape is the major cause of noise. The inherent unevenness of the magnetic coating, even in the best of tapes, always leaves a slight polarization of the magnetic particles after erasure, regardless of how complete erasure is. Therefore, as the loudness level of a recorded signal increases, tape noise increases proportionately.

There are other problems as well. Each time a tape is used, it wears away, however slightly, some of the oxide coating, thus decreasing the signal-to-noise ratio. Poor dispersion of the iron oxide particles creates dropout and noise. Too much residual magnetization after erasure due either to an erase bias frequency that is too high or too low, or to poor bulk erasing technique increases tape noise. A problem with the record bias will result in a recording that is not uniformly magnetized. A tape recording made at a loudness level that is too loud or too quiet will over- or underpolarize the magnetic particles, thereby creating loudness distortion or hiss.

The compressor and expander together can reduce most of these noise problems. However, they require very careful adjustment. Since it takes the combination of compression during recording and expansion during playback to reduce tape noise, it can be prohibitively expensive if you buy both to process all the signals in a multitrack recording. These two operations therefore have been combined into one unit called a **compander** (from its functions compression and expansion), more popularly known as a *noise reducer*.

Noise Reduction

Noise reducers vary in operation but are similar in principle. During recording, the input signal is compressed to keep it within the dynamic range of the tape. This increases the signal level and also the noise level, since the compression ratio is wide. Compression encodes the tape with a louder, noisier signal. During playback, the signal is decoded by expansion, thus returning it to its original level but with the noise considerably reduced since the signal gets through only when it is above the threshold and, therefore, louder than the noise (see **11-26**).

The two most commonly used **noise reduction systems** are Dolby and dbx. The Dolby A system, which is used in professional sound studios, divides the frequency spectrum into four bands with separate compression and expansion for each: (1) 80 Hz and below, to deal with rumble and hum; (2) 80 to 3,000 Hz, to deal with midrange noise; (3) 3,000 to 9,000 Hz; and (4) 9,000 Hz and above, to deal with hiss and modulation noise (see **11-27a, b, c**). Dolby A processes low-level signals and provides 10 dB of noise reduction from 30 to 5,000 Hz, increasing to 15 dB at 15,000 Hz.

A less expensive Dolby B system is used for less critical noise reduction (see **11-28**). It reduces high-frequency noise across a single band.

The dbx system processes high-level signals and operates on a single, full-frequency range band from 20 to 20,000 Hz (see **11-29**). Noise reduction across the band is 30 dB and more.

11-26 *How a noise reducer decreases noise in a tape recording.*

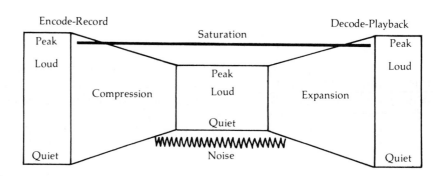

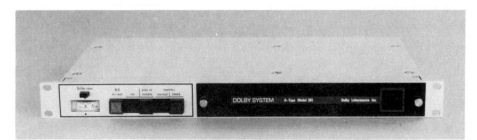

11-27a Dolby A one-channel noise reduction unit.

11-27b (Far left) Dolby A 16-channel noise reduction unit.

11-27c (Left) Dolby cinema processor used in dubbing theaters for the production of Dolby stereo film formats. It may also be used for the exhibition of all film formats.

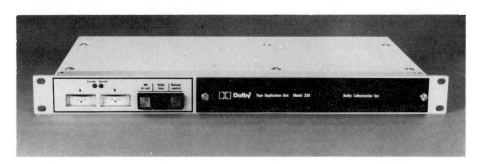

11-28 Dolby B noise reduction unit.

11-29 dbx four- and eight-channel noise reduction units.

Other Signal Processors

Several other signal processors are also available. A few of them are listed here:

Analog Time Unit—used to create many of the effects in science fiction, horror, and outer space films (see **11-30**).

Aphex Aural Exciter—like an equalizer in that it adds clarity and brilliance to sound but without increasing amplitude. It does not affect the lower frequencies, however (see **11-31**).

Harmonizer—can double, triple, and quadruple a signal, changing individual voicings into ensemble and choral effects (see **11-32**).

Pitch Transposer—produces an effect similar to the variable speed oscillator, but increases and decreases pitch across a wider range and with a cleaner sound (see **11-33**).

11-30 *Analog time unit.*

11-31 *Aphex aural exciter.*

11-32 *Harmonizer.*
(Harmonizer is a trademark of Eventide Clockworks.)

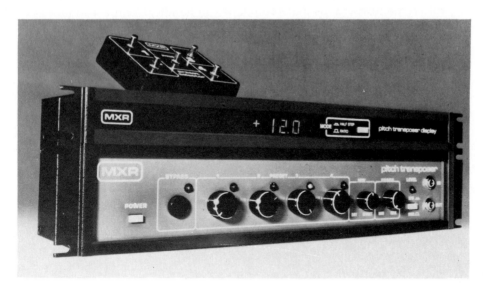

11-33 *Pitch transposer.*

Summary

1. Signal processing can alter the basic structure of an audio signal by changing its pitch, length, strength, attack, decay, and other features. Signal processing can also reduce electronic and tape noise and distortion.

2. Among the most common types of signal processing used are: equalizing, filtering, reverberation, delaying, phasing, flanging, limiting-compressing, and reducing noise.

3. Equalizing, perhaps the most commonly used type of signal processing, is accomplished with (a) a selectively variable equalizer, (b) a continuously variable or parametric equalizer, or (c) a graphic equalizer. Each has a different effect on the bandwidth curve of the frequencies adjacent to the frequency being equalized.

4. Filtering cuts off frequencies above, below, or at a preset point.

5. Reverberation produces different time delays, which affect the number of repeats in a signal, thus creating various degrees of aural spaciousness.

6. Delay is similar to reverberation except that a delayed signal can also be controlled to produce perceptually measurable repeats in a signal.

7. Phasing and flanging split a signal and slightly delay one part to create controlled phase cancellations that generate a pulsating sound.

8. Limiting and compressing help to bring the dynamic range of a signal to within the proportions that audio tape can handle. Compression helps to improve the sound quality in several other ways as well.

9. Noise reduction compresses the dynamic range of a signal as it is recorded on tape and expands the signal as it is played back. This reduces tape noise and increases the signal-to-noise ratio.

10. Other signal processors such as the pitch transposer, analogue time unit, and harmonizer can alter a signal by changing its speed, direction, quantity, or length.

12

*On-Location Production**

Today, going *on location*†—outside the studio—to cover news and sports, to promote a local sponsor or charity, to heighten realism, to add authenticity, and to provide settings that are difficult or impossible to reproduce in a studio is as commonplace as doing a production in the controlled environment of a studio. There was a time when few productions were done on location. The equipment was too heavy and cumbersome to move about with ease, transmission lines were difficult to set up, and the whole production was at the mercy of the weather.

Three developments have brought about the change to on-location production: (1) the equipment is much smaller and lighter, (2) it is easier to transmit a signal for broadcast, and (3) production techniques have become more sophisticated. This is not to say that on-location production is uncomplicated. It still requires planning, preparation, and a considerable amount of equipment.

Radio Equipment

The absence of the visual component cuts down on the amount of equipment you need in radio, compared with TV and film, and on the time that is necessary for preproduction planning and preparation. In many situations, such as broadcasting news and sports, a microphone and a tape recorder, or a transmission line, are sufficient. Even on remotes that require a more elaborate setup, radio equipment is compact, lightweight, and portable (see **12-1a, b**).

---

*Since the emphasis of this book is audio, this chapter will focus on those aspects of on-location production that relate to sound.

†In broadcasting, doing a production away from the studio is called a **remote**. It used to be known as a **NEMO**, the acronym for Not Emanating Main Organization.

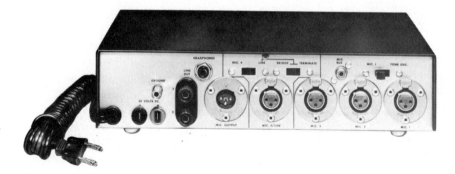

12-1a *Front and rear views of a portable microphone mixer. This particular mixer can combine and feed the input signals of four microphones.*

12-1b *Portable mixing consoles that can be carried in a case.*

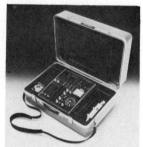

Television Equipment

All types of television programs are produced on location, from the simpler stand-up report of a newsperson to the more complex coverage of a football game, parade, or drama. The amount and type of equipment used for a production depend on how complicated the production is.

Two categories of on-location production are electronic news gathering (ENG) and electronic field production (EFP). Electronic field production can be divided into small-scale and large-scale operations.

ELECTRONIC NEWS GATHERING As recently as a few years ago, all television news gathered in the field was recorded on film. Film cameras were lightweight, portable, hand-held, and used on the move. The only TV cameras available were the large, heavy studio models. Processing film takes time, however, so news footage had to be shot long enough in advance of air time to allow for developing, screening, editing, and loading.

To speed the process, TV cameras with many of the same physical characteristics as portable film cameras and small, lightweight video tape recorders were developed. For news and for television in general, video tape has several advantages over film: (1) it is ready for playback immediately after recording, (2) its picture looks almost "live," (3) it can be coded for editing, and (4) it can be edited by computer. Video tape is gradually replacing film in the recording of TV news. The term *electronic news gathering* or *ENG* refers to news that is recorded with the new, portable video gear.

Basic ENG Equipment The basic equipment used for electronic news gathering consists of the following items:

TV camera—The camera can be one of the portable lightweight, battery-powered, hand-held, or shoulder-borne models developed for on-location operation (see **12-2a, b**).

12-2a *(Far left) Portable television camera.*

12-2b *(Left) Portable television camera with a built-in mount for a shotgun microphone.*

12-3a *(Right) Portable video tape recorder with a carrying handle.*

12-3b *(Far right) The same video tape recorder shown in 12-3a in a carrying case.*

12-4 *Portable ¾-inch cassette video tape recorder with a shoulder strap.*

Video tape recorder—Like the TV camera, battery-powered video recorders have been designed for portable use (see **12-3a, b**). The format preferred for ENG is the ¾-inch video cassette because it is easy and quick to load and unload (see **12-4**); however, portable VTRs are also capable of handling ½-, 1-, and 2-inch video tape.

Microphone—Since the audio in electronic news gathering usually involves a single reporter delivering a story or a reporter doing an interview, the hand-held, omnidirectional, moving-coil microphones or the new rugged condenser types with pop filters are preferred. In noisy environments, a cardioid is better than an omnidirectional pattern. If an interview is lengthy, it is probably better to take the time to set up two lavaliers. It could be annoying to the audience and interviewee to see one hand-held mike moved back and forth between reporter and guest for several minutes. Wireless microphones are usually not used in ENG because it takes too much time to set them up. A portable TV camera with a microphone built in allows one person to operate audio and video simultaneously. Although the built-in microphone is usually directional and can pick up sound from several feet away, any mike mounted on a fixed stand cannot adequately handle shots that change from one focal length to another. Unless you move the camera itself, it is difficult to adjust the sound for a change from, say, a medium shot to a close-up or a long shot.

Earphones—Perhaps the one piece of equipment most overlooked in on-location production is **earphones**. Regardless of the medium—radio, TV, or film—earphones are as important on location as loudspeakers are in the studio. *Earphones are the only reference you have to sound quality and balance*. Use the best earphones available, study their frequency response, and get to know their sonic characteristics. First-rate earphones are expensive (but worth it). They have a wide, flat response; they are sensitive; they have superb channel separation (for stereo); and their cushioned earpieces keep outside sound from leaking through. All these characteristics are essential in recording audio on location.

Power Supply—Most portable TV cameras and video tape recorders are powered by either batteries or standard AC electricity. In some units, the video tape recorder supplies power to both the VTR and the camera; in other units, the power supplies are separate (see **12-5a, b, c**). Several recorder units also come with a generator to charge the batteries.

12-5a *(Below, left) Battery power pack for video camera worn around the waist.*

12-5b *(Below, center) Battery power pack mounted to the back of a portable video camera.*

12-5c *(Below) Side view of the video tape recorder shown in **12-3a** with a battery power pack at lower left.*

ENG Mobile Unit   The basic ENG equipment usually requires a two-person team to operate: one person on video and one on audio. In many cases, the technical crew and the reporter cover assignments from a car.

One development that has made ENG so useful in the coverage of TV news is **microwave**—a system of wireless relays that transmit a TV signal live from the news scene back to the station. Since the microwave system is too large for a car, many TV stations have **mobile units**—vans that house the microwave system and also transport personnel and ENG equipment (see **12-6**).

Microwave systems link the mobile unit to the station, and the camera to the mobile unit (see **12-7**). The latter link is necessary when it is not possible to run a cable from the TV camera to the mobile unit because the van itself cannot get close enough to an event. Microwave transmission is also used in radio news as part of radio electronic news gathering (RENG).

12-6 *Cutaway diagram showing location of equipment in an ENG/EFP mobile unit.*

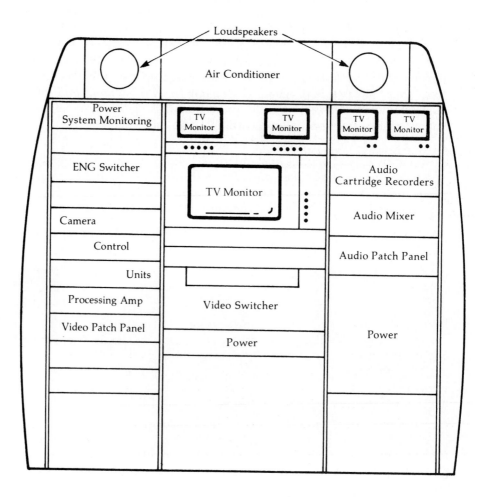

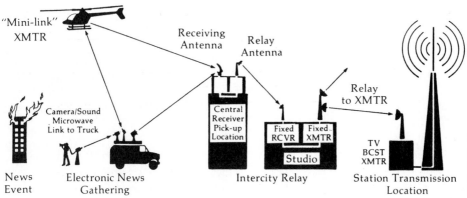

"Mini-link" XMTR

Receiving Antenna

Relay Antenna

Camera/Sound Microwave Link to Truck

Central Receiver Pick-up Location

Fixed RCVR | Fixed XMTR

Relay to XMTR

Studio

TV BCST XMTR

News Event

Electronic News Gathering

Intercity Relay

Station Transmission Location

12-7 *Microwave makes it possible to relay a wireless signal from the site of an event to the studio for broadcast or recording.*

ELECTRONIC FIELD PRODUCTION The major differences between ENG and electronic field production (EFP) are scale and purpose; however, in principle they are the same. They both make it possible to produce TV program material on video tape away from the studio. But whereas ENG is designed to cover news events quickly, EFP is used to produce non-news material such as entertainment programs, sports, documentaries, and commercials. Therefore, EFP generally requires more equipment, takes more time in production, and has better technical quality.

Small-scale EFP The main differences between small- and large-scale EFP are the amount of equipment and personnel used and the complexity of the production. Commercials and documentaries can be shot with a minimum of hardware and people, whereas a football game, parade, or the Academy Awards cannot. Small-scale EFP is closer to ENG; large-scale is more like a major studio production.

The following is the basic equipment used for electronic field production:

Cameras—The cameras are the same as those used in ENG. They may be hand-held and shoulder-mounted or mounted on tripods to achieve more controlled and better composed shots, since time is not so critical in EFP as it is in ENG (see **12-8**).

Video tape recorders—EFP incorporates most VTR formats, including ½-, ¾-, 1-, and 2-inch tape. One-inch tape is preferred because the picture and sound quality are relatively good, and compared with 2-inch tape, the reels are easier to handle and less expensive. The ¾-inch cassette, although easy to handle and inexpensive, does not give the same picture and sound quality as the 1-inch format.

Audio—Since small-scale EFP usually involves productions in which microphones should be unobtrusive and/or highly directional, shotgun mikes mounted on fishpoles or booms, wireless mikes, and lavaliers are generally preferred. It is also likely that a few microphones will be used

12-8 *Video cameras mounted on tripods for steadier and more controlled shots.*

that require a mike mixer (see **12-1a**) or a small audio console inside the van (see **12-1b**). Some directors may wish to use recorded music or sound effects to give the performers a better idea of the flavor or pace of the script, to aid in the timing of cues, or to save production time. Some EFP vans are therefore equipped with cartridge or reel-to-reel tape recorders.

Large-scale EFP Large-scale electronic field production involves taping or broadcasting an event, such as a football or baseball game, a parade, the Academy Awards, or the Miss America pageant, on the spot. As major productions, these events require the same technical support on location that large-scale productions require in the studio. A huge trailer, literally a studio-type technical facility on wheels, and the dozens of engineering and production personnel to go with it provide that support (see **12-9a, b**). The trailer contains all the equipment necessary to process and route signals from the many cameras and microphones that cover the event outside the truck and from the video and studio sources, such as instant replay, slow motion, and sound carts, inside the truck.

Telephone Lines

On-location broadcasts that must be transmitted across considerable distances are difficult to carry by microwave, since it would require hundreds of

12-9a *Production trailer used for large-scale remotes.*

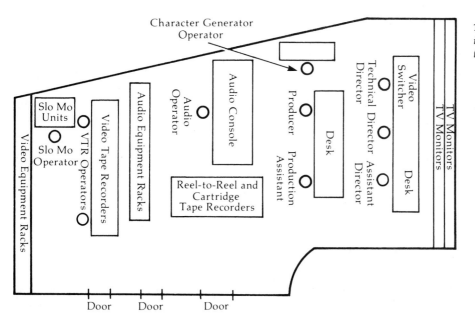

12-9b *Example of an interior layout of a large television production trailer.*

relay stations to get the signal from one area to another. Although using a satellite to beam signals for long-range transmission helps to solve this problem, on-location broadcasts are most often carried by telephone lines.

By placing an order with the telephone company, you can have various types of lines—audio and video, with wide or narrow bandwidths, permanent or temporary—connected from the broadcast site to the station. As the quality of the line and its usage increase, so does cost.

The line classifications for audio are:

AAA—50 to 15,000 Hz and continuous use   *Most Expensive*

AA—50 to 8,000 Hz and continuous use

A—100 to 5,000 Hz and continuous use

BBB—50 to 15,000 Hz and temporary use

BB—50 to 8,000 Hz and temporary use

B—100 to 5,000 Hz and temporary use

C—200 to 3,500 Hz and continuous use

D—200 to 3,500 Hz and temporary use

Film Equipment

Basically, the equipment used to film on location is the same as that used to film in a studio—a camera [lightweight models are used on location (see **12-10**)], a specially designed ¼-inch reel-to-reel tape recorder, microphones, lights, and so on. The difference between recording on film and recording on video tape is the way in which the picture and sound are synchronized. In film, synchronization is accomplished by either the single-system or the double-system recording method.

SINGLE-SYSTEM RECORDING In single-system recording, one camera records both picture and sound onto a single piece of magnetic stripe film (see **9-14**). Since sound and picture are recorded in one operation, the advantages of the single-system method are speed, easy operation, and efficiency. For these reasons, single-system recording is used in TV news. For other applications, it has a major disadvantage, however. Picture is recorded intermittently, one frame at a time, whereas sound must be recorded at a constant speed. Since this requires two separate mechanical actions, different parts of the camera must record the picture and sound (see **12-11**). Therefore, although the picture and sound are recorded simultaneously, they are not recorded at the same place on the film. Sound is several frames ahead of picture, which creates problems in editing (see **13-43**).

In filmed TV news, you often see a person's lips moving before you hear any sound, or you continue to hear sound after the lips have stopped moving (see Chapter 13). Although the editing results may not be as refined as an

12-10 *Lightweight 16-mm and 35-mm film cameras used for on-location shooting.*

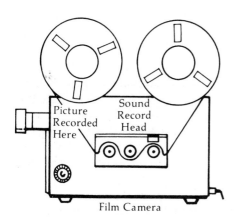

12-11 *In a single-system film recording, sound and picture are recorded simultaneously but at different places on the film.*

editor would like, they are acceptable for TV news where the need for immediacy takes precedence over production values.

DOUBLE-SYSTEM RECORDING In the *double-system method,* sound and picture are recorded in sync but separately; the camera records the picture and a specially designed ¼-inch reel-to-reel tape recorder records the sound (see **10-27**). After shooting, the audio is dubbed to full-coat magnetic film (see **9-14**), so the corresponding frames of picture and sound match. Since this makes editing much easier, most film productions shot for screen and television use double-system recording.

Two ways to synchronize the sound and picture in double-system recording are with a cable or an "umbilical" connected between camera and tape recorder (see **12-12**), and with a crystal oscillator in both camera and tape recorder (see **12-13**).

Cable Synchronization   In the "umbilical" or **cable** method of synchronization, the camera generates a pulse tone that runs through the cable, synchronizing the speed of the tape recorder with the speed of the camera. This tone is recorded onto the audio tape and keeps sound in sync with picture.

Crystal Synchronization   The main disadvantage of cable sync is that wherever the camera goes, the tape recorder must also go. **Crystal sync** does not require a cable. Both the camera and the tape recorder contain a crystal oscillator that

12-12   *Double-system film recording using a cable or "umbilical" to synchronize camera and tape recorder.*

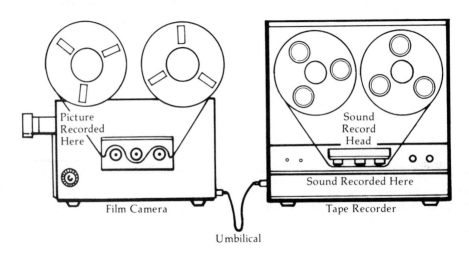

12-13   *Double-system film recording using an oscillator in the camera and tape recorder to synchronize sound and picture.*

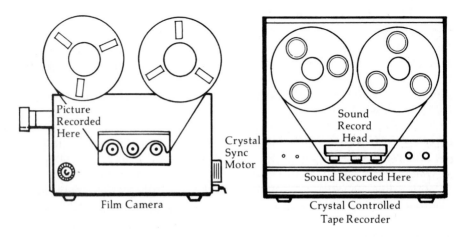

System	Head Displacement	Track Positions

12-14 *Head and track configurations for various sync pulse systems.*

regulates their motors to run at the same speed; they will stay in sync even if they are some distance apart. The oscillator in the tape recorder regulates tape speed to camera speed and also puts the synchronizing tone onto the tape.

Sync Tones   The tones that help to synchronize sound and picture are recorded in various ways, depending on the system used (see **12-14**). Nagra, with its *pilot tone* system, records two tones down the center of the tape superimposed over the main audio signal. These two tones are 180 degrees out of phase so they cancel each other during playback and do not interfere with the sound on the main track.

Other tape recorders used for double-system sound record pulse tones in different ways. *Perfectone* records two tones along the top and bottom edges of the tape with the sound track in between. *Ranger Tone* records one tone down the center of the tape but with a head whose azimuth is at a different angle

12-15 *Slate and clapstick.*

from that of the standard heads. This difference in azimuth ensures that the tone played back by the tone head will not be heard by the regular playback head. *Synchrotone* is used for stereo recording. It has a separate third track recorded down the center of the tape between the two stereo tracks.

Slating   One of the easiest but most important procedures in double-system sound recording is *slating*. Although the picture and sound are shot in sync, the editor has to know the precise point at which recording began to match them properly. For this purpose, a **clapslate** is used (see **12-15**). The clapslate is filmed just before each take, after the camera and the tape recorder have begun rolling. It serves two purposes. First, it displays the names of the production, director, and cameraperson; the number of the scene and take; the number of the sound take; the date; and whether the shot is interior or exterior. Second, on top of the slate is a clapstick, which can be opened and then closed quickly to produce a loud snapping sound. This sound is the sync mark that tells the editor at exactly what point to begin synchronizing sound with picture.

Sound Transfer: Audio Tape to Magnetic Film   Although the double-system method records the sound and picture in synchronization, there is no way to align ¼-inch audio tape and 16-mm (or 35-mm) film for editing; one format has sprocket holes and the other does not. The sound must be transferred to full-coat magnetic film. Then, with sound and picture in the same format and the same length, they can be aligned and edited frame to frame.

Transferring sound from ¼-inch tape to magnetic film requires two recorders: one to play back the audio tape and a magnetic film transfer recorder to rerecord the signal on full-coat film (see **12-16**). During transfer, the sync pulse on the audio tape controls the speed of the ¼-inch machine or the transfer machine, depending on the type of transfer system used, so that it matches the speed of the camera motor.

Cue Sheet   To avoid wasting time and money, make sure you prepare a cue sheet indicating the footage/frame count of the sound elements on the magnetic film (see **12-17**). Whether there is just a voice track or voice, music, and sound effects tracks, each will be on a separate roll of magnetic film. Write down the locations of the various parts of each track or you will spend most of your time searching for cues.

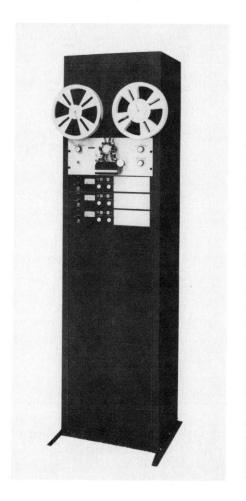 

12-16   *(Far left) Magnetic film insert transfer recorder/ reproducer. Sound from audio tape is dubbed to the insert transfer recorder, in or out of sequence. The reproducer plays it back. Some units are reproducers only. (Left) Another example of a magnetic film recorder/ reproducer. The recorder is to the left, and the reproducer is to the right.*

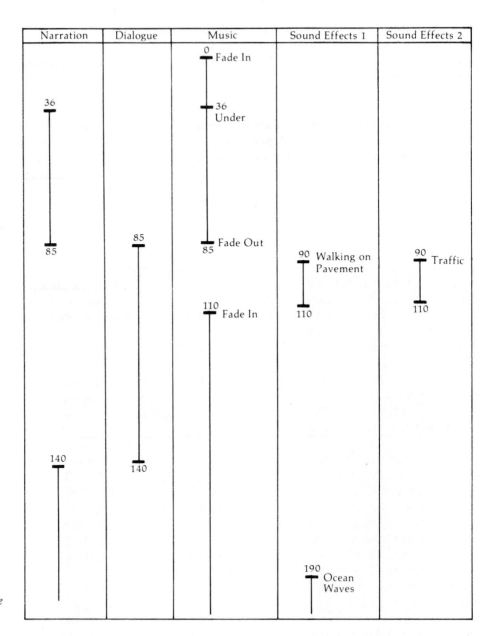

Narration	Dialogue	Music	Sound Effects 1	Sound Effects 2
		0 — Fade In		
36		36 Under		
85	85	85 Fade Out		
			90 Walking on Pavement	90 Traffic
		110 Fade In	110	110
140	140			
			190 Ocean Waves	

12-17 *Example of a cue sheet. The numbers indicate film footage.*

Preparing for On-Location Production

The importance of properly preparing for on-location production cannot be emphasized too strongly. Consider the loss of time and money, to say nothing of the inconvenience to all the people involved, if you have to hold up production because someone brought the wrong microphone, forgot the batteries for the tape recorder, neglected to pack the tool kit, planned to mount a heavy camera crane on soil that was too soft to hold it, chose a shooting site several days in advance of production without realizing that a building nearby was slated for demolition on the day of recording, scouted the shooting site at noon although the script called for the scene to take place at dusk, or selected a shooting site filled with goldenrod without checking whether any of the key people were allergic to pollen. Planning to shoot on location is a careful, meticulous procedure involving more than just decisions about production.

SELECTING A LOCATION In selecting a site, sound designers would prefer one with suitable acoustics indoors, and no distracting sounds outdoors. However, this rarely occurs away from the controlled environment of the studio. The first thing to understand about choosing a location is that you must be prepared to deal with unwanted sound. If possible, try to reduce the difficulties by suggesting to the director those sites with the fewest sound problems. Keep in mind, however, that where you shoot is determined by the demands of the picture, not by the demands of the sound.

The main challenge in doing a production on location is to record the principal sound source with little or no sonic leakage from either the acoustics or other sound sources. Therefore, you must judge a recording site on your ability to neutralize unwanted sound.

UNWANTED SOUND Unwanted sound is generated by many sources. Some are obvious, and some not so obvious: low-frequency rumble from traffic that becomes midrange hiss on a wet day, blowing sound from wind, clatter from an office that may be nearby, buzz from fluorescent lights, excessive reverb from rooms that are too live, jet roar from planes that fly over the production area, noise from construction, church bells that ring every hour on the hour, a far-off fog horn, clanking pipes, creaking floor boards, whine from an air conditioner, chirping from birds, barking from dogs, and so on.

Being aware of the problems is not enough, however; you have to know what, if anything, to do about them. For example, you can usually roll off low-frequency rumble from traffic, but the midrange hiss from wet tires on a wet surface is difficult to equalize out. Gentle wind presents little problem for a mike equipped with a pop filter and windscreen, but these filters will not completely offset the effect of noise from strong winds. If a room is reverberant, you can make it less reverberant by placing a lot of sound-absorbent material in the area and using tight, highly directional miking, but these techniques may not work in large, extremely reverberant spaces. If the director insists on a site where sound problems cannot be neutralized, you will have to record the audio in the studio during postproduction.

Two other considerations in choosing a production site with audio in mind are: (1) the available space—make sure the boom or fishpole operator has enough room to move with the action and still keep the microphone out of the picture; and (2) the power supply—if the production site does not have enough power outlets or wattage, plan to bring the main and backup power supplies.

PLANNING After a production location has been chosen, the next step is to decide what equipment and other essentials must be transported to the site. These decisions are based on the production itself, and the items usually fall into three categories:

Equipment—cameras, lights, microphones, cables, tape recorders, cotton swabs, head cleaner, demagnetizer, earphones, sound mixers, recording tape, film editing materials, gaffer's tape and masking tape, main and backup power supplies, stopwatch, rope, extra batteries and fuses, flashlights, tool kit.

Program—scripts, records, reel-to-reel and cartridge tapes.

Administrative—shooting schedule, chairs, tables, typewriters, pencils, dressing room accommodations, lavatory facilities, food, drink, transportation.

Microphone Technique

Each production done on location presents unique audio problems: noise, acoustics, microphone placement, microphone mobility, sound isolation, sound blend, and so on. With on-location recording, as with studio recording, good audio begins with good miking.

SPORTS In most sports broadcasts, audio provides three essential aural elements: (1) the sound of the announcers, (2) the sound of the crowd, and (3) the sound of the game action. To achieve the best results, mike each element separately and balance the levels of loudness at the mixer or audio console.

Miking the Announcers In sports broadcasting, the announcers have to be heard clearly, whether they project their voices over the constant din of a large, vocal crowd or speak quietly during a golf or tennis match. No microphone is better suited to meet both these demands than the headset mike (see **5-39**). Its design allows the mike to be positioned close to the announcer's mouth for optimal pickup of normal and quieter-than-normal speech. Its moving-coil element and built-in pop filter can withstand loud speech levels without overloading the mike. The unidirectional pickup pattern reduces sound leakages from outside sources, and the omnidirectional pattern adds more background color to the sound. Each earpiece can carry separate information—the director's cues on one and the program audio on the other; and the space in front of the announcer can be kept clear for papers, TV monitors, and other paraphernalia.

Miking the Crowd   The sound of the crowd is essential to the excitement of most sports events. The cheers, boos, and general hubbub punctuate the action, adding vitality to the event and making the home audience feel a part of things.

Usually the best microphone to use is a rugged moving-coil type with an omnidirectional pickup pattern, a pop filter, and, to be safe, a windscreen. This microphone can be exposed to any kind of weather. The omnidirectional pattern is preferred because (1) it blends the overall crowd sound, instead of concentrating it as would a unidirectional mike, and (2) it picks up more of the crowd's din, thus adding to the excitement and presence of the event.

With a crowd, as with any sound source, proper microphone placement directly influences the quality of the pickup. In baseball, football, and soccer stadiums, the crowd mike is usually hung outside the press box. This is because the press box is centrally located and, therefore, easy to get to, and it is usually situated at a good sound-collecting point (see **12-18**). If one mike is not sufficient to capture the crowd's intensity, use more. The key to getting good crowd sound is placing the mikes at points where the sound collects.

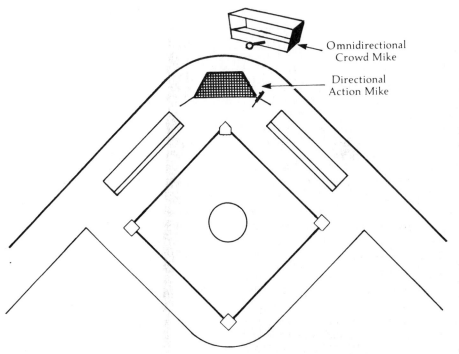

Omnidirectional
Crowd Mike

Directional
Action Mike

12-18 *Miking baseball. An omnidirectional microphone mounted outside the press box is at a good sound-collecting point for picking up crowd sound. It also makes the mike convenient to get to. To pick up the sound at home plate, mount a directional mike on the screen behind home plate and aim it toward the batter's box.*

In enclosed arenas used for basketball, hockey, and boxing, position the crowd mike at one of the balcony levels or hanging from the scoreboard or rafter, so long as it is not too far from the crowd. In basketball, mount shotgun mikes on the struts that support the backboard at each end of the court. These pick up the sound of both the crowd and the ball hitting the basket (see the next section). Since sound reverberates in an enclosed space, almost anywhere near the crowd is a good sound-collecting point. If the mike is too far from the crowd, the sound will decay significantly by the time it reaches the mike, thereby losing its punch, liveliness, and presence.

In golf and tennis, crowd response is different from that in baseball, football, basketball, hockey, and boxing. Golf and tennis require quiet during play, and when the crowd does react, it is more often with applause than with shouting.

Most golf broadcasts cover the last few holes of a round. Golf crowds follow the action by moving from hole to hole with a particular group of players. Out in the open, sound does not collect, so it is difficult to mount crowd mikes at reinforcing points, let alone place them for optimal sound pickup from groups of people whose number and position are always changing. Golf crowds are usually miked with directional microphones hung from trees. The shotgun's directional pattern can isolate and concentrate crowd reaction. Sometimes the microphones on hand-held cameras are used to expand the crowd sound.

12-19 *Miking football. To pick up the sound of the quarterback and hitting linemen, aim a parabolic microphone at the quarterback. The parabolic is usually better than a shotgun in this instance because it focuses the sound more precisely.*

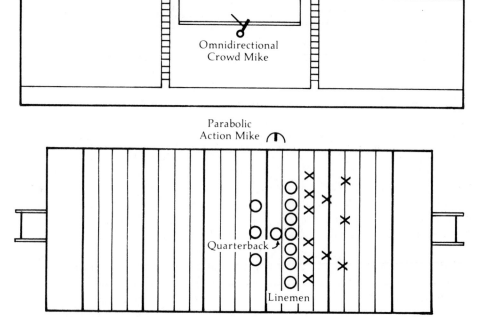

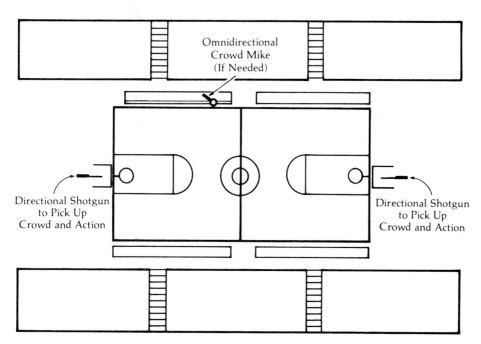

12-20 *Miking basketball. Directional mikes mounted on the support struts of each basket and facing the court pick up action and crowd sounds. If additional crowd sound is needed, place an omnidirectional mike on the scorer's table facing the court or hanging from the scoreboard. To pick up the sounds to go with shots, such as cheerleading or coach and players talking strategy at the bench, directional mikes on portable TV cameras work well. In all instances, microphones must be placed out of bounds.*

Tennis crowds usually sit either surrounding the court or to one side of it. They can be heard with an omnidirectional mike hung in the open from an overhang away from the public address system. No microphone should be placed near a PA system since it is difficult to separate and balance the sound of the system with the sound of the crowd (or with any other sound).

Miking the Action The sound of the action itself adds impact to a sports event—the crack of the bat on the ball in baseball, the signal calling of the quarterback and the crunch of hitting linemen in football, the slamming of bodies against the boards in hockey, the bouncing ball and squeaking sneakers in basketball, and so on. To capture these sounds, separate microphones, other than the crowd mike, are used. The mikes are mounted close to the area of play or are hand-held and pointed toward the action. There are different microphone placements for picking up action and crowd sounds in baseball, football, basketball, hockey, tennis, and golf (see **12-18** to **12-23**).

TALKS Recording someone speaking from a podium at an event such as a press conference, dinner, awards ceremony, or talk is almost an everyday assignment in broadcasting. In preparing for such an assignment, it is important to know whether you will be taking the sound from your own micro-

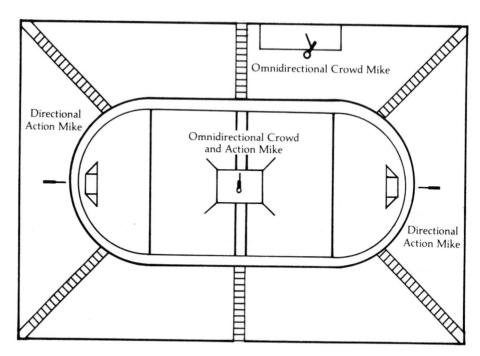

12-21 *Miking hockey. To pick up crowd sound, hang an omnidirectional mike outside the broadcast booth. In some arenas, the booth is high in the stands, so the crowd mike may be hung from the scoreboard or a rafter or used in addition to the one at the booth. The hanging microphone can be used to pick up action sounds on the ice, which can be enhanced with directional mikes behind each goal (and at the blue lines).*

12-22 *Miking tennis. The omnidirectional crowd mike is mounted from an overhang in the stands. Two hand-held shotguns cover the action on each half of the court, and shotgun mikes are placed on the ground on desk stands at the ends of the court pointed toward the players and net. A directional mike is placed on the judge's stand to hear the calls.*

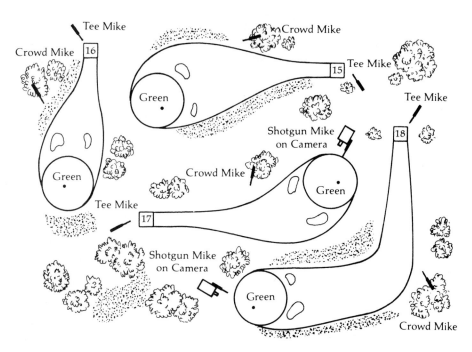

12-23 *Miking golf. To pick up crowd sound, directional mikes are mounted in trees as close to the crowd as possible without isolating any particular sound. Directional mikes on desk stands are placed behind the trees to pick up the sound of the drive. Other action sounds are picked up by the shotgun microphones mounted on portable cameras that get in close to cover play around and on the green.*

phone(s), from the house public address (PA) system, or from a common output feed, other than the PA system, called a multiple.

Setting Up Your Own Microphones　The cardioid microphone is usually best to use for a speaker at a podium. Its directional on-axis response focuses the sound from the speaker, and its 180-degree off-axis cancellation reduces unwanted room and audience noises.

The problem in using a directional microphone is that if the speaker moves his or her head from side to side, as often happens, the sound level will vary with the head movement. Therefore, two cardioid mikes are often used to provide a wider on-axis pickup and allow the speaker more freedom of movement. To avoid phasing problems, the microphones are placed at a 45-degree angle with their heads crossed or close together (see **12-24**). This technique increases the overall loudness level. Another technique is to put the mikes parallel to each other and close enough so that their cardioid patterns overlap, yet not so close that phasing problems are created. This technique will not increase overall loudness, however.

The advantages of setting up and using your own microphones are that you have control of the sound quality and exclusive use of the content. Nevertheless, there are situations in which you have little or no say in these matters and have to take your sound from a common source.

12-24 *Commonly used techniques when miking a speaker with two directional microphones. The mike placements in **a** and **b** add several decibels more loudness to the sound in the middle (of the left-to-right space) than the mikes in **c**, although the spaced mikes in **c** produce a more uniform left-to-right sound level. In terms of appearance, the technique shown in **a** is least used.*

a   b   c

Public Address Pickups   Talks delivered in many rooms and halls require a public address system so the audience can hear the speaker. The mike(s) for the PA system is at the podium. On occasion, adding your mikes to those already at the podium could create a clutter that may be visually detracting and also obscure the speaker from some of the audience. In such instances, you may have to take the audio feed from the PA system.

This entails patching into an output jack in the PA amplifier or PA control panel and feeding the signal to your mixer or console. It will not interfere with the loudspeaker sound since the PA feed from the podium mikes is split into two separate routing systems. Because many PA systems are not noted for their sound quality, this arrangement gives you some control over the audio. If the house technicians control the sound feed, however, which is often the case, it is a good idea to coordinate your needs with them in advance.

Multiple Pickups   Several stations often cover the same event. If they all set up microphones at the podium, not only would the clutter be unsightly, but also a good sound pickup might depend on how lucky you were in getting a mike close enough to the speaker. Although this often happens at news conferences, it is not ideal or preferred. If the facilities exist, it is better to take the sound from a **multiple**, or "mult" for short. A multiple (not to be confused with the multiple that interconnects jacks on a patch panel) is a **unity gain** amplifier—an amplifier with an output level that increases or decreases in proportion to its input level—with several mike level outputs. Each station then obtains a separate, quality sound feed without struggle by patching into one of the amplifier's output jacks. This type of feed is usually agreed to in advance by the stations involved and set up either cooperatively by them or by the sound people who operate the in-house audio system. This type of multiple is also known as a **presidential patch**.

Miking Speech Outdoors There is little or no reverberation outdoors unless hard surfaces are nearby, yet it is almost never absolutely quiet. Some sound is usually audible from atmospheric pressure, wind, animals, thunder, traffic, crowd, aircraft, and so on. For these two reasons, outdoor miking usually requires close mike-to-source proximity.

MIKING THE STAND-UP NEWS REPORT Most newspeople who report on camera from the scene of a news event use a hand-held, moving-coil microphone with a pop filter and/or windscreen. A hand-held mike is easier and quicker to set up than lavalier or wireless mikes. Moving-coil types stand up extremely well outdoors, and the pop filter or windscreen cuts down on unwanted plosive and blowing sounds.

Whether an omni- or unidirectional pickup pattern is used depends on how noisy the conditions are. In most instances, the omnidirectional mike is preferred. The speaker's body blocks much of the background sound, yet the mike picks up enough of it to give a sense of the environment. The closer you move an omnidirectional mike toward the speaker's mouth, the more you reduce background sound (see **12-25**). If conditions are too noisy, use a unidirectional mike. It reduces background sound considerably, especially if the mike is held close to the mouth (see **12-26**).

12-25 *(Far left) Holding an omnidirectional microphone at chest level usually creates an optimal mike-to-source distance (**a**). If background noise is high, its level can be reduced by decreasing the mike-to-source distance (**b**).*

12-26 *(Left) If background noise is too loud, use a directional microphone either several inches from the mouth (**a**) or close to it (**b**) depending on the performer's voice projection. Since the microphone is directional, it must be held at the proper angle if the performer is to be on-mike.*

MIKING DRAMA If a microphone must be out of the picture, as is the case in most dramatic productions involving dialogue, you have at least three choices: (1) to use a mike on a fishpole, (2) to use a wireless mike, or (3) to dub the dialogue in the studio during postproduction.

Mike on a Fishpole If the action takes place within a limited area, and there is little or no problem preventing unwanted sound from interfering with the desired sound, use a fishpole. You can maneuver it easily, get it relatively close to the sound source, and attach any type of shotgun mike to it (see **12-27**).

Wireless Microphone System When the shooting involves extended camera-to-source distances or considerable movement by the performers, assuming there is no problem with unwanted noise, try using a tie-tac mike with a wireless microphone system. Since the microphone itself is mounted like a lavalier and is omnidirectional, the performer is always on-mike.

Wireless systems are improving, but they still present some problems. Some systems are subject to dropout caused when the very high-frequency radio signals from the microphone's transmitter hit obstructions between the transmitter and the receiver. Other systems have limited frequency response and dynamic range. The best systems have reduced these problems.

12-27 *Using a fishpole with a directional microphone pointed at the performer's mouth from above (**a**) or below (**b**). The mike's position depends on the focal length and angle of the shot.*

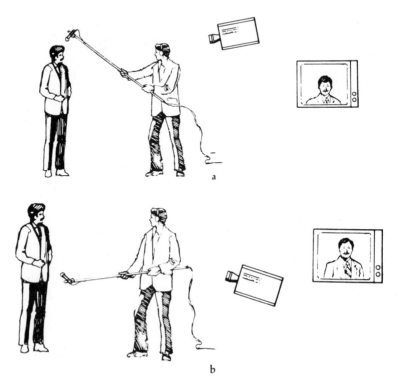

Nevertheless, make sure that (1) the transmitter and receiver are properly set up and tuned to ensure maximum signal strength and to cut down on signal drift; (2) the antennas are at least a few feet from obstructions, particularly metal (to prevent detuning), and 3 feet off the floor to avoid dropout; and (3) the antennas are vertical, since the signal is transmitted in a mostly vertical configuration.

Dubbing (or Looping)   Often, recording dialogue is done in a studio after shooting because of either too much noise at the production site or too much action to mike at once. This technique is known as **dubbing** (or **looping**). It involves taking short pieces of the exposed footage, splicing them into loops, projecting each loop over and over until the actors' dialogue is synchronized with their lip movements in the film, and then recording. This is a common procedure, particularly when films in one language are dubbed into another language. If the scene requires ambient or background sound, that is recorded separately and combined with the dialogue later.

cinema

MIKING MUSIC   Miking music on location usually depends on two factors: (1) the type of music involved, and (2) the quality of the acoustics, since most location music is played indoors. These factors may or may not be interdependent.

Classical Music   Ordinarily, classical music is recorded in a concert hall, presumably under good acoustic conditions. For this and other reasons—the need to capture the sound of the hall and the number of sound sources involved—miking every source is neither desirable nor recommended. Three common techniques in recording classical music on location are: (1) using two coincident mikes, (2) using a spaced pair of mikes several feet apart, and (3) using extra microphones in addition to the coincident or spaced pair in the rear of the hall for added reverb, or over certain sections of the orchestra to improve the music blend.

3 ways to mike classical

Coincident miking involves placing one cardioid microphone directly above another and, for music, at a 90- to 135-degree angle. This technique prevents phase differences in the sounds that reach the mikes, and preserves the balance in the left-to-right aural frame.

A spaced pair of mikes—two cardioids several feet apart—produces a wider and deeper sonic image than coincident microphones. You must use trial and error to determine (1) the best distance between the mikes to avoid phase problems caused by the sound traveling different distances to them and (2) how far from the stage the mikes should be, since every concert hall has different acoustics.

A general guideline in placing a coincident or spaced pair is: the closer the microphones are to the sound source, the sharper and drier is the sound; the farther they are from the sound source, the more diffused and reverberant is the sound.

Using extra directional mikes in addition to the two main microphones can enhance the sound's spaciousness if they are placed toward the rear of the hall. Adding extra mikes for reverb is a technique often used in halls that are too dry (see **12-28**). Extra mikes placed over the orchestra can enhance the sound blend in concert halls with acoustics that do not complement the sonic character of the music or can make the sound blend richer. Recordists may place microphones, say, over the strings and woodwinds if the brass is too predominant, or over a chorus that is not projecting because it is at the rear of the stage behind the orchestra. Sometimes extra mikes are needed to pick up solo instruments or voices (see **12-29**).

Pop Music   Most recordists use the multimicrophone technique to produce pop music on location regardless of the acoustics. Since so much pop music incorporates greatly amplified sound and since the electric instruments overpower the acoustic instruments, the music must be blended before it reaches the stage loudspeakers or the PA system. Miking each sound source permits several separate feeds to a mixer or a console, where the sound is balanced, equalized, and blended before the audience hears it.

Microphone selection and positioning are particularly important in producing pop music on location. Sound coming from the loudspeakers on stage or from the PA system should not feed back into the performers' mikes, otherwise it will produce that familiar and annoying high-pitched squeal. Most groups tightly mike each sound source with a unidirectional micro-

12-28 *Spaced directional microphones placed at the rear of the concert hall to pick up sound reflections add more reverb or "wetness" to the music.*

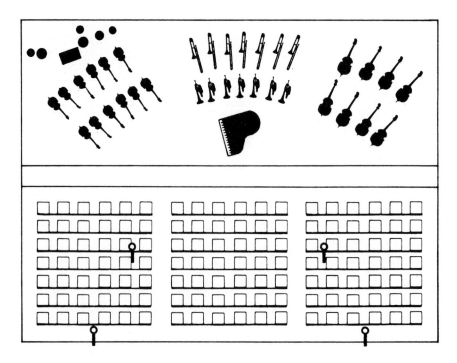

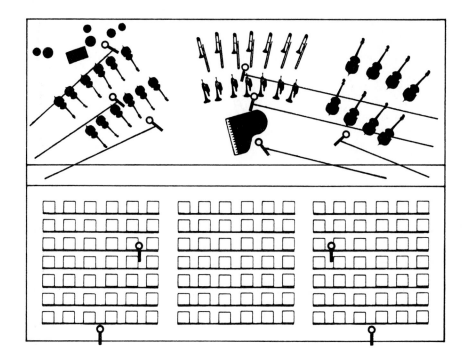

12-29 *Additional directional microphones placed above the main sound sources, or groups of sound sources, to enhance the overall music blend.*

phone; the directionality depends on the instrument, the acoustics, and the sound they want. To reduce the chance of feedback even further, some groups use a limiter to prevent sound levels from becoming acoustically unmanageable.

Many pop groups employ an audio person whose job is to blend the music during performances; indeed, this individual is as important to the group's overall sound as are the performers. When a pop group performs on television, the TV sound people often take their audio from the mix provided by the group's sound person.

VARIETY AND SPECIAL PROGRAMS Television shows with speech, music, and audience reaction, such as variety and awards programs and beauty pageants, use separate microphones for the main sound sources (see **12-30**).

Shows in which the sound is particularly complex require a separate remote truck just for the audio (see **12-31**). Some signal processing is almost always necessary, such as equalizing—to balance and blend the aural interaction between the sound of the performance and the acoustics; limiting/compressing—to control the dynamic range feeding the house PA system and the home TV receiver; and reverb—to add dimension to halls and theaters with dry acoustics.

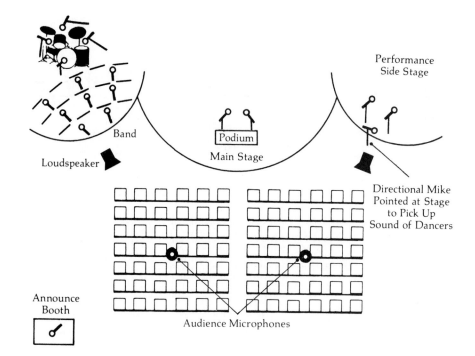

12-30 *Example of miking for an awards or variety program. All microphones are directional. Sounds from the audience mikes are blended. Notice how the dead sides of the microphones and loudspeakers are opposite each other. To avoid feedback into the audience mikes, the loudspeakers are above them.*

Performance
Side Stage

Loudspeaker

Band

Podium

Main Stage

Directional Mike
Pointed at Stage
to Pick Up
Sound of Dancers

Announce
Booth

Audience Microphones

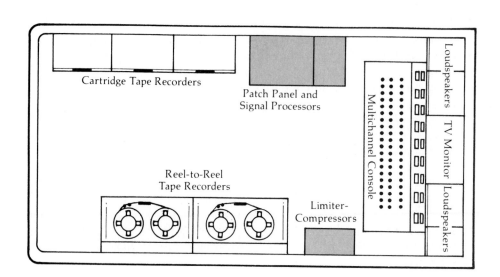

12-31 *Example of the layout of a mobile sound track.*

Cartridge Tape Recorders

Patch Panel and
Signal Processors

Reel-to-Reel
Tape Recorders

Limiter-
Compressors

Multichannel Console

Loudspeakers

TV Monitor

Loudspeakers

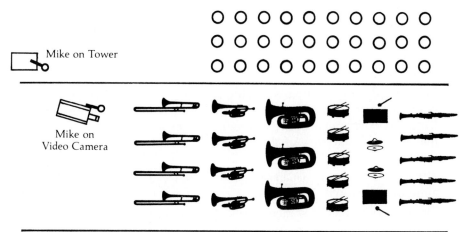

Mike on Tower

Mike on
Video Camera

12-32 *Miking a parade. Shotgun microphones hand-held from a specially built tower and mounted on a video camera pick up crowd and parade sounds. The mike on the tower is the main mike, and the one on the camera is used both to cover the shots it takes and to enhance the overall sound blend. Both microphones are on the same side as the cameras to avoid confusing the visual and aural images.*

Parades present the obvious but nevertheless difficult problem of covering an event that is spread over some distance and continuously moving. The key to good sound coverage is to mike each camera location with a long-reach shotgun microphone mounted on the same side of the street as the cameras to pick up the sounds of the parade and the crowd (see **12-32**). Sometimes a separate mike is used for the crowd.

Summary

1. Comparatively small, lightweight equipment has made it possible to record radio, television, and film productions on location with almost the same facility as recording productions in a studio.

2. In broadcasting, on-location recording involves producing material for either electronic news gathering (ENG) or electronic field production (EFP) using portable mixers, consoles, cameras, audio and video recorders, and mobile units. The main difference between ENG and EFP is that ENG covers news events, whereas EFP records the types of productions that take time to plan and produce.

3. Microwave transmission from a mobile unit makes it possible to transmit a signal from the location to the radio or TV station for recording or direct broadcast.

4. For a location broadcast such as an awards program or a sports event, telephone lines are used to feed the program to the station. The costlier the line, the better quality is the signal.

5. Film is recorded using either single system—sound and picture recorded simultaneously on the same piece of film—or double system—sound recorded by an audio tape recorder and film recorded by a camera separately but simultaneously and in synchronization.

6. In double-system recording, a slate is used to make a visible and audible sync mark on both tape and film. This helps in identifying and synchronizing scenes during their transfer from audio tape to magnetic film and in editing.

7. Preparing for on-location recording requires: selecting a location with a minimum of noise problems and determining what to do about the problems that exist; making sure where the power will come from; and deciding who will take care of the equipment, program, and administrative details.

8. Miking sports events usually requires three types of sound pickup: from announcers, crowd, and action.

9. Three ways to record someone talking from a podium are to: (a) set up and use your own microphones, (b) patch into the public address (PA) system, or (c) patch into a multiple pickup.

10. In miking someone outdoors, it is most important to record the sound on-mike and on-axis with as little interference as possible from background sounds. If there is too much background noise, the voice track(s) is dubbed in a studio during postproduction.

11. Miking music on location often depends on the type of music being played and/or on the acoustics in the hall. Music played by larger ensembles usually requires no more than a few mikes if the acoustics are good, and several mikes if the acoustics are mediocre. In pop music, regardless of the acoustics, the multimicrophone technique is used with the mike-to-source distance very close.

13

Editing

The art of editing (and it is an art in a sense) demands the ability to see a whole and build toward it while it is still in parts. It requires manual dexterity, a good "ear," and sensitivity to the aesthetics of sound. Yet, with all these abilities, the editor seldom gets recognition, because a good edit is never heard and the sign of success is the absence of audience response.

To be a successful editor, you should understand the purposes of editing and be able to use (1) the tools and materials of the trade; (2) the procedures for making a simple edit, cut, and splice; and (3) the techniques and aesthetic principles that govern the editing of speech, music, and sound effects.

Generally, there are several reasons for editing. Program segments may need rearranging, shortening, or cutting out altogether. Suppose a comedian ad libs so well about halfway through the taping of a show that the director wants to open with that segment. Editing makes such switches possible. Directors may need to record elements of a program out of sequence, which is common practice; editing makes this possible. It also makes it possible to record a segment several times and choose the best parts of each take. Editing can improve the pace as well as the timing of a program; it can eliminate mistakes, long pauses, coughing, "ahs," "ers," "ums," and other awkwardness. Parts of words can be transposed, music can be recomposed, and the character of a sound effect can be changed.

Types of Editing

Two ways to edit sound are (1) **cutting and splicing** tape, and (2) **electronic editing**—dubbing from one tape to another. Audio tape and sound on film are edited by cutting and splicing or by dubbing; video tape is edited by dubbing.

315

Cutting and Splicing Audio Tape

EQUIPMENT For cutting and splicing audio tape, you need the following items:

1. Cutting block
2. Marking pen or pencil
3. Razor blade
4. Splicing tape
5. Flat, clean surface

   Sometimes you also need these items:

1. Empty reel(s)
2. Leader tape
3. Cue sheet or script

CUTTING TOOLS Two cutting tools are recommended: the metal block (see **13-1**) and the Nagy guillotine splicer (see **13-2**). Both have several advantages over other types of splicers: (1) durability, (2) fast and accurate cutting and splicing, (3) easy visibility of the tape for close editing, (4) capacity—the block can hold at least 4 inches of tape at once—and (5) no necessity for trimming splicing tape. The guillotine splicer has the added advantages of an attached cutting blade, a built-in blade sharpener, and a mount for the splicing tape.

MARKING PEN OR PENCIL To mark the edit point on recording tape, use an indelible felt-tip pen or a very soft lead pencil. A bright color shows up best. Avoid grease pencils or any marking instruments that crumble or tend to leave residue; the particles could stick to or collect in the working parts of the tape recorder.

13-1 *(Right) Splicing block (mounted on head housing).*

13-2 *(Far right) Guillotine splicer with a holder for splicing tape and a built-in blade sharpener.*

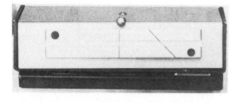

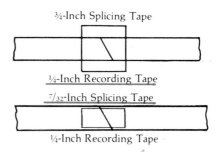

¾-Inch Splicing Tape

¼-Inch Recording Tape

⁷/₃₂-Inch Splicing Tape

¼-Inch Recording Tape

13-3 *(Far left) Precut splicing tab. With this type ("EdiTab" by EdiTall), pulling the dark end of the plastic cover lifts the splicing tape from the tab sheet. Once the splicing tape is pressed onto the recording tape, thus completing the edit, pulling the transparent end of the plastic cover separates it from the splicing tape.*

13-4 *(Left) The ⁷/₃₂-inch splicing tape leaves ¹/₆₄ of an inch between its edges and the edges of the recording tape; the ¾-inch splicing tape overlaps and must be trimmed.*

RAZOR BLADE   With the metal cutting block, use a single-edge razor blade to cut tape. Replace the blade often during lengthy editing sessions, before it gets dull and cannot cut cleanly. Razor blades also become magnetized after a period of time. Then, every time a magnetized blade touches the tape, it affects the magnetic information at that point on the tape. Whenever such a splice passes across the playback head, you hear a click or pop.

SPLICING TAPE   **Splicing tape** (and no other type of adhesive tape) is specially made to stick to recording tape without the adhesive bleeding to other tape layers or onto the tape recorder heads.

There are two types of splicing tape with different adhesive properties. One type (such as Scotch 41) sticks best to audio tape with shiny plastic backing and dull oxide surface. The other type (such as Scotch 620) is made for the newer tapes, like Ampex 406, 407, and 456 and Scotch 206, 207, and 250, with the dull plastic side and shiny oxide surface.

Individual, precut tabs of splicing tape are also available (see **13-3**). These tabs stick well, they can be used with any type of recording tape, and they speed up splicing.

Two widths of splicing tape are made for use with ¼-inch recording tape: ⁷/₃₂-inch and ¾-inch. The ⁷/₃₂-inch width is preferable because it does not require trimming (see **13–4**).

FLAT, CLEAN SURFACE   Have a flat, clean surface available near the editing area. Save deleted parts of the recording tape until your editing is finished. On a flat surface, you can keep bits of deleted tape in order and right side up, so that if you need a fragment, you can find it fast and be sure the sound is flowing in the right direction. To be even safer, write on a slip of paper what each piece of tape contains and put the slip beside the appropriate tape fragment. Be sure the working surface is clean; dust and dirt on tape can interfere with response and clog or damage the tape recorder's heads.

EMPTY REEL   Keep empty reels handy to store the outtakes (material deleted from a tape or film) until a project is done. You never know whether you will need some piece of deleted material, particularly if it is controversial. Also, label the contents of each reel.

LEADER TAPE   **Leader tape** is nonmagnetic plastic or paper tape used primarily for cueing (see **13-5**). When spliced between segments of recording tape, it provides an easy visual reference that allows you to spool quickly to the cut you want instead of having to listen for a cue point by constantly starting and stopping the tape (see **13-6**). Leader tape can also be spliced to both ends of recording tape to preserve these vulnerable points.

When you use leader tape for cueing, be sure that the beginning of the recorded sound starts immediately after the leader (see **13-7**). When this is done, an engineer can cue a tape without having to search for the first point of

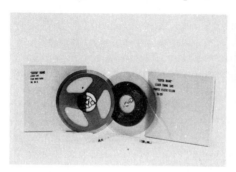

13-5   (Right) Paper and plastic leader tape.

13-6   (Far right) Light colored leader tape is visible between the tape segments.

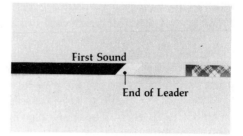

First Sound

End of Leader

13-7   Leader tape can serve as a visual reference to the beginning of a sound. Providing the sound is there, it makes cueing a tape easier and faster.

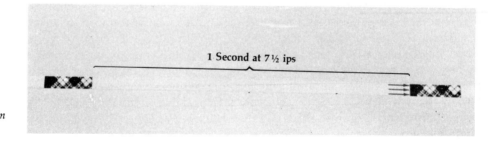

1 Second at 7½ ips

13-8   Leader tape that can also be used for timing.

```
        "We have to be aware, more aware than we have ever been before,

as aware as we can, that protecting our rights as handed down by the

founders of this great, proud, and diligent democracy is essential

to the future of (our) country. "
```

```
Outtakes

        aware, more aware than we have ever been before--

        proud, and diligent--

        the--

        of--

        country--

Intro-- We have to be as aware . . .
Outro-- . . . is essential to our future.


        Running time--0:09
```

13-9 Sample cue sheet used when editing tape. It can be laid out in any way that is convenient. The important information to have at your fingertips is what has been edited, what has been cut out (in case it is needed for legal purposes or to repair a faulty edit), the intro and outro lines, and the segment time.

sound. This is particularly helpful in pressure situations when time is at a premium.

You can use certain types of leader tape for timing (see **13-8**). If program material is on one reel and, say, commercials are being played from another sound source, you can place a timed leader in the program tape to coincide with the length of the commercials. With this technique, you do not have to stop and recue the program tape during commercial breaks.

Another feature of most timed leader tape is the arrows just before every other plaid marking. You can use the arrows to indicate the head end of the tape—that is, the direction in which the sound is going. The arrows are appropriate only for recordings that have all sound going in one direction.

We mentioned that leader tape is available in both plastic and paper. Paper is used mainly when extremely high sound quality is vital because, unlike plastic leader, paper does not build up static electricity when it is wound excessively. Static electricity can affect magnetically encoded information if it builds to strong enough proportions. Finally, avoid using transparent plastic leader, since it is sometimes hard to detect when it becomes twisted; also, it cannot be used for timing.

CUE SHEET Use a cue sheet when editing. Although there is no particular format, it should contain such information as (1) where edits have been made, (2) how long each outtake is, (3) where rearranged segments were originally located in the reel (assuming a long program), and (4) segment time and running time (see **13-9**).

Basic Procedures

Before cutting any important tape, make a duplicate—called a *dub*—of the original or master tape. Store the master, tails out, in a safe place, and use the dubbed tape for cutting and splicing. Then, if you make any serious mistakes in cutting, you can make another dub from the master. Of course, a dub is second-generation and loses something in sound quality. If you use high-quality, well-maintained equipment for dubbing, however, the loss in sound quality will be minimal and the trade-off—a slight loss in response for the sure safety of the original material—is worth it.

Try to record the master tape at 15 ips; if you cannot, then dub it at that speed. The faster a tape travels across the heads, the more spread out is the sound and the easier it is to edit (see **13-10**).

Let's go through the basic procedures, step by step, for making a simple edit, cut, and splice. A speaker greets an audience with "Good evening, (cough) ladies and gentlemen." The editing task here is to cut the cough. Once you decide what to edit, the next steps are to (1) determine exactly where the edit points will be, and (2) locate those points on the recording tape.

Assume that the speaker took two breaths, one after "evening" and one after the cough. For reasons that will be explained later, the edit points should fall after the first breath and immediately before "ladies" (see **13-11**). Once the edit points are chosen, you are ready to proceed with the cutting and splicing (see **13-12** to **13-23**).

Whatever sounds good

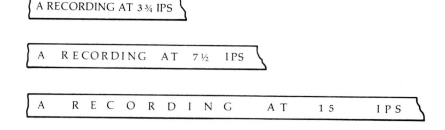

13-10 *The faster the tape recorder speed, the more spread out is the sound on the tape and the easier it is to edit.*

A RECORDING AT 3¾ IPS

A   RECORDING   AT   7½   IPS

A   R E C O R D I N G   A T   1 5   I P S

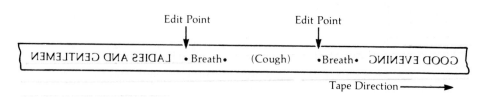

13-11 *Sounds to be cut and spliced with edit points indicated.*

Edit Point   Edit Point

LADIES AND GENTLEMEN   •Breath•   (Cough)   •Breath•   GOOD EVENING

Tape Direction ⟶

13-12 *After the tape has been threaded and wound close to the edit point, put the tape recorder in "Stop." In "Stop" (some machines have a pause, cue, or edit button), the playback head is "live" and the reel tension is disengaged. This allows you to hear what is on the tape and manually control the tape speed as you locate the precise edit point. You are making the initial cut after the first breath. With the edit point at the playback head, put your left hand on the feed reel and your right hand on the take-up reel. Then rock the tape back and forth until you hear exactly where the first breath ends, just before the sound of the cough.*

13-13 *When you locate the edit point, mark it with a marking pen or pencil. Make sure the mark is visible.*

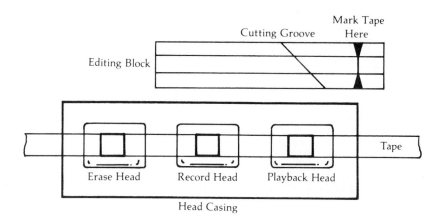

13-14 *You saw in* **13-13** *one way to mark tape—at the playback head. Unless you are highly skilled, this technique could result in the head being nudged out of alignment or, worse, damaged. A safer marking procedure is to establish a measured point close to the playback head and mark the tape there.*

13-15 *With the first edit marked, wind the tape to the second edit point and rock it until you locate the point just before you hear the "l" in "ladies." After locating the second edit point, mark it. Now you are ready to cut the tape.*

13-16 *Gently lift the tape from the playback head and place it in the channel of the cutting block with the first edit point on the diagonal groove.*

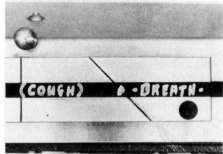

13-17 *Using a razor blade, cut the tape diagonally; a guillotine stroke usually cuts it easily without bending the tape ends into the cutting groove. A diagonal cut gives the sound a split second to become established in our hearing. A vertical (90 degree) cut hits the playback head all at once, and we hear the abrupt change from one edit to another as a pop, click, or beep. Also, the diagonal cut requires more splicing tape, thereby ensuring a stronger splice.*

13-18 *Gently remove the cut tape from the channel of the cutting block, find the second edit point, place the tape back in the channel over the diagonal groove, and cut on the mark.*

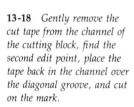

13-19   *Now you are ready to splice the two edits together.*

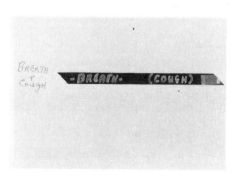

13-20   *Once you make the cuts, lay the deleted tape on a flat, clean surface. Write on a tab what has been edited and place the tab next to the fragment. Put an arrow on the tab to indicate the head end of the deleted tape.*

13-21   *Take the two tape ends and butt them together. Make sure that there is no overlap or space between them.*

13-22   *Take a piece of splicing tape, roughly ¹/₄-inch long, and place it so that ¹/₈-inch covers each tape end. Do not use less than ¹/₄-inch of splicing tape or the splice may break. Using your finger or a blunt instrument, press the splicing tape firmly onto the recording tape to ensure a strong splice. Make sure that no white "bubbles" appear on the splicing tape; they indicate that the splicing tape is not stuck firmly to the recording tape. Gently remove the tape from the cutting block and play it to check the edit.*

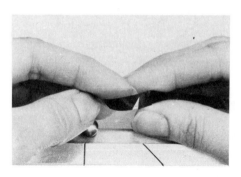

13-23 *If you need to undo a splice, grasp each end of the splice point, form a small loop, and work the tape back and forth until one side of the splice begins to loosen. Then peel away the recording tape. Do not reuse the splicing tape.*

Electronic Editing of Audio Tape

Another way to edit audio tape is by means of electronic editing (see **13-24**). The tape(s) you dub from—sometimes called the *slave(s)*—contains the program material; the tape you dub to is clean and becomes the *master*. The simplest way to accomplish electronic editing is by manual control.

Kwow

MANUALLY CONTROLLED ELECTRONIC EDITING Assume a reporter has recorded a news story in the field but the segments were taped out of order. The tape begins with an interview between, say, the mayor and the reporter, followed by a statement the mayor made that sets up the interview, followed by the reporter's open and close. Based on what the finished story should sound like, the taped segments are in a 3, 2, 1, 4 order.

To put these segments in the proper sequence by means of manually controlled electronic editing, you need two reel-to-reel tape recorders and a clean tape. You can also use cassette and cartridge recorders, but they are more cumbersome to work with. They do not edit as precisely as reel-to-reel machines, and the pulse tone on the cartridge recorder you dub to must be defeated (disconnected) or the tape will stop after each segment is played.

The procedure is as follows:

1. Thread the tape with the recorded material on one recorder (call it TR 1) and the blank tape on the other recorder (TR 2). Since you will dub from one machine to the other, they must be connected either by hard wiring or by patching.

2. Put TR 1 into "Playback" and TR 2 into "Record."

3. Cue the tape on TR 1 to the beginning of cut 3, the reporter's opening to the story. Try to leave a split second before the sound begins. Most professional quality audio tape recorders take at least that much time to reach full speed. By leaving a slight space before the first sound, you avoid starting it

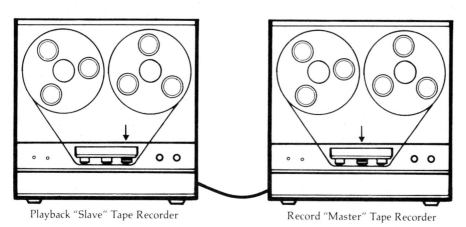

Playback "Slave" Tape Recorder   Record "Master" Tape Recorder

13-24 *Electronic editing involves dubbing segments that are out of order from one tape, or tapes, to another tape in the proper sequence.*

with a wow—that is, unless background sound is also on the tape. In that case, you have to preroll the playback tape to avoid wow. Prerolling involves starting the tape a few seconds before the cue so it has time to reach full speed. When it reaches the cue point, begin recording on the other machine.

4. Assuming the tape on TR 1 has no discernible background sound and that it is cued, start TR 2 in "Record," then start TR 1 in "Playback." Once cut 3 has been dubbed, stop both machines.

5. Recue TR 1 to the beginning of cut 2.

6. This time TR 2 must start recording at the point just after the conclusion of the reporter's open or there will be dead air between the segments. Put TR 2 in "Playback," cue the tape to the last sound in the reporter's open, put TR 2 back into "Record," and start both recorders at the same time.

7. Stop both recorders after cut 2 has been dubbed.

8. Recue TR 1 to be beginning of cut 1 and repeat steps 5, 6, and 7. Continue the same procedure with cut 4.

ASSEMBLE AND INSERT EDITING The type of electronic editing used in the preceding example is known as **assemble editing**—adding each program segment to a master tape in sequential order. It is also possible to **insert edit**—replace segment(s) on a tape without altering the other recorded material (see **13-25**).

In the reporter's story just edited, suppose that the mayor wants to update his statement, segment 2 on the assembled master, and both versions, the update and the original, take the same amount of time. (To insert edit, the

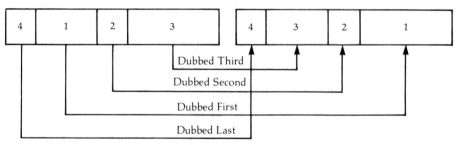

Assemble Editing

13-25 *In assemble editing, segments are dubbed in sequential order. In insert editing, they are not. However, the insert from the playback recorder and the location on the master tape to which it is dubbed must be the same length.*

Insert Editing

segment you insert and the one you replace must be exactly the same length.) Instead of assemble editing the entire story again, you can dub the new segment 2 in place of the old one without disturbing the other segments. To insert edit, the following steps are taken:

1. Cue the new segment 2 on a tape recorder and keep the recorder in "Playback."

2. On another recorder, cue the master to the beginning of the old segment 2 and then put the machine into "Record."

3. Start both recorders at the same time.

4. Stop the tape recorder with the master at the precise instant at which segment 2 ends, otherwise the machine will continue in "Record," erasing segment 3.

PUNCHING IN   If the space between segment 1 and the old segment 2 on the assembled master tape is too small to permit the tape recorder to reach full speed before recording, you will have to preroll the master—start it in "Playback" a few seconds before segment 2, and then **punch in** "Record" precisely at the point when segment 2 begins.

On most audio tape recorders, you punch in using the following procedure:

1. Start the machine in "Playback."

2. Hold in the start or play button until the insert point.

3. Press the record button at the insert point.

4. Stop the recorder, or take it out of "Record," after the insert has been dubbed.

Suppose, however, that the insert runs longer than the segment it is replacing. Let's say that the mayor's updated statement included some introductory remarks and that these remarks can be cut without detracting from the statement's overall meaning. Also suppose that the space on the tape between the end of the introduction and the beginning of the updated statement is too small to use as a cue point without wowing in the sound. To get a wowless insert edit, you will have to preroll not only the master tape but the insert tape as well.

This procedure requires that you do the following:

1. Rewind both tapes a sufficient distance so that they first reach full speed and then hit the cue point simultaneously.

2. Start both recorders in "Playback" at the same time.

3. Punch in "Record" at the edit point on the master.

4. Punch out of "Record," or stop the master, once the insert has been dubbed.

This is uncomplicated, but unless the two tape recorders run synchronously, which is unlikely even with the best machines, it is difficult to do precise dubbing.

Although manually controlled electronic editing of audio tape is possible, success depends on four factors: (1) the edit points are far enough apart with little or no audible background so the sounds do not wow in, (2) the tape recorders reach full speed quickly, (3) the machines can run synchronously if they have to, and (4) the relays on the start and record buttons are clean so they do not transmit clicking sounds onto the tape when they are activated. A fifth factor may be the speed of the operator's reflexes. Even if man and machine work well together, however, it is difficult to make tight, precise electronic edits manually.

Most of these problems have been worked out since the development of automatic and computer-assisted electronic editing and the SMPTE time code. These significant advances were motivated by problems in electronic editing of video tape that were similar to, but more serious than, those encountered in electronic editing of audio tape. For you to understand these advances more clearly, they must be discussed in relation to the problems that generated their development.

Electronic Editing of Video Tape

Although you can edit audio tape by either cutting and splicing or electronic editing, you have no such option with video tape. Cutting and splicing video tape is extremely difficult. The first problem is that the cuts must be made exactly between electronic frame lines, which are invisible to the naked eye, so the picture does not break up during playback. Second, since the video and audio heads are separated, picture and sound do not coincide on the tape. In editing video, you must take into account the effect on audio, and vice versa. Third, once any tape is cut, the danger of it breaking is greatly increased, thus making it unwise to use a spliced tape repeatedly. And fourth, video tape costs too much to reduce its playing time by using the cutting and splicing technique. Therefore, almost from its beginning, video tape has been edited by electronic means.

MANUALLY CONTROLLED ELECTRONIC EDITING   At first, electronic editing of video tape involved a manual dubbing procedure similar to the one used for manually controlled electronic editing of audio tape; the contents from one or more slave tapes were transferred to a master tape with an operator cueing the edit points, setting the playback and edit/record modes, and starting and stopping the tape recorders. Two significant differences between audio and video tape recording, however, make the manual electronic editing of video tape more difficult.

One difference is the control track (see Chapter 10) that synchronizes video playback. In assemble editing on video tape, each segment's audio and video are dubbed to the master along with their control track (see **13-26**). Since the control track works like sprocket holes on film, it must be recorded precisely to mark the beginning and end of each edit, otherwise the picture will tear as it passes from one edit point to another.

During insert editing, however, the control track on the insert is not dubbed, but is recorded onto a blank master tape before dubbing. This process is known as *recording black* (see **13-27**). It increases the possibility of trouble-free control tracks by making the control track at each edit point uniform, thus ensuring more stable edits.

Insert editing enables you to dub video and audio separately, something that is not possible with assemble editing. A disadvantage of insert editing is the long time it takes to record the control track before you can begin editing: a 30-minute tape takes 30 minutes; a 1-hour tape takes 1 hour to prepare; and so on. Most television production facilities have a stock of "black tape" on hand to meet day-to-day needs.

The other significant difference between electronic editing of video and audio tape is the time it takes the recorders to reach full speed. Modern, professional audio tape recorders take a split second, but even the best video tape recorders take several seconds; the usual preroll time is 10 seconds to ensure that the picture stabilizes.

This means that (1) the slave and master tapes must run in sync for sev-

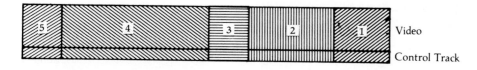

13-26 *In assemble editing video tape, each segment that is dubbed has its control track transferred also.*

Video

Control Track

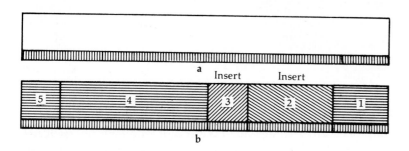

a   Insert   Insert

b

13-27 *To insert edit, a uniform control track first must be recorded on the video tape (a). This helps to ensure that the stability at the beginning and end of each insert will be the same (b).*

eral seconds before reaching the edit point regardless of how much space is between edits; (2) they must start at the same instant; and (3) the record button on the master must be punched in exactly at the beginning of the edit. "Laying down" a control track and insert editing a tape may reduce the chance of getting an unstable edit, but it does not overcome the problem of recorders running slightly out of sync, or an operator not punching in and out precisely at the right edit point.

AUTOMATICALLY CONTROLLED ELECTRONIC EDITING A number of devices—generally called **edit programmers**—allow you to perform these functions automatically (see **13-28**). By putting the appropriate command pulses on the cue tracks of the video tape (see Chapter 10), the edit programmer controls (1) the operation of the slave and master VTRs; (2) where the edit points punch in and out; and (3) in some units, the preroll starting point.

Edit programmers have different features, but basically they operate the same. To program an electronic edit, use the following procedure:

1. Locate the beginning and end of the edit on the playback VTR, and press the *player-in* and *player-out* buttons on the programmer unit at each edit point. (The commands on these buttons differ among programmers. The commands used here merely suggest the operation being performed.)

2. Locate the beginning of the cue point on the edit/record VTR and press the *recorder-in* and *recorder-out* buttons on the programmer.

3. If the edit programmer has a preroll control, it will automatically rewind both tapes to their preroll points. If it does not, cue the tapes manually.

4. Press the *execute* button. This starts both VTRs from the preroll point in sync and in "Playback." At the edit point, the master VTR will automati-

13-28 *(Right) This edit programmer controls the operation of the playback and master VTRs, the points where edits punch in and punch out, and the preroll starting points. It can run the tape in fast or slow motion, forward or backward, or hold it for still frame. This particular edit programmer is used with helical VTRs.*

13-29 *(Far right) Edit programmer showing the SMPTE time display in hours, minutes, seconds, and frames.*

cally switch into "Record." At the end of the edit, it automatically switches back into "Playback" or stops to avoid erasing any material already on the tape. Since the edit functions are programmed, you can rehearse the edit before recording to determine whether it is correct.

SMPTE TIME CODE   Automatically controlled electronic editing has solved most of the major problems in editing video tape: synchronization of VTRs; more accurate, precise, and stable edits; and automatic programmed control of the playback, record/edit, and preroll functions. It does not, however, provide a way to keep track of the edits after they are made. This makes it difficult to relocate and repeat them, which is often necessary in editing material from a variety of sources.

In 1970, the television, film, and audio industries agreed to a standardized coding system developed by the Society for Motion Picture and Television Engineers (SMPTE). This **SMPTE time code** gives each video frame a unique number in a language that any video or audio tape recorder equipped with a SMPTE time code system can read.

The number has eight digits—hours, minutes, seconds, and frames; the frame count runs from 1 to 29 since there are 30 video frames per second. The SMPTE code is recorded on the cue track and displayed on special monitors and digital counters (see **13-29**).

The SMPTE time code system makes it possible to do the following:

1. Code every electronic frame on any format of video tape
2. Program in and out edit cues to a thirtieth of a second
3. Relocate any cue sequentially or randomly
4. Repeat any edit exactly as it was programmed originally
5. Preset the preroll point to a thirtieth of a second
6. Synchronize as many tape recorders as a given control unit will allow

7. Rehearse any number of edits before recording
8. Use actual clock time or start from zero timing, forward or backward
9. Calculate times by adding or subtracting

FRAME-COUNT TIME CODE A less expensive alternative to the SMPTE time code system is the frame-count method of coding. It counts each electronic frame pulse on the control track and then converts these pulses into the same hour, minute, second, and frame numbers that are in the SMPTE code (see **13-30a, b**).

The advantages of frame-count coding are reduced expense and quicker editing of less complex material such as that usually recorded in ENG. Its disadvantages are that it does not code the tape itself, so tapes cannot be interchanged from one VTR to another without losing the coding, and that it is not as accurate as the SMPTE system.

COMPUTER-ASSISTED ELECTRONIC EDITING If the SMPTE and frame-count time code systems have made electronic editing easy and flexible, computer technology has made it virtually effortless in operation and limitless in its applications. Computer-assisted editing makes it possible to program all edits and edit operations, both simple and complex, by typing the commands for these events into a computer control unit (see **13-31**). The computer remem-

13-30a (Far left) A frame-count edit programmer.

13-30b (Left) A frame-count edit programmer used with ¾-inch video cassette recorders.

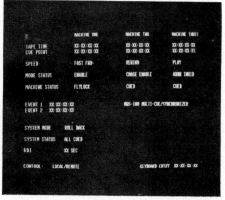

13-31 Computer control editing unit (far left) and cathode-ray tube display (left).

13-32a *Flow of commands in computer-assisted editing.*

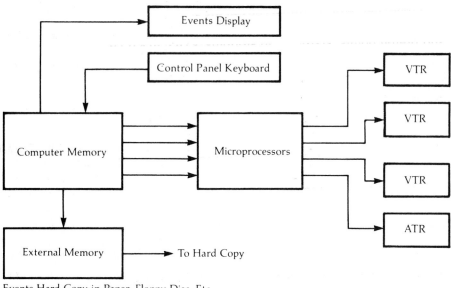

Events Hard Copy in Paper, Floppy Disc, Etc.

13-32b *Example of a hard-copy print-out of events.*

```
018   001   B   C      00:09:30:20  00:09:34:29  00:02:01:29  00:02:06:08
019   001   B   C      00:09:30:19  00:09:34:29  00:02:02:00  00:02:06:10
020   001   B   C      00:09:30:18  00:09:34:29  00:02:02:01  00:02:06:12
021   001   B   C      00:09:30:17  00:09:34:29  00:02:02:02  00:02:06:14
022   001   B   C      00:09:30:16  00:09:34:29  00:02:02:03  00:02:06:16
023   001   B   C      00:09:30:15  00:09:34:29  00:02:02:04  00:02:06:18
024   001   B   C      00:09:30:14  00:09:34:29  00:02:02:05  00:02:06:20
025   001   B   C      00:09:30:13  00:09:34:29  00:02:02:06  00:02:06:22
026   001   B   C      00:09:30:12  00:09:34:29  00:02:02:07  00:02:06:24
027   001   B   C      00:09:30:11  00:09:34:29  00:02:02:08  00:02:06:26
028   001   B   C      00:09:30:10  00:09:34:29  00:02:02:09  00:02:06:28
029   301   B   C      00:09:30:09  00:09:34:29  00:02:02:10  00:02:07:00
030   001   B   C      00:09:30:08  00:09:34:29  00:02:02:11  00:02:07:02
031   001   B   C      00:09:30:07  00:09:34:29  00:02:02:12  00:02:07:04
032   001   B   C      00:09:30:06  00:09:34:29  00:02:02:13  00:02:07:06
033   001   B   C      00:09:30:05  00:09:34:29  00:02:02:14  00:02:07:08
034   001   B   C      00:09:30:04  00:09:34:29  00:02:02:15  00:02:07:10
035   001   B   C      00:09:30:03  00:09:34:29  00:02:02:16  00:02:07:12
036   001   B   C      00:09:30:02  00:09:34:29  00:02:02:17  00:02:07:14
037   001   B   C      00:09:30:01  00:09:34:29  00:02:02:18  00:02:07:16
038   001   B   C      00:09:30:00  00:09:34:29  00:02:02:19  00:02:07:18
039   001   B   C      00:09:29:29  00:09:34:29  00:02:02:20  00:02:07:20
040   001   B   C      00:09:29:28  00:09:34:29  00:02:02:21  00:02:07:22
```

bers all commands, performs them at the touch of a button, and stores them for use at any time. The computer control unit comes with a cathode-ray terminal (CRT), which displays the events that have been programmed, and a teletypewriter, which prints a copy of the programmed events (see **13-32a, b**).

In addition to performing basic editing functions such as marking edit and preroll points, starting and stopping VTRs, insert editing, and time coding, all automatically on command, computer-assisted electronic editing makes it possible to process, mix, and integrate both audio and video.

Time Code and Computer-Assisted Editing of Audio Tape

The SMPTE time code system can also be used in editing audio tape. It is possible to (1) sync two or more audio tape recorders, (2) program them to punch in and punch out of edit cues automatically, (3) store the commands in a memory, and (4) code audio tape—all to a thirtieth of a second. (The same SMPTE code of hours, minutes, seconds, and frames used in editing video tape is used in editing audio tape. Since there are 30 video frames in each second, for audio simply count each frame number as a thirtieth of a second.)

It is also possible to sync audio recorders with video recorders (see **13-33a, b**). This eliminates at least one step in dubbing audio to video tape,

13-33a *Synchronizing a multitrack audio tape recorder with a video tape recorder using the SMPTE time code.*

13-33b *Synchronizer shown in* **13-33a** *enlarged.*

thereby improving the sound quality. For example, you can dub sound directly from a multitrack recorder by feeding the various tracks through an audio console, mixing them, and feeding the mix directly to the VTR in sync with the picture (rather than recording the mix on another audio tape and then dubbing it to video tape).

Digital Editing of Audio Tape

Digital audio tape recordings can only be electronically edited since there is no way to cut and splice pulses. The electronic editor reads the pulses recorded on the tape and converts them into a time code. In principle, the operation of a digital electronic editing system is similar to that of analog electronic editors (see **13-34**).

13-34 *The control module (right) that operates the digital audio tape recorders (far right) in electronic editing of digital audio recordings. Refinements in determining the edit points can be made by as little as one-thousandth of a second.*

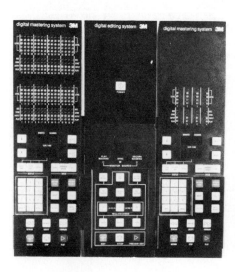

Editing of Sound Film

EQUIPMENT Sound film—magnetic full-coat, single magnetic stripe, and optical—is edited usually by cutting and splicing. Although the three film stocks differ, the equipment used to edit them is the same. That equipment includes the following (see **13-35**):

> *Editing table*—a table that (1) is large enough to hold all the editing equipment without the equipment being cramped; (2) provides some storage space for film, film reels, and other materials; and (3) is stable enough not to wobble.
>
> *Rewinds*—hand-operated metal shafts that hold the film reels and wind the film.
>
> *Viewer*—a small projector that displays the film images on its screen. You pull the film mounted on the rewinds through the viewer, forward or backward, at whatever speed you like.
>
> *Synchronizer*—a device with ganged, sprocketed wheels that locks in the film strips and keeps them in sync when winding and rewinding. A **synchronizer** also has a counter that measures the film in feet and frames.
>
> *Sound reader*—an audio/playback device, either contained in the viewer or attached to the synchronizer. A **sound reader** includes a playback head for magnetic and/or optical sound, and a small amplifier-speaker.
>
> *Horizontal editor*—a self-contained editing machine, also called a *flatbed*, that motor-drives the film reels, and combines the functions of the synchronizer, sound reader, and viewer (see **13-36**).
>
> *Film splicers*—devices that cut and splice film. The two types are **tape splicer** and **cement splicer.**

FILM SPLICING Tape splicing is done during rough editing to make temporary splices in picture film. It is easy and fast. Splices are bound with transparent tape and can be undone without damaging the film; frame loss is minimal. The major drawback of tape splicing picture film is that when it is projected,

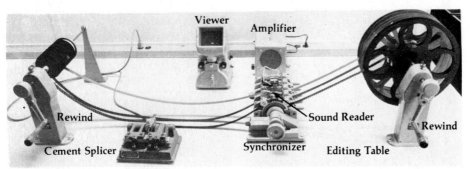

13-35 *16-mm film editing equipment.*

13-36 *Horizontal or flat-bed film editor. This unit holds picture and sound film reels and has a two-picture screen. This enables the editor to preview an edit before cutting the film.*

the splices are visible. Therefore, after final editing, the picture film must be permanently bonded with cement splices to mask the edits.

Magnetic film is edited only with tape, since visible splices are not a problem. Also, magnetic film, like audio tape, is cut on the diagonal, not on the vertical as is picture film (see **13-37** to **13-42**).

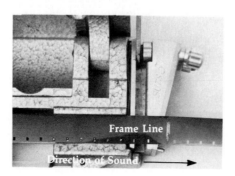

Frame Line

Direction of Sound

13-37 *In editing magnetic film, mark the first edit point (assume the sound is in a head-to-tail direction) to the right of the frame line. Place the sprocket hole on the frame line directly over the diagonal cutting edge of the tape splicer.*

13-38 *Using the guillotine blade, cut the magnetic film.*

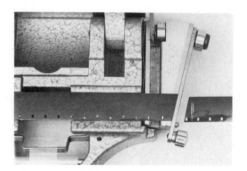

13-39 *Mark the second edit to the left of the frame line and place the sprocket hole directly over the diagonal cutting edge. Then cut the film.*

13-40 *Butt the cut edges of the film together by setting the sprocket holes on each strip across the registration pins at the bottom of the cutting plate. The edit marks indicate that the splice point is properly aligned. Splice the film with transparent mylar splicing tape.*

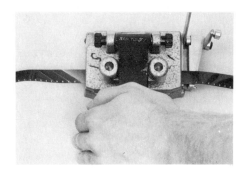

13-41 *Trim the splice by pressing the two cutting blades in the handle of the splicer through the splicing tape.*

13-42 *Remove the film from the splicer to check the splice for strength and to make sure the edges were trimmed cleanly.*

EDITING SINGLE-SYSTEM SOUND Recording single-system sound is done in one easy operation: picture and audio are recorded on the same piece of film at the same time (see Chapter 12). Editing single-system sound is not so easy, however. Picture and audio may be recorded simultaneously, but they are recorded at different places on the film. On super-8-mm magnetic stripe film, sound is recorded 18 frames ahead of picture; on 16-mm magnetic stripe film, it is recorded 28 frames ahead of picture (see **13-43**).* Therefore, sound for a

---

*On super-8-mm optical film, sound precedes picture by 22 frames; on 16-mm optical film, sound precedes picture by 26 frames.

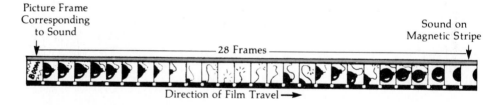

Picture Frame
Corresponding
to Sound

Sound on
Magnetic Stripe

— 28 Frames —

Direction of Film Travel →

13-43 *In single-system 16-mm magnetic film recording, sound precedes picture by 28 frames.*

given picture precedes that picture by roughly 1 second. If you edit a shot at the beginning of the picture, you lose part of the sound. Two ways to deal with this problem are blooping and double-chaining.

Blooping   Most editors prefer to edit single-system sound by cutting on audio at the beginning of the wanted shot and cutting on video at the end of it. To edit the statement "I enjoyed being here tonight," take the following steps:

1. Run the film through the viewer and sound reader.
2. Mark it (for cutting) at the sound head when you hear "I."
3. Mark it at the viewer when you see the person's mouth close after saying "tonight." If there is unwanted sound on the audio track, after the video, **bloop**—erase—it by passing a small demagnetizer, often called a *blooping pencil,* over the appropriate part of the magnetic stripe.

Follow the same procedure in editing optical sound film. Instead of using a blooping pencil to erase unwanted sound, however, cover the optical track with blooping tape or blooping ink (see **13-44**). (Optical sound film is usually edited when preparing a print for showing on television. It is no longer used during film production.)

The problem in editing single-system sound occurs when you have to splice together two different sound segments, or "bites." Although the procedure most often used is to cut from the beginning to the end of the audio in the first sound bite, and from the beginning of the audio to the end of the video in the second sound bite, **lip flap** is unavoidable. Lip flap occurs in the

Bloop Covering
Optical Sound Track

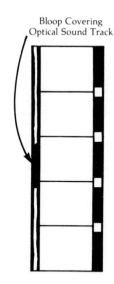

13-44   *(Above) To bloop an optical sound track, cover the appropriate section with a specially formulated blooping ink or cut a wedge from metallic blooping tape.*

13-45   *(Right) Film to be cut into A and B rolls for double-chaining.*

Reporter's On-Camera
Close from in front
of White House

President's
Statement

President Signing Bill
(Reporter's Voice-over)

Reporter's On-Camera
Open from in front
of White House

transition between the edits when a speaker is mouthing something different from what is heard, or when a speaker is obviously saying something but there is no audio.

Since lip flap usually lasts for only a second or two, it is tolerable in certain situations, such as in news reporting. If it looks too awkward, one way to cover it is by cutting to another shot, such as the crowd or the reporter. If this does not work, or if several different shots are involved, the editor usually prepares two separate reels of footage, an A and a B roll, for projection on two different projectors—**double-chaining** the film.

Double-chaining Suppose an edited film story includes the following elements: (1) a reporter's on-camera introduction from in front of the White House, (2) a cut to the President signing a bill as the reporter continues to voice over the picture, (3) a cut to the President making a statement about the bill, and (4) a cut to the reporter's closing from in front of the White House (see **13-45**). Use the following procedure to prepare the film for double-chaining:

1. Start with two equal-size strips of film leader (enough to thread through the projector): one for the A roll and one for the B roll.
2. Splice the reporter's on-camera open and voice-over to the A roll leader.
3. Continue the B roll leader to the point where the President is shown signing the bill.
4. Splice that shot into the B roll.
5. Splice the President's statement to the A roll and the leader that runs the length of the statement to the B roll.
6. Splice the reporter's close to the B roll and the leader that runs the length of the close to the A roll (see **13-46**).

A Roll

LEADER   President's Statement   Reporter's Voice-over   Reporter's On-Camera Open from in front of White House   LEADER

B Roll

LEADER   Reporter's On-Camera Close from in front of White House   LEADER   President Signing Bill   LEADER

13-46 *The A and B rolls of the film in* **13-45** *ready for double-chaining.*

To double-chain the A and B rolls, thread them into two projectors, start them at the same time, and feed the picture through the video console and the sound through the audio console. Double-chaining requires work and coordination, but it allows you to cut from one film to another, thereby covering awkward transitions and eliminating lip flap.

EDITING DOUBLE-SYSTEM SOUND Double-system recording is used in most film making, particularly when deadlines are more flexible than they are in news, for example. Since sound and picture are recorded on separate film rolls, double-system allows greater control and accuracy in editing than single-system recording.

Editing magnetic film is similar in technique to editing ¼-inch audio tape; you locate the edit, rock the film back and forth on the sound head to find the precise cutting point, and then mark, cut, and splice it. The main difference between editing audio film and editing audio tape is that film audio must be cut to sync with the picture.

To sync sound and picture, use the following steps:

1. Thread the picture film through the viewer, find the point where the clapsticks first come together, and mark the frame with an "X." The clapslate contains information about which scene and take it is.

2. Wind the magnetic film through the sound reader until you hear the corresponding scene and take announced. Then listen for the snap of the clapsticks coming together and mark the frame with an "X."

13-47 *Rolls of picture and magnetic film aligned in a synchronizer.*

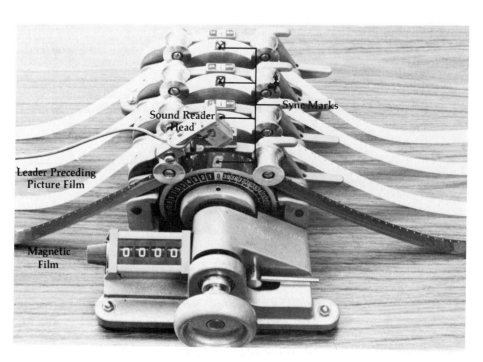

3. Align the rolls of film in the synchronizer and lock them in place (see **13-47**).

Now if you cut or add frames of sound, you can read the frame counter and cut or add a like number of frames of picture, always maintaining sync.

Techniques and Aesthetic Considerations

Upward = Question
Downward = Finality

Editing is matching—ambience, inflection, loudness, rhythm, key, and content. For instance, in a previous example, "Good evening, BREATH (cough) BREATH ladies and gentlemen," the cuts were made after the first breath and before "ladies." Why not cut after "evening" and before the second breath? A breath would still be there to preserve the rhythm. Does it matter which breath we use?

The difference is in the ambient sounds of the two breaths. For one thing, the cough is percussive, whereas "evening" is not. Thus, the reverberation after the first breath sounds different from the reverberation after the second breath. If "evening" were spliced to the breath after the cough, it would sound unnatural; the ambience does not match.

EDITING SPEECH The first thing to learn in editing speech is to recognize sounds at slow speeds—a skill you acquire only with experience. A "w" may sound like "woo," an "f" like a slight rush of wind, and an "s" like a click when they are rocked slowly across the playback head.

Some sounds are easier than others to recognize. Perhaps the easiest are those with striking power, such as "c," "d," "f," "k," "p," "s," "t," and "z": sounds with a hard attack identified by a click, pop, hiss, or buzz. The vowels "a," "e," "i," "o," and "u" are probably the most difficult to identify and separate. They lack any attack and usually blend with the other sounds in a word.

One way to locate vowels, or any sound that is hard to perceive, is to listen for differences in pitch. Suppose you want to cut between the "i" and "a" in "diamond." If you pronounce the word "dī' əmənd," the "i" is higher in pitch than the "a," and you can make a cut just before the pitch change.

Sometimes sounds are run together and cannot be separated in the usual way. If the word "deem" were mispronounced "dreem," you would have to delete the "r." Played (or rocked) in "Forward," however, the sound of the "r" runs into the sound of the "e" and is difficult to hear clearly. But if you reverse the tape and rock the sound backward, you may hear the point where the "ee" changes to the lower-pitched and more guttural "r."

Another technique used to cut between compound sounds, oddly enough, requires the eye instead of the ear. Remember that the VU meter responds to changes in voltage induced by acoustic energy. Thus, if you are unable to perceive a sound transition aurally, the VU meter may be able to "hear" it electrically. For instance, in the word "appoint," the "i" is often pronounced with somewhat more intensity than the "o," but it may be difficult to hear exactly where the change in level occurs. If the VU meter detects it, the needle will jump slightly at the transition between the "o" and "i," enabling you to see the edit point.

Matching Speech   Editing speech is matching similar or dissimilar sounds. Matching dissimilar speech sounds is easier, however, because they are usually distinct and flow more naturally.

Consider the sentence "Sound is both challenging and creative." If we delete "both," the edit will be made after "is" and before "challenging." The "s" will be spliced to the "ch" and, since they are different sounds, you will hear a distinct and natural rhythmic transition between "is" and "challenging."

Such is not the case with speech sounds that are similar. Suppose a speaker says, "I am, as you already know, more than happy to be here," and you want to remove "as you already know." At first glance, after the "am" and before "more" appear to be the edit points. But this could alter natural speaking rhythm, because most people do not pronounce separately adjacent words that begin and end with the same letter, such as "am more." The tendency is to slur them together so, in effect, one "m" serves both the "a" and the "ore": "amore." (You can test this by saying "and Donna" or "Joe's soda.") Therefore, one of the "m's" should be dropped to maintain the natural sound and rhythm. Probably the best place to edit is in the word "am," just after the "ă" and before the lips come together to form the "m" sound. Cutting between the "m" and "o" in "more" would be difficult and awkward.

This example assumes the speaker enunciated the "I" and "am" distinctly. What if the two words have been run together and the beginning of the "ă" sound is inaudible? As long as it does not change the speaker's style, cut the "m" in "am," making the contraction "I'm."

You can think of this technique as *editing on,* or *to, the same sound.* Another way to handle similar sounds that are adjacent is to *cut within a sound.* Suppose someone says "Nothing means more to me than my muse, or I should say, music." Obviously, the intention was to say "Nothing means more to me than my music." A quick look at the problem points to a cut between "my" and "muse" as the simplest edit. It could be; however, for the sake of illustration, let's say "my muse" is so slurred that there is no way to cut between the words. By editing within the sound common to both words, "s," you can maintain the natural sound and rhythm. Cut through the "s's" in "muse" and "music," and splice "mus" to "sic." Of course, the "mu" sound in both words helps to make this edit possible.

Matching Inflection   Still another common but difficult problem for the editor is matching inflection. Inflection is the nonverbal vocal sound that helps to define the meaning of a word or phrase in context. "How are you?" on paper indicates concern. But in saying it, you can change the meaning through inflection. For example, "How are you?" is often used as a greeting. From the inflection, you know whether it is a sincere concern for your welfare or just another way of saying "Hi."

Suppose you are editing a play or speech and the speaker says "How are you?," with the accent on "you" to express concern. For some reason, the "you" is garbled, and without this word it is not possible to use the phrase. If it is unimportant, there is no problem, but if it has to be kept, three alternatives are to (1) ask the person to deliver the line again, which may be impractical if not impossible; (2) go through the recording to hear whether the person said "you" elsewhere with the same or almost the same inflection; or (3) construct the word from similar sounds the speaker uttered.

To construct the word, you would have to listen for a "yoo" sound. Perhaps, with luck, the speaker may have said the word "unique," "unusual," or "continue." The "yoo" sound is part of each word, and if the phoneme and the inflection match, one of these "yoo's" may suffice.

Sometimes matching inflection is relatively easy. For instance, suppose two characters exchange these lines:

Character 1: Does it have to be that way? It doesn't have to.
Character 2: I just don't know.
Character 1: Well, it shouldn't have to be that way.

The director decides that C1 should not ask a question first but make a definite statement: "It doesn't have to be that way." C1 has said already "It doesn't have to," so we need a "be that way." To take that phrase from C1's question would mismatch the intended inflection and keep the statement a question, and an awkward one: "It doesn't have to be that way?" But the "be that way" in C1's reply is declarative and the downward inflection does make it a statement. Therefore, edit "It doesn't have to" from C1's first statement to "be that way" from C1's second statement.

Matching Backgrounds Editing speech recorded in different acoustic environments requires not only maintaining continuity of content and matching the speech sounds, but also matching the background sounds. For example, in editing two statements from the same speech when one was delivered over applause and the other over silence, or when one was delivered in a room full of people and the other was delivered after most of the audience had left, the edit will be obvious unless something is done to match the different backgrounds.

One way to make the transition from one statement/background to the other is by diverting the listeners' attention. In the second of the preceding examples, if the ambience during one statement was quiet when the room was filled with people, and the ambience during the second statement was reflectant when the room was almost empty, you could try to locate on the tape a cough, a murmur, someone accidentally hitting the microphone, or some other distraction. Splice the distractor between the two statements (the distractor would also contain some room background) so attention is called to it instead of to the obvious change in background sound.

Another technique used to match backgrounds is to mix one background with another to even them out. This assumes, however, that they were recorded "in the clear" before or after the event, which, by the way, should be standard procedure.

If there are rhythmic sounds in the background, such as a motor or a clock, take care to preserve these rhythms when editing. You may need a "chug" or a "tick" from another part of the tape to prevent any noticeable break in the background rhythm. Again, try to record the background sound separately to give you flexibility in editing.

Since on-location broadcasting is so common, the audience, to some extent, has grown used to abrupt changes in background sound and levels within the same program. Nevertheless, change should be motivated and not jarring. *The best thing to do during the recording is to anticipate the editing.*

EDITING MUSIC   Editing music is difficult to discuss in any detail because it involves using one language—the printed word—to explain another language—the notes, chords, rhythms, and other features of abstract, temporal sound. Although there is some similarity between editing speech and music, such as aural matching of space, rhythm, loudness, and inflection (intonation), there are also differences. Music contains so many simultaneous sonic elements that matching sounds is more complex and slight mistakes in cutting are more easily detected. In editing two pieces of music, you have to consider cutting on the right accent to maintain rhythm, tonality, relative loudness, and style. If any of these elements are aurally incompatible, the edit will be obvious.

You should have a good ear to edit music successfully. Assuming that, a few guidelines and techniques may be helpful. Generally, edits that heighten intensity cut together well, such as going from quiet to loud, nonrhythmic to rhythmic, or slow to fast. A transition from a seemingly formless or meandering phrase to one that is obviously structured and definite also tends to work.

Cutting to Resolution   Perhaps one of the most useful guidelines is to cut before an accent, downbeat, or resolution. Think of the final chord in a musical phrase or song. Although it resolves the music, it is the chord before it that creates the anticipation and need for resolution; it sets up the last chord. Edit on the anticipatory note, the one requiring some resolution, however brief, so that it leads naturally to the note being joined.

Preserving Rhythm   Most music has a time signature—2/4, 3/4, 4/4, 3/8, 6/8, etc.—that indicates the number of beats in each measure. In editing music, you have to preserve the beat or else the edit will be noticeable as a jerk or stutter in the rhythm. If you cannot read music or no score exists, try to get a sense of the rhythm by concentrating on the beat to determine the accents.

Matching Keys Just as most music has a time signature to regulate its rhythm, it also has a key signature—E major, B minor, etc.—which determines its overall tonality. Some keys are compatible; when you change from one to the other, it sounds natural or "in tune." Other keys are not, and splicing them together is jarring or sounds "out of tune," like the editing in some of the record offers on TV. Unless it is for effect, or if the picture justifies the change (discussed later in this chapter), edited music should sound consonant in order not to be noticed.

Matching Style and Texture Each type of music and musical group has a unique style and texture. This distinguishes the style of jazz from rock, or the texture of one voice from another although both may have identical registers, or one group from another although both may play the same instruments and music.

Editing from the same piece of music usually does not present a problem in matching style and texture as long as you follow the other guidelines for editing. If the music is from different sources, however, matching elements can be a problem.

Normally, you would not edit different styles—a piece of classical music to rock music just because they had the same rhythm, or a dance band to a military band just because they were playing the same song. The differences in sound would make the edits conspicuous and distracting.

Editing music of different textures is possible if there is some similarity in the music, instrumentation, and intensity. Cutting from one large orchestra to another or from one small ensemble to another can work if their sound intensities are similar, even if their playing styles and, to some extent, their instrumentation are not.

EDITING SOUND EFFECTS The main consideration in editing sound effects is to match perspective. If you splice the screech of tires to a car crash, the crash should sound as if it came out of the screeching tires. It sometimes happens, however, that the screech is heard close up and the crash far away, as if the sounds, although related, occurred in two different locations. The same thing happens in editing a police car or ambulance siren to the sounds of a screech and stop. The siren is heard in one perspective and the screech and stop are heard in another because either the levels or the ambiences are different.

Another example is editing rain and wind or wind, rain, and thunder to build a storm. Storms have varied intensities, and the force of each component should match; violent thunder and wind hardly go with a drizzle.

Editing Sound to Picture

In editing sound to picture, what has been said about matching applies only if it complements what is seen. Ordinarily, editing loud, fast symphonic music to a soft, quiet trio would be disconcerting, but if a picture cuts from a scene of violent destruction to one of desolation, the edit would make sense. In fact, it would make sense to cut from loud, jarring music to silence.

Changing from a dull tonality to a bright one is not recommended generally, but if the edit is played behind a change from night to day, the picture would justify it.

Editing two different styles, perhaps the most awkward type of change, is acceptable if the picture covers it. Cutting from hard rock and roll to Indian raga offends even our imagination, but not if the picture cuts from a shot of the Hell's Angels riding through town to a shot of oxen being driven through an Indian village.

Persistence of Sound

Our ability to retain precise visual information is far better than our ability to retain precise auditory information. This makes editing sound, particularly music, more difficult than editing picture. If you try to remember the pitch or rhythm of musical segments in two different parts of a tape, by the time you wind from one to the other, the pitch will be different or the rhythm will be off.

This is known as *persistence of sound* and, with most humans, it is very limited. A few things can be done to lessen the problem, however. Make rough cuts of the music segments you are editing, splice them together, and put them on a single reel. This reduces the distance and hence the time between them. Another technique is to make two tapes of the music and use two recorders. When the tape you are editing is at one point in the edit, cue the second tape to the other edit point. In checking to make sure the edit works and in trying to determine the exact cutting points, you can play them almost as they would sound if spliced.

Listening Fatigue

Editing for long periods of time can create listening fatigue—reduced ability to perceive or remember the nuances of sound. (This type of psychological fatigue can occur during any long listening sessions.) If you suffer from listening fatigue during editing, rhythm, inflection, tonality, and other features of sound are continually mismatched, cuts are slightly off, and it is difficult to keep track of what should be edited to what.

One way to extend the time before listening fatigue sets in is to work in a quiet acoustic environment, and with no predominance of midrange frequencies since they tend to tire the listener faster. If a recording or loudspeaker system has too much midrange, equalize the monitor playback by slightly boosting the lower frequencies anywhere between 50 and 150 Hz, and the frequencies above 12,000 Hz. This balances the sound and reduces its harshness and intensity. You can also attenuate the frequencies between 1,000 and 3,500 Hz, but this may reduce the sound's intelligibility.

Summary

1. Editing tape and film permits the rearranging, shortening, or deleting of elements in a production. It allows elements to be recorded out of sequence and as often as necessary.

2. Two types of editing are cutting and splicing and electronic editing.

3. The materials used to cut and splice tape are: a cutting block; a marking pen or pencil; a razor blade; splicing and leader tape; an empty reel(s); a flat, clean surface; and a cue sheet or script.

4. The materials used to edit tape electronically are: two tape recorders, one to play back and one to record and play back; a slave tape(s) containing the material to be edited; and a clean master tape used to record the material during editing.

5. Cutting and splicing are done manually. Electronic editing can be done manually or automatically. In automatic electronic editing, tape recorders can be programmed to start and stop on cue, perform the edit, and code the tape—all at the touch of a button.

6. Electronic editing involves either assemble editing—dubbing the program elements in sequential order, or insert editing—dubbing the program elements in any order. To assemble edit video tape, the control track on the playback tape can be used to stabilize the picture at the edit points. To insert edit, it is necessary to record a control track on the blank master tape before dubbing, thus creating more stable edits.

7. Film is edited by cutting and splicing using an editing table, rewinds, viewer, synchronizer, sound reader, horizontal editor, and film splicer.

8. Film is spliced with tape for temporary splices, or with cement for permanent splices.

9. Film editing involves either single- or double-system sound. In single-system, sound is several frames ahead of the picture. In editing, this creates a slight overlap in either audio or video, causing lip flap, which usually lasts for a second or two. If it lasts longer, the film can be edited into two rolls, A and B, and double-chained. In double-system, sound is put on magnetic film and edited the same way as audio tape. Having audio on magnetic film makes it possible to edit sound in sync with picture.

10. The key to editing audio is matching sound: speech, inflection, rhythm, pitch, loudness, style, texture, and other features.

11. Mismatching of sound makes an edit obvious unless the sound is being edited to a picture and the picture justifies the edit.

12. Generally, edits that heighten intensity will work, such as cutting from quiet to loud, nonrhythmic to rhythmic, slow to fast, formless to structured, or nonmelodic to melodic.

14

Additional Production Techniques and Procedures

Music and Sound Effects

Many productions require music and sounds to **underscore**—emphasize or define—the ideas and emotions in a script. The preferred way of obtaining music is to compose and record it to suit the individual needs of a production. This is beyond the budget and time constraints of many producers, however. As an alternative, music from prerecorded libraries is available, for a fee, on tape or disc.

MUSIC LIBRARIES The philosopher Susanne Langer wrote that music is a tonal analogue to forms of human response, bearing "a close logical similarity to conflict and resolution, speed, arrest, terrific excitement, calm, dreamy lapses. . . ."[*] Music libraries are developed with those relationships in mind. They provide original music composed to evoke a wide range of human emotions and information: sadness, happiness, conflict, melancholy, liveliness, danger, the future, the eighteenth century, ancient Rome, the military, the Far East, the city, the country, and many others.

Music libraries provide music in a variety of different styles and textures. Compositions are arranged for orchestras of various sizes, dance and military bands, rock and jazz groups, trio, solo instrument, synthesizer—virtually any instrument or combination of voicings necessary to evoke an idea or emotion.

USING FAMILIAR MUSIC Each selection in a prerecorded music library is original. Familiar music tends to trigger memories associated with it, which could compete with or distract from the main information. Familiar music usually

---

[*]Susanne K. Langer, *Feeling and Form* (New York: Scribner's, 1953), p. 27.

does not compel so much concentration as unfamiliar music, and this could also reduce the overall impact of the communication. Sometimes using familiar music is justified and effective, but the decision to use it should come only after careful consideration. It should not be used because it is an easier way to provide underscoring.

"CANNED" MUSIC   One problem with music libraries is that sometimes the music sounds obviously prerecorded or **canned**. This canned sound may be due to sonic deficiencies in the presence or brilliance ranges, too much mid-range, stilted and mechanical performances, or bad composing. Since some music libraries are better than others, ask to hear a demonstration disc or tape before you buy.

SOUND EFFECTS   Sound effects usually include all sounds except speech and music, such as aircraft, animals, acoustic ambience, bells, buzzers, whistles, clocks, crowds, rain, footsteps, impacts, machines, and personal movement effects—clothes rustling and chairs creaking. Three ways to collect sounds are by (1) recording them from live sources, (2) creating them, and (3) using pre-recorded sound effects libraries.

Recording Live Sound   There are two ways to record live (also called *natural*) sound: as part of the overall action and separately. Suppose you are recording a scene that involves two actors conversing inside a room, near a door, at street level. During their conversation, the telephone rings, a crowd shouts from outside, and there is a knock on the door (see **14-1**). If the acoustics are excellent, a unidirectional microphone mounted on a boom or fishpole may be able to pick up the actors' voices and the sounds clearly and in their proper perspective. Recording everything at once is certainly easier and more economical than recording it all separately. This is not always possible, however.

The acoustics may be bad or you may decide, after taping, that the knock on the door should be stronger, the telephone ring sharper, and the crowd quieter. If everything has been recorded at once, changing one sound may affect the other sounds as well. Therefore, you would probably have to go to the time and expense of rerecording the entire scene to obtain the effects you want.

In this and similar situations, the preferred technique is to concentrate on recording the speech, since verbal content usually conveys the main information. Then, after recording the dialogue, tape each other sound separately on-mike at an optimal level. When the separately recorded tracks are combined into a single track, you have maximum control over each element; adjusting the loudness or frequency of one sound will have no effect on the other sounds.

This is not to suggest that in recording speech, however tightly the performers are miked, other sounds will not leak through. They will leak, but

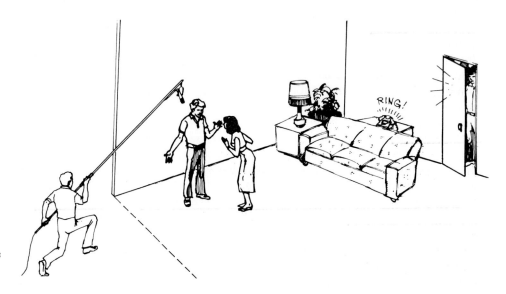

14-1 *Using one microphone to pick up dialogue and sounds in proper balance is usually very difficult even in spaces with good acoustics.*

they will be in the background and can serve as references when mixing in the better-quality sounds.

One technique used to record sounds, particularly when foreground and background sounds are taped at the same time, is to use two unidirectional microphones and a stereo tape recorder. Suppose you are recording a performer on a noisy street. Since it is important to hear the speaker as clearly as possible, a highly directional mike close in is the best choice. If the sound of the environment is important to the reality of the scene, however, placing a highly directional mike close to the performer could reduce the level of the street sounds to the point where they seem far away and not part of the same space, or they do not reflect the intensity of what the picture is showing (assuming a visual medium).

With a stereo tape recorder, you can use one mike to make a tight, clean recording of the speaker with a minimum of street sounds, and use the other mike to record the street sounds at full loudness. At the studio, you can dub the two stereo tracks onto a single track, mixing in just enough street sounds to establish the presence and intensity of the aural environment without interfering with the intelligibility of the speaker.

Sometimes sounds recorded on location are not usable or location recording is not possible. In these circumstances, recordists at major studios have several "live" sound sources available to record, including a **foley stage**—a stage that contains various kinds of surfaces such as water, pavement, brick, wood, and cardboard (see **14-2**).

Creating Sound Effects   Recording sounds from live sources is perhaps the most accurate, if not always the most convenient, way of obtaining them. There are occasions when recording natural sound is impractical, however. If you need the sound of a large forest fire, you obviously cannot set one or wait for one to break out; or you may need the sound of footsteps on snow, but you live in Miami; or you need the sound of a cow being milked, but live nowhere near a farm. Since most production facilities do not have foley stages or other sources for natural sound, you can either create the sounds yourself or use prerecorded sound effects.

Creating your own sounds can be fun and the results are sometimes better than the effects in recorded libraries. Many sound effects in radio drama are created this way. It does take time, however, and may involve some expense. The appendix contains a list of some commonly used sounds and ways to create them.

Sound Effects Libraries   Sound effects libraries are collections of sounds recorded on tape or disc and available for purchase. The advantage of sound effects libraries is that for one fee you have dozens of sounds at your fingertips; some may be very difficult to obtain or inconvenient to produce. The

14-2 *Foley stage used for recording sound effects. This stage has a miniature pool and 14 different surface units.*

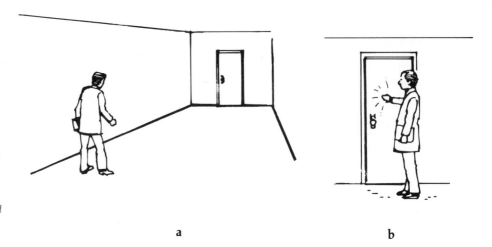

14-3 *The ambience or "room tone" complementing the sounds in shots a and b should reflect and define the differences between the two visual spaces. Shot **a** should have more ambience than shot **b**.*

a   b

disadvantages are that the effects may sound "canned" and the ambiences in the various recordings may not match each other or those you need in your production.

Regarding the latter disadvantage, suppose you have the sound of footsteps walking toward a door and then the sound of knocking. If the ambience from the footsteps is highly reverberant and the ambience from the knocking is not, the audience will perceive the two actions as being in two different locales, especially if they are used in radio. If there is a picture, sound and picture will not match unless the shot of the person walking is a long shot—showing more space—and the shot of the knocking is a close-up—showing less space (see **14-3**).

Some sound effects libraries purposely provide different ambiences for specific applications: footsteps on a city street with reverb to put you in town among buildings, and without reverb to put you in a more open area; or a gunshot with several echoes to suggest a weapon fired in hills or mountains, and with a few or no echoes to suggest a very open, flat space. Whether the ambiences in a sound effects collection are there by design or by accident, always audition sounds in advance to make sure they match the appropriate elements in your production.

TITLES AS REFERENCES   Titles in music and sound libraries are often not precise enough to be used as guides for selecting material. For example, what does "Jelly Walker" tell you about a piece of music, or what does "Crowd reaction at a soccer game" tell you about a sound effect? Most good libraries provide short descriptions of each effect to give you an idea of its content (see **14-4a,b** and **14-5**). Even so, always listen before you choose.

ROMANTIC (Orchestral)

Cat. No.	Title	Description	Time	Composer
LPC 1026B●	PRAIRIE SUNSET	†Slow evocative theme featuring **strings** and **woodwind**.	3.16	Robert Farnon
LPC 1029A	PARIS BY CANDLELIGHT	†Melodic **waltz** by strings, accordion and orchestra.	1.58	Jos Cleber
LPC 1029B	ELIZABETH OF GLAMIS	**Tranquil** work opening with theme by **oboe**; at 2.35 second theme by strings returning at 3.05 to oboe. Quiet ending.	5.23	Eric Coates
LPC 1030A	PICTURE PARADE	†**Glamorous** theme by full orchestra in **slow** free tempo. Big opening and ending.	2.56	Jack Beaver

COMEDY MUSIC

Cat. No.	Title	Description	Time	Composer
LPC 1049A●	RHINO RIDE	†**Humorous** theme by **tuba** with brass, woodwind and rhythm. **Jaunty** medium tempo.	1.07	Sam Fonteyn
LPC 1050A●	LONG JOHN SILVER	†**Humorous rhythmic** theme by **brass** in bouncy medium tempo.	0.56	Oswald Cheesman
LPC 1051A●	GUMBOOTS	†**Catchy** medium-tempo theme by **piccolo** with guitars and rhythm. Brass and piano also featured.	2.49	Lee Mason
LPC 1052A●	SLOOPY	†**Light perky** theme in **medium-fast** tempo featuring **woodwind**, brass and rhythm.	2.16	James Clarke

ELECTRONIC

Cat. No.	Title	Description	Time	Composer
C 947B●	TELESONICS Pt. 4	**Dramatic effects**		Robert Sherlaw Johnson
		1. Deep 'plodding' theme.	0.27	
		2. Mounting tension.	0.13	
		3. Mounting tension.	0.10	
		4. Mounting tension.	0.08	
		5. Eerie 'sliding' effect.	0.45	
		6. Eerie 'sliding' effect.	0.45	
C 963A	WEIRD SUSPENSE	**Slow dramatic** atmosphere with distant harpsichord theme.	1.26	Roger Roger
C 963A	WEIRD TENSION	**Slow dramatic** atmosphere with harpsichord theme and effects.	1.31	Roger Roger
LPC 1033A●	WEIRD SOUNDS No. 1	**Heavy dramatic** effects in medium-fast tempo. Various cutting points.	2.19	Georges Teperino

14-4a *Examples of titles and descriptions of library music.*

PASTORAL MUSIC - VOL 1
CIS 5018

Side 1

1. WINTER JASMINE 2′ 20″ C.951B
(Farnon; Buchel)
Slow wistful theme by solo flute and oboe with strings, harp and celeste.

2. BY THE WILLOWS 2′ 55″ C.706A
(Horace Shepherd)
Light melody by strings and woodwind in medium tempo.

3. FLUTE IN DESOLATION 1′ 09″ C.895B
(Robin Stephenson)
Lonely theme by flute accompanied by vibraphone.

4. SPRINGTIME IDYLL 2′ 59″ C.585B
(Montague Phillips)
Gentle orchestral theme in slow lilting tempo. Woodwind and strings featured.

5. AN AUTUMN SUNSET 1′ 29″ C.727A
(Charles Williams)
Quiet orchestral melody featuring oboe and clarinet solos and short horn passage.

6. GOLDEN HARVEST 2′ 30″ C.598B
(Roger Roger)
Gentle orchestral piece in slow rhythmic tempo throughout. Solo instruments featured.

7. OAKS FROM ACORNS 3′ 14″ C.600B
(Jack Beaver)
Slow theme opening with solo flute and strings, building to full orchestra with main theme on strings.

8. BY THE RIVERSIDE 1′ 23″ C.876B
(Roger Roger)
Restful piece by woodwind, strings and harp.

9. INTRODUCTION AND PASTORAL 2′ 46″ C.768B
(Arnold Steck)
After swift build-up for opening title, at 0′ 30″ slow sweeping theme by strings and brass. Further cutting point at 1′ 40″.

Side 2

1. AUTUMN IDYLL 3′ 03″ C.733A
(Malcolm Williamson)
After quiet introduction by two flutes, at 0′ 25″ gentle melodic theme by oboe and harp. At 1′ 17″ strings take up theme.

2. THE SEASONS 3′ 33″ C.1005B
(Paul Kass)
Slow melancholic theme by woodwind, horn and strings.

3. SONG OF THE TORRENT 2′ 24″ C.575B
(Felton Rapley)
Quiet opening in free tempo suggesting rippling water. At 0′ 53″ restful waltz theme to end. Woodwind and strings.

4. COOL SHADE 1′ 23″ C.882B
(Roger Webb)
Tranquil theme featuring oboe and horn with strings.

5. WAVING CORN 2′ 30″ C.706B
(Charles Williams)
Slow gentle theme by strings and woodwind.

6. QUIET COUNTRYSIDE 2′ 55″ C.341A
(Peter Yorke)
Restful piece in slow free tempo. Strings and woodwind.

7. MOORLAND HEATHER 1′ 52″ C.884B
(Walter Stott)
Slow theme featuring oboe, strings and harp.

8. LATE AUGUST 2′ 30″ C.883A
(Eugene Cines)
Quiet haunting melody by strings and woodwind. Cutting point at 1′ 00″.

9. COUNTRY TOWN 1′ 29″ C.880B
(Charles Williams)
Jaunty piece on unison strings in medium tempo.

MARCHING AND WALTZING - VOL 1
CIS 5019

Side 1

1. OVER TO YOU 2′ 50″ C.489A
(Eric Coates)
Bright medium-paced march by full orchestra.

2. CRINOLINES AND CANDLELIGHT 2′ 20″ C.684A
(Roger Roger)
Elegant quick waltz with strong melody on unison strings.

3. OUT OF TOWN MARCH 2′ 12″ C.508B
(Robert Farnon)
Bright swinging march with predominant brass. Medium tempo.

4. THE TRAPEZE WALTZ 2′ 44″ C.773B
(Sidney Torch)
Humorous waltz with main theme on strings and novel percussion.

5. DRUM MAJORETTE 2′ 13″ C.643B
(Arnold Steck)
Rousing medium-paced march by full orchestra. Opening suitable for titles.

6. THE WESTMINSTER WALTZ 3′ 17″ C.507B
(Robert Farnon)
Melodic waltz featuring lush strings in medium-slow tempo. Opening and ending features chime effects by strings.

7. COMMONWEALTH MARCH 2′ 33″ C.628A
(Walter Stott)
Slow stately march with fanfare opening and ending.

Side 2

1. DERBY DAY 2′ 24″ C.464A
(Robert Farnon)
Lively march in medium bouncy tempo. Brass predominant.

2. SWEET SEVENTEEN 2′ 42″ C.499A
(Eric Coates)
Melodic concert waltz by full orchestra. Quick tempo.

3. WELLINGTON BARRACKS 3′ 05″ C.346A
(Haydn Wood)
Bright quick march by full orchestra.

4. THE YOUNG BALLERINA 2′ 35″ C.400B
(Charles Williams)
Light delicate waltz featuring strings.

5. MUSIC EVERYWHERE 2′ 55″ C.363B
(Eric Coates)
Quick march by full orchestra. Opening and ending suitable for titles.

6. SOPHISTICATION WALTZ 2′ 45″ C.383A
(Robert Farnon)
Glamorous waltz in slow tempo featuring lush strings.

7. MONTMARTRE MARCH 2′ 45″ C.631B
(Haydn Wood)
Bright medium-paced march by full orchestra.

14-4b *Examples of titles and descriptions of library music.*

BACKGROUNDS

Section 3

Catalog Number	Subject	Description	Tape Reel #3-1 Time
_____3-033	FACTORY--In steady operation.		0:28
_____3-034	ELECTRICAL GENERATING PLANT--In steady operation.		0:33
_____3-035	NEWSPAPER PRINTING PLANT--In steady operation		0:39
_____3-036	ROAD BUILDING--Has bulldozer, trucks, tractor, etc., sounds.		1:04
_____3-037	ROAD BUILDING--Has bulldozer, trucks, tractor, etc., sounds--also workers' voices.		1:02

BELLS--BUZZERS--WHISTLES

Section 4

Tape Reel #4

Catalog Number	Subject	Time
_____4-018	CHURCH BELLS--Large type--two tones.	0:10
_____4-019	SLEIGH BELLS--Various tempos.	0:37
_____4-020	ORIENTAL TEMPLE BELL--Medium type--one strike and long ring.	0:11
_____4-021	SCHOOL BELL--Clanging fast and constantly.	0:12
_____4-022	ORIENTAL TEMPLE BELL--Medium type--one strike and long ring.	0:07

FOOTSTEPS

Section 12

Tape Reel #12

Catalog Number	Subject	Time
_____12-020	MAN--Walking slowly on wooden surface-- squeaky shoes.	0:14
_____12-021	MAN--Walking at medium pace on hard surface.	0:19
_____12-022	MAN--Running on wooden surface.	0:04
_____12-023	MAN--Walking slowly on crunchy surface.	0:14
_____12-024	MAN--Walking slowly on wooden surface-- with spur sounds.	0:16

14-5 *Examples of titles and descriptions of recorded sound effects.*

EXTENDING A SOUND LIBRARY BY VARYING PLAYING SPEED   Since pitch and duration are inseparable parts of sound, it is possible to change the character of any recorded sound by varying the speed of a tape recorder or turntable. This technique will not work with all sounds; some will sound obviously unnatural—either too drawn out and guttural or too fast and falsetto. For sounds with sonic characteristics that do lend themselves to changes in pitch and duration, however, the effects can be remarkable.

The sound effect of a low-pitched, slow, mournful wind can be changed to a ferocious howl of hurricane force by increasing its playing speed. The beeps of a car horn followed by a slight reverb at, say, 7½ ips or 45 rpm can become a small ship in a small harbor at 3¾ ips or 33⅓ rpm, or a large ship in a large harbor at 1⅞ ips or 16 rpm. Hundreds of droning bees in flight can be turned into a squadron of bombers by decreasing the playing speed of the bee sound, or turned into a horde of mosquitoes by increasing its playing speed. Decreasing the playing speed of cawing jungle birds will take you from the bush to an eerie world of science fiction. The possibilities are endless and the only way to discover how flexible sounds can be is to experiment.

USING VARIABLE SPEED TAPE RECORDERS AND OSCILLATORS   Often it is not possible to produce the sonic changes you need using the fixed speeds of a turntable or tape recorder. To make a sound natural, you may have to play an effect at, say, 38 rpm or 9 ips.

Variable speed tape recorders are available with a control that increases or decreases the tape speed to various rates between the recorder's fixed speeds (see Chapter 10). An even wider variety of speed changes is possible with a **variable speed oscillator**—a device that you can attach to either a tape recorder or a turntable (see **14-6**).

RECORDING SOUND BACKWARD   Another way to alter the characteristics of a sound is to record it backward. Although no tape recorder runs in reverse at a constant speed suitable for recording, and a record head cannot be activated in "Rewind," you can record backward by threading the tape around the

14-6   *Variable speed oscillator.*

14-7 *Threading technique used to record/play tape backward at a standard speed—7½ ips, 15 ips, etc.*

capstan and pinch roller so the tape feeds from right to left (see **14-7**). After recording, simply rethread the tape in the normal way and the sound will play backward.

Copyright

By law, any recorded material that is **copyrighted** may not be played over the air, copied (dubbed), or used for most nonprivate purposes without permission from the licenser—that is, the company or individual holding the rights to the recorded material. Broadcasters, for example, pay fees to such major licensers as Broadcast Music, Inc. (BMI); the American Society of Composers, Authors, and Publishers (ASCAP); and the Society of European Stage Authors and Composers (SESAC) for the right to play commercial recorded music on the air. These licensers then apportion the fees—called *royalties*—to the performer, composer, lyricist, publisher, and recording company. The rights to music and sound libraries, however, usually belong to the companies that distribute them. Fees are paid to these companies and apportioned by them as royalties to their talent.

When you buy a music library, you pay a set fee for it. (You usually have the option of buying all or part of a collection.) Purchasing the library entitles you only to its acquisition, however; it does not entitle you to its use. For that you must pay another fee that is determined on the basis of **needle drops**—the number of times you use sound from any cut or any portion of a cut. If you use 1 second of music or play an entire selection from beginning to end, each counts as a needle drop, although the charge would vary with how much of each selection was used (see **14-8**).

SCHEDULE OF LICENSE FEES

FOR FILMS (Either Television or Non-Theatric, but not both)

$ 30.00 per needle drop
$100.00 maximum fee for 10 minutes or less duration—
$150.00 maximum fee for 11-15 minutes or less duration—
$200.00 maximum fee for 16-30 minutes or less duration—
$375.00 maximum fee for 31-60 minutes or less duration—

COMBINED Television and Non-Theatric Films (When applied for together)
35% more than film fees above.

FOR THEATRICAL FILMS

$ 50.00 per needle drop
$ 250.00 maximum fee for 15 minutes or less deduction—
$ 500.00 maximum fee for 30 minutes or less duration—
$1000.00 maximum fee for Feature Length Film

COMMERCIALS

$50.00 per needle drop (Radio or Television)

All of our licenses are granted for the entire world. At above maximum rates music from all of our catalogs can be used intermixed for unlimited needle drops in the same film.

APPLICATION FOR LICENSES for each use must be made within 14 days after dubbing. Fees are payable with applications.

QUOTATIONS for pay or subscription TV or Video Cassette are available upon request.

Rates are subject to change without notice.

BACKGROUND AND MOOD MUSIC LIBRARY

14-8 *Example of a schedule of license fees for needle drops.*

After a production is completed, you fill out a clearance form (see **14-9**) listing all the needle drops in a production, and then you pay whatever fee the licenser's rate card indicates. The licenser will then send you written permission to use, for profit, its music in your production. If you use any of the same music in another production, you have to pay another needle drop fee.

CBS RECORDS / EZ CUE
An Activity of Columbia Special Products

CBS RECORDS/EZ CUE LIBRARY
51 W. 52 STREET / NEW YORK, N. Y. / 10019

AGREEMENT made this   day of   19   by and between Columbia Special Products, a service of CBS Records, a Division of Columbia Broadcasting System, Inc., 51 West 52 Street, New York, New York 10019 (herein called "Columbia") and

(herein called "Licensee").

In consideration of the mutual covenants herein contained, the parties hereto have agreed and do agree as follows:

1. Columbia hereby grants to Licensee a non-exclusive, irrevocable license to re-record the following listed recorded composition or compositions

Titles	Copyright Owner	Composer	Catalog No.

(herein called the "composition" or "compositions") as part of, either in synchronization or in timed relation with, or as background for

Type	Title

(herein called the "program").

2. For all of the rights herein granted by Columbia, Licensee shall pay Columbia the sum of and the receipt by Columbia of such sum shall be a condition precedent to the grant of any rights to Licensee hereunder.

3. Licensee shall have the right to exhibit the program by means of direct projection throughout the world in perpetuity and to broadcast, transmit and exhibit the program by means of radio or television and radio or television devices, methods and improvements, now or hereafter developed, throughout the world in perpetuity; provided, however, that Licensee will not exhibit or authorize the program to be exhibited in any theater, auditorium or other place to which an admission fee is charged. The word "broadcast," as used in this Agreement, means the broadcast, transmission and exhibition of the program by means of radio and television and radio and television devices, methods and improvements, now or hereafter developed, excluding any means or method of subscription, pay or toll television whether now known or hereafter developed.

4. The license herein granted is a license to re-record for simultaneous performance with the program only and does not authorize or permit any other use, it being understood that performing rights licenses will be secured from any person, firm or corporation or other legal entity having the legal right to issue such licenses on behalf of the owner of such rights in the respective territories in which the composition or compositions, as re-recorded hereunder, may be performed; provided, however, that Columbia hereby grants to Licensee for the duration of the following period, the right to perform, and to authorize others to perform, the composition or compositions as a part of any broadcast, transmission or exhibition of the program permitted under paragraph 3 hereof; any period or periods in which non-dramatic radio or television performing rights, as applicable, in the composition or compositions are not owned by, or available for license through, either the American Society of Composers, Authors and Publishers or Broadcast Music, Inc.

5. Columbia warrants only
(i) that Columbia is the owner of the rights herein licensed; and either
(ii) that the composition or compositions were not recorded in the United States or Canada, or
(iii) there is no agreement between Columbia or any other person and any labor union or guild, nor is there any other agreement, restricting or limiting (whether by requiring the payment of a fee or in any other way) the use of the composition or compositions, as re-recorded hereunder, in any manner permitted under paragraph 3 hereof, and the license herein granted is given without other warranty or recourse, except that if such warranty is breached, Columbia shall repay to Licensee the consideration heretofore paid hereunder.

6. Licensee will indemnify and hold harmless Columbia from and against any and all suits, claims, demands, damages, liabilities, costs and expenses, including reasonable counsel fees, arising out of the breach by Licensee of any warranty or agreement made by Licensee herein or arising out of the manner and extent of use of the program by Licensee.

7. All rights and uses in the composition or compositions not herein granted are expressly reserved to Columbia.

8. Columbia may assign its rights hereunder in full or in part to any person, firm or corporation and this Agreement may be assigned by any assignee thereof.

9. This Agreement and all matters or issues collateral thereto shall be governed by the laws of the State of New York applicable to contracts performed entirely therein.

10. This Agreement contains the entire understanding of the parties hereto relating to the subject matter herein contained, and this Agreement cannot be changed or terminated orally.

11. If any provision of this Agreement as applied to either party or to any circumstance shall be adjudged by a court to be void or unenforceable, the same shall in no way affect any other provision of this Agreement, the application of such provision in any other circumstances or the validity or enforceability of this Agreement.

IN WITNESS WHEREOF, the parties hereto have executed this Agreement as of the day and year first above written.

COLUMBIA SPECIAL PRODUCTS
A Service of CBS Records
A Division of Columbia Broadcasting System, Inc.

By...   By...
Licensee

14-9 *Example of a release form.*

Often a production contains so many needle drops that the copyright fee is prohibitive. In such cases, many licensers charge a flat rate.

Some organizations such as educational institutions, small production companies, and many broadcasting stations do not generate enough in copyright fees to make the sale of a music library worthwhile to the licenser.

Therefore, many licensers sell their libraries to such organizations for a flat, yearly copyright fee. This clears the music for blanket use. Such an arrangement may be renewed each year; when it terminates, most licensers require return of the library.

Obtaining the clearance rights to use sound effects libraries is usually handled in one of two ways.

1. You purchase the library and pay the copyright fee on a needle drop basis, similar to the way music clearances are handled. The rights to sound effects usually cost less than music rights.
2. The licenser gives blanket clearance at the time of purchase and no additional fee is required.

Dubbing from Record to Tape

Convenience and record preservation are two reasons for dubbing from disc to tape. However, when you dub down a generation—recopy a recording—the signal-to-noise ratio worsens (see **14-10**). Generally, this loss is more acute when dubbing from disc to tape than when dubbing from tape to tape, since the sound on a record is already several generations down (see **14-11**). On one hand, therefore, dubbing a record to a tape brings it down still one more generation. On the other hand, continuous use of a record and the resulting susceptibility to scratches, clicks, and pops may reduce its sound quality even more than by dubbing it to tape.

DUBBING TO CARTRIDGE TAPE   When dubbing from record to tape or from tape to tape, you have a choice of two formats (not including cassette): cartridge and reel to reel. Provided the program material is not long, cartridge tape is

14-10   *The effect that dubbing has on sound quality.*

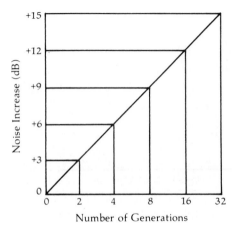

easier and faster to work with (see Chapters 9 and 10). If material is longer than about 3 minutes, however, you should consider dubbing it to reel-to-reel tape. Remember that with most cartridge machines, once a cart is put into "Play" (or "Start"), it has to wind through its entire length to get back to the starting point. This could be time-consuming during rehearsals and sound level checks, and when mistakes are made.

An exception to this is sound that is the same and continuous, such as a background of ocean waves during a beach scene, or crowd noise during a game. Such recorded sounds can be stopped and started at any point during the playing of a cartridge tape without sounding unusual.

DUBBING TO REEL-TO-REEL TAPE   In dubbing to reel-to-reel tape, it is best to begin recording the sound a few seconds after the tape has started spinning in order to prevent the sound from wowing in—gradually reaching full speed. Any reel-to-reel recorder, no matter how good, takes at least a split second to reach full speed. Video tape recorders require a 10-second roll-down to make sure that picture and sound lock in at the correct speed.

CUEING REEL-TO-REEL TAPE FOR PLAYBACK   When playing back tape on reel-to-reel recorders, it may be difficult to use a preset roll-down time since some machines have no footage or time counter; you can use a clock, of course. One technique recordists use to make sure the audio tape hits the heads at the proper speed is to splice plaid marked leader tape to the magnetic tape for timing (see Chapter 13). The distance between each marking is 7½ inches or 1 second at 7½ ips.

Another technique is to spin the freely rotating tape guide roller manually and at high speed before starting the recorder (see **14-12**). This helps propel the tape to full speed after you hit the "Play" button.

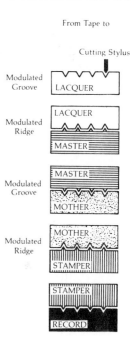

From Tape to

Cutting Stylus

Modulated Groove — LACQUER

Modulated Ridge — LACQUER / MASTER

Modulated Groove — MASTER / MOTHER

Modulated Ridge — MOTHER / STAMPER

STAMPER / RECORD

14-11 *The steps in making a record.*

14-12 *Spinning the tape guide roller by hand helps the tape to reach full speed more quickly. (Some tape recorders may not have this type of tape guide roller.)*

Using Calibrated Equipment

When you record a signal on tape, it usually goes through the console first. Make sure the VU meters on the console and on the tape recorder are adjusted or **calibrated** to show the same readings. If they do not, you have no idea whether the signal level passing through the console is the same as the one being recorded, and vice versa. This could result in a poor signal-to-noise ratio and in a signal being over- or undermodulated.

Tape Loops

Sometimes you may need a continuous effect that has to last several seconds, such as an idling car engine, wind, or a drum roll. Since many prerecorded effects last only a few seconds, there are two alternatives. If the recorded effect is, say, 5 seconds long and you need 60 seconds of it, you can (1) dub it to reel-to-reel tape 12 times and edit out the spaces between each dub to make the sound continuous, or (2) make a tape loop.

To make a tape loop, dub a few seconds of the effect to reel-to-reel tape, cut the tape at the beginning and end of the recording, and splice the two ends together. Be sure to follow the editing guidelines recommended in Chapter 13 and make the edit at a point where it will not be aurally conspicuous. For one way to play a tape loop, see **14-13**.

14-13 *A tape loop and one way it can be played.*

Take two precautions in using a tape loop. First, the tape length, before splicing, should be no longer than a few feet, otherwise the loop will be unwieldy on the tape recorder. Second, regardless of how good the edit and splice are, if the loop plays too long it will become evident that the effect is not continuous but repetitious.

Backtiming and Dead Rolling

All recordings, both tape and record, have a fixed total time; it may be 3:13, 2:21, 1:00, 0:12½, or something else. Suppose you use a recorded theme song that is 3:00 long to close a program that runs exactly 28:50. To get the theme to end when the program ends, it would have to start at 25:50. Subtracting the time of an individual item from the total time of a program or program segment is known as **backtiming.**

Consuming 3:00 of a program with just theme is usually a waste of time, however. If it is important that the theme end when the program ends, you can still backtime it to start, in this case, at 25:50. Just do not open the pot. The recording will **dead roll**—play with no sound feeding through—until you are ready for it. At that point, fade in the sound; since it started at the right time, it will also end on time.

Headroom

In Chapter 3 in the discussion about levels, we suggested that for optimal results it is usually best to ride the gain between 60 and 100 percent of modulation. Most major sound studios record and process a signal to reduce gross fluctuations in the dynamic range during playback. This allows the operator to preset an optimal playback level without having to worry about the sound being over- or undermodulated. Maintaining levels between 60 and 100 percent of modulation during recording is not always possible, however.

Suppose that in a dramatic scene, a distraught man is alternately shouting and sobbing at a woman who is responding in a quiet, controlled voice trying to calm him. In such a scene, the level changes would be wide and acute and very difficult to ride. Putting a limit on the sound is not always preferred or recommended because it reduces sound quality. Blocking may not permit proper microphone placement to compensate for the widely fluctuating levels.

Most recordists in a situation like this use the technique of maintaining **headroom.*** Headroom is the difference in level between the loudest sound and the rest of the sounds. If the loudest sounds in the scene just described are the shouts of the man, you would set them at zero level (100 percent of

---

*The term *headroom* is also used to refer to how much increase in level a tape, amplifier, or other equipment can take, above working level, before overload distortion occurs.

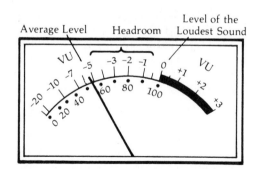

14-14 *Example of adjusting for headroom.*

modulation), regardless of the other levels. If the average level of the scene is −5 VU (55 percent of modulation), then you have a headroom of 5 VU or 45 percent of modulation (see **14-14**). The advantages of maintaining headroom are that it makes riding the levels less critical in situations where the dynamic range is wide and changes quickly, and it keeps both dialogue and ambience in perspective.

Concerning perspective, by using headroom in the preceding scene, the woman's level will be quite a bit lower than the man's because she has a less powerful voice and is speaking softly. Increasing her loudness level during the quiet passages, however, will also increase her ambience disporportionately to the man's. This creates different background noise levels between the two actors and different spatial relationships as well. If levels are in the mud, you can make slight adjustments in microphone placement, actor placement, or voice projection.

Recording Narration

Ambience is also a consideration when recording narration since it is part and parcel of the sound. Usually narration is taped, edited, and then added to the other program elements. Often a script does not call for a narrator to speak continuously but to take pauses to allow for other types of aural and visual information. In editing narration, therefore, the natural tendency is to splice in blank, unused magnetic tape or leader tape where the narrator is not speaking. This technique causes ambience changes in the narrator's track, however. The changes are often subtle, but they are perceptible as differences in the openness and closeness of the aural space. Even if the narrator is recorded in a quiet studio, the change could be noticeable.

In taping narration (or drama), take time to record the ambience separately; after the narrator finishes recording, keep the tape rolling for a while. Then in the editing you can maintain a consistent background sound by splicing in the recorded ambience during the pauses in the narration.

Taping Off the Telephone

In this era of instant communication, the telephone is indispensable not only to obtain information but also to transmit it directly from the source to tape or broadcast. In using a telephone for these purposes, there are three considerations: (1) whether both ends of a conversation are important, in which case you would have to pick up sound from both the earpiece and the mouthpiece; (2) whether only the information you are listening to is important, in which case you would have to pick up sound from just the earpiece; and (3) whether only the information you are feeding through the phone is important, in which case you would transmit sound through just the mouthpiece.

PICKUP FROM BOTH THE EARPIECE AND MOUTHPIECE The best way to broadcast or record a phone conversation, in terms of convenience and sound quality, is to wire the telephone to the console. This enables you to amplify and control the loudness of the phone's sound, mix it with sound from other sources, and feed it to tape or air with just the flick of a switch. Most stations have this type of phone connection in their control rooms and studios. (In telephone talk shows, the arrangement is somewhat different in that conversation is fed first through a delaying system to prevent undesirable language or comments from getting on the air.) In a newsroom where several telephones and news-people are collecting information, however, this type of phone connection is impractical.

A device called a **phone coupler** is small and easily wired to the inside of the phone. One end of the coupler has a connector that plugs into a tape recorder. The coupler requires a special phone handle with a push button in it (see **14-15**). When the button is pushed, you can record from both the mouthpiece and the earpiece; when it is released, only sound from the earpiece will feed through. The sound quality from the phone coupler is as good as you can get without going through the console.

PICKUP FROM THE EARPIECE As we said, one way to pick up sound from an earpiece is to use a phone coupler and not depress the button in the phone

14-15 *Phone coupler.*

Soft Iron
Windings

Wire Connecting Earpiece
to Tape Recorder

14-16 *Induction phone patch fitted to earpiece.*

handle. Another device that picks up sound from the earpiece is the induction phone patch, which you can make yourself or buy from an electronics store.

The induction phone patch is an insulated coil of soft iron with a few windings of heavy wire attached to a cable, and a connector (see **14-16**). The coil fits over the earpiece and picks up the low-level sound vibrations. These vibrations are amplified to usable proportions usually by feeding them to a tape recorder. The sound quality is not good, but it is acceptable.

FEEDING SOUND THROUGH THE MOUTHPIECE The need to feed sound through just the mouthpiece usually occurs when a reporter phones in a story from the field. The easiest way to make the feed is for the reporter to talk into the mouthpiece and have the sound recorded or broadcast from the earpiece at the studio.

Due to logistics or personal preference, however, many reporters use cassette tape recorders as electronic notepads and record their story in the field before phoning it in. One method they use to feed the recording via telephone is to (1) screw off the phone's mouthpiece, (2) remove the microphone that is inside, (3) take a cord with alligator clips on one end and a connector on the other, (4) attach the alligator clips to the two exposed metal prongs, (5) plug the connector into the output of the tape recorder, and (6) put the recorder into "Play" (see **14-17**). However, new pay phones have mouthpieces that cannot be unscrewed.

14-17 *One way of feeding sound through the mouthpiece of a telephone is to (1) screw off the mouthpiece, (2) remove the microphone inside (right), (3) attach alligator clips on one end of a wire to the two exposed metal prongs, and (4) plug the connector on the other end of the wire into a tape recorder (far right).*

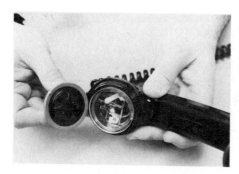

14-18 *An induction patch that connects to the telephone mouthpiece.*

A less awkward way to accomplish the same thing is with an induction patch that attaches to the mouthpiece (see **14-18**). To obtain sound of acceptable quality, however, it does have to feed to an amplifier or tape recorder.

LAW AND ETHICS OF TELEPHONE RECORDING   The Federal Communications Commission (FCC) has developed regulations that apply to the recording and airing of information obtained over the telephone. They include the following:

1. You may not broadcast any part of a respondent's comments without his or her permission.

2. You may tape a conversation without permission. However, it is ethical to at least let the person know what you are doing and always preferable to obtain permission.

3. You may quote from a taped conversation so long as it is "on the record" and the material is not aired directly from the tape. If the interviewee says that a statement is "off the record," it is utterly unethical to use it in sum or substance.

Overdubbing

the means by which takes overdubbing place

Sel sync (see Chapter 10) has made overdubbing one of the most convenient *mixing together* and often used production techniques in audio. Overdubbing is recording *"Sel-sync makes overdubbing possible"* new material on a separate track(s) while listening to the replay of a previously recorded track(s) in order to synchronize the old and new material.

Overdubbing makes it possible to tape various elements in a recording separately and at different times. This facilitates a greater degree of sound control over each track, alleviates the need to have all the elements ready for recording at the same time, and allows a few performers to do the work of many.

BUILDING A RECORDING Although overdubbing allows flexibility in scheduling performers, the order in which you tape them is often not so flexible. For example, if you record a pop music group consisting of drums, bass guitar, lead guitar, piano, and vocal, you should tape certain instruments before others.

Standard procedure is to record the rhythm tracks first to ensure that everyone's timing will be the same. If there is a vocal, record the rest of the background or accompaniment during the next stages of the session. The vocal is usually taped last, since it is most likely the focus of the music and needs the other elements in place for proper tonal balance and perspective. Therefore, the group would record the drums first or along with the bass, the lead guitar and piano next, either separately or together, and the vocal last.

CLICK TRACK When timing is absolutely critical—as when syncing a music track to a motion picture, when the beat is not well defined, or when the basic rhythm instruments do not come in until after the music has begun— recordists use a **click track** to maintain timing and rhythm. A click track is a separately recorded audible tape track that plays the appropriate rhythm, usually from the sound of a metronome recorded on one of the available 4, 8, 16, or 24 tracks. The beat is fed to the performers through their earphones. In recording film sound, the click track may be on one of the magnetic stripes. If a metronome is not available, clicking drum sticks together will also work, although it is difficult for a musician to maintain a precise rhythm if he or she has to keep it up for very long.

avoid using outside tracks for most important tracks

TRACK ASSIGNMENT It usually does not make much difference what elements are assigned to which track, but it is a good idea to record information that is particularly valuable or difficult to rerecord on the inside tracks of the tape, away from the outer edges. Sometimes the edges can fray from scraping against improperly aligned tape guides or the sides of defective tape reels. On, say, an 8-track tape, this could damage tracks 1, 2, 7, and 8; on a 16-track tape, tracks 1, 2, 15, and 16 could be lost; and so on. Deciding which tracks are more important depends on the recording, but it is usually obvious. Drums are harder to record than, say, trumpets; it would be more difficult to rerecord a soloist who has flown in for a session than to rerecord performers who live in the vicinity; a vocalist usually requires more time and attention than most instruments.

It is also helpful to put the same instruments or groups of instruments on adjacent tracks, such as the various parts of a drum set, strings, woodwinds, and rhythm instruments. This makes it easier to see and coordinate their relative levels of loudness (see **14-19**).

BOUNCING TRACKS Regardless of how many tracks are available, sometimes you need more. One way to increase the capacity of a multitrack tape recorder is by **bouncing tracks**—combining two or more previously recorded tracks onto a single unused track.

14-19 *Putting similar instruments or groups of instruments on adjacent channels makes it easier to coordinate their processing.*

Suppose you have an 8-track machine and want to record 12 instruments separately: bass drum, snare drum, tom-toms, hi hat cymbal, overhead cymbals, bass, guitar, piano, violin, viola, French horn, and vocal. By bouncing tracks, you can first record the drums onto tracks, say, 2, 3, 4, 5, and 6, and then rerecord and combine them onto a single available track (assume the drums are mono). You combine them by (1) putting tracks 2 through 6 into sel sync, monitoring them from the record head;* (2) feeding each track to a separate channel at the console for balancing and mixing; (3) assigning each channel to the same open track, say, track 8; and (4) recording. This frees tracks 2 through 6, and by adding tracks 1 and 7, you have enough open tracks to record the seven other instruments.

Perhaps an easier way to accomplish this is through a *live mix.* A live mix is done during the recording session by feeding the appropriate instruments to separate channels at the console and delegating each channel to the same tape track (or two, for stereo).

If you bounce tracks, do not use adjacent tracks for the transfer. In the previous example, you would not bounce tracks 2, 3, 4, 5, and 6 to either track 1 or 7.

The separation between tracks of a multitrack tape recorder is not wide. If you put a track in "Record" that is next to one of the tracks playing back, it could result in the live record head picking up unwanted crosstalk from the adjacent playback track, especially if the signal level is high. Furthermore, if the live head is picking up sound across the head from the adjacent track and also internally via the normal recording process, that is, through the head, it will create a feedback loop and, hence, a squeal.

PUNCHING IN Conventional cut and splice editing is not possible with multitrack recording, since there is no way to cut into any one track without cutting

---

*With state-of-the-art recorders, there should be no discernible loss in sound quality in reproduction from the record head compared with the playback head. With older machines, the playback quality of the record head is 2,000 to 5,000 Hz poorer than the quality from the playback head.

into the other tracks as well. If part of a performance has a mistake in it or is of poor quality, most multitrack recorders have electronic means that allow you to rerecord any portion of any track without affecting the rest of the recording. This technique is called punching in.

You punch in by putting the recorded tracks into sel sync, playing them back to the performer(s) through earphones, and, when it is time to rerecord over the defective portion of a track, switching that track to "Record." After the appropriate section has been rerecorded, take the track out of "Record" either by stopping the machine or by switching the track back into sel sync or "Play." Punching in is a very clean way to edit electronically. It is quick and leaves no sound pulses on the tape. It does require perfect timing, however, or you could erase some of the good material, too.

FOLDBACK LEVELS Any overdubbing requires that you feed the recorded tracks to the performers as they tape the new tracks. This is done through the foldback (earphone) system (see Chapter 3).

Some performers like the sound level in the earphones to be loud, particularly with high-energy music. This could have a detrimental effect on the intensity of the performance, however. As the loudness in the earphones increases, performers without realizing it have the tendency to "lay back," reducing their own output level.

If you run into this problem, provide whatever foldback levels are wanted, but after the playing begins, gradually reduce the loudness to a comfortable level. Usually the energy of the performance will increase proportionately and the performer will be none the wiser.

Tape Preparation: Recording Tone, Leadering, Labeling

When a tape is ready for broadcast or shipment, certain procedures help ensure that the recorded material will not be damaged, misplaced, or reproduced incorrectly. Record a reference tone(s) on the tape, leader the tape, and label it.

RECORDING TONE When a tape is played, the playback levels should be the same as the recording levels for optimal reproduction. The person playing the tape is often not the one who recorded it, however. Therefore, standard procedure is to record reference tones before the program material to indicate the loudness level of the recording. This allows any operator to preset the fader control to the correct loudness level.

Reference tones are pure tones (sine waves) generated by an oscillator (see Chapter 3) and recorded at 0 VU (100 percent of modulation). It is usually best to record three tones: a low-frequency tone, 50 or 100 Hz; a midrange tone, 1,000 Hz is standard; and a high-frequency tone, 10,000, 12,000, or 15,000 Hz. Some recordists use only the 1,000-Hz tone. If you use Dolby noise reduction, add the Dolby reference tone generated by the Dolby A unit itself. There is no specified length of time for a reference tone; generally, 20 to 30 seconds for each one is adequate.

LEADERING TAPE After you finish recording the program material and the reference tones, leader the tape. Splice 4 to 6 feet of tape to the front and tail ends of the magnetic tape to protect the recording at these exposed and vulnerable points. Use color-coded leader to tell which end is which. Then separate different segments within the tape with leader to provide a visual means of identifying where material begins and ends (see **13-6**). If a reel of tape contains two different selections of program material and reference tones, the order of elements should be as follows:

1. Four to six feet of leader tape
2. Reference tones
3. A foot or two of leader tape
4. Cut 1
5. A foot or two of leader tape
6. Cut 2
7. Four to six feet of leader tape (spliced after the last sound decays)

LABELING The last step in tape preparation is *labeling*—putting the essential information about the recording on the tape box, placing a cue sheet (if needed) inside the box, and attaching some identification to the reel. The information on the box should include the following:

1. Title of program, song, cuts, etc.
2. Producer or director
3. Artist or client
4. Duration of the material
5. Tape speed
6. Tape type and thickness (if it is not printed on the box)
7. Format (full-track mono; two-channel, two-track stereo; two-channel, four-track stereo; etc.)
8. Tape wind—heads or tails out
9. Type of noise reduction (Dolby, dbx), if any

If the recording requires a cue sheet, place it inside the tape box. On the cue sheet should be information such as the first and last lines of segments that contain speech, how the end of a segment stops (with an abrupt cut, fade, etc.), the segment time or the total time, any sudden changes in loudness level, and other peculiarities.

NATIONAL PUBLIC RADIO QUALITY CONTROL REPORT FORM

2025 M Street, N.W. • Washington, D.C. 20036 • (202) 785-5400

SERIES NAME: _____ PROGRAM TITLE: _____ No._____ of_____

SOURCE: _____ FOR: ☐ NPR ☐ ST-Mono ☐ ST-Stereo ☐ Ordered ☐ Speculation

TYPE: ☐ Live ☐ Tape ☐ Cart ☐ Cassette ☐ Disc ☐ Mono ☐ Stereo ☐ Full ☐ ½ 'A' ☐ ½ 'B'

RESULTS: ☐ Accepted for Technical Quality
☐ Rejected for Technical Quality (see below)
☐ Accepted If Certain Items are Fixed (see "must fix" below)
☐ Accepted, Some Items could be Improved in the Future (see "could fix" below)

	REJECTED	MUST FIX	COULD FIX	GOOD		REJECTED	MUST FIX	COULD FIX	GOOD
'BOOMY'	☐	☐	☐	☐	TAPE STOCK	☐	☐	☐	☐
'PEAKY'	☐	☐	☐	☐	INTELLIGIBILITY	☐	☐	☐	☐
'MUDDY'	☐	☐	☐	☐	SIGNAL TO NOISE	☐	☐	☐	☐
BASS EQUALIZATION	☐	☐	☐	☐	BUZZ OR HUM	☐	☐	☐	☐
TREBLE EQUALIZATION	☐	☐	☐	☐	POOR LIMITING	☐	☐	☐	☐
CONTROL OF LEVELS	☐	☐	☐	☐	COMPRESSION	☐	☐	☐	☐
MIKING	☐	☐	☐	☐	AMBIENT NOISE	☐	☐	☐	☐
WOW AND FLUTTER	☐	☐	☐	☐	ERASURE	☐	☐	☐	☐
NOISE	☐	☐	☐	☐	DROP OUTS	☐	☐	☐	☐
TAPE HISS	☐	☐	☐	☐	'POPS AND CLICKS'	☐	☐	☐	☐
PRE OR POST ECHO	☐	☐	☐	☐	TIMING	☐	☐	☐	☐
DISTORTION	☐	☐	☐	☐	WARPING	☐	☐	☐	☐
STEREO PHASING	☐	☐	☐	☐	DOUBLE AUDIO	☐	☐	☐	☐
STEREO BALANCE	☐	☐	☐	☐	'UP-CUTTING'	☐	☐	☐	☐
EDITING	☐	☐	☐	☐	SPEED	☐	☐	☐	☐
SPLICING	☐	☐	☐	☐	CROSSTALK	☐	☐	☐	☐
HEAD AZIMUTH	☐	☐	☐	☐	HEAD CONFIGURATION	☐	☐	☐	☐
ROOM ACOUSTICS	☐	☐	☐	☐	LEADERING	☐	☐	☐	☐
MIXING	☐	☐	☐	☐	PRESENCE	☐	☐	☐	☐

REPAIR METHOD: ☐ EQ ☐ Notch ☐ Remix ☐ Re-edit ☐ Rerecord ☐ Dub/Fix Gain
☐ Boost HF ☐ Cut HF ☐ Boost Mid. ☐ Cut Mid. ☐ Boost LF ☐ Cut LF

COMMENTS: _____
_____
_____
_____
_____
_____

Audition By:_____ Date:_____ Corrected By:_____ Date:_____
Audition By:_____ Date:_____ Accepted By:_____ Date:_____

RETURN TO SOURCE

14-20 *This quality control report form lists several elements that are important to a well-prepared tape recording.*

On the reel itself, paste a label with some identification on it. Any one or combination of the following will do: the name of the program, the producer, and the name and address of the place where it was recorded. If the tape and tape box get separated, as they sometimes do, it would then be easy to return the right tape to the right box.

Finally, try not to use reels smaller than 7 inches; 5- and 3-inch reels could create problems with tape tension and result in an uneven wind. Also, put on a reel only the tape containing the recording, not any leftover blank tape.

Quality Control

The sound on a tape recording obviously should be as good as possible. See **14-20** for an idea of what one broadcast operation looks for in a tape recording.

Summary

1. Music libraries provide original music to underscore the ideas and emotions in a script, such as character, happiness, conflict, danger, and love.

2. Sound effects also help to emphasize and define actions in a script. Three ways to produce sounds are by (a) recording them from live sources, (b) creating them manually, and (c) using recorded sound effects libraries.

3. A sound can be changed by varying its playing speed and, hence, its pitch, recording it backward, or feeding it through a signal processor (see Chapter 11).

4. Most recordings are copyrighted and may not be used unless a fee is paid to the licenser. In the case of music libraries, the fee usually is based on the number of needle drops in a production. With sound libraries, fees may be paid based on needle drops or for blanket use.

5. If you use material from a disc repeatedly, it is better to dub it to a tape for convenience, preservation of the record, and consistent sound quality.

6. If sound is fed through the console as it is recorded on tape, the console and tape recorder must be calibrated to make sure the VU meters on each show the same readings.

7. In recording material with wide and rapid changes in dynamic range, it is difficult to keep the VU meter averaging between the recommended levels of 60 and 100 percent of modulation. Maintaining headroom keeps aural elements in perspective without increasing ambient noise or distorting.

8. To record from the telephone, connect it to the console or to a phone coupler to pick up sound from both the earpiece and the mouthpiece. Attach an induction coil to the earpiece to pick up only sound being received. Use alligator clips or an induction coil for the mouthpiece only to send sound to tape or broadcast.

9. Overdubbing facilitates greater control over each sound element, alleviates the need to record all elements at the same time, and allows a few performers to do the work of many.

10. If there are more sound sources than available tracks to record on, <u>bounce tracks.</u>

11. <u>In preparing a tape for broadcast, record cutting, or shipment, it should have a reference tone(s) preceding the material on the tape, leader tape at the head and tail and between the cuts of the recording tape, and adequate labeling.</u>

15

Mixing Sound

In most environments, you hear not one but several different sounds simultaneously: the instruments of an orchestra; traffic and sirens outside an office; conversation with music in the background; waves breaking against a shore, sea gulls, and children frolicking at a beach.

The same is true in audio production. Much of the time, you are working with several sounds at once: a voice over music for a disc jockey show or spot announcement; various instruments in an ensemble for a music recording; or voices, music, and sound effects for a television or film production. In audio, combining different sounds into a natural and integrated whole is called a *mix*, and the process of obtaining a mix is known as the *mixdown*.

Mixing Procedures

Most recordists today use a separate channel and track for each sound component to have more sonic control during taping. Regardless of how many different channels and tracks they use, however, at some point all the sounds must be mixed down—combined by rerecording—into mono or stereo.*

In most music mixdowns, the procedure involves rerecording from 2-, 1-, or ½-inch tape to ¼-inch tape and then transferring the sound from ¼-inch tape to disc (see **14-11**). Sometimes, to improve the dynamic range, the tape stages are eliminated and the music is recorded **direct to disc** (which is the way cylinders and records were made before the invention of wire and tape recording).

---

*Although it has existed for some time, quadriphonic (four-channel) recording is not included here since it has never caught on and, as a result, the technology and the art are moribund. The problem is that no agreement can be reached about which of two existing formats, **discrete** and **matrix** (see Glossary), should be standard. Consumers have been unwilling to invest in either format since the software made for one is not compatible with the other.

Mixing TV sound involves either first recording onto multitrack tape and then mixing down to video tape, or doing a "live" mix during video taping and feeding the sound directly to video tape. Although the first alternative involves an extra tape generation, it does permit better overall control of the sound.

The final stages of film mixing begin with the transfer of everything recorded on audio tape to full-coat magnetic film. Then all mag film tracks are fed through a multichannel console for rerecording onto either a full-coat master for mono, or a multistripe mag film master (usually three-stripe) for stereo. The master then goes to the lab, where it is combined with picture on an optical or magnetic sound track.

In addition to combining tracks into mono or stereo, the mixdown has the following other purposes:

1. To enhance or **sweeten** the sounds through equalization and other signal processing
2. To blend the sounds
3. To balance levels
4. To add any special effects
5. To create the acoustic space artificially (if necessary)
6. To position the sounds within the aural frame

[handwritten margin note: "sweeten" = enhancing a recorded sound through equalization and various other signal processing techniques. PURPOSES OF MIXDOWN]

Music Mixdown

SWEETENING AND BLENDING The first step in mixing down music is to evaluate and determine the positive and negative attributes of the recording. Then, as needed, equalize or sweeten each element separately by boosting frequencies—adding more "sizzle" to a cymbal sound, "fatness" to a snare sound, "edge" to a vocal, "brightness" to an alto saxophone; or by attenuating frequencies—reducing the string noises of a bass, the "bottom" in the sound of a bass drum, the "pinging" sound of guitar strings, the scratchiness of a violin, and so on. Keep in mind, however, that equalizing should be used to touch up the aural canvas, not to repaint it.

In recording sessions that do not meet expectations, a producer or engineer will sometimes say, "Don't worry about it, we can fix it in the mixdown." With all the sophisticated signal processors available, however, the mixdown cannot change a mediocre performance into a good one or compensate for poor microphone placement. In most instances, it is the quality of the recording session that determines the overall quality of the mix.

SUGGESTED PROCEDURE There are several ways to equalize during a mixdown. A common approach is to (1) work with a single track at a time until each sounds acceptable; (2) start with the rhythm tracks, then go to the other accompanying tracks, and equalize the lead voicings last; (3) listen to all the

[handwritten margin note: WAYS TO EQUALIZE: (1) Work single tracks (2) work rhythm tracks, then acompanying tracks, vocals last (3) Listen to all tracks for total sound blend (4) Change individuals to complement overall sound.]

tracks together for the sound blend; and (4) change any individual equalized settings to complement the overall blend.

As you go through these steps, remember three things. First, since equalizing often involves boosting frequencies, it can mean more noise. Therefore, be careful, particularly when increasing some of the unpleasant frequencies in the midrange and high end.

Second, try to avoid using the same frequencies too often. For example, on one channel you may increase by 4 dB at 5,000 Hz the sound of a snare drum to make it crisper, then on another channel you increase 2 dB at 5,000 Hz to make a cymbal sound fuller, and on a third channel you increase 3 dB at 5,000 Hz to bring out a vocal. If you consider each channel separately, there has been very little equalizing at 5,000 Hz, but the cumulative boost at the same frequency could unbalance the overall blend.

Third, to achieve a satisfactory blend, you may have to change the sounds of individual elements in ways that could make them unpleasant to listen to by themselves. For example, the frequencies between 1,000 and 3,500 Hz make most vocals intelligible. One way to make a vocal clear and stand out from its instrumental accompaniment, while maintaining the overall blend, is to boost it a few decibels in the 1,000 to 3,500 Hz range and decrease the accompaniment a few decibels in the same range. Together they should sound quite natural. Separately, however, the vocal will be harsh and thin and the accompaniment will sound muddy and lifeless.

EQUALIZING: HOW MUCH, WHERE, AND WHEN? One question most often asked of a recordist is: "What kind of a sound will I get on this instrument if I equalize so many decibels at such and such a frequency?" The question suggests that there are ways to predetermine equalization. *There are not!* Consider the different things that can affect sound. For a guitar: what is it made of; is it acoustic or electric; are the strings steel or gut, old or new, played with a metal or plastic pick or with the fingers; is the guitarist heavy- or light-handed; are there fret sounds; is the guitar miked and with what type of microphone; how are the acoustics; what type of song is being played; what is the spatial placement of the guitar in the mix; and so on? These influences do not even include personal taste, the most variable factor of all.

The best way to approach equalization is to (1) know the frequency ranges of the instruments involved, (2) have a basic idea of what each octave in the audible frequency spectrum contributes to the overall sound, (3) listen to the sound in context, and (4) have a good idea what you want to achieve before starting the mixdown. A few other tips are the following:

1. Equalizing will alter a sound's harmonic structure.
2. Very few people, even under ideal conditions, can hear a change of 1 dB or less, and many people cannot hear changes of 2 or 3 dB.
3. Avoid large increases or decreases in equalizing.
4. Do not use equalizing as a substitute for better microphone selection and mike placement.

5. Do not increase or decrease too many tracks in the same frequency range.

6. An absence of frequencies above 600 Hz adversely affects the intelligibility of consonants; an absence of frequencies below 600 Hz adversely affects the intelligibility of vowels.

7. Equal degrees of equalizing between 400 and 2,000 Hz are more noticeable than equalizing above or below that range (remember the equal loudness curves).

8. Most amplified instruments do not have ranges higher than 7,500 Hz; boosting above that frequency usually adds only noise.

9. Equalize with an awareness of the frequency limits of the medium in which you are working.

[handwritten in margin: Know]

PLACING THE MUSICAL ELEMENTS IN AURAL SPACE Once you have finished equalizing and have achieved a satisfactory blend of all the voicings, the next step is to position the various elements in aural space. In multitrack recording, each element is recorded at an optimal level and on a separate track. If all the elements were played back in the same way, it would sound like they were coming from precisely the same location. In reality, of course, this is not the case. Therefore, you have to position each musical component in an aural frame by setting the levels of loudness to create front-to-back perspective, or depth, and panning to establish left-to-right stereo perspective. In setting levels, the louder a sound the closer it seems, and conversely, the more quiet a sound the farther away it seems. In panning, there are five main areas: left, left center, center, right center, and right (see 3-22).

[handwritten in margin: Louder = closer]

There are many options in positioning various elements of an ensemble in an aural frame, but three factors are usually considered in the decision: (1) the aural balance, (2) how the group usually arranges itself when playing before a live audience, and (3) the type of music being played.

[handwritten in margin: Three factors in positioning various elements: (1) aural balance. (2) how the group is usually arranged (3) type of music]

Sounds and where they are placed in aural space have different effects on perception. In a stereo field, some of these effects are: the sound closest to the center and to us is the most predominant; a sound farther back but still in the center creates depth and a balance or a counterweight to the sound that is front and center; sound placed to one side usually requires a similarly weighted sound on the opposite side or else the left-to-right aural space will seem unbalanced; and the more you spread sound across the aural space, the larger the sound sources will seem.

This is not to suggest, however, that all parts of aural space must be sonically balanced or filled at all times; that depends on the ensemble and the music. A symphony orchestra usually positions 1st violins to the left of the conductor, 2nd violins to the left center, violas to the right center, and cellos to the right. If the music calls for just the 1st violins to play, it is natural for the sound to come mainly from the left. To pan the 1st violins left-to-right would establish a stereo balance, but it would be poor aesthetic judgment and it would disorient the listener.

To illustrate aural framing in a stereo field, assume that a pop music group was recorded on eight tracks as follows:

Track 1—Bass   Track 5—Low end of piano

Track 2—Bass drum   Track 6—High end of piano

Track 3—Left side of drum set   Track 7—Vocal

Track 4—Right side of drum set Track 8—Guitar

For a few ways to position this ensemble, see **15-1a, b, c.** In reality, the music has to be the determining factor.

CREATING ACOUSTIC SPACE ARTIFICIALLY Due to the common practice of miking each sound component separately (for greater control) and closely (to reduce leakage), many original multitrack recordings lack a complementary acoustic environment. In such cases, the acoustics usually are added in the mixdown by artificial means using signal processing devices such as reverb and digital delay (see Chapter 11).

If you add acoustics in the mixdown, do it after equalizing, since it is difficult to get a true sense of the effects of frequency changes in a reverberant space, and after panning, to get a better idea of how reverb affects positioning. Avoid giving widely different reverb times to various components in an ensemble, or it will sound as if they are not playing in the same space, unless

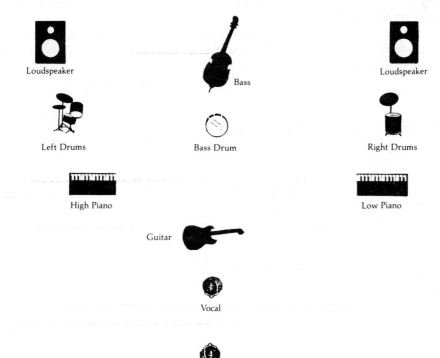

15-1a *This spatial arrangement takes full advantage of stereo spacing, placing sound sources wide and deep. The sound will be open and airy. Notice that the bass and bass drum are positioned center rear and together to anchor the sound and enhance their blend. The piano is behind the guitar on the assumption that it accompanies throughout the song. The guitar is behind the vocal to provide accompaniment and be close enough front and center for solos when the vocalist is not singing. (Note: In reality there is no "hole" in the sound of the piano or the drums. Also, the left and right drums are more often reversed. See also 15-1b).*

Loudspeaker

Loudspeaker

Bass

Left Drums

Bass Drum

Right Drums

High Piano

Low Piano

Guitar

Vocal

Listener

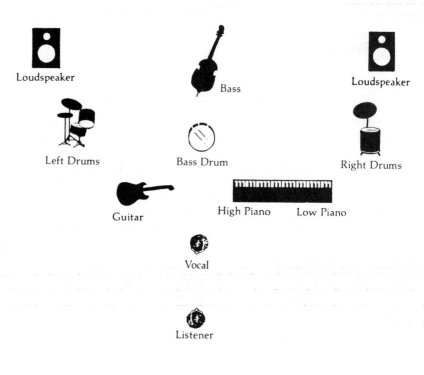

15-1b *This spatial arrangement maintains stereo perspective but repositions the guitar and piano for a better balance if they both play solos as well as accompany.*

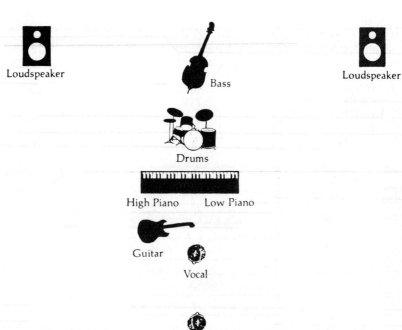

15-1c *This closer arrangement changes the open sound for a tighter, more intense sound. The piano also could be positioned to the right of the vocal.*

it is for special effect. Also, the two stereo channels should have the same amount of reverb, otherwise the spatial weight will be unbalanced.

Automated Mixdown

Mixing various sounds to mono or stereo from several different tape or film tracks is an exacting and tedious process. It requires dozens of tape replays and hundreds of adjustments to get the right equalization, reverberation, blend, spatial balance, timing of inserts, and so on. Comparing one mix with another is difficult unless settings are written down (which is time-consuming) so that controls can be returned to previous positions if necessary. It is not uncommon to discard a mix because someone forgot to adjust one control, or to decide after a few days to change a few settings and have to set up all the controls again. Mixing down one song can take many hours.

Much of this tedium has been eliminated from the mixdown by automated consoles with computer systems that remember and recreate any loudness or EQ setting or change in setting made during a mixdown. Three different operations are involved in programming an automated console: write, read, and update. In the **write mode**, controls function normally. As the operator makes the various control adjustments, the positional information is fed to and stored in the computer. In the **read mode**, the information stored in the computer is retrieved and the programmed controls operate automatically. In the **update mode**, any control setting can be changed by

15-2a *Example of a computer control unit used to automate faders on a console.*

15-2b *Automated fader controls on a multichannel console.*

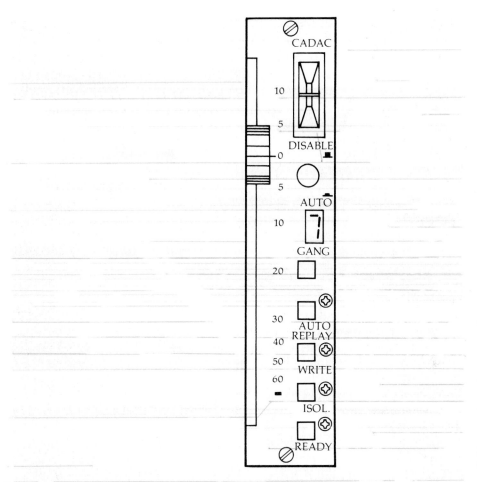

15-2c *Another example of an automated channel fader.*

switching it into the write mode without disturbing any other setting (see 15-2a, b, c).

Mixing a Sound Track

Audio for TV, film, and radio production often contains a combination of speech, music, and sound effects. Although the considerations in recording and mixing down these elements are similar to those in recording and mixing down music, working with different types of sounds in various combinations involves aesthetic relationships different from those that influence mixing music. These relationships are affected by loudness levels, how sounds are established, transitions, balance, perspective, intelligibility, and the presence of a picture.

Establishing Sound

In audio, level can mean two things: (1) the amount of electric energy objectively measured by a VU meter, and (2) the loudness of a sound as you perceive it. The VU reading is always important to keep sound from going in the mud or in the red. In mixing, however, the aesthetic relationship of one sound to another is also important and that judgment is subjective, based on what you hear. You, not a meter, ultimately decide whether sounds are at the right level of loudness and in the proper perspective.

Before determining and setting a level, you have to establish—start—the sound. The two ways to do it are at full (not loudest, but optimal) level and fading it in. Each requires a different technique and produces a different aesthetic effect.

Starting a sound at full volume means that the instant it begins, you hear it at its correct level relative to the rest of the sound. If the beginning of a piece of music has a level of −6 VU, about 50 percent of modulation, that is how loud it should be when it starts.

To establish a sound at its full volume, you must know what its VU reading is before it begins, otherwise it may start too quietly or blast in, thus requiring quick adjustments after the sound has begun. Such sudden changes often call attention to themselves and divert audience attention from the program material. To avoid this type of uneven start, standard procedure is to take a level—audition the sound before broadcasting or recording and, once you have obtained the desired loudness, note where the pot is in relation to the VU reading.

Starting sound at full volume should not be an arbitrary decision because it creates certain effects depending on the sound's attack. It can (1) direct attention, (2) clearly define or punctuate the beginning of a sequence, (3) establish the character of a sequence, or (4) provide the impetus for a sequence.

The **fade-in**—gradually increasing the level of loudness from inaudibility to full volume—is another way of establishing a sound. When you accomplish the fade-in by gradually turning up the pot, it is a simple technique. But the rate and smoothness of the operation do influence audience response. A slow fade-in usually implies duration, or building action. If the fade-in is too slow, the effect may be tedious. This is particularly so in radio, where there is no visual material to justify an effect and help engage attention. In visual media, however, the appropriate picture, say, a distant image gradually coming closer, could very well cover a slow fade-in and make it meaningful.

A very quick fade-in is usually not recommended even with an appropriate accompanying picture. It tends to jolt the listener to attention and its suddenness can be distracting. It may also sound like sloppy production. If a sound should be established quickly, start it at full volume; the resulting effect is cleaner.

Regardless of how fast or slow the fade-in is, it must be smooth. The ear can detect a change in level as little as 3 VU, especially if the sound is predominantly midrange. This means there should be no sudden movements of the pot* or uneven step changes in the loudness level; the effect is unnatural and distracting.

It is easier to discuss the technique of a smooth fade-in than it is to articulate what constitutes a fade-in that is too slow, too fast, or just right. Like so many aspects of audio, this judgment can be made only by listening to the effect in relation to the material's content and pace.

Aesthetically, a fade-in engages attention more gradually than establishing sound at full volume. It is not so definitive, nor does it punctuate; rather it eases the listener into the sound. The "feel" is softer, and the sense of motion and impetus is less acute.

Transitions

Although the way you start a sound establishes its initial impact, most sound is continuous and constantly changing. The changes or transitions help to create a production's pace or rhythm. In audio, three techniques are used to make transitions: segue (pronounced "seg-way") or cut, fade-out–fade-in, and crossfade.

Segue is a musical term that means "follow on." In radio, it has come to refer to the playing of two or more recordings—tape or record—with no live announcing in between. In a broader sense, segue is analogous to the term **cut** used to describe transitions in TV and film. In this context, cutting from one element to another means establishing a picture or sound immediately after the previous picture or sound stops and doing it all at once, not gradually. In discussing the effects of this particular type of transition, we will use the broader term cut.

The cut is standard language for a small related change within the same time, place, or action, such as cutting from someone waking up, to washing, to eating breakfast; or cutting from a striking match and the eruption of a flame to an alarm sounding at a fire station. Cutting creates transitions that are sharp and well defined, picking up the rhythm of sequences and giving them a certain briskness. Cutting also tightens the pace of a production because the change from one sound (or picture) to another is quick. Due to its aesthetic value, the cut is also used for larger transitions, such as cutting from a person walking out the door at the beginning of the day to coming back in at the end of the day, or from the eruption of flames to some charred remains.

---

*The pot should be well maintained and clean. Otherwise signals passing through it may crackle from dirt in the mechanism, or sound may cut in and out as you open and close the pot.

Cut is like a tape edit or take

The cut, in effect, butts two different sounds or groups of sounds together; in that regard, it is like a tape edit. Like the edit, you have to give some thought to whether the effect is natural. Cutting from a fast, loud record to one that is very slow and quiet, or vice versa, may be too abrupt; seguing two songs in keys that are incompatible may create a transition that has unwanted dissonance; or cutting from a commercial for a liquor store to a public service announcement for Alcoholics Anonymous may present a problem of taste.

Drama and documentary provide more of an opportunity to make unnatural cuts because the action or picture can cover the transition, like cutting from a furious storm to the quiet calm of its aftermath, or from a deeply moving love scene to a raucously funny bachelor party. The cut has both an informational and an aesthetic function and either justifies its use.

More emotional

ANOTHER Time place, etc.

The **fade-out–fade-in** is a transition used to make a clearly defined change from one time, place, and action to another. Aesthetically, it is gentler than the cut, and it gives a stronger sense of finality to a scene that is ending and a sense of beginning to the scene fading in.

slow w/silence = complete break

In TV and film, the rate of the fade-out–fade-in depends on the picture. Generally, however, the type of fade you use provides not only an aesthetic effect but an informational one as well. A slow fade-out and fade-in with silence between suggests a complete break from one action to another. The change is rather marked because it so obviously and deliberately stops one scene and starts another, and also because it changes the pace or rhythm of the material. You could use this type of transition to bridge the time between a student going off to college as a freshman and graduation, or to bridge the action between a police car's hot pursuit of bank robbers trying to get away and the thieves being booked at the police station.

fast = shorter lapses of time

Faster fades suggest shorter lapses of time, smaller changes of location, or fewer events in a series of actions. They still provide a definite break in the presentation, but their quicker rate implies that less has happened. A fade-out–fade-in to bridge the time between going off to college and graduation should be longer than the transition that bridges the time between going off to college and returning home for the Thanksgiving vacation. You should not, however, consider these guidelines as prescriptive. There are no formulas for how long transitions should be relative to the scenes they bridge; it is a matter of what "feels" right.

★ Best to crossfade at the music's climax

The **crossfade**—gradually fading out one sound as you fade in another—is another transition used for smaller changes in time, locale, and action, although you can vary the length of these changes somewhat by increasing or decreasing the duration of the crossfade. Informationally, the crossfade accomplishes the same thing as the fade-out–fade-in, but aesthetically it is softer, more fluid, and graceful. It also maintains rather than breaks rhythmic continuity and pace.

Crossfade is softer, more fluid, and more graceful than a fade-in/out

Maintains continuity and pace

You can produce the crossfade in a number of ways depending on the loudness levels of the sounds when they cross. Usually it is more aesthetically satisfying to cross the sounds at the moment they are at full and equal loudness. This keeps audience attention "stage center" with no loss of focus or gap in continuity, which could occur if the crossfade were made at lower levels. Crossfading at too low a level could sound like a sloppy fade-out–fade-in.

Layering Sound

The techniques and aesthetics related to establishing sound and transitions apply whether you are working with one sonic element or several. If two or more sounds are involved, however, there are additional principles to consider.

In audio, combining sounds is commonly referred to as *mixing*, although the term *layering* is more to the point. A mix suggests a blend in which the ingredients lose their uniqueness in becoming part of the whole. Although blending is important, you also have to (1) establish the main and supporting sounds to create focus or point of view, (2) position the sounds to create relationships of space and distance, (3) maintain spectral balance so the aural space is properly weighted, and (4) maintain the definition of each sound. These considerations relate more to layering than to mixing. Layering involves some of the most important aspects of aural communication—balance, perspective, and intelligibility.

BALANCE AND PERSPECTIVE In layering, some sounds are more important than others; the predominant one establishes the focus or point of view. The commercial an announcer reads usually is louder than any accompanying mood music, since the main message is likely to be in the copy. In a racing scene with the sounds of speeding cars, a cheering crowd, and dramatic music defining the excitement, if you want to focus on the race, the sound of the speeding cars should dominate. The crowd and the music should be in the background with the music under to provide the dramatic support. To establish the overall dramatic excitement of the event, the music probably would create that point of view best. Therefore, the speeding cars and cheering crowd should be layered under the music as supporting elements.

Whatever the combination of effects, establishing the main and supporting sounds is fundamental to good production, indeed, to good dramatic technique. In audio, you create the focus or point of view by balancing levels—making them louder or softer relative to their importance, thereby establishing perspective—the relationship of sounds to each other and to the overall communication.

In layering, the loudest sound or the one with the most presence is usually the most important. By being louder and closer, it compels attention; the disc jockey introducing a record keeps the voice level higher than the music level; a singer with a level louder than an accompanying orchestra's level is in front of the ensemble; the main conversation at a party is focused and understandable because it is louder and more present than the other conversations.

Level not only establishes focus but also helps to create distance. If thunder is louder than the sound of children playing, a storm seems imminent. The reverse would place the storm farther away, thus suggesting that the children had time to head for shelter.

DOPPLER EFFECT   Sometimes you can create distance by varying pitch. Have you ever noticed that as a moving sound source, such as a train, car, or siren, gets closer its pitch gets higher, and as it recedes its pitch gets lower? This phenomenon is known as the **Doppler effect** (named for its discoverer, C. J. Doppler, an early nineteenth-century Austrian physicist). Varying the pitches of sounds, using a variable speed tape recorder or variable speed oscillator (see Chapters 10 and 14), can help to create the illusion of increasing or decreasing distance.

INTELLIGIBILITY   Level is important to sound balance and aural perspective, but level alone cannot keep all the sound clear and understandable. Imagine the sound track for a gothic mystery thriller. The scene: deep night, a sinister castle on a lonely mountaintop high above a black forest silhouetted against flashes of lightning. You can almost hear the sound: rumbling, rolling thunder; ominous bass chords from an organ, cellos, and double basses; low-pitched moan of wind.

The layering seems straightforward, depending on the focus: music over wind and thunder to establish the overall scariness, wind over thunder and music to focus on the forlorn emptiness, and thunder over wind and music to center attention on the storm about to break above the haunting bleakness.

With this particular mix, however, setting the appropriate levels may be insufficient to communicate the effect. The sounds are so much alike—low pitched and sustained—that they may mask—cover—each other, thereby creating a combined sound that is "thick" and muddy, lacking in clarity. This adversely affects intelligibility—the distinctiveness of each sound in the mix. Usually when elements in a mix are unintelligible, it is because too many of them are sonically alike in pitch, rhythm, loudness, intensity, envelope, timbre, or style. In the gothic mix, the frequency range, rhythm, and envelope of the sounds are too similar: low pitched, legato, weak in attack, and long in sustain.

One way to layer them more effectively would be to make the wind a bit wilder, thereby sharpening its pitch. Instead of rolling thunder, start it with a sharp crack and shorten the sustain of the rumble to separate it from any similar sustain in the music. These minor changes would make each sound more distinctive, with little or no loss in the overall effect on the scene.

This technique also works in complex mixes. Take a war scene: soldiers shouting, cannons booming, rifles and machine guns clattering, jet fighter planes diving to the attack, and intense orchestral music dramatically underscoring the action. Although there are six different elements, they are distinctive enough to be layered without losing their intelligibility.

The pitch of the cannons is lower than that of the rifles and machine guns; their firing rhythms and sound envelopes are also different. The rifles and machine guns are distinct because their pitch, rhythm, and envelope are not the same either. The pitch of the jets may be within the same range as that of the rifles and machine guns, but their sustained, roaring type of "whine" is the only sound of its kind in the mix. The shouting soldiers have varied rhythms, regardless of any similarities in pitch, envelope, and intensity; and the timbres of the human voices are easily distinguishable. As for the music, its timbres, blend, and intensity are different from the other sounds. Remember, too, that the differences in loudness levels help to contribute to the clarity of this mix.

DIALOGUE Seeing lip formations aids in making dialogue intelligible. When people speak at a distance, the difficulty in seeing lip movements and the reduced loudness inhibit comprehension. Therefore, in film and particularly in TV, it is better to "cheat" a bit with the loudness levels to make the sound easier to perceive and let the picture compensate for any aural-visual discrepancy.

Take a scene in which two people are talking as they walk in the countryside and stop by a tree. The shot as they are walking is a long shot (LS), which changes to a medium close-up (MCU) at the tree (see **15-3**). Reducing the loudness in the LS to match the visual perspective would actually interfere with comprehension because the lip movements would be difficult to see. The better technique is to ride the levels at almost full loudness and let the picture establish the distance and perspective. Psychologically, the picture establishes the context of the sound. This also works in reverse.

15-3 *Normally the sound for a long shot or medium long shot would not be as loud as the sound for a closer shot. A train seen far off should sound far off. The sound of a rider coming closer should grow louder. However, these obvious relationships of level to spatial perspective do not necessarily apply if dialogue is involved. In these two shots, sound in the long shot should be loud enough to compensate for the reduced intelligibility that results from the viewer not being able to see the lip movements of the actors.*

In the close-up, there must be some sonic change to be consistent with the shot change. Since the close-up does not show the countryside but does show the faces better, you can establish the environment by adding ambience to the sound track. In this case, the sound (ambience) will establish the unseen space in the picture. Furthermore, by adding the ambience, the dialogue will seem more diffused. This creates a sense of change without interfering with comprehension, since the actors' lip movements will be much easier to see.

Sound-Picture Relationships

Sound and picture complement and supplement each other in several ways that can be broadly grouped into two categories: informational and emotional.

INFORMATIONAL FUNCTIONS   An informational function relates to cognitive responses such as learning a fact, idea, or concept. A few examples of informational functions of sound in relation to picture follow.

Define the Intensity of an Action—As a wave builds and then crashes, the loudness of the crash helps to define the wave's size and power. In cartoons, sound defines the extent of a character's running, falling, crashing, skidding, chomping, and other actions. Rapid knocks on a door indicate urgency; pounding suggests a threat.

Depict Character or Personality—A dark, brooding theme or a hissing sound can characterize the "bad guy." Tender music can indicate a gentle, sympathetic personality. Strong, rhythmic music can suggest the relentless character who will destroy the character depicted by thin-sounding, syncopated music.

Articulate Point of View—The picture shows a man apologizing to a woman for his many past wrongs. Her look is stern and unforgiving. The music underscoring the scene is gentle and sympathetic, indicating her true feelings. A boxer dances around the ring throwing up his hands to the crowd and his opponent in gestures of invincibility and anticipated victory. The music underscoring the scene is low-keyed and hesitant, indicating the fighter's concern for his ability. Two lovers meet and embrace on a busy street to a cacophony of loud traffic sounds and blaring car horns, suggesting that perhaps all is not well between them.

Establish Counterpoint—Revelers flitting from party to party in apparent good cheer are counterpointed with music that is monotonous and empty. A horror that compels a scream is counterpointed with silence when the character opens his mouth to let out the scream, suggesting something beyond the unspeakable. Football players shown blocking, passing, and running are counterpointed with ballet music to underscore the grace and coordination of the athletes.

Recall the Past or Foretell the Future—A theme used to underscore a tragic crash is repeated to recall the incident. A person is shown standing on a shore looking out to sea. The sound track recreates bits of conversation, sounds, and music from a luxury cruise taken years earlier during which something pivotal occurred. A soldier kisses his girl goodbye as he goes off to war, but the background music indicates he will not return. A happy, hopeful, aspiring actor is shown arriving in the big city to seek fame and fortune while the music foreshadows failure and tragedy.

Establish Locale—Familiar sounds and music evoke the Orient, the American West, old Vienna, Russia, Hawaii, the city, the country, and other environments.

EMOTIONAL FUNCTIONS An emotional function relates to affective responses such as feeling or mood. A few examples follow.

Create an Atmosphere, Feeling, or Mood—Birdsong and gentle, melodic music can create the atmosphere of a serene wooded glen. A beautiful, romantic theme can evoke the feeling of love. Loud, triumphant music can stimulate the feeling of victory or success. The breeze blowing through sails and the creaking of a ship can suggest a feeling of loneliness.

Punctuate an Emotional Highlight—A dramatic chord underscores shock or a moment of decision. A theme enhances that flash of recognition between boy and girl when their eyes first meet. The scariness of sinister music builds to a climax behind a scene of sheer terror, and there is fright when the final chord crashes. A sliding trombone, clanking percussion, or a cawing heckelphone underscores the humor of a comic highlight.

Dozens of other sound-picture relationships exist. Those listed here are designed to suggest possibilities; they are not formulas.

Summary

1. The mixdown is the stage of production when the various recorded sound tracks are sweetened by equalizing and other signal processing, blended, balanced, positioned in the aural frame, and combined into mono or stereo.

2. One procedure in mixing down is to evaluate the positive and negative attributes of the recording, work with one track at a time until each sounds acceptable, and blend and balance the sounds together. This may involve changing individual settings in favor of the overall mix.

3. When equalizing, avoid large increases or decreases in equalization, do not increase or decrease too many tracks at the same frequency, and do not use equalizing as a substitute for better microphone selection and placement.

Equalizing between 400 and 2,000 Hz is more noticeable than equalizing above and below that range. Be sure to equalize with an awareness of the frequency limits of the medium in which you are working.

4. When you add artificial reverberation, do it after signal processing and panning since it is difficult to get a true sense of the effects of frequency and positional change in a reverberant space. Also, avoid giving widely different reverb times to the various components in an ensemble or sound track unless they are supposed to sound as if they are in different acoustic environments.

5. In mixing a sound track that consists of speech, music, and sound effects, the aesthetic relationships of these elements are affected by levels of loudness, how the sounds are established, transitions, balances, perspective, intelligibility, and the presence of a picture.

6. Sound complements and supplements picture in several ways, both informationally and emotionally.

7. Informationally, sound can (a) define the intensity of an action, (b) depict character or personality, (c) articulate point of view, (d) establish counterpoint, (e) recall the past or foretell the future, and (f) establish locale.

8. Emotionally, sound can create an atmosphere, feeling, or mood and punctuate an emotional highlight.

Appendix

Manually Produced Sound Effects

This is a list of selected sound effects and how to produce them. Since these effects are simulated, they may require some refinement beyond the suggestions provided.

AIRPLANE   **Prop:** Hold stiff cardboard against an electric fan. **Jet:** Turn on a high-pitched vacuum cleaner or electric sweeper.

* **ANIMALS**   **Cat:** This is easily done vocally. Listen and try to imitate. **Cow:** Do vocally or with a small bellows-type toy. **Dog:** Do vocally. **Horse:** *Hooves:* Clap halved coconut shells together or on a packed surface. *Snorting:* Take a deep breath, close the lips lightly, and as you force the air out of the lungs, relax the lips and allow them to vibrate freely. *Whinny:* Do vocally. **Monkey:** Dampen the cork from a smooth-sided bottle and rub the side of the bottle with the cork in hard, fast, short strokes.

ARROW   **Through Air:** Swish a stick through the air. **Hitting Target:** Throw darts into a dart board.

BABY CRYING   This is done by a high-pitched voice crying into a pillow.

BASEBALL HIT WITH BAT   Strike a thick, hollowed-out piece of wood with another piece of wood.

* **BELLS**   **Church, Fight, Fire, School Bell:** These can all be made on an old automobile brake drum. Set the drum on a piece of wood so that the flange is facing up and is free to vibrate. Try striking with various wooden and metal strikers for different tones; also strike in various rhythms to get the effect of various bells. **Dinner Bell and Emergency Bell:** These are usually rung much faster than the other bells. To get the speed necessary, suspend by a cord a piece of strap iron or small-diameter pipe bent into a U shape. With a small piece of metal, rapidly strike back and forth

---

*Asterisked entries in appendix are from *Radio and Television Effects* by Robert B. Turnbull. Copyright, 1951, by Robert B. Turnbull. Reprinted by permission of Holt, Rinehart and Winston.

inside the inverted horseshoe. **Electric Bells:** These may be purchased inexpensively and should be mounted on wood for greater resonance. The dry-cell setup is handy, but the batteries eventually run down. An AC setup is good but calls for an AC cord to an outlet.

BIRD CALLS   Bird calls can be made by an imitator. A warbling sound that simulates the twittering of a canary can best be done with a small bird whistle of the type that holds water.

BIRD WINGS (FLAPPING)   Flap flat pieces of canvas near the microphone.

＊**BLOOD PRESSURE SPHYGMOMANOMETER**   The sound of the gadget that is strapped on the arm to take blood pressure is easily simulated by placing a finger over the nozzle end of an atomizer, then rapidly squeezing the bulb. Work close to the mike on this.

＊**BLOWS**   **On the Head:** (1) Strike a pumpkin with a mallet. (2) Strike a large melon with a wooden mallet or a short length of garden hose. (3) Strike a baseball glove with a short piece of garden hose. **On the Chin:** (1) Lightly dampen a large powder puff and slap it on the wrist close to the mike. (2) Hold a piece of sponge rubber in one hand and strike with the fist. (3) Slip on a thin leather glove and strike the bare hand with the gloved fist.

BOAT   **Row Boat:** *Oar locks:* Use real oar locks or a rusty hinge. *Rowing:* Dip a wooden paddle into a tub of water or blow lightly and rhythmically into a glass of water through a straw. **Canoe:** Sound of paddling is the same as rowing. **Ship:** *Gangplank:* Use a ratchet wrench. *Anchor:* Rattle a chain; let an object fall into a tub of water. *Flapping sails:* Flap a piece of canvas or paper near microphone. *Creaking of boat:* Twist a leather belt. *Putting up sails:* Run rope through a pulley, occasionally flap a piece of cloth.

BONES RATTLING   A good effect may be produced by suspending wooden sticks with strings from a board. Manipulate the board so that the sticks clank together for the macabre illusion of rattling bones.

BOTTLE   To open, (1) press two plungers together and pull suddenly apart; or (2) open mouth, snap cheek with finger.

＊**BREAKING BONES**   (1) Chew Life Savers close to the mike. (2) Twist and crunch wooden boxes. (3) Snap small-diameter dowel rods wrapped in soft paper. (4) Snap small pieces of hardened isinglass.

＊**BREAKING EGGS**   Take a 6-inch square of very coarse sandpaper and fold the corners in toward the center, the rough side up. Lay in the palm of the hand and suddenly squeeze.

BREEZE   Fold two sections of newspaper in half, then cut each section into parallel strips. Sway the strips gently close to the mike.

BROOK BABBLING   Blow air through a straw into a glass of water. Experiment by using varying amounts of water and by blowing at varying speeds.

BULLET   For a bullet hitting a wall, strike a book with the flat side of a knife handle.

CAMERA CLICK   Snap the switch on a flashlight.

CHOPPING WOOD   Chop a piece of 2-by-4 wood with a small hatchet near the microphone.

CIGARETTE For lighting a cigarette, draw a toothpick against sandpaper.

* **CLOCKS** (1) Use various clocks. (2) Use a metronome for a steady beat. (3) Collect striker mechanisms for a variety of tones. (4) A cuckoo-clock effect is produced by a whistle or a small bellows mechanism. (5) Strike a suspended and undamped steel spring with a padded mallet.

COAL CARS The sound of small loaded cars approaching can be made by rolling a pair of roller skates over a piece of iron, starting off-mike and bringing them as close as desired. A little gravel sprinkled on the iron may help the effect.

* **COCKTAIL** Shake some bits of broken glass in a small amount of water in a closed coffee can.

COINS CLINKING Some coins cannot be used because they produce a high-frequency sound that may be lost in transmission. Use nickels, quarters, half-dollars, and dollars. Lead washers are used successfully sometimes.

COLLISION **Fenders Colliding:** Drop a knife into a slightly tipped tub so that the knife will rattle a little after landing. **Locomotive and Automobile:** (1) Let air out of a tire. (2) Shake broken glass in a small box. (3) Crush wooden boxes. (4) Drop a stove pipe on its end into a tub. **Old Truck and Street Car:** Drop broken glass from a height into an empty tub that is slightly suspended.

COW BEING MILKED Squirt a water pistol into an empty metal container.

* **CRASHES** (1) Metallic crashes can be done by piling a collection of tin and metal scraps into a large tub and dumping. To get a sustained crash, shake and rattle the tub until the cue for the pay-off crash. (2) Wooden crashes can be done by smashing large wooden containers close to the mike. The impact must come before the crash.

* **CREAKS** (1) Twist and squeeze a Dixie cup close to the mike. (2) Mount a rusty hinge between two blocks of wood. Twist so that the hinge binds, then slowly open or close the hinge. (3) For the creak of a ship rubbing against a wharf, rub an inflated rubber balloon close to the mike.

* **CRICKETS** Run a fingernail along the fine teeth of a pocket comb. Remember, the sound should alternate—loud then soft.

CROWDS Let several people stand at a distance from the microphone, and several closer to bring through "front" speeches. Be careful not to let the sound of the crowd increase too regularly.

* **CURTAINS** The principal sound of drawn curtains is the sound of rings sliding on rod, not the fabric. String several washers or wooden or metal rings on a 2-foot length of dowel or metal rod. Space the rings evenly apart, then sweep them together from one end to the other.

DESTRUCTION NOISES General destruction noises can be simulated by crushing and breaking wooden boxes close to the microphone. In the background you may want the sound of breaking glass (drop a box filled with broken glass).

* **DIGGING AND SHOVELING** Fill a small wooden box with several inches of dirt and add several small rocks for realism. Use a small shovel or fireplace ash scoop. Force the shovel into the dirt with a slanting motion. The bottom of the box (inside) should be covered with an old piece of carpet to cut down on wood resonance.

DISHES   Use whole dishes in a natural way. The common advice to shake or rattle broken pieces does not prove satisfactory. For washing dishes, swish dishes in water.

DOORBELL   Use a real doorbell.

DOOR KNOCKER   Screw one side of a large door hinge to a block of wood. Rap the wood with the loose wing of the hinge.

∗**DOORS**   **Squeaky Door:** Use rusty hinges, if possible, attached to a miniature door, or twist a leather belt or billfold. Some old wooden chairs will give the squeak you need. **Smashing Door:** Crush a wooden box. **Closing Door:** Use a miniature or close a real door very lightly. Have regulation catches attached to the miniature. **Iron Door:** For the hollow clang of iron doors opening, draw an iron skate over an iron plate. Rattling a heavy chain and a key in a lock adds to the effect. The principal sound heard on a door close or open comes from the lock and jamb. Half-size doors may be built, paying particular attention to the hardware for different types. **Elevator Door:** Run a roller skate over a long, flat piece of metal. **Jail Door:** The characteristic sound of an iron door is the noise when it clangs shut. For this, clang two flat pieces of metal together, then let one slide along the other for a moment, signifying the bar sliding into place. **Screen Door:** The distinctive sound comes from the spring and the rattle of the screen on the slam. Secure an old spring, slap it against a piece of wood, then rattle a window screen. Or use a miniature, including screen and catches. **Stone Doors:** Slide a large block of cement on a large flat slab of cement. At the end of the slide, tip the block to one side and then let it fall back. This signifies the close of the door. **Swinging Doors:** These can be simulated by swinging a real door back and forth between the hands. Let the free edge strike the heels of the hands. Watch the timing.

∗**DRAWERS**   Slide two pieces of wood together. Put a small crosspiece on one so that the other will hit it at the end of the slide, indicating the close.

∗ **ECHOES**   (1) Suspend a solid wastepaper basket or any other good-sized container horizontally so that the open end faces the diaphragm of the microphone. The actor then stands behind the mike so that most of his voice goes into the container and then is reflected back into the microphone. (That part of the voice which is reflected lags enough behind the sound waves which go directly into the microphone to give a muffled hollow effect.) (2) To give the voice a hollow ghostlike sound, place one end of a 10-foot length of 2-inch pipe about 2 feet from the microphone. The actor will then speak into his hands, which he cups over the other end of the pipe.

∗ **ELECTRIC MOTORS**   (1) Remove the bag from a vacuum cleaner and run the motor. (2) Use an electric mixer or juicer. (3) Sometimes a hair dryer sounds satisfactory.

∗ **ELECTRIC SPARK**   Rub two blocks of sandpaper-covered wood together in one long fast stroke.

ENGINES   A toy steam engine operated near the mike gives a fairly good imitation of a large steam engine.

FALLING BODY   (1) Dropping a squash provides the dull, sickening thud of a body hurtling to the sidewalk. (2) By dropping a sack half filled with sand on the studio floor, you can produce the sound of a body or a heavy object falling to the ground or floor.

* **FALLING INTO WATER**   The important thing is to get the impact of the hit on the surface of the water. To simulate this effect, however, reverse the procedure this way. Secure a large washtub or wooden tub. Fill it about three-quarters full of water. Get a very large can or a bucket. Sink the bucket until it is full of water, then turn it over but keep it submerged. With the bottom side up, yank it sharply out of the tub. If it is necessary to keep the hands dry, get a 3-foot length of pipe and at one end fasten a round disc of wood about 1 foot in diameter. Place the end with the wood in the bottom of the tub, then yank sharply upward.

FIGHTING SOUNDS   Whack a sponge with the fist.

FIRE   (1) Crumple stiff paper or cellophane near the mike or pour salt from the shaker on stiff paper. (2) For the roar of flames, blow lightly through a soda straw into liquid at the mike. (3) The breaking of the stems of broom straws or the crushing of wrapping paper gives various effects of crackling fire.

FIRE ENGINES   Use sirens, horns, clanging bells, etc.

* **FISHING**   (1) To indicate fishing, use the occasional "sing" of the reel. Clamp the reel to some surface near the mike, then take the string and rapidly run it out as needed. (2) To indicate a caught fish, flop about an empty hot-water bottle or a folded inner tube.

FLOOD   Blow into a glass of water through a soda straw.

* **FOOTSTEPS**   **Cement:** Use hard-heeled shoes on composition stone. **Gravel:** Fill a long shallow box with gravel and have someone actually walk on it. **Leaves:** Stir corn flakes in a small cardboard box with fingers. Match the rhythm of walking. **Mud:** In a large wash pan, place several crumpled and shredded newspapers. Paper towels work fine. Leave very little water in the pan. Simulate walking by using the palm of the hand for footsteps. **Snow:** Squeeze a box of cornstarch with the fingers in the proper rhythm. The effect works better if cornstarch is put into a chamois bag. **Stairs:** Use just the ball of the foot in a forward sliding motion. Do not use the heel.

* **GAMBLING SOUNDS**   (1) Use cards and chips. (2) For a crap table, roll dice inside an open violin case.

* **GEIGER COUNTER**   Twist the knob of a heavy spring lock.

* **GLASS CRASHES**   Place an accumulation of broken glass and crockery in a flour sack. Drop it on the floor and then shake.

GLASSES   The clinking of glasses can be made by setting glasses down on wood at intervals. Water poured into them gives the effect of a bartender filling them up.

GUN COCK   Use a real weapon, unloaded.

HAIL   Drop rice onto glass, tin, or a thin board.

HANDCUFFS   To lock or unlock, turn the key in a flimsy padlock, or scrape a nail against a hinge or another nail or piece of metal.

* **HAND PRESS**   A small hand-operated printing press may be simulated by holding a wooden folding chair by the back and rhythmically opening and closing the seat of the chair. An old rattly chair works best. This same effect may be used for a hand loom.

HARNESS   Rattle a belt buckle.

HINGES SQUEAKING   Squeaking noises can be made by turning wooden pegs in holes drilled in a block of wood to make a snug fit; twisting a cork in the mouth of a bottle; or twisting a piece of leather.

HOOF BEATS   Horse on a Hard Road: A pair of coconut shells clapped together in proper rhythm gives the "clippety-clop" sound. **Horse Crossing Bridge:** Hold mouth open, snap cheeks with fingers. **Horse on Soft Ground or Turf:** Rubber suction cups or half coconut shells clapped slowly in a box containing earth give a very satisfactory effect. Eraser on a pencil bounced on a book also gives a good sound.

HORSE AND WAGON   Run roller skates over fine gravel sprinkled on a blotter of beaver board.

ICE CRACKLING   Styrofoam crumpled near a mike gives the effect of crackling ice.

ICE JAM CREAKING   Twist an inflated balloon.

KEY GRATING   If possible, use a large key in an actual lock. The more rusty the lock, the better.

* **KNIFE THROW**   The sound of a knife being thrown and hitting the wall a couple of inches from the hero is done in three parts: (1) The flight through the air is done by a swish stick. (2) The thud of the knife hitting is done by sharply stabbing a bayonet or large heavy knife into a block of soft wood. (3) The quiver of the knife after it hits is made by placing a flexible table knife on a flat wooden surface or table so that about 2 inches of the blade rests on the table, with the rest of the blade and handle extending over the edge. Press the table end of the knife firmly against the table, then sharply hit the free end so that it will vibrate. Practice will determine the right pressure on the blade and the amount of overlap on the table. The three steps must be done very rapidly.

LETTER   To open, tear a piece of paper.

LIGHT SWITCH   Snap fingers or use an old light switch.

LOCKS   Use real locks or a nail against a hinge.

MACHINERY, HEAVY   (1) A motor mounted on a light board and placed close to the mike gives the effect of much larger mechanisms at work. (2) Run roller skates across a desk or table. (3) Roll a heavy can on a table. (4) Fasten a wooden wheel with rough edges in a frame. Turn it by an attached handle, and grind this against wood. (5) Use a lawnmower.

MOTORBOAT   Certain rattles of the ratchet type used on Halloween if operated slowly and near the mike produce a satisfactory sound of a motorboat.

* **PHONE BOOTH DOOR**   Unfold and fold the leg of a card table.

PORCH SWING   Rock an old swivel chair rhythmically.

* **POURING A DRINK**   (1) Always touch the edge of the glass with the bottle to establish the sound. (2) For a comedy effect, use the long glass tube that covers the paper cups on a water cooler. A pitcher of water used with this tube gives a terrifically big drink.

RAIN   (1) For mild rain, rub the microphone stand with excelsior. (2) Let salt or fine sand slip through fingers or through a funnel onto cellophane, or pour water from a sprinkling can into a tub with some water already in it.

RAPPING   Strike a desk with an ordinary gavel.

RIVETING MACHINE   Hold stiff paper firmly against the blades of a cheap fan.

ROAR OF RIVER   Fill a large washtub half full of water and draw a flat paddle through the water. A little experimenting will determine the speed and vigor necessary to give the proper volume and quality of sound. As a precaution against getting a metallic sound, line the tub with a piece of canvas.

✻ **ROBOT**   For a robot walking, use a 3-by-5 metal file case. Hold it in a vertical position with the open end up, and bang it against a walking surface in a slow definite rhythm. Leave the drawer in the case.

ROCK CRASHING   Drop rocks onto other rocks in a box. To lengthen a crashing sound, have more than one person drop the stones.

✻ **ROULETTE WHEEL**   (1) A toy or party roulette wheel works very well. (2) To improvise, cut a circular piece the size of a biscuit cutter out of the bottom of a large wooden salad bowl. Insert a tin biscuit cutter open side up in the hole. Place a marble in the wooden bowl and rotate briskly. On cue, slow down the speed of the rotation and allow the marble to drop into the biscuit cutter.

SHIP   Moving Ship: Twist the resined screw handle of a broom into and out of a socket; flap a cloth lightly for a sailboat. **Ship Sailing on Water:** With a little ingenuity, you can rotate an ordinary hair brush on the surface of a bass drum to give the sound of the waves breaking away from the boat. **Ship Signal Bells:** Pull back the hammer of a doorbell and snap.

SHOTS   (1) Close a book smartly. (2) Shots are usually done with a small tambourine-like frame with a membrane, to which is attached a pliable metal spatula. When the spatula is bent back away from the membrane and then quickly snapped against it, the sound is like a shot. (3) Another good way is to strike a padded leather cushion with a thin, flat stick or with a whip. (4) Prick a balloon with a pin. (5) A shot similar to that of heavy artillery may be produced on a bass drum or tympani. (6) If the whistling sound of the bullet or shell is desired, it may be produced vocally by whistling close to the mike.

SHUTTERS   (1) To close, drop a small board lightly against a wooden box. (2) To flap, at irregular intervals, slam two pieces of wood together twice.

SIDEWALK   To walk on a sidewalk, sprinkle fine gravel lightly on a blotter, walk lightly.

✻ **SIZZLE**   To get the sound of a sizzle like someone backing into a hot stove, put a heated electric iron into a very shallow pan of water. The same may be done with a soldering iron. (Unplug it first.)

SLAP   A slap is easily made by slapping the hands together. Be careful not to get this too close to the mike, or it will sound like an explosion.

SNOW   For walking in snow, squeeze cornstarch in a gloved hand.

SPLASH   Drop a flat block of wood into a tub of water off mike.

✻ **SQUEAKS**   (1) Twist a leather wallet close to the mike. (2) Use a squeaky swivel office chair. (3) Twist a Dixie cup in a sideways motion. (4) Draw a violin bow across the edge of a styrofoam container. (5) Twist a dampened tight-fitting cork in a bottle.

✻ **SQUEAL**   The dominant sound of a squeal is caused by friction. (1) Twist a metal cup (like the top of a thermos jug) on an unglazed pottery plate. (2) Twist and scrape various bits of metal against metal.

SUBWAY TURNSTILE   Use a ratchet wrench.

* **SURF**   (1) Rub a stiff scrubbing brush with a rotary motion over the head of a drum or tympani. (2) Also try rolling a few beans on a window screen or drum head. (3) A splash cradle could be used for this effect. It consists of a watertight box mounted on rockers and containing 2 or 3 inches of water. Rock the cradle back and forth slowly, allowing the water to swish from side to side.

SWORD   (1) Clash and scrape knives. (2) A dueling scene can be made more convincing by clashing iron rods together.

TELEGRAPH INSTRUMENTS   Use real ones or use a typewriter. In using a telegraph key, remember that sending an intelligible message as part of a radio broadcast is prohibited by law.

TELEPHONE   Use equalizer and filter frequencies below 400 Hz and above 4,000 Hz.

THRESHING MACHINE   Use roller skates, motor, electric fan, geared motor, or other metallic sounds combined with a baby rattle.

THUNDER   (1) Rumble a large sheet of tin easily. (2) Beat stiff parchment, stretched on a frame, with a bass drum stick.

TIME BOMB   Use a ticking alarm clock.

TOM-TOM   (1) Beat the end of an oatmeal box with a dull instrument. (2) Beat a tambourine or drum dully. (3) Beat stiff parchment on a frame.

UNDERBRUSH NOISES   Twisting a bundle of straw, excelsior, or recording tape near the mike gives the effect of something astir in the underbrush.

WAGON   Move a box filled with loose blocks of wood.

WATERFALL   (1) Rustle tissue paper. (2) Tear paper evenly. (3) Blow through a straw into a glass of water. (4) Let water fall from a small hose into a tub. (5) Pour water evenly from a teakettle.

* **WHIP CRACK**   Sharply slap two thin boards together.

WHISTLE   For a steamboat whistle, there are square boxlike whistles about a foot long on the market which are used in major studios for this effect. If one of these is not available, a boy or a man can be found, who by cupping his hands over his mouth and making a "who-o-ing" sound several times some distance off-mike can simulate this effect. Also, by blowing into an ordinary section of pipe held just below the lower lip, a ship's whistle may be effected. Of course, the "blower" must vocalize the correct tone as he blows.

WIND   A flywheel of wands rotated by a high-speed electric motor gives a fairly good effect.

* **WINDOW**   Slide one block of wood on another.

WOOD SPLINTERING   Crush wooden boxes or crates.

Glossary

ACOUSTICS   The science that deals with the behavior of sound and sound control. The sound qualities of a studio.

AMBIENCE   Sounds such as reverberation, noise, and atmosphere that are background to the main sound.

AMBISONIC   Manufacturer's term to describe a microphone's "surround sound" pickup.

AMPLIFIER   A device that boosts the power of an electric signal.

AMPLITUDE   The magnitude of a sound wave or electric signal.

ANALOG RECORDING   A method of recording in which the wave form of the recorded signal resembles the wave form of the original signal.

ASSEMBLE EDITING   Dubbing segments from one tape or tapes to another tape in sequential order.

ATTACK   The way a sound begins—that is, by plucking, bowing, striking, blowing, etc. The first part of the sound envelope.

ATTACK TIME   The length of time it takes a limiter or compressor to respond to the input signal.

ATTENUATOR   Another term for potentiometer, fader, gain control, or loudness control.

AUDITION   1. A system on the console through which sound can be fed and heard without it going on the air. 2. A talent tryout.

AUDITORY CANAL   The channel that directs sound from the outer ear to the eardrum.

AUDITORY NERVE   The nerve in the inner ear that transmits sound waves to the brain.

AZIMUTH   Alignment of the record and playback heads so that their center lines are parallel to each other and at right angles to the direction of the tape motion passing across the heads.

BACKTIME   Method of subtracting the time of a program segment from the total time of a program so that the segment and the program end at the same time.

BALANCED LINE   A line (or circuit) with two conductors of equal voltage.

BANDWIDTH   The difference between the upper and lower frequency limits of an audio component. The upper and lower frequency limits of AM radio are 535 and 1,605 kHz; therefore, the bandwidth of AM radio is 1,070 kHz.

BANDWIDTH CURVE   The curve shaped by the number of frequencies in a bandwidth and their relative increase or decrease in level. A bandwidth of 100 to 150 Hz with 125 Hz boosted 15 dB forms a sharp, narrow bandwidth curve; a bandwidth of 100 to 6,400 Hz with a 15-dB boost at 1,200 Hz forms a more sloping, wider-bandwidth curve.

BASS ROLL-OFF   Attenuating bass frequencies. The control—for example, on a microphone—used to roll off bass frequencies.

BIAS CURRENT   An extremely high-frequency AC current, far beyond audibility, added during a tape recording to linearize the magnetic information.

BIDIRECTIONAL MICROPHONE   A microphone that picks up sound to its front and back and is dead at its sides.

BINAURAL MICROPHONE HEAD   Two omnidirectional condenser microphones set into the ear cavities of an artificial head. Theoretically, this arrangement picks up sound as humans hear it.

BINAURAL SOUND   Sound recorded using the binaural microphone head, or a similar miking arrangement, and reproduced through two separate earphone channels.

BLAST FILTER   (See Pop filter)

BLOCKING   Plotting actor, camera, and microphone movements in a production.

BLOOPING   Erasing or masking optical or magnetic stripe sound with a small demagnetizer (blooping pencil), metallic blooping tape, or blooping ink.

BOARD   Audio mixing console.

BOOM   A long, counterbalanced, projectable steel pole mounted on a special tripod or pedestal with a microphone on one end and an operator at the other end.

BOUNCING TRACKS   Transferring two or more previously recorded tape tracks to a single track, thus allowing rerecording on the previously used tracks.

BULK ERASER   A demagnetizer used to erase an entire roll of magnetic tape without removing it from its reel. Also known as a "degausser."

BUS   A mixing network that combines the outputs of other channels.

CABLE SYNCHRONIZATION   A way of synchronizing the operating speeds of a film camera and an audio tape recorder. A sync pulse tone feeds through the cable (also called an "umbilical") that connects camera and recorder.

CALIBRATE   Adjusting equipment—for example, a console and a tape recorder—with a standard so that their measurements are similar.

"CANNED" MUSIC   Music that sounds obviously recorded.

CAPACITOR   A device capable of storing an electric charge.

CAPACITOR LOUDSPEAKER   (See Condenser loudspeaker)

CAPACITOR MICROPHONE   (See Condenser microphone)

CAPSTAN   The shaft that rotates against the tape, pulling it across the heads at a constant speed.

CARBON MICROPHONE   A low-quality, high-impedance microphone with a carbon element.

CARDIOID MICROPHONE   A unidirectional microphone with a heart-shaped pick-up pattern.

CARTRIDGE   1. The transducing element in a record player that converts mechanical energy into electric energy. 2. The plastic housing for a continuous-loop tape.

CARTRIDGE TAPE   A continuous-loop audio or video tape.

CARTRIDGE TAPE RECORDER   A device specially designed to record and/or reproduce sound or sound and picture on a cartridge tape.

CASSETTE TAPE   A reel-to-reel audio or video tape enclosed in a plastic container.

CASSETTE TAPE RECORDER   An audio or video tape recorder specially designed to play cassette tape.

CELLULOSE ACETATE   A plastic film base used for magnetic tape.

CEMENT SPLICER   A splicer used to bond film splices permanently.

CERAMIC MICROPHONE   A low-quality, high-impedance microphone with a ceramic element.

CHANNEL   A single, complete signal path through a system.

CHROMIUM DIOXIDE   A compound of magnetic particle oxide used on some cassette tape to increase the output level.

CLAPSLATE   A slate used in synchronizing sound and picture during filming and editing. The slate carries information such as scene and take number, production title, and whether the shot is taken indoors or outdoors. A pair of hinged boards on top of the slate clap together producing the sound that is used to synchronize picture and sound.

CLICK TRACK   A specially recorded track of rhythmic measurements used to maintain the beat and timing of musicians or conductor.

CLOSED-LOOP TAPE SYSTEM   A tape transport system with two capstans and pinch rollers, one on each side of the head assembly. Also known as the "isolated" or "iso" loop system.

COERCIVITY   The magnetic force field necessary to reduce a tape from saturation to full erasure. This value is expressed in oersteds.

COINCIDENT PAIR OF MICROPHONES   Two microphones, usually unidirectional, crossed one above the other and at an angle for stereo recording.

COMPANDER   Contraction of the words *compressor* and *expander* that refers to the devices that compress an input signal and expand an output signal to reduce noise. Also refers to a noise reducer.

COMPRESSION   1. Reducing a signal's output level in relation to its input level to minimize distortion. 2. Drawing together of vibrating molecules, thus producing a high-pressure area. (See Rarefaction)

COMPRESSION RATIO   The ratio of the input and output signals in a compressor.

COMPRESSION THRESHOLD   The level at which a compressor acts on an input signal and the compression ratio takes effect.

COMPRESSOR   A signal processor with an output level that decreases as its input level increases.

CONDENSER LOUDSPEAKER   A loudspeaker that transduces electric energy into acoustic energy electrostatically.

CONDENSER MICROPHONE   A microphone that transduces acoustic energy into electric energy electrostatically.

CONSOLE   An electronic device that amplifies, processes, and combines input signals and routes them to broadcast or recording.

CONTACT MICROPHONE   A microphone that attaches to a sound source and transduces the vibrations that pass through it.

CONTROL ROOM   Room used by the audio operator, who is sometimes the performer, or the director and staff to control and process audio and video signals during a production.

CONTROL ROOM, POSTPRODUCTION   A room that houses the equipment used in sweetening and editing a recorded production.

CONTROL TRACK   The track on a video tape that controls and synchronizes the video frames. It is essential for editing.

COPYRIGHT   The exclusive legal right of an author, composer, playwright, publisher, or distributor to publish, produce, sell, or distribute his or her work.

CROSSFADE   Fading in one sound source as another sound source fades out. At some point the sounds cross at an equal level of loudness.

CROSSOVER FREQUENCY   The frequency at which the high frequencies are routed to the tweeter(s) and the low frequencies are routed to the woofer(s).

CROSSOVER NETWORK   The device that separates the high and low frequencies for routing to the tweeter(s) and woofer(s).

CROSSTALK   Unwanted signal leakage from one signal path to another.

CRYSTAL MICROPHONE   A low-quality, high-impedance microphone with a crystal element.

CRYSTAL SYNCHRONIZATION   Synchronizing the operating speeds of a film camera and an audio tape recorder by using a crystal oscillator in both camera and recorder. The oscillator generates a sync pulse tone.

CUE   1. To prepare a record or tape for playback and to start at the first point of sound. 2. (See Audition) 3. A verbal command or hand signal to begin.

CUE TONE   A pulse recorded onto a cartridge tape that stops the tape, after recueing, at the beginning of the recording.

CUE TRACK   The track on video tape used to record the information that codes the video frames for editing.

CUT   1. An instantaneous transition from one sound or picture to another. 2. The sound (modulated) bands on a record. 3. To make a disc recording.

CUTTING AND SPLICING   Editing tape or film by physically cutting the material and joining the cut ends with splicing tape.

CYCLES PER SECOND   (See Hertz)

DEAD ROLL   Starting a record or tape with the pot turned down all the way.

DECAY   The decrease in amplitude after a stimulus has been removed from a vibrating object.

DECAY, RATE OF   The evenness or unevenness with which a sound decays.

DECAY TIME   The length of time it takes a sound to die away.

DECIBEL   A relative and dimensionless unit to measure the ratio of two sound intensities.

DE-ESSER   A compressor that reduces sibilance.

DEGAUSSER   (See Bulk eraser)

DELAY   The time interval between a sound or signal and each of its repeats.

DELEGATION SWITCH   The control on the console that routes an input to a channel.

DIALOGUE LOOPING ROOM   A studio in which dialogue is recorded and synchronized to picture. The film is cut into loops and shown over and over so the performers can synchronize their lip movements with the lip movements in the film.

DIFFUSION   The scattering of sound waves.

DIGITAL RECORDING   A method of recording in which the recorded signal is encoded on the tape in pulses and then decoded during playback.

DIRECT INSERTION   Taking the signal from an electric instrument and plugging it directly into the console.

DIRECT SOUND   Sound waves that reach the listener before reflecting off any surface.

DIRECT TO DISC   Making a record by sending the signal directly from the microphones through the console to the disc-cutting machine and bypassing the tape altogether.

DISCRETE QUADRIPHONIC REPRODUCTION   A system that records and reproduces quadriphonic sound using four separate channels. (See Matrix quadriphonic reproduction)

DISTORTION, FREQUENCY   Nonlinear distortion that occurs when frequencies that are present at the input are not present, or equally reproduced, at the output.

DISTORTION, HARMONIC   Nonlinear distortion caused when an audio system introduces harmonics to a signal at the output that were not present at the input.

DISTORTION, INTERMODULATION   Nonlinear distortion that occurs when different frequencies pass through an amplifier at the same time and interact to create combinations of tones that are unrelated to the original sounds.

DISTORTION, LOUDNESS   Distortion that occurs when the loudness of a signal is greater than the sound system can handle.

DISTORTION, SPATIAL   Distortion that occurs when sound sources are reproduced out of aural position in comparison with the way they were recorded or panned.

DISTORTION, TRANSIENT   Distortion that occurs when a sound system cannot reproduce sounds that begin with sudden, explosive attacks.

DOPPLER EFFECT   The perceived increase or decrease in frequency as a sound source moves closer or farther from the listener.

DOUBLE-CHAINING   Running A and B film rolls at the same time on two film chains to allow cutting from one to the other without lip flap.

DOUBLE-SYSTEM RECORDING   Filming sound and picture simultaneously but separately with a camera and a tape recorder. (See Cable synchronization and Crystal synchronization)

DOUBLING   Mixing slightly delayed signals with the original signal to create the effect of several sound sources where there was only one.

DRIVE SYSTEM   The system in a turntable that drives or spins the plate.

DROPOUT   A sudden attenuation of sound or loss of picture due to an imperfection in the magnetic coating.

DRY SOUND   A sound devoid of reverberation. (See Wet sound)

DUBBING   Transferring sound from one tape to another.

DYNAMIC MICROPHONE   A microphone that transduces energy electromagnetically. Moving-coil and ribbon microphones are dynamic microphones.

DYNAMIC RANGE   The range between the quietest and loudest sounds a sound source can produce without distortion.

EARLY REFLECTIONS   (See Echo)

EARPHONES   A pair of electro-acoustical transducers held to the ears by a plastic or metal headband. They may be mono, stereo, quad, or switchable between the two or three formats.

ECHO   The perceptible repetition of a sound.

ECHO CHAMBER   A specially built room with reflectant surfaces and a loudspeaker through which sound feeds, reverberates, and is picked up by a microphone that feeds the reverberant sound back into the console.

EDIT CONTROL   The control on a tape recorder that disengages the take-up reel but keeps the rest of the tape transport system working, thus enabling unwanted tape to spill off the machine.

EDIT PROGRAMMER   A device that connects to a playback and edit/record video tape recorder and automatically controls their operation in preroll cueing, edit auditioning, and performing the edit by punching in and punching out.

ELASTICITY   The capacity to return to the original shape or place after deflection or displacement.

ELECTRET MICROPHONE   A condenser microphone with a permanently charged element.

ELECTRONIC EDITING   Editing by dubbing from a playback or "slave" tape recorder to a record/edit or "master" tape recorder.

ELECTRONIC FIELD PRODUCTION   Video tape production done on location involving program materials that take some time to produce. Also known as EFP.

ELECTRONIC NEWS GATHERING   Video production done on location, sometimes taped and sometimes live, but usually with a news-type deadline. Also known as ENG.

EMULSION   The light-sensitive coating on film that produces the image.

EQUALIZATION   Altering the frequency/amplitude response of a sound source or sound system.

EQUALIZER   A signal processing device that can boost, attenuate, or filter the frequency response in a sound source or sound system.

EQUAL LOUDNESS CURVES   Graphs that indicate the sensitivity of the human ear to various frequencies at different loudness levels. Also known as Fletcher-Munson curves. (See Robinson-Dadson curves)

EQUIPMENT NOISE   Noise produced by all the components in a recording system except the tape. (See Noise, System noise, and Tape noise)

ERASE HEAD   Electromagnetic transducer on a tape recorder that automatically demagnetizes a tape before it reaches the record head when the recorder is in the record mode.

EXPANDER   A signal processor that expands dynamic range.

FADE-IN   Gradually increasing the loudness of a signal level from silence (or from "black" in video).

FADE-OUT   Gradually decreasing the loudness of a signal level to silence (or to "black" in video).

FADE-OUT–FADE-IN   A transition usually indicating a marked change in time, locale, continuity of action, and other features.

FADER   Potentiometer.

FEEDBACK   A loud squeal or howl caused when the sound from a loudspeaker is picked up by a nearby microphone and reamplified. Also caused when the output of a tape recorder is fed back into the record circuit.

FILM   A flexible, cellulose-base material with a light-sensitive emulsion containing sprocket holes.

FILM, MAGNETIC FULL-COAT   Sprocketed film containing one track of sound only and no picture.

FILM, MULTISTRIPE MAGNETIC   Sprocketed film containing several magnetic stripes of sound and no picture.

FILM, SILENT   Film with sprocket holes down both its sides containing picture only.

FILM, SOUND   Film with sprocket holes down one side, an optical or magnetic stripe sound track down the other side, and picture between.

FILTER   An electric network that attenuates a selected frequency or band of frequencies.

FLANGING   Combining a direct signal and the same signal slightly delayed, and continuously varying their time relationships.

FLETCHER-MUNSON CURVES   (See Equal loudness curves and Robinson-Dadson curves)

FLOOR PLAN   A scale drawing of a studio showing the location of cameras, microphones, lights, sets, and props for a production.

FLUTTER   High-frequency distortion, about 6,000 Hz and above, caused by very short, rapid variations in tape speed that result in similar variations in sound pitch and amplitude. (See Wow)

FM MICROPHONE   Wireless microphone.

FOLDBACK   The system in a multichannel console that permits the routing of sound through a headphone monitor feed to performers in the studio.

FOLEY STAGE   An area containing various types of surfaces used to create and record sound effects.

FOOTAGE COUNTER   An indicator on an audio or video tape recorder that displays the amount of tape that has been used. It may or may not measure in actual feet. (See Tape timer)

FOUR-WAY SYSTEM LOUDSPEAKER   A loudspeaker that divides the high frequencies in two and the low frequencies in two, sending each of the four groups of frequencies to a separate speaker.

FREQUENCY   The number of times per second that a sound wave repeats itself. Now expressed in hertz (Hz), formerly expressed in cycles per second (cps).

FREQUENCY RESPONSE   A measure of an audio system's ability to reproduce a range of frequencies with the same relative loudness. It is usually represented in a graph.

FREQUENCY SPECTRUM   The range of frequencies audible to human hearing: about 20 to 16,000 Hz.

FUNDAMENTAL   The lowest frequency a sound source can produce. Also called "primary frequency" and "first harmonic."

GAIN CONTROL   Potentiometer.

GAUSS   A unit that measures the amount of magnetization remaining on a tape after erasure.

GRAPHIC EQUALIZER   An equalizer with sliding controls that gives selective equalization in narrow bandwidths. It gives a graphic representation of the response curve chosen.

GROOVE   The track cut into a record. Grooves are either modulated, with sound, or unmodulated, without sound.

GUARD BAND   The space between tracks on an audio tape recorder head to reduce crosstalk.

HANGING MICROPHONE   Any microphone hung from a beam, lighting grid, or other support and used in situations that are difficult to mike with other types of microphone mounts.

HARD WIRED   Description of pieces of equipment wired to each other. (See Patch panel)

HARMONICS   Frequencies that are whole-number multiples of the fundamental.

HARMONIZER   A signal processing device that generates various effects including delay and doubling. Trademark of Eventide Clockworks.

HEADROOM   1. The difference in level between the loudest sound and the average loudness of the other sounds during recording. 2. The amount of increase in loudness level that a tape, amplifier, or other piece of equipment can take, above working level, before overload distortion occurs.

HEADSET MICROPHONE   A microphone attached to a pair of earphones; one earphone channel feeds the program and the other earphone channel feeds the director's cues.

HEADS OUT Having the program information at the head or outside of the reel of tape or film ready for playback or projection.

HEADSTACK A multitrack tape head.

HEIGHT One of the adjustments made when aligning the heads on an audio tape recorder. This adjustment aligns the height of the heads with the recording tape.

HELICAL VIDEO TAPE RECORDING Video tape recording that uses one or more rotating video heads that engage the tape wrapped at least partially around the head drum. Video is recorded in slanted tracks across most of the tape's width. Also known as "slant track recording."

HEMISPHERIC DIRECTIONAL MICROPHONE A microphone that picks up sound from a hemispheric direction.

HERTZ Unit of measurement of frequency; numerically equal to cycles per second.

HIDDEN MICROPHONE A microphone placed in a flower pot, lamp shade, pen holder, or other spot to hide it from view. Sometimes used when it is impractical or unnecessary to set up a boom microphone.

HIGH END The treble range of the frequency spectrum.

HIGH-OUTPUT TAPE High-sensitivity tape.

HIGH-PASS FILTER A filter that attenuates frequencies below a selected frequency and allows those above that point to pass.

HYPERCARDIOID MICROPHONE Unidirectional microphone that has a narrow angle of sound acceptance at the front, is dead at the sides, and is slightly sensitive at the rear.

IMPEDANCE Resistance to the flow of alternating current (AC) in an electric system.

INDIRECT SOUND Sound waves that reflect from one or more surfaces before reaching the listener.

INNER EAR The part of the ear that contains the auditory nerve, which transmits sound waves to the brain.

INPUT 1. The point to which signals feed into a component or sound system. 2. Feeding a signal to a component or sound system.

INSERT EDITING In electronic editing, inserting a segment between two previously dubbed segments. Also, electronic editing segments out of sequential order.

IN THE MUD Sound level so quiet that it barely "kicks" the VU meter.

IN THE RED Sound level so loud that the VU meter "rides" over 100 percent of modulation.

INVERSE SQUARE LAW The acoustic situation in which the sound level changes in inverse proportion to the square of the distance from the sound source.

IRON OXIDE The magnetic constituent of most recording tape. Actual name: gamma ferric oxide.

JACK Receptacle or plug connector leading to the input or output circuit of a patch panel, tape recorder, or other electronic component.

LATER REFLECTIONS (See Reverberation)

LAVALIER MICROPHONE Microphone worn around the neck or attached to the clothing.

LEADER TAPE   Nonmagnetic tape spliced to the beginning and end of a tape and between segments to indicate visually when recorded material begins and ends.

LEAKAGE   Unwanted sound from one sound source being picked up through the microphone of another sound source.

LIMITER   A compressor with an output level that remains the same, regardless of the input level.

LIP FLAP   Lip movement in the video when there is no sound in the audio. Usually seen in film recorded with single-system equipment.

LOOPING   Recording dialogue in synchronization with a picture. (See Dialogue looping room)

LOUDNESS   Subjective perception of amplitude.

LOUDSPEAKER   A transducer that converts electric energy into acoustic energy.

LOW END   The bass range of the frequency spectrum.

LOW-OUTPUT TAPE   Low-sensitivity tape.

LOW-PASS FILTER   A filter that attenuates frequencies above a selected frequency and allows those below that point to pass.

LOW-PRINT-THROUGH TAPE   Low-sensitivity tape.

MASTER CONTROL   The room to where audio and video outputs from other control rooms are fed for final adjustments before distribution to recording or broadcast.

MASTER POT   The pot that controls the combined signal level of the individual channels on a console.

MATRIX QUADRIPHONIC REPRODUCTION   A system that reproduces quadriphonic sound by encoding two signals each on two channels during recording and decoding them into four separate signals during playback.

METAL-PARTICLE TAPE   Tape specially made for cassette tape recorders with a high coercivity and sensitivity compared with other cassette tapes.

MICROPHONE   A transducer that converts acoustic energy into electric energy.

MICROWAVE   Wireless point-to-point relay of a signal.

MIDDLE EAR   The part of the ear that transfers sound waves from the eardrum to the inner ear.

MIDRANGE   The part of the frequency spectrum to which humans are most sensitive; the frequencies between, roughly, 300 and 4,000 Hz.

MIKE-TO-SOURCE DISTANCE   Distance between a microphone and its sound source.

MIL   One thousandth of an inch.

MILKING THE AUDIENCE   Boosting the level of an audience's sound during laughter or applause.

MIX   The product of a rerecording session in which several separate sound tracks are combined through a mixing console in mono or stereo.

MIXDOWN The procedure of sweetening, positioning, and combining several separately recorded tracks into mono or stereo.

MOBILE UNIT A car, truck, or trailer equipped to produce program material on location.

MODULATION 1. Impressing sound (or picture) on disc, tape, or film. 2. In broadcast transmission, superimposing a sound wave on the carrier wave.

MONAURAL Literally means "one ear." Often used as a synonym for "monophonic."

MONITOR Loudspeaker used in a sound facility.

MONITOR SYSTEM Internal sound system in a console that feeds signals to the monitor loudspeakers.

MONOPHONIC Refers to a sound system with one master output channel.

MOVING-COIL LOUDSPEAKER A loudspeaker with a moving coil element. The coil is wrapped around a diaphragm suspended in a magnetic field.

MOVING-COIL MICROPHONE A microphone with a moving coil element. The coil is wrapped around a diaphragm suspended in a magnetic field.

M-S MIKING For middle-side; a technique using a cardioid microphone pointed toward the sound source and a bidirectional microphone with its dead sides perpendicular to the cardioid mike and facing the sides of the sound source. The outputs of the microphones must be specially wired.

MULTIDIRECTIONAL MICROPHONE Microphone with switchable pickup patterns.

MULTIMICROPHONE TECHNIQUE Microphone technique using several microphones to pick up sound sources individually or in small groups.

MULTIPLE 1. On a patch panel, jacks interconnected to each other and to no other circuit. They can be used to feed signals to and from sound sources. 2. An amplifier with several mike level outputs to provide individual feeds, thereby eliminating the need for many.

MUTE Cut off a sound.

MYLAR The DuPont Company name for polyester. (See Polyester)

NEEDLE DROP Taping a cut or part of a cut from a recorded music library for use in a production. Fees for permission to use the music for any purpose are based on the number of needle drops used. Fees are paid to the holder of the copyright.

NEMO The acronym for Not Emanating Main Organization, the term that used to indicate a remote broadcast.

NOISE Any unwanted electric disturbance, other than distortion, that occurs at the output of a sound system. (See Equipment noise, System noise, and Tape noise)

NOISE GATE An expander with a threshold that can be set to reduce or eliminate unwanted low-level sounds, such as room ambience, rumble, and leakage, without affecting the wanted sounds.

NOISE REDUCTION SYSTEM Designed to reduce noise in an audio recording system, usually at the tape or film stage.

NOTCH FILTER   A filter capable of attenuating an extremely narrow bandwidth of frequencies.

OCTAVE   The interval between two sounds that have a frequency ratio of 2 to 1.

OERSTED   A unit of magnetic force.

OFF-MIKE   Not being within the optimal pickup pattern of a microphone.

OMNIDIRECTIONAL MICROPHONE   Microphone that picks up sound from all directions. Also called a nondirectional microphone.

ONE-WAY SYSTEM LOUDSPEAKER   Loudspeaker system with one speaker to reproduce all frequencies.

ON-MIKE   Being within the optimal pickup pattern of a microphone.

OPEN-LOOP TAPE SYSTEM   Tape transport system with one capstan and a pinch roller usually located to the right of the head assembly.

OSCILLATOR   A device that generates pure tones or sine waves.

OUTER EAR   The portion of the ear that picks up and directs sound waves through the auditory canal to the middle ear.

OUTPUT   1. The point from which signals feed out of a component or sound system. 2. Feeding a signal from a component or sound system.

OVERDUBBING   Recording new material on a separate tape track(s) while listening to the replay of a previously recorded tape track(s) in order to synchronize the old and new material.

OVERLOAD   Feeding a component or system more loudness than it can handle and thereby causing overload distortion.

OVERTONES   Harmonics that may or may not be multiples of the fundamental. Subjective response of the ear to harmonics.

PAD   An attenuator inserted into a component or system to reduce level.

PAN POT   A potentiometer that changes the loudness level of a sound between two channels. Abbreviation for panoramic potentiometer.

PARABOLIC MICROPHONE SYSTEM   A system that uses a concave dish to focus reflected sound into a microphone pointed at the center of the dish.

PARAMETRIC EQUALIZER   An equalizer in which the bandwidth of a selected frequency is continuously variable.

PATCH CORD   A short cord, or cable, with a plug at both ends used to route signals in a patch panel.

PATCHING   Using patch cords to route or reroute signals by connecting the inputs and outputs of components wired to a patch panel.

PATCH PANEL   An assembly of jacks to which are wired the inputs and outputs of the audio components in a sound studio. Some of these jacks are then wired to each other to create permanent or normaled signal paths.

PEAK PROGRAM METER   A meter that responds to the loudness peaks in a signal.

PERCENTAGE OF MODULATION   On a VU meter, a measure of the amount of current passing through a channel or group of channels.

PHANTOM POWER SUPPLY   A circuit that sends DC power to a condenser microphone, thereby eliminating the need to use batteries to generate the microphone's voltage.

PHASE The time relationship between two or more sounds reaching a microphone or signals in a circuit. When this time relationship is coincident, the sounds are *in phase* and their amplitudes are additive. When this time relationship is not coincident, the sounds or signals are *out of phase* and their amplitudes are subtractive.

PHASING An effect created by splitting a signal in two and time delaying one of them.

PHONE COUPLER Device used to feed both ends of a telephone conversation to a tape recorder. A push button in the handle of the telephone can cut off the sound feeding into the mouthpiece if sound from only the earpiece is being recorded.

PICKUP ARM (See Tone arm)

PICKUP PATTERN (See Polar response pattern)

PINCH ROLLER On a tape recorder, the spring-loaded, free-spinning rubber wheel that holds the tape against the capstan. Also called "capstan idler," "pressure roller," and "puck."

PINNING When the needle of the VU meter hits against the peg at the right-hand corner of the red. Pinning is to be avoided since it indicates too high a loudness level and it could damage the meter.

PITCH The subjective perception of frequency.

PITCH TRANSPOSER A signal processor that varies the pitch of sounds.

PLATE On a turntable, the flat, metal surface on which the record is placed. The plate is usually covered with felt or rubber to protect the record.

PLAYBACK HEAD Electromagnetic transducer on a tape recorder that converts magnetic energy into electric energy.

PLOSIVE A speech sound that begins with a transient attack, such as "p" or "b."

POLAR RESPONSE PATTERN The graph of a microphone's directional characteristics as seen from above. The graph indicates response over a 360-degree circumference in a series of concentric circles, each representing a 5-dB loss in level as the circles move inward toward the center.

POLYESTER Durable, plastic-base material used in most recording tape made today. (See Mylar)

POP FILTER Foam rubber windscreen placed inside the microphone head. Particularly effective in reducing sound from plosives and blowing.

POTENTIOMETER A device containing a resistor that is used to vary the output voltage of a circuit or component.

PREAMPLIFIER Device that boosts very low-level signals to usable proportions before they reach the amplifier. Abbreviated preamp.

PRESENCE Perception of a sound as being close and realistic.

PRESENCE RANGE Those frequencies in the frequency spectrum that give sound the quality of closeness and realism; roughly from 2,000 to 8,000 Hz.

PRESIDENTIAL PATCH (See Multiple)

PRESSURE PAD On a turntable, the free-spinning rubber disc that engages the capstan and spins the plate.

PRESSURE ZONE MICROPHONE A pressure-calibrated electret transducer designed to eliminate the time difference between direct and reflected sound waves. Abbreviated PZM microphone. Trade name of Crown International, Inc.

PRINT-THROUGH   Unwanted transfer of a magnetic signal from one tape layer to an adjacent tape layer.

PROGRAM SYSTEM   External system in a console that feeds signals to broadcast or recording. Also called "Master system" and "Air system." (See Monitor system)

PROXIMITY EFFECT   Disproportionate increase in the bass frequencies of a unidirectional microphone as the mike-to-source distance decreases.

PSYCHOACOUSTICS   Study of the subjective perception of sound stimuli.

PUNCHING IN   Inserting material into a recording by rolling the tape recorder in the playback mode and putting it in the record mode at the insert point.

PZM MICROPHONE   (See Pressure zone microphone)

QUADRIPHONIC MICROPHONE   Two pairs of directional microphone capsules, feeding four separate outputs, built into one housing.

QUADRIPHONIC SOUND   System of recording and reproducing sound using four separate channels and four separate loudspeakers. Also called "quad."

QUADRUPLEX VIDEO TAPE RECORDING   System of recording that encodes the video transversely across the tape. (See Helical video tape recording)

RADIO MICROPHONE   Wireless microphone.

RAREFACTION   Drawing apart of vibrating molecules to produce a low-pressure area. (See Compression)

READ MODE   Mode of operation in an automated mixdown when the console controls are operated automatically by the data previously encoded in the computer. (See Update mode and Write mode)

RECORD HEAD   Electromagnetic transducer on a tape recorder that converts electric energy into magnetic energy.

RECORDING TONE   Procedure of recording reference tones before taped program material to give the operator playing back the tape an idea of where to set levels.

REEL-SIZE CONTROL   (See Tension control)

RELEASE TIME   The length of time it takes a limiter or compressor to return to its normal level after the signal has been attenuated or withdrawn. Also known as recovery time.

REMOTE   A broadcast or recording done away from the studio on location.

RERECORDING ROOM   A good-sized room with a projector, screen, magnetic sound reproducers called "dummys," and a magnetic sound recorder. The projector and dummys are interlocked to synchronize sound and picture. The dummys feed each sound element to the console, where the sound track is mixed and sent to the recorder.

RETENTIVITY   Measure of a tape's ability to retain magnetization after the force field has been removed. Retentivity is measured in gauss—a unit of magnetic energy.

REVERBERATION   Repeated reflections of a sound wave after the sound source has ceased vibrating.

REVERBERATION TIME   The time it takes a sound to decrease to one-millionth of its original intensity, or 60 dB-SPL.

REVERB RETURN   1. Channel through which a signal passes on its way from the reverb unit to the console. 2. Control that adjusts the loudness of the reverberant signal.

REVERB SEND   1. Channel through which a signal passes on its way to the reverb unit from the console. 2. Control that adjusts the loudness of the dry signal on its way to the reverb unit.

RIBBON LOUDSPEAKER   A loudspeaker with a ribbon diaphragm suspended in a magnetic field.

RIBBON MICROPHONE   A microphone with a ribbon diaphragm suspended in a magnetic field.

RIDING THE GAIN   Adjusting the levels during recording or playback.

ROBINSON-DADSON CURVES   Equal loudness curves plotted by averaging the results obtained from a large number of listeners. They are gradually replacing the original curves plotted by Fletcher-Munson. (See Equal loudness curves)

SCORING STAGE   Large studio with a projector and screen where the music sound track for a motion picture is recorded and synchronized.

SCRAPE FLUTTER FILTER   A cylindrical, low-friction, metal surface, usually installed between the heads, to reduce flutter.

SEARCH-TO-CUE   Device on a tape recorder that programs cue points so that in Fast Forward or Rewind the recorder automatically stops at the appropriate place on the tape.

SEGUE   Playing two recordings, one after the other, with no live announcement in between.

SELECTIVE SYNCHRONIZATION   (See Sel sync)

SEL SYNC   Changing the record head into a playback head to synchronize the playback of previously recorded material with the recording of new material. Trademark of Ampex Corporation.

SENSITIVITY   Measurement of a tape's output level capability relative to a standard reference tape.

SHOCK MOUNT   A device that isolates a microphone from mechanical vibrations. It can be attached externally or built into a microphone.

SHOTGUN MICROPHONE   A highly directional microphone with a tube that resembles the barrel of a rifle.

SIBILANCE   The annoying hissing sound produced by overaccenting "s," "z," "sh," "ch," and other similar sounds.

SIGNAL FLOW   The path a signal follows from its sound source to its destination.

SIGNAL PROCESSOR   A device that alters some characteristic of a sound, such as frequency, amplitude, phase, or quantity.

SIGNAL-TO-NOISE RATIO   The ratio between the signal level and the noise level of a component or sound system. Usually signifies the amount of signal that can be generated before noise is introduced. The wider the signal-to-noise ratio, the better.

SINGLE-SYSTEM RECORDING   Recording film picture and sound in a camera simultaneously but at different places on the film.

SLATE/TALKBACK The part of a talkback system that feeds sound to tape. It is used to record verbal identification of the material being taped, the take number, and other information just before each recording.

SLIP CUE Holding onto a record that is cued while the turntable is spinning and then letting it go at the appropriate time.

SMPTE TIME CODE Standard code used to edit tape. The code is in eight digits representing hours, minutes, seconds, and frames. Although developed for video tape editing, hence, the "frames," it can be used to edit audio tape since frame time can be converted to a thirtieth of a second.

SOLO MUTE A control on a multitrack console that automatically cuts off all signals feeding the monitor system except those signals feeding through the channel that the solo mute control activates.

SOUND ABSORPTION COEFFICIENT A measure of the sound-absorbing ability of a surface. This coefficient is defined as the fraction of incident sound absorbed by a surface. Values range from 0.01 for marble to 1.0 for the materials used in an almost acoustically dead enclosure.

SOUND CHAIN The audio components that carry a signal from its sound source to its destination.

SOUND ENVELOPE The attack, sustain, and decay of a sound.

SOUNDFIELD MICROPHONE SYSTEM Multidirectional microphone that can be adjusted to pick up in omnidirectional, bidirectional, cardioid, hypercardioid, stereo, or quad patterns.

SOUND PRESSURE LEVEL A measure of the pressure of a sound wave, expressed in decibels.

SOUND READER A playback head attached to a viewer or synchronizer and wired to an amplifier enabling a film editor to hear a magnetic or optical sound track.

SOUND STAGE A film studio used to record picture and sound.

SOUND TRANSMISSION CLASSIFICATION A rating that evaluates the effectiveness of barriers in isolating sound. Abbreviated STC.

SOUND WAVE A series of compressions and rarefactions of molecules set in motion by a vibrating sound source and radiating from it.

SPACED PAIR OF MICROPHONES Two microphones, usually directional, spaced from several inches to several feet apart, depending on the width of the sound source, for stereo recording.

SPEED CONTROL On a turntable, tape recorder, or film camera, the control that selects the speed at which these devices operate.

SPLICING TAPE A specially made adhesive tape that does not ooze, is nonmagnetic and pressure sensitive, and is used to join cut ends of audio tape and magnetic film.

STANDING WAVE A sound wave perceived as stationary, which is the result of a periodic sound wave having a fixed distribution in space. The result of interference of traveling sound waves of the same kind.

STEREO MICROPHONE Two directional microphone capsules, one above the other, with separate outputs, encased in one housing.

STEREO MIKING   Using only two microphones, or microphone capsules, usually directional, to pick up sound from an ensemble. Sometimes ambience or blending microphones may be added.

STEREOPHONIC SOUND   Two-channel, two-loudspeaker sound reproduction that gives the listener the illusion of sonic depth and width. Sometimes additional channels and loudspeakers are used to enhance the spaciousness of the sound.

STROBE   Any of various instruments used to adjust a moving, rotating, or vibrating object by making it appear stationary. Abbreviation for stroboscope.

STUDIO   1. A room in which the talent performs during a production or program. 2. Any room or group of rooms used for the performance, production, and processing of a program (or film) for recording or broadcast.

STYLUS   The needle, generally diamond tipped, that transmits modulations from a record groove to the cartridge. (See Cartridge)

SUPERCARDIOID MICROPHONE   Unidirectional microphone with a slightly narrower angle of sound acceptance than a cardioid microphone, little sensitivity at the sides, and some sensitivity at the rear.

SUSTAIN   That part of a sound envelope just after the attack and before the beginning of the decay.

SWEETENING   Enhancing the sound of a recording with equalization and various other signal processing techniques, usually during the mixing stage(s) of a production.

SYNCHRONIZER   1. Device with sprocketed, ganged wheels that locks in the film reels of picture and sound so they can be wound in synchronization during editing. 2. Device that regulates the operating speeds of two tape recorders so they run in sync.

SYNC PULSE   The pulse or tone that synchronizes tape recorder speed and film camera speed in double-system recording.

SYNC PULSE HEAD   The head on an audio tape recorder used in double-system recording that records the sync pulse on the tape.

SYSTEM MICROPHONE   Interchangeable microphone capsules of various directional patterns that attach to a common base. The base contains a power supply and a preamplifier.

SYSTEM NOISE   The total noise produced by a recording system.

TAILS OUT   Having the end of the material on a tape or film at the head of the reel.

TAKE-UP IDLER   A spring-loaded control on a tape recorder that can activate or deactivate the transport without the machine being turned on and off.

TALKBACK   System that permits communication from a control room microphone to a loudspeaker or earphones in the studio.

TANGENCY   One of the adjustments made when aligning the heads of an audio tape recorder. This adjustment aligns the forwardness of the heads so the tape meets them at the correct pressure.

TAPE GUIDES   Grooved pins or rollers mounted at each side of the head assembly to position the tape correctly on the head during recording and playback.

TAPE LOOP   A tape with the ends spliced together.

TAPE NOISE   Noise generated by the tape in a recording/reproducing system. (See Equipment noise, Noise, and System noise)

TAPE RECORDER   A mechanical-electronic device that encodes and decodes audio and video information on a magnetic tape.

TAPE SPLICER   A device used to cut and splice magnetic tape or film.

TAPE TIMER   An indicator on an audio or video tape recorder that displays the amount of tape used in hours, minutes, and seconds. (See Footage counter)

TAPE TRANSPORT   The mechanical portion of the tape recorder mounted with motors, reel spindles, heads, and controls that carry the tape at a constant speed from feed reel to take-up reel.

TENSION CONTROL   A two-position switch that adjusts the torque to the feed and take-up reels to compensate for different sizes of reels and hubs.

THREE-TO-ONE RULE   A guideline used to reduce the phasing caused when a sound reaches two microphones at slightly different times. It states that no two microphones should be closer to each other than three times the distance between one of them and its sound source.

THREE-WAY SYSTEM LOUDSPEAKER   A loudspeaker that divides the high from the low frequencies and then divides the high frequencies again, sending each group of frequencies to three separate speakers.

TIE-TAC MICROPHONE   A lavalier microphone with a clasp or pin that attaches to a tie or other piece of clothing.

TIMBRE   The unique quality or color of a sound.

TONE ARM   The arm on a turntable that houses the cartridge and stylus. It must be balanced and weighted so the stylus sits in the groove and tracks across the record properly.

TRACK   The path on magnetic tape along which a single channel of information is recorded.

TRANSDUCER   A device that converts one form of energy into another.

TRANSFORMER   A device used to match the impedances of high- and low-impedance components or systems.

TRANSIENT   A sound that begins with a sharp attack followed by a quick decay.

TRANSMITTER MICROPHONE   Wireless microphone.

TRIM   1. To attenuate the loudness level in a component or circuit. 2. The device, usually so called on a console, that attenuates the loudness level at the microphone/line input.

TURNTABLE   The system that plays a disc recording.

TWEETER   The informal name of a loudspeaker that reproduces high frequencies. (See Woofer)

TWO-WAY SYSTEM LOUDSPEAKER   A loudspeaker that divides the high from the low frequencies, sending the highs to a tweeter and the lows to a woofer.

ULTRACARDIOID MICROPHONE   A directional microphone with a very narrow angle of acceptance, very little sensitivity at the sides, and some sensitivity at the rear.

UNBALANCED LINE   A line (or circuit) with two conductors of unequal voltage.

UNDERSCORE   Using music or sound to provide informational or emotional enhancement to narration, dialogue, or action.

UNIDIRECTIONAL MICROPHONE   A microphone that picks up sound from one direction. Also called "directional."

UNITY GAIN   Gain in output level equal to the gain in input level.

UPDATE MODE   Mode of operation in an automated mixdown when an encoded control can be recoded without affecting the coding of the other controls. (See Read mode and Write mode)

VARIABLE SPEED CONTROL   Device on an audio tape recorder that alters the playing speed to various rates of the recorder's set speeds.

VARIABLE SPEED OSCILLATOR   Device that can be used to vary the speed of a turntable or tape recorder.

VELOCITY   The speed of a sound wave: 1,130 feet per second at sea level and 70 degrees Fahrenheit.

VIDEO TAPE   A plastic base coated with magnetic particles, transverse or slanted, used to record video and audio signals. (Magnetic particles on audio tape are horizontal.)

VOLUME CONTROL   Potentiometer.

VOLUME UNIT   A measure that is related to a human's subjective perception of loudness.

VOLUME UNIT METER (VU)   A meter calibrated in volume units and percentage of modulation.

WAVELENGTH   The length of one cycle of a sound wave. Wavelength is inversely proportional to the frequency of a sound; the higher the frequency, the shorter is the wavelength.

WET SOUND   A sound with reverberation. (See Dry sound)

WINDSCREEN   Foam rubber covering specially designed to fit over the outside of a microphone head. Used to reduce plosive and blowing sounds. (See Pop filter)

WIRELESS MICROPHONE SYSTEM   System consisting of a microphone with an antenna. The signal is picked up by a small transmitter carried on the person using the mike. The transmitter sends the signal over a distance of as much as a few hundred yards to a receiver, which feeds the signal to a mixer or console.

WOOFER   Informal name for a loudspeaker that reproduces the bass frequencies. (See Tweeter)

WOW   1. Low-frequency distortion, usually below 6,000 Hz, caused by very short, rapid variations in tape speed causing similar variations in sound pitch and amplitude. (See Flutter) 2. Starting the sound on a record or tape before it reaches full speed.

WRAP   One of the adjustments made when aligning the heads of an audio tape recorder. This adjustment aligns the head so it is in full physical contact with the tape.

WRITE MODE   The mode of operation in an automated mixdown during which controls are adjusted conventionally and the adjustments are encoded in the computer for retrieval in the read mode. (See Read mode and Update mode)

XLR CONNECTOR   Commonly used male and female microphone plugs with a three-pin connector.

X-Y MIKING   Coincident miking.

ZENITH   One of the adjustments made when aligning the heads of an audio tape recorder. This adjustment aligns the vertical angle of the heads so they are perpendicular to the tape.

Index